Banking Sector Liberalization in India

Contributions to Economics

www.springer.com/series/1262

Further volumes of this series can be found at our homepage.

Jan-Egbert Sturm/Timo Wollmershäuser (Eds.)
Ifo Survey Data in Business Cycle and Monetary Policy Analysis
2005. ISBN 978-3-7908-0174-3

Bernard Michael Gilroy/Thomas Gries/Willem A. Naudé (Eds.)
Multinational Enterprises, Foreign Direct Investment and Growth in Africa
2005. ISBN 978-3-7908-0276-4

Günter S. Heiduk/Kar-yiu Wong (Eds.)
WTO and World Trade
2005. ISBN 978-3-7908-1579-5

Emilio Colombo/Luca Stanca
Financial Market Imperfections and Corporate Decisions
2006. ISBN 978-3-7908-1581-8

Birgit Mattil
Pension Systems
2006. ISBN 978-3-7908-1675-4

Francesco C. Billari/Thomas Fent/Alexia Prskawetz/Jürgen Scheffran (Eds.)
Agent-Based Computational Modelling
2006. ISBN 978-3-7908-1640-2

Kerstin Press
A Life Cycle for Clusters?
2006. ISBN 978-3-7908-1710-2

Russel Cooper/Gary Madden/Ashley Lloyd/Michael Schipp (Eds.)
The Economics of Online Markets and ICT Networks
2006. ISBN 978-3-7908-1706-5

Renato Giannetti/Michelangelo Vasta (Eds.)
Evolution of Italian Enterprises in the 20th Century
2006. ISBN 978-3-7908-1711-9

Ralph Setzer
The Politics of Exchange Rates in Developing Countries
2006. ISBN 978-3-7908-1715-7

Dora Borbély
Trade Specialization in the Enlarged European Union
2006. ISBN 978-3-7908-1704-1

Iris A. Hauswirth
Effective and Efficient Organisations?
2006. ISBN 978-3-7908-1730-0

Marco Neuhaus
The Impact of FDI on Economic Growth
2006. ISBN 978-3-7908-1734-8

Nicola Jentzsch
The Economics and Regulation of Financial Privacy
2006. ISBN 978-3-7908-1737-9

Klaus Winkler
Negotiations with Asymmetrical Distribution of Power
2006. ISBN 978-3-7908-1743-0

Sasha Tsenkova, Zorica Nedović-Budić (Eds.)
The Urban Mosaic of Post-Socialist Europe
2006. ISBN 978-3-7908-1726-3

Brigitte Preissl/Jürgen Müller (Eds.)
Governance of Communication Networks
2006. ISBN 978-3-7908-1745-4

Lei Delsen/Derek Bosworth/Hermann Groß/Rafael Muñoz de Bustillo y Llorente (Eds.)
Operating Hours and Working Times
2006. ISBN 978-3-7908-1759-1

Pablo Coto-Millán; Vicente Inglada (Eds.)
Essays on Transport Economics
2006. ISBN 978-3-7908-1764-5

Christian H. Fahrholz
New Political Economy of Exchange Rate Policies and the Enlargement of the Eurozone
2006. ISBN 978-3-7908-1761-4

Sandra Gruescu
Population Ageing and Economic Growth
2007. ISBN 978-3-7908-1905-2

Patrick S. Renz
Project Governance
2007. ISBN 978-3-7908-1926-7

Christian Schabbel
The Value Chain of Foreign Aid
2007. ISBN 978-3-7908-1931-1

Martina Eckardt
Insurance Intermediation
2007. ISBN 978-3-7908-1939-7

George M. Korres (Ed.)
Regionalisation, Growth, and Economic Integration
2007. ISBN 978-3-7908-1924-3

Kerstin Groß
Equity Ownership and Performance
2007. ISBN 978-3-7908-1933-5

Ulrike Neyer
The Design of the Eurosystem's Monetary Policy Instruments
2007. ISBN 978-3-7908-1977-9

Christian Roland

Banking Sector Liberalization in India

Evaluation of Reforms and Comparative Perspectives on China

Physica-Verlag
A Springer Company

Series Editors
Werner A. Müller
Martina Bihn

Author
Dr. Christian Roland
christian_roland@yahoo.de

ISBN 978-3-7908-1981-6 e-ISBN 978-3-7908-1982-3

ISSN 1431-1933

Library of Congress Control Number: 2007935678

Cover design: WMXDesign GmbH, Heidelberg

Printed on acid-free paper

9 8 7 6 5 4 3 2 1

springer.com

Foreword

Reforms of the financial and banking sector are of utmost importance for emerging economies as well as economies in transition especially due to the fundamental importance of these sectors for economic development processes. In this context, the extent of government intervention in these areas plays an important role, which has been controversially discussed in the literature. While market optimists assign a very restricted to the government and argue that a market-determined banking and financial system will have sustainable positive effects on the allocative and dynamic efficiency and eventually economic growth, market pessimists point out that, particularly in less developed countries, emerging economies as well as economies in transition, the government should assume an active role (at least) in the phases of reform and transformation. In that case, the government is particularly supposed to address market failure, but also to bring about an economically effective and politically feasible sequencing and timing of institutional and economic reforms in the overall economy. Empirical investigations regarding the dichotomy of market and state have not yet yielded clear analytical results or straightforward policy recommendations.

Starting from this controversy, this book addresses the reform and development process in India since the mid-1980s and compares it with the Chinese reform process which has been taking place since the end of the 1970s. Thereby, the author chooses two of the currently most intriguing reform countries, both of which are amidst a comprehensive transformation process from a state-led economy towards a liberalized market economy.

The analysis actually represents a comparative, empirically oriented, yet theoretically sound country study. Its overall objective is to undertake a comprehensive, profound assessment of the distinct transformation steps in the Indian banking sector and to compare this with corresponding reform and transformation steps in China. More specifically, the study pursues the goals

- to identify the potential reasons for government intervention into the banking sector of a country as well as for financial-market liberalization;

- to discuss the crucial policy recommendations of general transformation studies in the context of the transformation of the banking sector;
- to link transformation studies and the works about financial-market liberalization and thereby to craft a theoretical framework for the liberalization of the banking sector in a transformation country;
- to discuss the necessary extent of government activities in the banking sector;
- to identify suitable indicators for assessing banking sector reforms;
- to compare the status and the consequences of banking sector reforms in India and China; and
- to discuss necessary steps for further reaching reforms of the banking sector in these countries.

In the course of his study, the author succeeds in accomplishing these objectives in an impressing differentiated, independent, and innovative way.

As a key outcome of this book, the reader will recognize and acknowledge that the dichotomy of the market and the state regarding the transformation of a banking sector exists only seemingly. In fact, an active role of the government proves to be a key factor during the transition towards a market-determined financial and banking system, i.e. in an environment characterized by market and coordination failure.

The author does not develop a novel theoretical approach for systemic transformation. Rather, Christian Roland suitably links two strands of theory in an impressing way: he combines the theoretical transformation studies with the works on financial market and banking sector liberalization and develops thereby a theoretically founded concept which can also be applied in empirical analyses. This approach to analyze banking sector reforms in a transformation context is successfully applied to India and China and brings about novel insights and policy implications. In this context, it is remarkable that the author explicitly focuses on the *process* of liberalizing the banking sector as well as complementary reform steps in other sectors. This process has not yet been explored in the research community.

To conclude: "Banking Sector Liberalization in India" is, without doubt, one of the best books on the economics on policy, particularly banking sector, reform in emerging economies. It is a must-read not only for scholars interested in financial sector reform, but also for those interested in the region and, of course, for all students of economic transition. The book is a concisely written, excellent addition to the everlasting debate on the role of institutions and policies for economic development. The author's judgements and recommendations are based on actual policy alternatives which are available to policymakers rather than on theoretical reference models. By demonstrating the central role of institution building and highlighting the crucial complementary role which governments need to play in order to support the emergence of markets, the study provides a sound theoretical analysis and instructive empirical evidence, which will enhance readers' understanding of reforms in India and China.

Joachim Ahrens
Professor of International Political Economy
European Business School International University
Oestrich-Winkel, Germany
and
Private University of Applied Sciences Goettingen
Goettingen, Germany

Preface

This book was written during my time as a doctoral student at the European Business School, Oestrich-Winkel from 2004 until 2006. A number of people have supported me during this journey – my special thanks go to them.

First and foremost, my gratitude goes to my "doctoral fathers" Prof. Dr. Jürgen Bunge and Prof. Dr. Joachim Ahrens. They gave me a great degree of freedom in pursuing the topic, while at the same time sharing their insights and experiences with me. Professor Bunge's advice in late 2003 was invaluable: at a time when most people were still focusing exclusively on China, he suggested to look at India and compare it to China, and thus showed clear foresight of the emerging importance of India on the global stage. Being his last doctoral student, he showed great personal interest in the development of this thesis. Professor Ahrens helped me greatly in shaping the theoretical foundations of this book and always had an open ear to my questions.

I have benefited tremendously from a research trip to India in 2005. Many people have taken the time to share their knowledge on the Indian banking sector with me. These include Dr. Anand, Ms. Das and Dr. Ram Mohan (State Bank of India); Mr. Dixit, Mr. Gadgil, Mr. Gupta and Mr. Otte (Deutsche Bank India); Mr. Steinrücke (Indo-German Chamber of Commerce); Mr. Menon and Mr. Umamaheshwaran (Development Credit Bank); Prof. Vaidya (Indira Gandhi Institute of Development Research); Dr. Kohli and Mr. Wattleworth (International Monetary Fund); Dr. Patnaik (Indian Express); Prof. Varma and Dr. Ram Mohan (Indian Institute of Management Ahmedabad); Dr. Basu (World Bank); Prof. Correa and Prof. Nadkarni (University of Mumbai); Mr. Puri, Mr. Sengupta and Mr. Thomas (McKinsey & Company).

Their perspectives on the changes in the industry have helped me tremendously to gain deeper insight into the sector. Special thanks go to Professor Sunder Ram (NMIMS) who met several times with me, Dr. Leichtfuß (McKinsey & Company, now The Boston Consulting Group) for facilitating my trip to India, and Mr. Tahilyani (McKinsey & Company) for being my point of contact while in Mumbai and helping me in setting up some of the interviews.

From my friends, Timo Schretzmair helped with the proofreading and provided helpful inputs, Jens Wimschulte always took the time to discuss new approaches with me, while Dirk Eichler ensured that I would get sufficient time away from my desk through our tennis matches.

Last, but certainly not least, I have to thank my parents Agnes and Gregor Roland, and my brother Björn for their support during my years of study. My spouse Leonie Staude was a constant source of encouragement and motivation throughout the time I was writing this book. Furthermore, she helped me advance my thinking on the topic by pointing to flaws in my argumentation, and spotting errors in the text. I dedicate this book to my family and Leonie.

Christian Roland

Table of contents

Abbreviations..........XV

1 Introduction..........1
1.1 Original problem and objectives..........1
1.2 Methodology..........6
1.3 Categorization of topic..........8
1.4 Definition of key terms..........9
1.4.1 Liberalization..........10
1.4.2 Banking sector and financial sector..........10
1.5 Structure of the thesis..........13

2 The Indian banking sector..........17
2.1 Development of the Indian banking sector..........17
2.1.1 Development from 1947 to 1991..........17
2.1.2 Development from 1991 to 2005..........20
2.1.2.1 Background and goals of reforms..........20
2.1.2.2 Reform areas..........23
2.2 Current structure of the banking system..........37
2.3 Political, economic and institutional environment of the banking sector..........42
2.3.1 Political environment..........42
2.3.2 Economic environment..........43
2.3.3 Institutional environment..........46
2.4 Conclusion..........48

3 The Chinese banking sector..........51
3.1 Development and structure of the banking sector..........51
3.1.1 Development of the banking sector..........51
3.1.2 Structure of the banking sector..........56
3.2 Major reform areas and status of the sector..........58
3.3 Similarities and differences to the Indian banking sector..........64
3.4 Conclusion..........67

4 Banking sector functions and coordination 69
4.1 Functions of the banking sector.. 69
4.1.1 Mobilization of resources.. 70
4.1.2 Allocation of resources.. 71
4.1.3 Fostering economic growth...................................... 72
4.2 State involvement in the banking sector............................... 74
4.2.1 Reasons for state involvement.................................. 75
4.2.1.1 Economic goals... 75
4.2.1.2 Developmental goals.................................. 78
4.2.1.3 Political goals... 79
4.2.2 Instruments of state involvement............................... 81
4.3 The financial liberalization hypothesis.................................. 84
4.4 Evaluation of financial liberalization................................... 88
4.4.1 Financial liberalization, savings and capital formation...... 88
4.4.2 Financial liberalization, financial development and growth.. 91
4.4.3 Financial liberalization and banking sector performance... 96
4.4.4 Financial liberalization and financial crisis.................... 98
4.5 Conclusion.. 101

5 Management of transformation processes............................ 103
5.1 Classification of transformatory changes and applicability to India... 103
5.1.1 Definition of transformatory changes.......................... 104
5.1.2 Applicability to the banking sector and India............... 107
5.2 Initial policy recommendations for transition countries 109
5.3 Elements of transformation processes 111
5.3.1 Liberalization... 111
5.3.2 Stabilization.. 113
5.3.3 Privatization.. 115
5.3.4 Institution building... 118
5.3.5 Structural change.. 122
5.4 Management of transition processes.................................. 124
5.4.1 Speed of reforms... 124
5.4.2 Sequencing and timing of reforms............................. 127
5.5 Differences in transformation processes in India and China...... 129
5.6 Conclusion.. 134

6 Framework for banking sector liberalization......................... 137
6.1 Overview and special considerations................................. 137
6.2 Transformation of the banking sector................................. 140
6.2.1 Basic requirements for banking sector liberalization...... 140

6.2.2 Process elements for banking sector liberalization......... 141
6.2.2.1 Liberalization of price and volume restrictions... 142
6.2.2.2 Stabilization of banks.............................. 144
6.2.2.3 Bank privatization.................................. 146
6.2.2.4 Institutional infrastructure of the banking sector. 148
6.2.2.5 Structural change of the banking sector........... 152
6.2.3 Speed, sequencing and timing of banking sector reforms..154
6.2.3.1 Speed of reforms...................................154
6.2.3.2 Sequencing and timing of reforms....................155
6.2.4 Political-economy considerations for banking sector liberalization..156
6.3 Measurement of process and results of banking sector liberalization... 159
6.3.1 Identification of process and result indicators.............. 159
6.3.2 Construction of a liberalization index.......................169
6.3.3 Effects of market failure on indicators 171
6.4 Macroeconomic effects of banking sector liberalization...........180
6.5 Conclusion... 183

7 Evaluation of banking sector liberalization in India and China... 185
7.1 Qualitative evaluation..185
7.2 Quantitative evaluation..195
7.2.1 Sector level...195
7.2.2 Macroeconomic level..217
7.2.2.1 Econometric specification and data description.. 217
7.2.2.2 Results of statistical tests........................... 222
7.3 Conclusion... 240

8 Policy recommendations and implications of research findings...243
8.1 Summary of goals and results.......................................243
8.2 Policy recommendations..248
8.3 Limitations of research approach....................................253
8.4 Perspectives for future research......................................254

Appendix... 257

References.. 275

Abbreviations

ABC	Agricultural Bank of China
AMC	Asset Management Company
BFS	Board of Financial Supervision
BOC	Bank of China
CAMEL	Capital adequacy, Asset quality, Management soundness, Earnings and profitability, and Liquidity
CBRC	China Banking Regulatory Commission
CCB	China Construction Bank
CEE	Central and Eastern Europe
CPI	Consumer price index
CRAR	Capital to risk-weighted assets ratio
CRR	Cash Reserve Ratio
DFI	Development Financial Institution
GDP	Gross Domestic Product
GOI	Government of India
ICBC	Industrial and Commercial Bank of China
ICOR	Incremental capital-output ratio
IFS	International Financial Statistics
IMF	International Monetary Fund
NBFC	Non-Banking Financial Company
NDTL	Net demand and time liabilities
NPL	Non-performing loan
PBOC	People's Bank of China
PRC	People's Republic of China
PSB	Public Sector Bank
RBI	Reserve Bank of India
RMB	Renminbi
ROA	Return on Assets
Rs	Indian Rupee
SBI	State Bank of India
SLR	Statutory Liquidity Ratio
SOCB	State-owned commercial bank
SOE	State-owned enterprise
WTO	World Trade Organization

1 Introduction

1.1 Original problem and objectives

A banking sector performs three primary functions in an economy: the operation of the payment system, the mobilization of savings and the allocation of savings to investment projects. By allocating capital to the highest value use while limiting the risks and costs involved, the banking sector can positively influence the overall economy and is thus of broad macroeconomic importance.[1]

There is broad consensus in the literature that the mobilization of savings and the allocation of capital have positive repercussions on the overall economy.[2] This suggests two questions: Under which coordination mechanism – state or market – does the banking sector best perform its functions? And how can a country move towards this coordination mechanism given the associated adjustment costs of the change?

From both a development and a political perspective on state involvement, the state is better suited than the market to ensure that the banking sector performs its growth-enhancing functions. A government can achieve this either through either direct ownership of banks or with restrictions on the operations of banks. It is argued that the government can ensure a better economic outcome than the market, for example by channeling savings to strategic projects that would otherwise not receive funding or by creating a branch infrastructure in rural areas. In this context, active government involvement in the banking system is the trigger for the growth-enhancing effect.[3]

---

[1] See Bonin and Wachtel (1999), p. 113; Jaffe and Levonian (2001), p. 163; Rajan and Zingales (1998), p. 559; Wachtel (2001), p. 339.

[2] See Bonin and Wachtel (1999), p. 113; King and Levine (1993), p. 719; Levine (1997), p. 691; Quispe-Agnoli and McQuerry (2001), p. 22; Wachtel (2001), pp. 357-359.

[3] See Arun and Turner (2002c), p. 93; Denizer, Desai and Gueorguiev (1998), p. 2; Gerschenkron (1962), pp. 19-22; La Porta, Lopez de Silanes and Schleifer (2002), p. 266f.

The proponents of financial liberalization take an opposite stance. They argue that imposing repressive policies such as artificially low real interest rates, directed credit programs and excessive statutory pre-emptions on banks can have a negative effect on both the volume and the productivity of investments, which in turn inhibits economic growth. Removing these repressionist policies and giving more weight to market forces will, it is argued, stimulate financial development and promote stronger economic growth.[4]

These two opposing views and the effects of banking sector liberalization are subject to much debate in the literature. The majority of empirical studies support the view that repressive policies have a negative effect on both the banking sector and the economy as a whole. These studies recommend that repressionist policies be abolished and banks privatized to reduce the government's influence in the sector. Less clear, however, is how to best manage the change of the coordination mechanism from state to market. This is especially important given the perils of the liberalization process – McKinnon (1991) notes that "liberalizing a highly repressed economy has been likened to walking through a minefield: your next step might be your last"[5]. While studies investigating the effects of financial liberalization abound, there is a distinct lack of research into how to actually conduct a liberalization program. There is still no clear outline of how to best manage the transition from a state-directed to a market-based banking sector.[6]

India's recent history exemplifies the tensions between the two different views. After increasing government involvement from the 1960s until the end of the 1980s, India's banking sector is now transforming from state direction to a market base. Prior to 1991 India's banking sector showed a significant degree of state ownership and extensive regulation, among others of the allocation of credit and the setting of interest rates. Following the balance of payments crisis in 1991, structural reforms were introduced that were a clear departure from the previous economic policy, in which the state was supposed to take the "commanding heights" of the economy.[7]

---

[4] See Demetriades and Luintel (1997), p. 311; Denizer, Desai and Gueorguiev (1998), p. 3; King and Levine (1993), p. 730; McKinnon (1991), p. 12; Shaw (1973), p. 3f.

[5] McKinnon (1991), p. x.

[6] See de Gregorio and Guidotti (1995), p. 433f.; Fry (1997), p. 768f.; King and Levine (1993), p. 734f.; Wachtel (2001), pp. 357-359.

[7] See Acharya (2002), pp. 2-4; Budhwar (2001), p. 552; Forbes (2001), p. 5; Mohan (2004), p. 851; Singh (2003), p. 1f.

The blueprint for the initial reforms was the report of the Narasimham Committee published in 1991. Subsequent steps have included the deregulation of interest rates, the easing of directed credit rules under the priority sector lending arrangements, the reduction of statutory pre-emptions and the lowering of entry barriers for both domestic and foreign banks.[8]

Yet despite these reforms, the state still plays an important direct role in the Indian banking sector.[9] One of the major goals of the current ruling coalition is to achieve a sustainable growth rate of 7-8%.[10] In fact this may be difficult, or even impossible, since a higher degree of state involvement is commonly associated with lower growth. The questions at hand are therefore how far the reforms have actually proceeded, what their effects on the banking sector and the economy have been so far, and what further reforms are necessary. The Deputy Governor of the Reserve Bank of India has stressed the importance of finding answers to these questions:

"India has had more than a decade of financial sector reforms during which there has been substantial transformation and liberalisation of the whole financial system. It is, therefore, an appropriate time to take stock and assess the efficacy of our approach. It is useful to evaluate how the financial system has performed in an objective quantitative manner. This is important because India's path of reforms has been different from most other emerging market economies: it has been a measured, gradual, cautious, and steady process, devoid of many flourishes that could be observed in other countries."[11]

Evaluating India's reform experience yields a number of insights into changes in the banking sector. However, it is difficult to identify clear lessons learned, as it is not always straightforward to distinguish factors that have a general application from those that are specific to India. One solution is to compare India's reform experience and its outcomes with that of

---

[8] See Bhide, Prasad and Ghosh (2001), p. 7; Hanson (2001a), pp. 5-7; Shirai (2002a), p. 54.

[9] For example Public Sector Banks still account for about 80% of bank assets, foreign banks are bared from taking majority ownership of privately owned Indian banks until April 2009 and the 40% target for credits to priority sectors has remained unchanged. See Bowers, Gibb and Wong (2003), p. 85; Gupta and Jayakar (2005), p. 60; Hanson (2001a), p. 7; Reserve Bank of India (2004b), p. 60.

[10] See La Porta, Lopez de Silanes and Schleifer (2002), p. 26f. One of the main priorities of the United Progressive Alliance government elected in 2004 is achieving a sustainable growth rate of 7-8% over a period of 10-15 years to significantly reduce poverty. See Gupta (2005), p. 116; United Progressive Alliance (2004), p. 2.

[11] Mohan (2004), p. 851.

other countries, which will help to identify peculiarities of the liberalization process in India.

A prime candidate for such a comparison is the People's Republic of China. Like India, China is in the process of creating a more market-based banking system. Since the opening up of its economy in the late 1970s, China has been trying to reform its banking system. This has been achieved first by creating commercial banks and later by a gradual easing of restrictions such as interest rate controls. China and India thus face a similar reform agenda, and a comparison of the two countries in terms of banking sector liberalization may reveal a number of interesting insights.[12]

The thesis of this study – based on the policy changes that have occurred in the banking sector and the literature on financial liberalization – is that India has proceeded faster with reforms than China, but still needs to make progress in creating a market-based system. Even when allowing for market failure arguments, the reforms in India have not been far-reaching enough, especially as far as state-owned banks are concerned. The positive liberalization effects on the sector and on the economy as a whole thus remain limited, jeopardizing India's economic growth targets. Transformation studies offer a framework that can be transferred to the banking sector, allowing us to flesh out the changes required to the allocation and coordination mechanism. The objectives below briefly describe the issues that must be addressed in order to test the thesis of this study.

Objective 1: *To review potential reasons for state involvement in a country's banking sector and the rationale for financial liberalization*
According to the proponents of financial sector liberalization, a banking sector can fulfill its functions of mobilizing and allocating savings better if repressive policies are removed. However, there are several arguments from economic, developmental and political standpoints that state involvement in the banking sector has a positive effect. This study consequently attempts to review the basic rationale for liberalizing the banking sector, given its function in the economy, and look at the differing views on the role of the state.

Objective 2: *To review key policy recommendations of transformation studies in the context of the transformation of a banking sector*
Since the beginning of the transition in the Central and Eastern European countries, a vast amount of different and at times conflicting policy rec-

[12] An in-depth discussion on the comparability of the banking sectors in India and China follows in section 3.3.

ommendations has been given. This thesis attempts to review the key policy recommendations on how to transform a banking sector and discuss which of these recommendations have proven successful given the historical experience of transition countries.

Objective 3: *To integrate transformation studies and financial liberalization studies and thus provide a framework for banking sector liberalization*
Transformation studies and financial liberalization studies both deal with changing the prevailing coordination mechanism from plan to market.[13] These approaches have complementary elements, such as recommendations concerning the timing and sequencing of reforms. Integrating the two concepts is likely to provide a more holistic picture on how to transform a banking sector.

Objective 4: *To discuss the necessary extent of state involvement in the banking sector*
The focus of both transformation and financial liberalization studies is the change from a state-controlled coordination mechanism to market-based system. While these changes lead to a significant reduction of direct state involvement in the economy, they do not imply the complete retreat of the state. This is because "state" and "market" are not discrete variables, but rather constitute two opposite ends of a continuum.[14] The extent to which a country can shift along the continuum depends on the overall economic order as well as sector-specific issues such as the existence of market failures.[15] Under the assumptions that market failures are more prevalent in developing countries and that banking is even in the most developed countries characterized by market failures, it is necessary to define a level of state involvement that ensures the proper functioning of the market.[16]

Objective 5: *To identify a set of indicators for evaluating banking sector reforms*
The purpose of indicators is to give guidance to decision makers. This is especially important during the complex task of transforming the banking

[13] See Csaba (1993), p. 100; Gibson and Tsakalotos (1994), p. 579; Wagener (1996), p. 2.
[14] See Kloten (1991), p. 8f. The continuum problem is discussed by Pryor (1985), pp. 18-20.
[15] Market failures can be caused by information asymmetries that can for example lead to credit rationing as shown by Stiglitz and Weiss (1981). See Aschinger (2001), pp. 66-68 for a general overview of market failures.
[16] See Stiglitz (1996), p. 14f.; Stiglitz (2004), p. 21.

system. The objective is to develop a set of indicators based on transformation and financial liberalization studies that can be used to evaluate the process of reforms and their results.

Objective 6: *To compare and evaluate the status and effects of banking sector reforms in India and China*
A set of indicators is used to evaluate reforms in the banking sector in India. This evaluation looks at both the progress of reforms and their outcomes along several dimensions. In addition, a comparative perspective to the reforms of the Chinese banking sector is taken.

Objective 7: *To discuss further necessary steps for banking sector reforms in India and China*
This objective is achieved by discussing the current status of liberalization in India and China and comparing it to policy recommendations given by transformation studies and the literature on financial sector liberalization.

This thesis advances the existing literature in four areas. First, insights from transformation studies and the literature on financial liberalization are integrated with each other to mould a framework for managing banking sector liberalization. Second, the progress of the transition of the Indian banking sector is evaluated using a comprehensive set of indicators, rather than using a single indicator or looking at a specific aspect of the reforms. Third, while it is generally acknowledged that market failures affect the potential degree of liberalization, this study attempts to incorporate them explicitly in its evaluation of the reforms. And fourth, although many studies have previously compared the performance of the Indian and the Chinese economies, there is a dearth of comparative investigations of their banking sectors.

1.2 Methodology

It is not the goal of this thesis to develop a new theory of either system transformation or financial liberalization. Rather, elements of existing theories are integrated and applied in a new context – the liberalization of the banking sectors in India and China.

To address the research objectives, a multi-method approach combining qualitative and quantitative research methods is employed. Transformation studies and financial liberalization studies are integrated in order to develop propositions on how to liberalize a banking sector. These propositions then form the basis for a discussion of how the reform process should be managed. Indicators are identified for the process elements and the results that are expected based on causal relationships. Subsequently, these form the basis for a quantitative evaluation of the reforms. Finally, the process indicators are integrated to construct a process index.

The process index is constructed in line with the steps identified by transformation studies for evaluating the progress of reforms, their current status and further steps necessary. With the help of econometric methods, the process index can be used to test the effects of liberalization, for example on saving rates, capital accumulation and financial development over time. Wherever possible, data for both India and China for the period 1980 to 2004 is included. However, since better data is available for India, some analyses use data from 1960 to 2004, which allows a clearer evaluation of the effects of different policy regimes.[17]

The results of the qualitative and quantitative evaluations of the reform process form the foundation for recommendations on further steps for banking sector liberalization. They are also used to identify aspects of the political and economic environment that are peculiar to India and that might affect this process.

Since the main research focus of this thesis is on India, this thesis provides an in-depth country case study as opposed to a cross-country study. From a methodological point of view this is in line with a growing recognition that country case studies are an important complement to the still dominant cross-country case studies since they allow for a more careful consideration of specific political, economic and institutional circumstances.[18] The inclusion of China as a comparator country allows combining the advantages of an in-depth country case study with the greater ability to deduct generalizations of cross-country studies.

---

[17] In addition, this will help to account for the growing evidence that the acceleration of India's economic growth already began in the 1980s, and not in the 1990s as commonly assumed. See DeLong (2003), p. 195f.; Rodrik and Subramanian (2004), p. 6.

[18] See Bell and Rosseau (2001), p. 154; Kirkpatrick (2005), p. 633; Ram (1999), p. 173.

1.3 Categorization of topic

The theoretical foundations of the thesis are transformation studies and financial liberalization studies.

The first theoretical framework to explain and guide the transition in Central and Eastern Europe was the so-called "Washington Consensus", whose main policy recommendations focused on the triad of liberalization, stabilization and privatization. However, these policy recommendations came under intense scrutiny soon after the start of the transition for offering a "one-size-fits-all" model of transformation. It was claimed that this neglected the importance of institution building as well as the need for structural change in the transformation countries.[19]

Despite considerable discussion in the literature following the Washington Consensus, there is still no agreement as to a general theory of transformation. Since it is beyond the scope of this thesis to propose such a theory, the focus will instead be on the key elements necessary to manage a transformation process, with emphasis on the transformation of the banking sector.[20]

Financial liberalization studies date back to the seminal works of McKinnon (1973) and Shaw (1973). The basic argument is that freeing a financial sector from repressionist policies, such as interest rate controls or directed credit rules, will enable the sector to perform its functions of mobilizing savings and allocating capital more efficiently. This then has a beneficial impact on growth. The positive effects of financial liberalization and the negative effects of financial restraints are generally accepted in the literature.[21]

However, the link between financial liberalization and economic growth has been subject to intense debate over the last years. An important factor here is market failures, which affect the degree of state involvement

---

[19] See Csaba (1997), p. 8; Ghose (2000), p. 2; Murrell (1995), p. 175; Rodrik (2000), p. 86; Roland (2001), p. 32; Seliger (2002), p. 41; Stiglitz (1999), p. 30; Stiglitz (2004), p. 22.

[20] See Ahrens (1994b), p. 18; Pickel (2002), p. 113; Schulders (1998) p. 3; Seliger (2002), p. 51; Wagener (1996), p. 5. There are several related approaches that can help explain transformation and its problems, such as public choice theory, new institutional economics, development economics, political-economy arguments and ordo-liberalism. These approaches will be referred to where appropriate.

[21] See McKinnon (1973), pp. 1-3; Shaw (1973), p. 3f.

needed. Thus, it is still open to debate how much state involvement is necessary in the banking sector in order to promote economic growth.[22]

Financial liberalization studies and transformation studies are to a certain extent complementary; both, for example, are concerned with the transition from a state-dominated system to a market-based one. Within this, financial liberalization studies emphasize why changing the coordination mechanism provides benefits whereas transformation studies focus more on how to manage the transformation process. A unifying element in both approaches is the desire to overcome the limitations of state involvement, which supposedly inhibits economic growth. Furthermore, as regards managing these changes, both approaches address issues such as the timing and sequencing of reforms.

This thesis attempts to integrate these common elements to form a framework for the evaluation of the liberalization of the banking sector. These insights are then applied to the banking sectors in India and China, which are cases in point for banking sectors currently undergoing liberalization.

1.4 Definition of key terms

For the sake of clarity it is necessary to first define three key terms used in this study: "liberalization", "banking sector" and "financial sector".[23] This is done in the following sub-sections.

It is also necessary to point out two Indian peculiarities. First, the fiscal year in India is distinct from the calendar year and runs to the end of March. For example, official publications use the form of "2002-03" to refer to the fiscal year 2002, which runs from April 2002 to March 2003. Since most of the international data used for comparison purposes covers the calendar year, the simplifying assumption has been made that data for the fiscal year is equivalent to that for the calendar year (i.e. data for 2002-03 is treated as if it were year-end data for December 2002). Second, in India the numerical units *lakh* ("100,000") and *crore* (10,000,000, or 100 *lakh*) are commonly used. Thus, for example, twenty million Indian rupees may be referred to as two crore.

---

[22] See for example Arestis and Demetriades (1997); Balassa (1990); King and Levine (1993); Levine (1997); Rajan and Zingales (1998).

[23] A discussion of the terms "transformation" and "transition" follows at the beginning of section 5.1.1.

1.4.1 Liberalization

In relation to the banking sector of a country, the term "liberalization" can be used in both a narrow and a broad sense.

In the narrow sense, financial liberalization refers to the removal of repressionist policies, especially interest rate restrictions and direct credit rules. Since these constitute price and volume restrictions, liberalization in the narrow sense can be essentially thought of as the restoration of the price and allocation mechanism in the financial sector. Williamson and Mahar (1998) define liberalization in this narrower sense as "[...] giving the market the authority to determine who gets and grants credit and at what price."[24]

In its broader sense, the term liberalization refers to a range of different economic policies designed to open up the banking sector.[25] In this sense, liberalization is the process through which market forces as opposed to the government gain importance in allocating resources and setting prices.[26] Liberalization of the banking sector in this broader sense can thus be understood "[...] as a set of operational reforms and policy measures designed to deregulate and transform the financial system and its structure with the view to achieving a liberalized market-oriented system within an appropriate regulatory framework."[27]

In this thesis, liberalization is used both the narrower and the broader sense. The general topic of this thesis is liberalization in the broad sense, since it focuses on the overall set of policies needed to change the coordination mechanism of a banking sector. Liberalization is used in the narrow sense to refer to the easing of repressionist policies such as interest rate restrictions and directed credit rules. In its narrow sense, liberalization is just one of the necessary policy steps needed to transform the banking system.

1.4.2 Banking sector and financial sector

Before discussing the difference between the "banking sector" and the "financial sector", it is necessary to define what institutions make up the banking sector.

Banks, like for example non-bank financial intermediaries or credit unions, can be categorized as financial institutions. The distinguishing feature

[24] Williamson and Mahar (1998), p. 2.

[25] See Raje (2000), endnote 1.

[26] See Quispe-Agnoli and McQuerry (2001), p. 3.

[27] Johnston and Sundararajan (1999), p. 2f. (quoted from Quispe-Agnoli and McQuerry (2001), p. 3).

of banks from other institutions is that they can both receive deposits and grant loans. In addition, they generally hold a banking license issued by a regulatory authority, which makes them subject to banking supervision. A further type of formal financial institutions are development financial institutions. These institutions mostly have a relatively narrow business scope that distinguishes them from commercial banks – in general, they try to foster the development of a certain sector and cannot take deposits. Semi-formal financial institutions provide certain banking services but do not hold a banking license. They include non-bank financial intermediaries like insurance companies, investment banks, finance companies, pension funds and also credit unions, for example. Furthermore, informal financial institutions are, for example, self-help groups or moneylenders that operate outside of government regulations.

For the purposes of this study, the banking system includes formal and semi-formal financial institutions (Figure 1).[28] The main research focus of this thesis is commercial banks in the formal sector, which make up the banking sector of a country. The reason for this focus is that better data is available for these banks, and policy changes such as financial liberalization are geared towards the formal sector, so the main effects can be expected here.

The terms "banking sector" and "financial sector" are often used interchangeably. In fact, a distinction should be made between the two. While the banking sector comprises only the commercial banks of a country, the financial sector consists of both the banking sector and securities markets. Thus, the banking sector is in fact a sub-section of the financial sector.[29]

Although this thesis focuses on the banking sector, it will also be necessary in places to refer to the financial sector as well. In fact, findings for the financial sector should also apply to the banking sector of a country. This is because banks are the major player in the financial sector, particularly in developing countries. Securities markets, on the other hand, are of relatively minor importance. Accordingly, the financial system of these countries is often described as "bank-based". This is true for both India and China, where the banking sector accounts for over 80% of the funds flowing through the financial sector. In this case, then, banking and financial sector are virtually identical and it can be assumed that the effects of liber-

[28] See Freixas and Rochet (1998), p. 1; Krahnen and Schmidt (1994), p. 35. Sometimes an argument is made that formal and informal sources of finance are functionally equivalent. This however is not the case since informal finance is generally insufficient to fund large-scale projects. See Huang (2006), p. 300.

[29] See Platek (2002), p. 9.

alization in the financial sector largely coincide with those in the banking sector.[30]

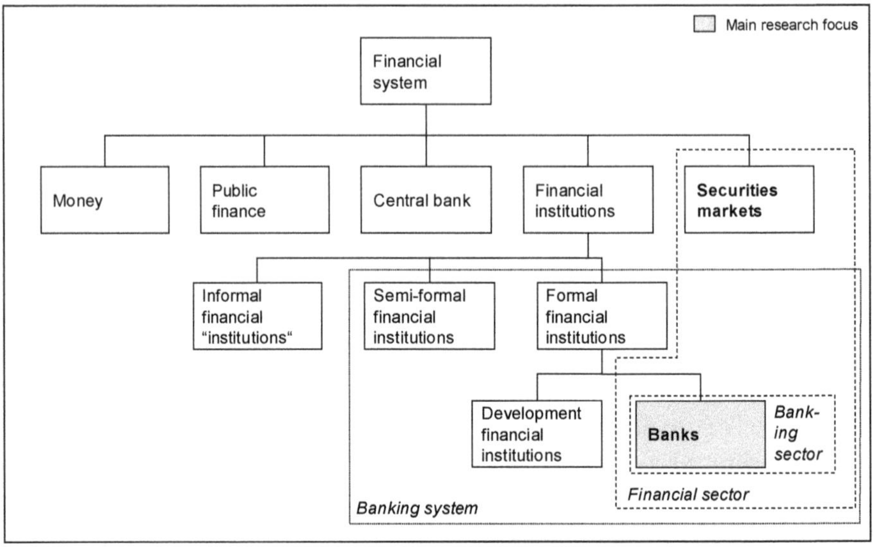

Fig. 1. Differentiation between financial sector and banking sector[31]

Furthermore, even though the financial sector is often discussed in the context of financial liberalization, the banking sector is a good proxy for this as most early adjustments actually occur there.[32]

The main focus of this thesis is on formal sector institutions, as discussed above. Semi-formal sector institutions such as cooperative banks, non-bank financial intermediaries and donor-sponsored programs, as well

---

[30] See Berglof and Bolton (2002), p. 92; Indian Banks' Association (2003), p. 9; Mohan (2006a), p. 17; McKinsey Global Institute (2006b), p. 27; Quispe-Agnoli and McQuerry (2001), p. 2; Werner (1999), p. 5. Commercial banks are the most important players in these countries since development financial institutions such as agricultural banks are also comparatively small. See Fry (1997), p. 754.
The importance of securities markets increases when a country becomes more advanced economically. An important reason is that banks are generally supervised by the state and thus offer better protection for small investors when regulatory and contractual enforcement institutions in securities markets are weak. See Berglof and Bolton (2002), p. 92.

[31] Author's presentation based on Krahnen and Schmidt (1994), p. 7 and Platek (2002), p. 9.

[32] See Fry (1997), p. 754; Quispe-Agnoli and McQuerry (2001), p. 1.

as informal sector "institutions" such as money lenders or rotating saving and credit associations, are largely excluded from the analysis.[33]

1.5 Structure of the thesis

The structure of this thesis can be seen in Figure 2. Chapters 2 and 3 deal with the development of the banking sector in India and China. These chapters precede the discussion of the theoretical framework of the thesis so that it is possible to connect the theoretical underpinning with the experiences of the two countries.

Chapter 2 provides a detailed overview of the Indian banking sector. The starting point is the development of the banking sector since Independence in 1947. This is necessary in order to gain an understanding of changes in the policy environment. However, the main focus is on policy changes after 1991, which are the basis for the later evaluation of the reforms. Banking sectors are closely integrated with the rest of the economy; therefore the structure and political, economic and institutional setting of the banking sector are also presented.

Chapter 3 provides an overview of the Chinese banking sector. The main issues covered are the development of the sector over recent decades and the current reform areas. As for India, an overview of the structure of the sector is provided. Even a cursory look at developments in India and China reveals that there are, in fact, numerous differences between the two. Therefore, to determine whether a common assessment of the two countries is meaningful, the issue of comparability with the Indian banking sector is also discussed.

Chapter 4 focuses on financial liberalization. It begins by presenting the functions of a banking sector that include the mobilization of savings and the allocation of capital. These functions can be provided under different coordination mechanisms ranging from "state" to "market", as the two extremes, which both have advantages and disadvantages. Therefore, first an overview of arguments for state involvement and possible instruments for the state is given. This is followed by a discussion of the main elements of the financial liberalization hypothesis of McKinnon and Shaw, as an argument for market coordination of the banking sector. As there are compelling theoretical arguments for both the state and the market as the predominant coordination mechanism of the banking sector, chapter 4 con

[33] For an overview see Krahnen and Schmidt (1994), p. 7.

cludes with a detailed overview of the empirical evidence on their relative merits.

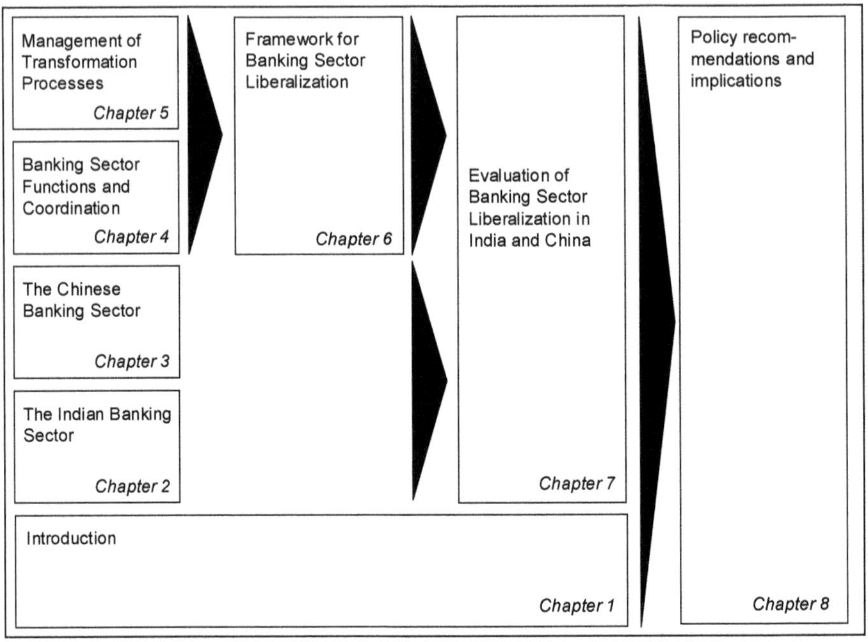

Fig. 2. Structure of the thesis

The main emphasis of the financial liberalization literature is on the advantages of one particular coordination mechanism. Little advice is given on how to achieve it. This void can be filled by transformation studies – the major focus of chapter 5. The starting point here is the initial recommendations of the Washington Consensus and the additional recommendations based on the experience of the transition countries. Chapter 5 discusses the necessary elements of the transformation process – such as liberalization, privatization and institution building; it also discusses issues in the management of the transition from a state-dominated to a market-based system, such as speed and sequencing of reforms. The focus is on the level of the overall economy as the necessary basis before the insights can be applied to the banking sector.

Chapters 4 (on financial liberalization) and 5 (on transformation studies) form the basis for chapter 6, in which a framework is developed for managing the transformation of a banking sector. The recommendations of transformation studies generally apply to the overall economy, so they must first be adapted to the level of the banking sector. After this, the process elements of transformation studies serve as the structure for deriving propositions for managing the liberalization of a banking sector. Besides the derivation of qualitative proposition, possible indicators for the process and results along the process steps are identified. As discussed, market failures are an important factor in developing countries like India and China. Since they influence both the reform steps and the evaluation of the results, they are also discussed in detail. Finally, chapter 6 presents some hypotheses on the macroeconomic effects of liberalization.

The propositions and indicators from chapter 6 are used in chapter 7 for a comprehensive evaluation of banking sector reforms in India and China. The discussion of the results forms the basis for recommendations for further reforms and policy changes.

The final chapter summarizes the main findings of this study and gives recommendations for further reforms. It also attempts to determine which findings are due to country-specific factors and which apply equally to other settings.

2 The Indian banking sector

This chapter gives an in-depth overview of the Indian banking sector and its structural setting. The focus is on the development of the sector since 1947, with special emphasis on the reforms that have taken place since 1991. Furthermore, it examines the structural setting of the Indian banking sector and its political, economic and institutional environment.

2.1 Development of the Indian banking sector

The Indian banking sector has undergone several major policy changes since Independence in 1947, at which time it had a relatively market-friendly system. With the creation of the State Bank of India in 1955 and two waves of bank nationalization in 1969 and 1980, the state gained considerable influence over the sector. This influence was subsequently reduced after an external crisis in 1991. The following sections describe these developments as well as their underlying causes.

2.1.1 Development from 1947 to 1991

When India achieved independence in 1947, its banking system was already fairly well developed. The Reserve Bank of India (RBI) had been established in 1935 following the passing of the Reserve Bank of India Act in 1934. At the end of 1947, over 600 commercial banks were operating in India.[1] However, soon after Independence the view gained prominence that the banks founded in colonial times were biased in favor of working-capital loans for trade and large firms, and against extending credit to small-scale enterprises, agriculture and ordinary citizens.[2]

To counter these imbalances, the 1951 *Committee of Direction of All India Rural Credit Survey* recommended founding an integrated state-

[1] See Cygnus Economic & Business Research (2004), p. 5; ICRA (2004), p. 4; Reddy (2002b), p. 337.

[2] See Joshi and Little (1997), p. 110f.; Shirai (2002c), p. 8.

partnered commercial bank in order to stimulate banking development and credit extension to rural constituencies. This was the starting point for the nationalization of commercial banks in India. The Government of India assumed ownership of the Imperial Bank of India and, in 1955, it was established as the State Bank of India (SBI) to ensure better coverage of the banking needs of larger parts of the economy and the rural population. In 1959, the State Bank Group was founded by adding eight state banks to the SBI.[3]

Despite progress in the 1950s and 1960s, the creation of the SBI was felt to be insufficient: the banking needs of small-scale industries and the agricultural sector were still not covered adequately. This was partly due to the close ties commercial and industry houses maintained with the established commercial banks, which gave them an advantage in obtaining credit. Furthermore, there was the perception that banks should play a more prominent role in India's development strategy by mobilizing resources for sectors that were considered a priority for economic development. As a consequence, in 1967 the Indian government imposed a policy of social control over banks with the aim of forcing changes in the management and distribution of credit by commercial banks.[4]

Following the Nationalization Act of 1969, the 14 largest public banks with deposits above a certain cut-off point were nationalized. This measure raised the Public Sector Banks' (PSB) share of deposits from 31 to 86%. The two main objectives of this first wave of nationalization were rapid branch expansion and the channeling of credit in line with the priorities of the five-year plans.[5] To achieve these objectives, the newly nationalized banks received quantitative targets for the expansion of their branch network as well as targets for the percentage of credit that they had to extend to priority sectors.[6]

Besides introducing priority sector lending, the government raised the statutory liquidity ratio (SLR) and cash reserve ratio (CRR) for banks,

[3] See Bhide, Prasad and Ghosh (2001), p. 3f.; Cygnus Economic & Business Research (2004), p. 5; Hanson (2001b), p. 261; Kumbhakar and Sarkar (2003), p. 406f.; Reddy (2002b), p. 337.

[4] See ICRA (2004), p. 5; Reddy (2002b), p. 338; Shirai (2002c), p. 8.

[5] The launch of the first Indian five-year plan was in 1951. The plans provided a general framework for the allocation of capital and lined out key policies such as "import substitution", but were not as extensive as the five-year plans in the Soviet Union or in China. See Jalan (2005), p. 46f.

[6] See Arun and Turner (2002a), p. 184; Bhide, Prasad and Ghosh (2001), p. 4; Hanson (2001a), p. 2; Joshi and Little (1997), p. 111; Kumbhakar and Sarkar (2003), p. 407; Reddy (2002b), p. 338.

which gave it greater control over banks' funds.[7] The consequence was that "[...] companies became dependent on government banks for short-term capital and on financial institutions funded by the banks, for long-term capital. In this way the government monopolized the access of private – and government – companies to private savings".[8]

From 1975 onward the SBI and the nationalized banks were required to set up and sponsor regional rural banks. This had to be done in partnership with individual states. The goal was to provide low-cost financing and credit facilities to the rural population.[9]

In 1980 the nationalization of six more banks raised the public sector's share of deposits to 92%. The rationale for this second wave of nationalizations was the increasing importance of state control over the banking system as a means to ensure priority sector lending, to reach the poor through a widening branch network, and to ensure funding of rising public deficits.[10]

However, the policies that were supposed to promote a more equal distribution of funds also led to inefficiencies. To counter these inefficiencies, attempts to deregulate the sector were made from the second half of the 1980s. This included the introduction of Treasury Bills, the creation of money markets, and the partial deregulation of interest rates. In 1985, there was a gradual increase in interest rates on government bonds to better reflect supply and demand. The following year, a 182-day Treasury Bill was introduced. In 1988, the Discount and Financial House of India was established with the purpose of enhancing liquidity in the financial market. As part of the simplification of interest rate categories, ceiling lending rates and ranges in minimum rates were unified in 1988 and a new minimum lending rate introduced. In 1989, the maximum interest rate on call money was liberalized and commercial paper and certificates of deposit introduced.[11]

With hindsight, the reforms enacted between 1985 and 1989 can be seen as paving the way for the reforms of the 1990s. They were more far-reaching than the isolated reforms of the 1960s and 1970s, which were of-

---

[7] The SLR refers to funds that have to be kept in cash or government bonds, the CRR is a percentage of funds that have to be deposited with the RBI. In section 2.1.2.2.1, a more detailed description of the SLR and CRR follows.

[8] Desai (1999), p. 14.

[9] See Deolalkar (1999), p. 61.

[10] See Arun and Turner (2002a), p. 184; Hanson (2001a), p. 2f.; Kumbhakar and Sarkar (2003), p. 407.

[11] See Bhide, Prasad and Ghosh (2001), p. 5; Shirai (2002c), p. 9.

ten reversed soon after their introduction. However, the reforms were not enough to ensure an efficient distribution of funds.[12]

India's banking system prior to 1991 was an integral part of the government's spending policies. Through directed credit rules and statutory preemptions it was a captive source of funds to prop up the fiscal deficit and promote key industries. With the CRR and the SLR more than 50% of savings either had to be deposited with the RBI or to be used to buy government securities. Of the remaining savings, 40% had to be directed to priority sectors as defined by the government. Besides these restrictions on the use of funds, the government also had control over the price of the funds, i.e. the interest rates on savings and loans. This changed at the beginning of the 1990s when a balance-of-payments crisis triggered a number of far-reaching reforms.[13]

2.1.2 Development from 1991 to 2005

Although some reforms were initiated during the 1980s, the 1991 crisis marked a turning point for the Indian banking sector. To gain an appreciation of the triggers for change, the background and goals of the reforms are first presented below. This is followed by a description of the policy changes in the six main reform areas.

2.1.2.1 Background and goals of reforms

The impetus for the changes in the Indian banking sector and the rest of the economy was a balance-of-payment crisis in 1991. The reforms that followed the crisis were unquestionably more comprehensive than previous reform attempts. While the reforms of the 1980s had aimed at improving the functioning of the sector within the existing coordination framework, the reforms of the 1990s marked a fundamental break with the past. Before turning to the changes that have taken place in India's banking sector, it is worth looking at the economic environment at the start of the reforms and the events immediately leading up to them. The distortions that triggered the changes were not, in fact, confined to the banking sector. There were also problems in other parts of the economy and these had further repercussions on the problems in the banking sector.

In the 1980s, India's fiscal deficit grew from 6 to 8.4% of GNP. This was due to higher public spending, financed by India's central bank. As a

[12] See Panagariya (2004), p. 5.
[13] See Mukherji (2002), p. 39.

consequence, inflationary pressures increased. As an additional means to obtain funds, the government increased the CRR and SLR so that private funds could be used to pay for public consumption. This, in turn, led to a crowding out of private investment.[14]

With this expansive fiscal policy, India's current account deficit increased significantly in the 1980s. While the current account deficit stood at an average of 25% of exports from 1982 to 1984, it increased to an average of 40% of exports in the period from 1985 to 1990. The shortfall in the balance-of-payments was covered by borrowing from the International Monetary Fund (IMF) and from commercial sources. India's exchange rate policy is partially to blame for the deficit, at least for the period from 1982 to 1985. Between 1979 and 1981 the real exchange rate appreciated by 15% and stayed at that level for the next four years. The result was an almost complete stagnation of exports. However, the main culprit for the structural problems was the deterioration of fiscal discipline, as described above.[15]

The full extent of the structural problems was exposed at the start of the Gulf War in early 1991. The war led to an increase in oil prices, cut off Iraq as an export market for Indian goods and stopped the remittances from Indians working in Kuwait. The result was a major balance-of-payment crisis during which foreign exchange reserves dropped to less than the cost of two weeks' imports. Gold reserves had to be flown to London as collateral for loans. Other factors aggravating the situation in India were a general slowdown in world trade due to recessions in developed countries, the breakup of Eastern Europe, and tight liquidity in global capital markets.[16]

But these external factors were only the trigger of the balance-of-payment crisis: the root causes lay elsewhere. The events of the 1990s exposed the structural problems created by India's economic policies in previous decades, such as its inward-looking nature and its mistrust of foreign direct investment. Consequently, India's inability to receive capital from the international markets to cover its current account deficit was not necessarily an exogenous shock but at least partly a result of the previously pursued macroeconomic policies. The balance-of-payments crisis also showed that the economic policies of the time were out of line with the changing

[14] See Desai (1999), p. 20; Oschinski (2003), p. 7.

[15] See Joshi and Little (1997), p. 14f; Oschinski (2003), p. 7.

[16] See Desai (1999), p. 24; Oschinski (2003), p. 7; Singh (2005), p. 4f.

environment. Indeed, in many ways the crisis of the 1990s facilitated radical change because the old order had been discredited.[17]

The banking sector in India also suffered from severe structural problems. The major issues were summarized by the *Narasimham Committee* that was charged with proposing reforms for the sector:

"despite impressive quantitative achievements in resource mobilisation and in extending credit reach, several distortions have, over the years, crept into the financial system, especially in respect of allocation of financial resources. [...] Several factors have contributed to this [...] but perhaps the most important among them has been the impact of policy induced rigidities such as an excessive degree of central direction of their [the banks'] operations in terms of investments, credit allocations, branch expansion, and even internal management aspects of the business."[18]

These policy-induced rigidities severely undermined the viability of the banking sector. Joshi and Little (1997) characterize the sector as it was in 1991 as "[...] unprofitable, inefficient, and financially unsound".[19] By international standards, Indian banks were extremely unprofitable, despite a rapid growth in deposits. In the second half of the 1980s, the average return on assets (ROA) was around 0.15%. The return on equity was considerably higher at 9.5%, but this merely reflected the low capitalization of banks. While capital and reserves stood at about 1.5% of assets in India, the level in other Asian countries stood at about 4 to 6%.

Moreover, these differences do not take into account the fact that India at the time did not utilize the tighter internationally recognized income recognition and loss provisioning standards, which would further deteriorate the relative position of Indian banks.[20] Policies used by the state to gain influence over the banking sector between the 1960s and the mid-1980s, including statutory pre-emptions, interest rate controls and priority sector advances, adversely affected the performance of the banking sec-

[17] See Halbach and Helmschrott (1994), p. 34; Joshi and Little (1997), p. 14. In fact, before the economy was opened up, other policy measures such as increasing restrictions or restraining growth were tried unsuccessfully to stabilize the economy. See Desai (1999), p. 8.

[18] Government of India (1991), p. 3f.

[19] Joshi and Little (1997), p. 111.

[20] See Joshi and Little (1997), p. 111. In addition to their weak financial performance, the banks also provided a very low quality of service despite a large personnel overhang. See Halbach and Helmschrott (1994), p. 53; Joshi and Little (1997), p. 112.

tor.[21] As a result, despite the reform efforts of the mid-1980s, India's banking sector was still highly regulated and financially repressed.

The objective of the banking sector reforms after 1991 was in line with the overall goals of the concurrent economic reforms. They aimed to open up the economy, give a greater role to market forces in setting prices and allocating resources, and increase the role of the private sector. Specific objectives were abolishing repressive policies, creating a productive financial sector, increasing the profitability and efficiency of Public Sector Banks, providing institutions with operational and functional autonomy, enabling price discovery through the deregulation of interest rates, and promoting financial stability. By overcoming the shortcomings and distortions of the previously heavily administered banking sector, the reforms hoped to give the private sector better access to financial savings, reduce interest rates and distortions in credit allocation, and ultimately aid economic growth.[22]

2.1.2.2 Reform areas

The *Narasimham Committee* provided the blueprint for the initial reforms in the banking sector following the balance-of-payment crisis in 1991. The reforms enacted can be grouped into three large areas. First, reforms liberalizing the sector by dismantling interest rate controls and reducing the statutory pre-emptions that required banks to hold government securities. Second, reforms increasing competition in the industry by granting licenses to new banks and lowering restrictions on the expansion of foreign banks. And third, reforms that improved financial soundness, such as the introduction of capital adequacy requirements and the strengthening of bank supervision.[23] A detailed description of each area is given below.

2.1.2.2.1 Statutory pre-emptions

An important step towards a more efficient and market-oriented banking sector was the lowering of the CRR and the SLR.

---

[21] See Demetriades and Luintel (1997), p. 314f.; Shirai (2002c), p. 8.

[22] See Arun and Turner (2002a), p. 183; Guha-Khasnobis and Bhaduri (2000), p. 335f.; Hanson (2001a), p. 5; Mohan (2004), p. 852; Shirai (2002c), p. 7; Werner (1999), p. 6.

[23] See Ahluwalia (2002), p. 81.

The CRR is a percentage of Reservable Liabilities[24] that banks[25] have to keep with the RBI. During the 1960s and 1970s the CRR was mostly below 5%, but by 1991 it had increased to its maximum legal limit of 15% (Figure 3). The high CRR was identified as one of the main causes of low profitability and high interest rate spreads in the banking system; accordingly, it was gradually reduced in line with the recommendations of the *Narasimham Committee*. From a peak of 15% in 1991, it declined gradually to a low of 4.5% in June 2003. In October 2004 it was increased to 5% to counter inflationary pressures, but the RBI so far remains committed to decreasing the CRR to its statutory minimum of 3%.[26]

The SLR refers to the reserves that banks have to keep in cash, government bonds or other approved securities. It is calculated as a percentage of the higher of net demand and time liabilities (NDTLs) or reservable liabilities. At its peak in February 1992, the SLR stood at 38.5%, slightly below the legal limit of 40%. Since then it has been gradually lowered to the statutory minimum of 25%, its level since October 1997 (Figure 3).[27]

Lowering the SLR was expected to reduce the captive market for government bonds, forcing the government to pay higher interest rates due to the lower demand for its securities. Contrary to expectations, however, banks have not reduced their holding of government bonds. In March 2004, banks held SLR securities at a level of 41.3% of NDTLs; this fell slightly 38.4% in March 2005.[28]

---

[24] Reservable Liabilities are net demand and time liabilities less all liabilities exempted from statutory reserve requirements. See Shirai (2002c), p. 11.

[25] Regional Rural Banks are not required to deposit the CRR. See Shirai (2002c), p. 11.

[26] See Ghose (2000), p. 199; Government of India (1991), p. 26f.; Reserve Bank of India (2004b), p. 10; Shirai (2002c), p. 12.

[27] See Ghose (2000), p. 199; Reserve Bank of India (2004b), p. 10; Shirai (2002c), p. 12.

[28] See Government of India (1991), p. 25; Reserve Bank of India (2004b), p. 10; Reserve Bank of India (2005c), p. 3; Shirai (2002c), p. 12. The interest-rate environment contributed to the increased demand for government securities, since banks could profit from falling interest rates. See Sy (2005), p. 3.

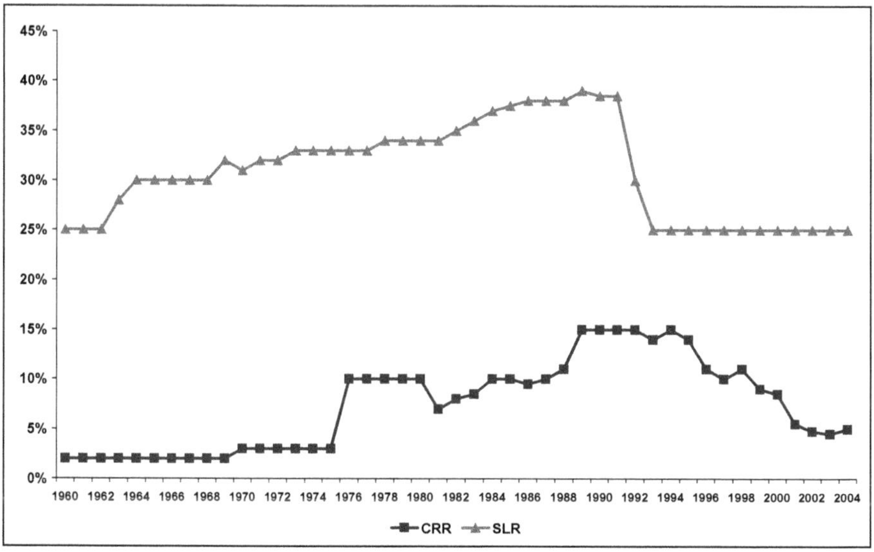

Fig. 3. Development of CRR and SLR[29]

Reducing the CRR and the SLR gave banks increased flexibility to determine both the volume and the terms of lending. It also enabled a shift in monetary policy from direct controls to indirect market-based instruments.[30]

Despite reductions in the CRR and SLR, the combined share of funds that flows to the government today stands at about 30%. Banks serve as sort of "quasi-fiscal instruments"[31] for the government. Further reductions of the CRR and SLR will therefore depend on a lowering of the budget deficit.

2.1.2.2.2 Priority sector lending

Since 1969, Indian banks have been required to allocate a predetermined portion of credit to specific end-users – the so-called priority sectors – so as to extend the geographical and functional reach of bank credit. Priority sectors include sectors areas as agriculture, small-scale industry, small

[29] Demetriades and Luintel (1997), p. 320; Reserve Bank of India "Report on Trend and Progress of Banking in India", various issues. The 25% SLR ratio was between 1993 and 1997 applied to increases over deposits on a base date. See Hanson (2001a), p. 4.

[30] See Kamesam (2002), p. 379; Reddy (2002a), p. 364; Reserve Bank of India (2003), p. 11.

[31] Bhattacharya and Patel (2004), p. 17.

transport operators and the export sector. Thus, it favors areas that are most likely to suffer from a shortage of credit because of a lack of credit history, high risks and high relationship maintenance costs for banks. In 1985 the target for priority sector advances in India increased to 40% of net bank credit. At the same time, additional sub-targets were introduced for sectors such as agriculture (18%), small-scale industry (10%) and weaker sections of the population (10%).[32]

As early as 1985, the *Report of the Committee to Review the Working of the Monetary System* observed that loans extended to priority sectors had relatively low interest rates. This was identified as one of the main reasons for the low profitability of the banking system. Advances in the priority sector furthermore led to an expansion of different credit and interest rate categories depending on the sector, the size of the credit, and the use of the funds. Thus in the fiscal year 1989-1990 more than 50 credit categories were in place. Naturally, this increased the complexity – and cost – of doing business for banks and borrowers alike.[33]

The directed credit program helped to broaden the reach of bank credit. However, the adverse effects on banks included a reduction of the quality of the loan portfolio, an increase of non-performing loans (NPLs), and lower profitability. As a result the *Narasimham Committee* recommended reducing directed credit from 40 to 10%.[34] This recommendation has not been implemented and the targets of 40% for domestic banks and 32% for foreign banks have remained. Although the nominal target has remained unchanged, the burden of directed credit has been reduced by expanding the definition of priority sector lending to include for example information technology companies and by liberalizing lending rates on credit in excess of Rs 200,000. These measures have increased the profitability of priority sector loans. Shortfalls in meeting the priority sector targets can be compensated through loans to certain development financial institutions.[35]

The issue of priority sector credit remains controversial. Sectors such as agriculture, road and water transport operators and small-scale industries

---

[32] See Ganesan (2003), p. 14; Government of India (1991), p. 27; Raje (2000), p. 28; Reserve Bank of India (2004b), p. 16; Shirai (2002c), p. 18.

[33] See Ganesan (2003), p. 14; Joshi and Little (1997), p. 130. Hanson (2001b) reports that in 1988 the overview of the various lending rates covered ten pages. See Hanson (2001b), p. 246.

[34] See Government of India (1991), p. 29 and p. 44.

[35] See Hanson (2001a), p. 8; Reserve Bank of India (2004b), p. 16; Shirai (2002c), p. 18. Priority sector lending requirements for foreign banks stand at the current level of 32% since 1993. The sub-targets for foreign and domestic banks are different as well. Foreign banks for example have a 10% target for the export sector, which is not the case for domestic banks. See Shirai (2002c), p. 18.

often suffer for various reasons from a lack of credit from the formal sector, which may hinder economic development. These issues will be discussed in detail in section 6.3.3.

2.1.2.2.3 Interest rate deregulation

Prior to the reforms, interest rates were used to cross-subsidize different sectors of the economy. To achieve this objective, the interest rate structure had grown increasingly complex. Moreover, both lending and deposit rates were set by the RBI and rates on postal savings were set by the government. The deregulation of interest rates was a major component of the banking sector reforms aimed at promoting financial savings and the growth of the organized financial system.[36]

The government-set lending rate for loans in excess of Rs 200,000, which accounts for over 90% of total advances was abolished in October 1994. At the same time banks had to announce a prime lending rate that under RBI guidelines had to take into account the cost of funds and transaction costs. For loans under Rs 200,000, interest rates can be set freely since April 1998 as long as they do not exceed the prime lending rate. Easing the priority sector lending requirements (see above) also reduced the number of rate categories. In addition, interest rates on priority sector credit rates were gradually liberalized.[37]

On the deposit side, there was a gradual liberalization for the rates on all term deposits, which account for 70% of total deposits. Deposit rate liberalization started in 1992, when an overall maximum rate for term deposits was fixed. From October 1995 onward, interest rates for term deposits of two years were liberalized. This threshold was reduced to one year in 1996, while the minimum maturity was lowered from 46 days to 30 days, which was further reduced to 15 days in 1998 and 7 days in 2004. Term deposit rates were fully liberalized in 1997. As of 2005, the RBI only sets the interest rate for non-resident Indian deposits and the savings deposit rate. The RBI's stated rationale for continuing to set the deposit rate is that households in rural and semi-urban areas hold the bulk of these deposits.

[36] See Arun and Turner (2002b), p. 437; Government of India (1991), p. 46; Sen and Vaidya (1997), p. 75; Singh (2005), p. 18; Varma (2002), p. 10.

[37] See Arun and Turner (2002b), p. 437; Hanson (2001a), p. 8; Hanson (2001b), p. 250f.; Reserve Bank of India (2005c), p. 15; Shirai (2002c), p. 13. An early attempt to liberalize loan rates actually started in 1988 by turning the maximum rate on non-directed credit into a minimum rate. See Hanson (2001a), p. 8.

For all other deposits above 15 days, banks are free to set their own interest rates.[38]

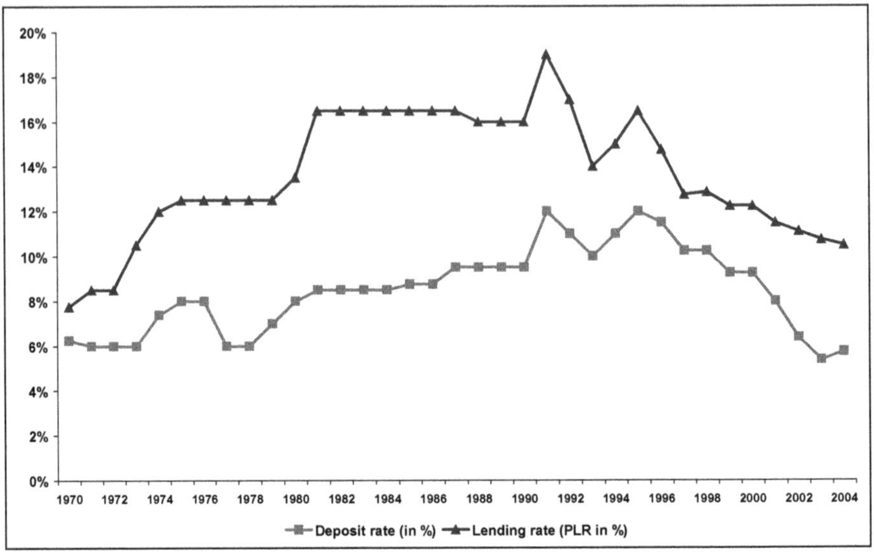

Fig. 4. Development of nominal interest rates[39]

The deregulation of interest rates marked an important move towards market-oriented banking as it gave banks the flexibility to devise their own deposit and lending rate structures. This increased the level of competition, as interest rates can now be used by banks to differentiate themselves in the marketplace. With increased competition, banks cannot cross-subsidize between different activities and customers as easily as before, which means that they have had to become better at assessing and pricing risk. In addition, the lifting of interest rate restrictions has benefited customers by lowering lending rates and reducing the spread between deposit and lending rates (Figure 4).[40]

2.1.2.2.4 Entry regulations

Two important measures to infuse more competition into the banking system in India were entry deregulation and the deregulation of branch restric-

[38] See Mohan (2006b), p. 2; Reserve Bank of India (2005c), p. 14; Shirai (2002c), p. 13f.
[39] See Reserve Bank of India (2005a); Shirai (2002c), p. 10.
[40] See Hawkins and Mihaljek (2001), p. 3; Reserve Bank of India (2004b), p. 11.

tions. Before the start of the 1991 reforms, there was little effective competition in the Indian banking sector for at least two reasons. First, the detailed prescriptions of the RBI left banks with a limited degree of freedom to differentiate themselves in the marketplace. Regulated interest rates are a case in point. And second, India had strict entry restrictions for new banks, which effectively shielded the incumbents from competition.[41]

In 1993 the RBI issued guidelines concerning the establishment of new private sector banks. It specified six major requirements for setting up a bank. These were as follows: to maintain paid-up capital of at least Rs 1 billion; to list shares on stock exchanges; to fulfill priority sector credit requirements; to have a ceiling of one percent of total voting rights held by a single foreign shareholder; not to set up a subsidiary or mutual funds for at least three years; and to use modern infrastructure facilities to provide good customer service. Foreign banks have three options to conduct business in India. They can operate either through wholly-owned subsidiaries, through branches, or through a subsidiary with a foreign investment below 74% in an Indian private bank.[42]

With the lowering of entry barriers, competition has significantly increased since the beginning of the 1990s. Nine new private banks have entered the market after the introduction of the new entry guidelines at the beginning of 1993. In addition, over 20 foreign banks have begun operations in India since 1994. By March 2005, the new private sector banks and the foreign banks had a combined share of almost 25% of total assets.[43]

The deregulation of entry requirements and the subsequent arrival of new players has benefited the Indian banking system. Following the market entry of new private sector and foreign banks, most PSBs upgraded their customer service standards and technology, as well as their risk management skills, so as to be able to compete. A further advantage of the entry of foreign banks has been the exposure of unsustainable lending practices at some domestic banks, such as lending to chronically loss-making enterprises, which were not viable anymore in the new competitive environment.[44]

---

[41] See Deolalkar (1999), p. 60; Joshi and Little (1997), p. 148; Kamesam (2002), p. 380; Reddy (2002b), p. 340.

[42] See Reserve Bank of India (2005b), p. 1; Shirai (2002c), p. 19f. The ceiling on individual shareholding was increased to 10% after the amendment of the Banking Regulation Act in 1994. See Shirai (2002c), p. 20.

[43] See Arun and Turner (2002b) p. 439; Hanson (2001a), p. 6; ICRA (2004), p. 23; Reserve Bank of India (2005c), pp. 231-233; Shirai (2002c), p. 20.

[44] See Fitch Ratings (2003), p. 2; Koch (1998), p. 76f.; Reserve Bank of India (2004b), p. 167.

It was originally expected that the government would lift the barriers to foreign banks entering the market, allowing global operators to acquire controlling stakes in Indian banks. However, the requirements on foreign banks wanting to acquire Indian banks instead increased at the beginning of 2005 with the issuing of a two-phase roadmap by the RBI. According to this roadmap, between 2005 and 2009 foreign banks may acquire a maximum of 74% of those private sector banks the RBI identifies as in need of restructuring. The situation will be reviewed in Phase two of the roadmap will start in April 2009 with an evaluation of the experiences of the first phase. Depending on the outcome of this review, foreign banks may be allowed to list their wholly-owned subsidiaries on the stock-market if they ensure that resident Indians own at least 26% of the equity.[45]

Entry barriers were also lowered through changes in branch restrictions. As mentioned above, the extension of banking services to larger parts of the population was one of the main priorities of the policy of social control of banking from 1967 onward. In terms of the number of bank branches – up from about 8,250 in 1969 to over 68,000 in 2005 – significant progress has been made. The main thrust for this came from rural branches, that increased by about 30,000 branches. At the same time, the average population served per branch fell from 64,000 to 16,000. Yet despite this, only around 60% of India's adult population have a bank account, a figure that compares to over 90% in developed countries.[46]

In line with the recommendations of the *Narasimham Committee*, the RBI changed its licensing policy in 1992 to give banks greater autonomy in opening, transferring and closing branches. Banks may now shift branches within the same locality, open special branches, convert non-viable rural branches into satellite offices and open extension counters without prior approval from the RBI. Regulations were eased still further in 1993-94, when banks received permission to close one loss-making branch in rural centers. The prerequisites are that the area is not left "unbanked" – this means that at least two other commercial banks have to maintain branches there, mutual consent must be reached, and the RBI must approve the closure.[47]

Quantitative branch licensing restrictions were also eased. In 1995-96, the RBI gave banks complete discretion to open branches if they meet a capital adequacy ratio of nine percent, have earned a net profit for three

---

[45] See Gupta and Jayakar (2005), p. 60; Indian Banks' Association (2003), p. 19; Reserve Bank of India (2005b), p. 2.

[46] See Leeladhar (2006), p. 75; Reserve Bank of India (2004c), p. 1; Reserve Bank of India (2005c), p. 101.

[47] See Fitch Ratings (2003), p. 3; Shirai (2002c), p. 21.

consecutive years, and have NPLs of less than 15%. In 1998-99, foreign banks also received permission to open twelve branches a year instead of eight.[48]

Lowering entry barriers has led to a more competitive environment. While the incumbent banks now have increased flexibility to expand their operations, they also face greater competition following the appearance of new private banks and foreign banks. However, despite the increase in competition, the PSBs have until now been able to defend their dominant position. Several factors account for this. First, the new entrants have needed time to scale up their operations, which is a multi-year task. Second, the sheer size of the state-owned banks means that they are the default partner in large credit deals; new entrants have not had the balance sheets and the sophistication to handle large transactions. Third, the government required state-owned banks to open branches in rural and semi-urban areas in line with its policy of social banking. It can be assumed that many of these branches are only marginally profitable, or even make a loss; accordingly profit-oriented private banks will not enter these markets.[49] However, overall these branches provide the state-owned banks with a relatively steady flow of business, which helps to compensate for lost market share in other areas. A likely scenario is that the new entrants will make further gains in urban markets – where it is easier to establish a presence – while state-owned banks will remain important players in the banking sector.

2.1.2.2.5 Prudential norms

The banking sector is vulnerable to systemic crises that may arise from problems at a single institution. Therefore, it is commonly recognized that the banking sector needs supervision and protection to guarantee a certain degree of stability. The establishment of explicit deposit insurance schemes or lender of last resort facilities to provide liquidity in times of crises are common government responses to enhance the stability of the system. However, these measures are not sufficient in themselves and must be complemented by bank regulation and supervision.[50]

[48] See Shirai (2002c), p. 21.

[49] The average sum of deposits and credit in rural branches stood at about Rs 870,000 (approximately EUR 14,900 based on an exchange rate of 58.54 Rs/EUR as of June 30th 2006) in 2004, which is likely to be insufficient to cover costs. In comparison, the volume of deposits and credit was 4.7 times higher in urban branches and about 15 times higher in metropolitan branches. Calculations based on Reserve Bank of India (2004a), p. 3.

[50] See Joshi and Little (1997), p. 115; Reserve Bank of India (2004b), p. 24.

On the question of prudential norms and the supervisory system, the *Narasimham Committee* recommended strengthening and upgrading the system.[51] The strengthening of the prudential and supervisory framework started with the guidelines on income recognition, asset classification and provisioning issued by the RBI in 1992-93. Capital adequacy rules were also introduced. Since then, there have been continuous efforts to enhance the transparency and accountability of the banking sector. These have included requirements for increased disclosures in the annual reports of banks, allowing stakeholders to make a better risk-return assessment.[52]

A further important step was the adoption of the Basel Accord Capital Standards in April 1992.[53] An 8% capital adequacy ratio was introduced in phases between 1993 and 1996, according to banks' ownership and the scope of their operations.[54] Following the recommendations of the *Narasimham Committee* the regulatory minimum capital adequacy ratio was later raised to 9%.[55] As of March 2005, all but two commercial banks met the capital adequacy requirements; the capital adequacy ratio for the banking sector stands at 12.8%.[56]

Significant changes also occurred in the rules guiding the recognition of non-performing loans. Loans with unpaid interest of two quarters are now defined as non-performing, as opposed to four quarters in 1992-93. For accounting purposes, non-performing loans are classified as either substandard, doubtful, or as a loss, with provisioning requirements attached to this

[51] See Government of India (1991) pp. 51-59.

[52] See Chipalkatti and Rishi (2003), p. 2f.; Reserve Bank of India (2004b), p. 24; Shirai (2002c), p. 21.

[53] The Basel Accord Capital Standards were introduced in 1988 and – among others – include provisions for the amount of equity capital banks should hold based on their risk exposure.

[54] See Joshi and Little (1997), p. 117; Shirai (2002c), p. 21f. The 8% capital adequacy ratio is based on risk-weighted assets. At least half of the capital has to be tier 1 capital (equity and disclosed reserves). Tier 2 capital includes among others hybrid debt capital instruments. The risk-adjusted assets include both on- and off-balance sheet items and receive risk weights of 0%, 20%, 50% and 100%. See Basel Committee on Banking Supervision (1997), p. 23f.; Santos (2000), p. 17.

[55] See Reserve Bank of India (2000), p. 5. The *Narasimham Committee* had suggested to increase the minimum capital to risk assets ratio from 8% to 10% to account for the increased off-balance sheet exposure of banks. See Government of India (1998), p. 22.

[56] See Reserve Bank of India (2005c), p. 95. The rating agency Fitch estimates that the effective level of NPLs in India could be twice as high as reported due to less stringent classification norms. See Fitch Ratings (2003), p. 4.

classification.[57] Even though these changes mark an improvement, the accounting norms for recognizing NPLs are still less stringent than those of developed economies, where a loan is already considered non-performing after one quarter of outstanding interest payments.[58]

Besides improving capital adequacy standards and accounting norms, the RBI has also attempted to strengthen the supervisory authority by establishing the Board of Financial Supervision (BFS) in 1994 as part of the RBI. The BFS has the dual task of ensuring that commercial banks have adequate internal control systems and performing off-site inspections to ascertain the financial condition of commercial banks in the periods between on-site visits. The BFS triggers supervisory action as needed. The improvements in the prudential and supervisory framework were also accompanied by a paradigm shift from micro-regulation of the banking sector to a strategy of macro-management. This has resulted in a shift of the supervisory role from on-site inspections to off-site surveillance, with a corresponding increase of risk-based supervision.[59]

A further step in enhancing the regulatory structure was the adoption of the CAMEL framework by the RBI in 1999-2000. This is a rating model based on a bank's capital, assets, management, earnings and liquidity. It aims to allow a more accurate assessment of the performance of individual banks and the overall strength of the banking system.[60]

The upgrading of the framework of prudential norms and supervision after 1991 has led to an overall strengthening of the banking sector. After

---

[57] See ICRA (2004), p. 22f.; Joshi and Little (1997), p. 117; Shirai (2002c), p. 22. Loans are classified as substandard if they have been non-performing for up to two years and require a 10% provision. If the loan has been non-performing for more than two years, it is classified as doubtful and a provision of between 20-50% is made. To be classified as a loss, a loan has to be certified as a loss by an external auditor. In this event a 100% provision for the loan is made. See ICRA (2004), p. 22f.

[58] See Madgavkar, Puri and Sengupta (2001), p. 114.

[59] See Indian Banks' Association (2003), p. 29; Joshi and Little (1997), p. 117f; Reddy (2002a), p. 364; Reddy (2002b), p. 340; Reserve Bank of India (2004b), p. 24f.; Singh (2005), p. 23.

[60] See Shirai (2002c), p. 23. The acronym CAMEL stands for Capital adequacy, Asset quality, Management soundness, Earnings and profitability, and Liquidity. Commonly, the sensitivity to market risk is included as a sixth component of the framework. See International Monetary Fund (2000a), pp. 4-9 for a detailed description of the elements of the framework.

gradual improvements in the supervisory system over the last years, it now largely meets international standards.[61]

2.1.2.2.6 Public Sector Banks

At the end of the 1980s, operational and allocative inefficiencies led to a deterioration of Public Sector Banks' profitability. Enhancing the performance of PSBs was thus an important reform task in ensuring the stability of the financial system.[62]

In its report, the *Narasimham Committee* suggested to significantly reduce the number of PSBs.[63] However, the government decided against liquidation, which would have involved significant losses accruing to either the government or depositors, and opted instead to maintain and improve operations. This was done in order to provide a good starting basis before possible privatization.[64] The subsequent restructuring measures for PSBs were threefold and included recapitalization, debt recovery and partial privatization.

At the beginning of the 1990s, Indian banks had accrued a significant level of NPLs due to directed lending practices and poor risk management (Figure 5). In 1993, NPLs stood at 23.2% of gross advances and 11.8% of total assets so that India's banking sector was technically insolvent.[65] As a consequence, prior to any privatization, the balance sheets of PSBs had to be strengthened by means of capital injections.

In the fiscal years 1991-92 and 1992-93 the Government of India provided almost Rs 40 billion to clean up the balance sheets of PSBs. Between 1993 and 1999 another Rs 120 billion was injected into nationalized banks through the issuance of bonds with fixed coupon rates. In total, the recapitalization amounted to 2% of gross domestic product (GDP).[66]

---

[61] See Bhide, Prasad and Ghosh (2001), p. 28; Mukherji (2002), p. 40. For a comprehensive overview of applicable prudential norms in the Indian banking sector see Reserve Bank of India (2004b), pp. 206-210.

[62] See Kamesam (2002), p. 377; Reddy (2002a), p. 358.

[63] See Government of India (1991), p. 67.

[64] See Shirai (2002c), p. 26.

[65] See Deolalkar (1999), p. 66f.

[66] See Reddy (2002a), p. 359; Reserve Bank of India (1999), section 5.1; Reserve Bank of India (2001b), p. 26. Table 13 in the appendix provides an overview of the recapitalization amounts.

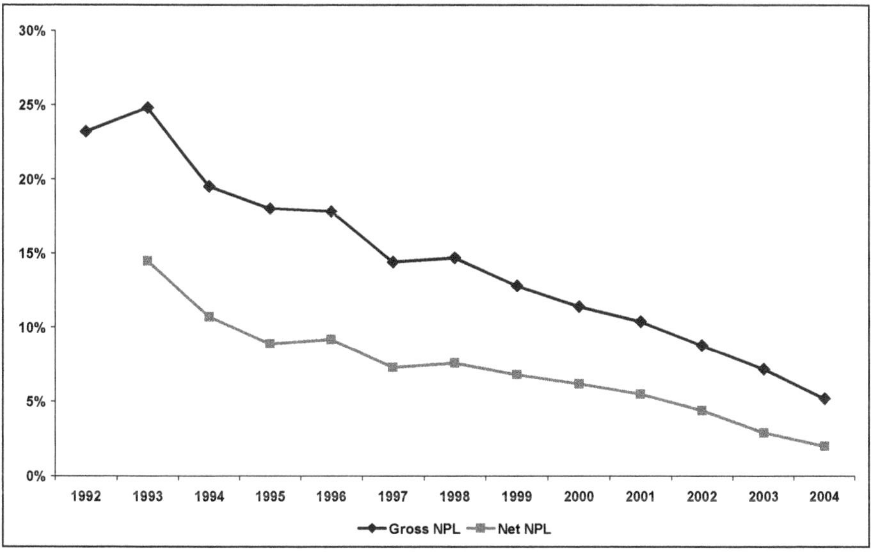

Fig. 5. NPL level in India as percent of total loans[67]

However, the RBI itself recognized that recapitalization programs were not only costly to the public budget but are also highly uncertain in their outcome, resulting in significant moral hazard.[68] In an attempt to overcome these problems, after 1992-93 performance obligations and commitments were outlined in a Memorandum of Understanding with banks receiving a capital injection. Yet despite the memorandums, the inherent moral hazard problems could not be resolved: banks faced no penalty despite frequently failing to meet performance targets.[69]

The need to recapitalize PSBs was to a large extent caused by NPLs. Debt recovery was therefore an important part of the reform package. Bankruptcy is one of the central features of capitalist economies due to the limited liability feature of corporations. To be able to deal with the consequences of bankruptcy in an orderly fashion, comprehensive laws are necessary to mitigate the consequences of bankruptcy.[70] In the case of India, the lack of a comprehensive bankruptcy law combined with directed lending practices was one of the major causes for the high level of NPLs at the

[67] See Muniappan (2002), p. 2f.; Reserve Bank of India "Report on Trend and Progress of Banking in India", various issues. Note: (1) values for 1992-1996 include only PSBs; (2) net NPLs are gross NPLs less provisions made for non-performing loans.

[68] See Reserve Bank of India (2001b), p. 24.

[69] See Mukherji (2002), p. 40; Reserve Bank of India (1999), sections 5.2 and 5.4.

[70] See Stiglitz and Bhattacharya (1999), p. 114.

start of the reforms. The speedy enforcement of creditors' claims was impossible, which in turn led to a further deterioration of banks' balance sheets.[71]

The first step in improving the recovery of bad loans was the passage of the "Recovery of Debts Act" in 1993. This led to the setting up debt recovery tribunals in major cities. However, the effectiveness of the tribunals was rather weak at first because their constitutionality had been challenged in court. As of June 30, 2004, the tribunals had adjudicated about 28,000 cases out of 63,600, with an overall recovery rate of about 30%. Due to these unsatisfactory results, in July 2004 a working group was charged with coming up with suggestions to improve the functioning of the debt recovery tribunals.[72]

Another step forward in the faster recovery of NPLs was the 2002 "Securitisation Bill" that allowed banks to seize collateral if payment in full was not made by the borrower within 60 days of receipt of a notice. However, like the debt recovery tribunals, the bill was challenged in court. In 2004 the Supreme Court ruled that parts of the bill were unconstitutional, making the recovery of NPLs more difficult for banks.[73]

Recapitalization and debt recovery are also necessary to prepare banks for a privatization. Prior to 1991, the government owned all commercial banks with the exception of 22 relatively small private sector banks and the foreign banks. This dominant role declined somewhat following the partial privatization of several PSBs in the 1990s. In 1993, the SBI Act was amended to promote partial private shareholding. The SBI became the first PSB to raise equity in the capital markets. After the 1994 amendment of the Banking Regulation Act, other PSBs were allowed to offer up to 49% of their equity to the public. Since then, 20 PSBs have been partially privatized. At the end of 200%, the government continued to hold over 80% of the overall paid-up capital of nationalized banks and had at least a 51% stake in every nationalized bank.[74]

---

[71] See Ahluwalia (2002), p. 82; Madgavkar, Puri and Sengupta (2001), p. 114; Reserve Bank of India (2001a), p. 11. Equally important is that adequate bankruptcy laws can reduce incentives for deceptive practices by borrowers. Consequently, bankruptcy laws are not only important to clean up the bad loans of the past, but also to prevent them in the future. See Buiter, Lago and Rey (1999), p. 146.

[72] See Reserve Bank of India (2004b), p. 35; Reserve Bank of India (2005c), p. 37; Shirai (2002c), p. 25.

[73] See Center for the Advanced Study of India (2004), p. 33; Reserve Bank of India (2004b), p. 35.

[74] See Arun and Turner (2002b), pp. 436-442; Bhide, Prasad and Ghosh (2001), pp. 7-13; Economist Intelligence Unit (2005), p. 10; Fitch Ratings (2003), p. 2;

Partial privatizations have largely been used to raise new funds for PSBs. Despite the dilution of the government's ownership position, it continues to be the dominant shareholder and can still exercise extensive control. Since individual shareholders are subject to a 10% cap on total voting rights, it is unlikely that greater non-governmental influence will appear. Even if the minimum government stake were lowered to 33% – as proposed by the former BJP-led National Democratic Alliance government – PSBs would be likely to remain under government control and thus retain their character as public enterprises.[75]

The problems of the Public Sector Banks illustrate the interrelated nature of the reforms needed in the Indian banking sector. Mandatory branch expansion to rural areas and priority sector credit have led to a lower profitability of banks, a higher level of non-performing loans and a weaker capital base. However, from a developmental point of view the rural branches are needed to provide banking services to large parts of the population and priority sector credit may be needed to overcome the credit constraints of certain sectors. Reforming the banking sector therefore does not only have an economic dimension, but also a political and a developmental one that have to be considered.

2.2 Current structure of the banking system

After the overview of the development of the Indian banking sector since 1947, this section focuses on the structure of the banking system as it presents itself today. In many respects the current structure can be directly related to the policies described in the previous sections, including the nationalization of banks in 1969 and 1980 and the opening up of the banking sector for new players after 1991.

In India, the most important intermediaries in the banking system today are scheduled commercial banks, co-operative banks, development financial institutions (DFI) and non-bank financial companies. The large state-owned and private-sector banks that form part of the scheduled commercial banks are the most visible representatives of the banking system. While the scheduled commercial banks hold more than 80% of the banking

Hanson (2001a), p. 8; ICRA (2004), p. 23; Saez and Yang (2001), p. 80; Shirai (2002a), pp. 54-56; Shirai (2002c), p. 26. An overview of the government holdings in state-owned banks can be found in Table 14 in the appendix.

[75] See Ahluwalia (2002), p. 82; ICRA (2004), p. 23f.

system's assets, they represent a minority in terms of numbers.[76] The main focus of this study is scheduled commercial banks; however, a brief description of the four most important types of institutions will enable a better overview of the structure of the banking system in India.

Scheduled commercial banks

Scheduled banks are banks that fulfill the two provisions of section 42 (6) of the RBI Act. First, it must maintain paid-up capital and reserves of more than Rs 500,000. Second, it must satisfy the RBI that its business is not conducted in a manner that is detrimental to depositors' interests.[77] Scheduled banks can be either commercial banks or co-operative banks. While scheduled banks have to fulfill certain provisions in line with the RBI Act, the advantage of the status is that they have access to credit from the RBI.[78]

As of March 2005, there were 284 scheduled commercial banks in India. These can be further divided into four subcategories: public sector banks, private sector banks, foreign banks, and regional rural banks (Figure 6). The 28 public sector banks can be further grouped into those banks that were nationalized in 1969 and 1980 and the State Bank of India Group.[79] The 29 private sector banks comprise the old private sector banks that were in existence before 1994 and the new private sector banks that entered the market after 1994. In 2005, 31 foreign banks held the status of scheduled commercial bank.

With 196 institutions, the regional rural banks form the largest group among the scheduled commercial banks. They were set up from 1975 onwards with the aim of enhancing the availability of credit for the rural population. The SBI and the nationalized banks were required to set up these institutions together with individual states.[80]

[76] See Reserve Bank of India (2005c).

[77] See Reserve Bank of India Act 42 (6).

[78] See Fitch Ratings (2003), p. 7.

[79] Besides the earlier foundation of the SBI, a major difference between the nationalized banks and the SBI is their ownership. Whereas the Indian government is the majority owner of the nationalized banks, the RBI is the majority shareholder of the SBI.

[80] See Deolalkar (1999), p. 61.

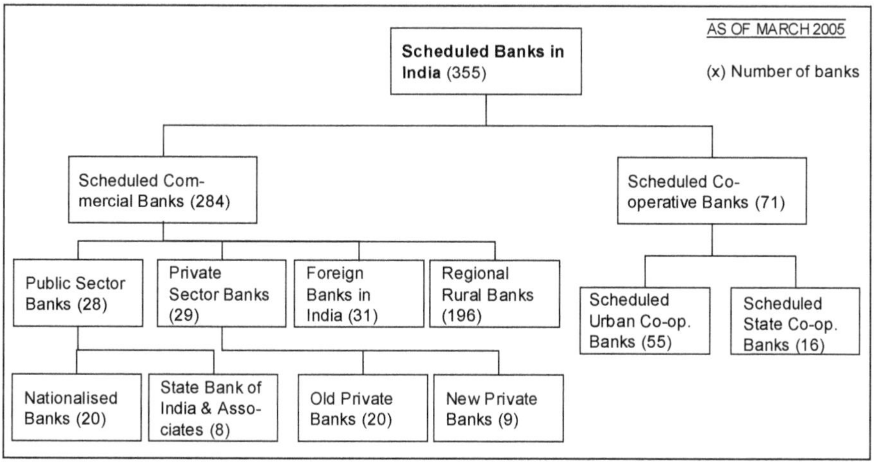

Fig. 6. Overview of scheduled banks in India[81]

Co-operative banks

There are two main differences between commercial and co-operative banks. First, the RBI exerts only partial control over co-operative banks, since the Banking Regulation Act is not fully applicable to them. Second, co-operative banks – as their name implies – function on the basis of cooperation, so profits are not their primary motive.[82] Currently there are almost 107,000 rural co-operative credit institutions and 2,000 urban co-operative banks in India, holding about 11% of the assets in the banking system. Only a small fraction of these co-operatives – some 71 in total – have the status of scheduled banks with the ensuing responsibilities and benefits. The formal co-operative banking structure dates back about 100 years to the Agricultural Credit Co-Operative Societies Act of 1904. The co-operative banks are an important instrument in bringing financial services to the rural constituencies. Their focus is on mobilizing deposits and handing out agricultural and rural credit.[83]

A fairly new aspect of the co-operative sector is the microfinance movement. It follows up on previous attempts to improve the access of India's poor to financial services. Despite efforts such as the creation of the network of rural co-operative banks in the 1950s and the nationalization of commercial banks from 1969 onward, the poor still have to rely to a large extent on informal sources of finance such as moneylenders. The formal microfinance program in India started in 1992 and has made considerable

[81] See Reserve Bank of India (2005c).
[82] See Deolalkar (1999), pp. 64-66.
[83] See Reserve Bank of India (2005c), p. 108.

progress. Its nucleus are self-help groups that are linked with non-governmental organizations and commercial banks ("Self-Help Group-Bank Linkage") to provide very basic banking services to disadvantaged groups of the population. Through innovative contractual structures and organization forms, microfinance institutions can extend small, uncollateralized loans to poor households that would otherwise be excluded from the formal banking system. In addition, many microfinance institutions also offer saving facilities. Despite the progress made over the last years – 1.6 million self-help groups were participating in the Self-Help Group-Bank Linkage Programme by March 2005 – most of India's poor still have no access either to formal finance or to semi-formal microfinance, and instead have to rely on moneylenders, friends or relatives for credit.[84]

Development financial institutions

Development financial institutions (DFIs) play an important role in providing broader access to financial services and enhancing competition in the banking system. Most DFIs were funded as part of India's development strategy to provide long-term financing for certain sectors. Currently, they hold about 5% of the banking system's assets.[85]

The first DFI, the Industrial Finance Corporation of India, was established in 1948. This was followed by the Industrial Credit and Investment Credit Corporation of India in 1955 and the Industrial Development Bank of India in 1964. Other DFIs serve particular sectors of the economy or special purposes, such as the National Bank for Agriculture and Rural Development, the Export Import Bank of India, the National Housing Bank, and the Small Industries Development Bank of India. Based on their geographical coverage, financial institutions can be classified as either all-India or state-level institutions.[86]

Over the last years, the importance of DFIs has decreased due to increased competition in the market, reduced access to concessional funds, and problems with the traditional client base due to excess industrial capacity and increased imports.[87]

[84] See Basu and Srivastava (2005), p. 138f. and p. 150; Morduch (2000), p. 617; Reserve Bank of India (2005c), p. 129f.; Swain (2002), p. 18.

[85] See Reserve Bank of India (2005c), p. 139.

[86] See Deolalkar (1999), p. 62f.; Reserve Bank of India (2005c), p. 140; Sunder Ram (2001), p. 56.

[87] See Basu (2005), p. 8.

Non-banking financial companies
The majority of non-banking financial companies (NBFCs) are private sector entities. They can be categorized according to their primary activities into equipment leasing companies, hire purchase companies, loan companies, and investment companies. As of mid-2005, over 13,000 NBFCs were operating in India. Their asset share in the banking system is negligible at about 1%. They are regulated according to chapter III B of the Reserve Bank of India Act of 1934.[88]

During the 1990s, the number of NBFCs grew rapidly thanks to less stringent regulation compared to banks. Unlike banks, NBFCs did not face cash, liquidity, or priority sector requirements. In addition, they were exempt from minimum capital requirements. After a strong growth in the number of NBFCs in the 1990s, several regulatory initiatives attempted to align the regulation of NBFCs with that of banks and improve protection for depositors. These initiatives included compulsory registration, prudential regulations, investment norms, disclosure standards, and the tightening of the supervisory oversight.[89]

The banking system's structure with its emphasis on state-owned commercial banks and development financial institutions reflects the state-dominated development strategy of the 1960s and 1970s. It lies beyond the scope of this thesis to determine if this structure is still appropriate for India's economy. However, it is important to discuss the effects of the structure of the banking system on the reforms. Here, it can be argued that those elements of the banking system that were necessary to help develop India and create a nationwide bank network – i.e. large state-owned banks that were not operating purely on commercial principles – now make reforms for the overall system more difficult. Disrupting state-owned banks would affect large parts of the population and the economy. The scarcity of alternative providers of banking services makes comprehensive reform of the sector more difficult. For example, the threat to let a major bank fail would not be credible because this would leave large parts of the population without formal banking services.

Of course, the structure of the banking system is not the only determinant of performance. The external environment in which the sector is embedded also plays an important part. Accordingly, the following section attempts to explore the political, economic and institutional factors influencing the banking sector.

---

[88] See Reserve Bank of India (2005c), p. 139 and pp. 149-152.
[89] See Basu (2005), p. 7; Reserve Bank of India (2004b), p. 146.

2.3 Political, economic and institutional environment of the banking sector

A country's banking sector is tightly integrated into the overall political, economic and institutional setting. These factors influence the conduct and performance of the banking sector by providing incentives and restraints. To allow a better appreciation of the overall environment of the banking sector in India and its influencing factors, the following subsection examines the political, economic and institutional setting in more detail.

2.3.1 Political environment

India is a federal state with a demarcation of duties and funds between the center and the States. At both levels separate legislative, executive and judicial arms of government exist. Important functions that are assumed at the central level include money supply, external borrowing, international relations, defense, national highways and airways, as well as functions whose provision involves significant scale economies. The center and the States jointly undertake functions that affect several States or issues with major developmental potential – such as economic planning, education and welfare. Matters with statewide implications are assigned to the States.[90]

This federal setting has important implications for the current reform process. As a federal democracy, India has to implements reforms slower than other countries. However, the federal system has ensured both a wider and deeper sharing of the reform impulses. Despite periodic setbacks, it is thus likely that the overall reforms will continue This is shown by the fact that the seven consecutive governments between the start of the reforms in 1991 and 2006 have not reversed any major economic decisions and have continued pursuing the overall reform agenda.[91]

The rise of single-state parties represents an important change in the overall political setting and is likely to have repercussions on economic reforms. It has led to a proliferation of state-level considerations at the expense of national issues.[92] Echeverri-Gent (2001), for example, argues that the fragmentation of the national party system poses challenges not only for coalition politics, but also for economic reforms because an overarching coordination mechanism is lacking. When the Congress Party dominated both the central and state governments, it could coordinate policies

---

[90] See Rao (2002), p. 4f.

[91] See Mukherji (2002), p. 59; Singh (2003), p. 9.

[92] See Echeverri-Gent (2001), p. 3; Jalan (2005), p. 89.

across different levels of government. This is no longer possible in the current fragmented political landscape.[93]

2.3.2 Economic environment

After Independence in 1947, India focused on accelerating economic growth in order to achieve social justice and economic self-sufficiency. Under Nehru and his successors, governments saw their role not only as supplying the infrastructure and regulatory framework for economic activity, but also as actively shaping economic development. Investment planning was exercised through Five Year Plans and became an important tool for implementing the development strategy. This strategy was marked by a duality between the public and private sectors of the economy, since in some sectors investments were made through public enterprises, while in others the private sector was supposed to take the lead. Public enterprises were effectively shielded from competition from the private sector.[94]

The private sector was also highly regulated through detailed licensing requirements – the so-called "license-raj" system. India relied on the bureaucracy it had inherited from the British to manage both the public and the private sector. Despite the approach of state-led development that was inspired by the Soviet Union, India never abandoned market structures completely.[95]

This regime prevailed at least until the early 1980s, when the attitude of the top political leadership shifted toward a more market-friendly policy framework. The average GDP growth rates per decade reflect the changes of the economic policies. While the average growth rate stood at 4.1% during the 1960s and 3.1% during the 1970s, it increased significantly to 5.8% in the 1980s. During the 1990s, the growth rate declined slightly to 5.5% before accelerating to an average of 6.4% at the beginning of 2000 (Figure 7). The main factors behind the increase in the growth rate at the beginning of the 1980s were loan-financed imports, increased public investments and a rise in exports in textiles and chemicals.[96]

---

93 See Echeverri-Gent (2001), p. 5.
94 See Datta-Chaudhuri (1990), p. 29f.; Oschinski (2003), pp. 3-5.
95 See Datta-Chaudhuri (1990), p. 29; Mukherji (2002), p. 31.
96 See Rodrik and Subramanian (2004), p. 4; Swamy (2005a), p. 81. See Kohli (2006a) and Kohli (2006b) for a detailed discussion of the political-economy factors leading to India's growth acceleration.

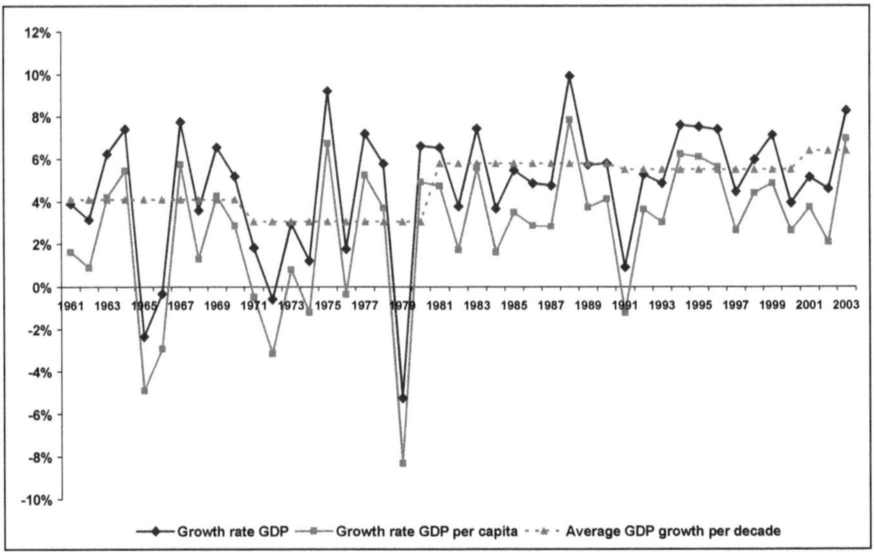

Fig. 7. GDP and GDP per capita growth rates[97]

Budget deficits persist at the level of central government and the states despite the increasing growth rate. For the central government, the average budget deficit in 1993 stood at about 5.5%, with a downward trend since then (Figure 8). While central government's finances have improved somewhat, those of the states have deteriorated. Today, the aggregate budget deficit remains at 8-9% of GDP.[98] The high budget deficits stem in part from the political competition that led to expensive campaign promises to important interest groups. For example, subsidies from state governments amount to about 10% of GDP, the majority going to power, irrigation, transport and higher education. And as expenditure has grown, tax revenues as a percentage of GDP have steadily declined since the mid-1980s.[99]

[97] Author's calculation based on International Monetary Fund (2006b).
[98] See Acharya (2002), p. 11; Government of India (2006); Pandit (2005), p. 135f.
[99] See Deutsche Bank Research (2006), p. 2; Echeverri-Gent (2001), p. 9.

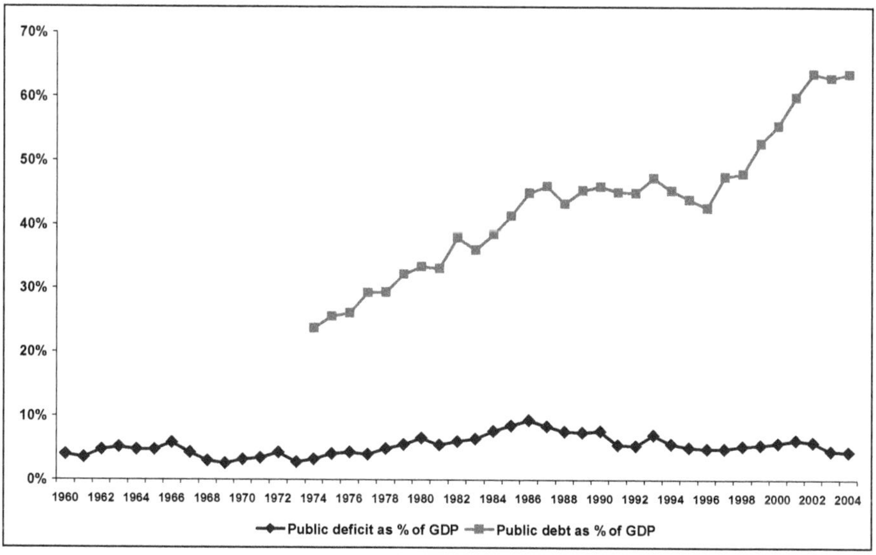

Fig. 8. Fiscal deficit and debt as a percentage of GDP[100]

The effect of the fiscal deficit on the banking sector and the economy as a whole is that the government pre-empts a large share of financial savings that could otherwise go to the private sector. In addition, government demand also puts upward pressure on interest rates.[101]

With high public deficits, the level of domestic debt as a percentage of GDP has steadily increased despite the acceleration of GDP growth. At the beginning of 2000, the level of domestic debt crossed the 50% mark for the first time (Figure 8). Servicing the debt makes fiscal consolidation harder and takes away funds for investment in other areas.

Another important element in economic policy is capital mobility. The extent to which the capital account is liberalized is important for banks since capital flows can affect exchange rates, interest rates, savings and investments. India's overall reform strategy in the financial sector has included a limited opening of the capital account. Prior to 1991, the capital account was largely closed, with capital flows being restricted through far-reaching administrative controls that were influenced by the balance-of-payment situation and exchange rate movements. With the improvement of the balance-of-payments situation in 1992-93, the capital account was partially liberalized for Indian companies; they are now allowed to obtain funds from international bond markets so that larger companies can bypass

[100] See Government of India (2006); International Monetary Fund (2006b).

[101] See Basu and Srivastava (2005), p. 146; Mukherji (2006), p. 6; Pandit (2005), p. 136.

the banking system to obtain funding. Capital flows by residents are still forbidden or highly restricted. Consequently, the choice for investment opportunities remains largely domestic, which creates a certain degree of stability for the banking sector.[102]

The exchange rate system is also a key factor in a country's economy. Its significance relates to the "unholy trinity" – the incompatibility of having a fixed exchange rate, an open capital account, and discretion over domestic monetary policy. Especially the combination of a fixed exchange rate and an open capital account can in the case of capital inflows lead to monetary expansion and inflationary pressures that also affect bank lending.

Economic liberalization in India also included changes in the management of the exchange rate. From an adjustable nominal peg tied to a basket of currencies in the pre-reform area, India has moved to a largely market-determined exchange rate in March 1993. Consequently, India today has a fairly high degree of monetary policy independence and foreign exchange fluctuations should not overly affect the banking sector. [103]

2.3.3 Institutional environment

The institutional setting of the banking sector in India is largely influenced by the RBI and the central government. The RBI is the main regulatory authority for the Indian banking sector. Under the Banking Regulations Act of 1949, it has extensive powers for licensing, supervising and controlling banks.[104]

While the Banking Regulations Act provides the general legal and institutional framework for banking regulation, the Banking Companies Acquisition & Transfer of Undertaking Acts of 1969 and 1980 are the enabling acts for nationalization. These acts also provide the legal basis for the operation and management of state-owned banks. In addition, the Indian Parliament has also directly established some banks, including the State Bank of India in 1955, the Industrial Development Bank of India in 1964, the Export-Import Bank of India in 1981, the National Bank for Agricultural and Rural Development in 1982, and the National Housing Bank in 1987.[105]

While the RBI is charged with the ongoing supervision and control of the banks, the nationalized banks are ultimately accountable to the Indian

[102] See Joshi and Little (1997), p. 166f.; Kohli (2001), p. 3; Mohan (2006b), p. 4f.

[103] See Kohli (2001), p. 7 and p. 11; Mohan (2006b), p. 6f.

[104] See Cygnus Economic & Business Research (2004), p. 5; Fitch Ratings (2003), p. 5.

[105] See Fitch Ratings (2003), p. 5.

Parliament since the shares are held by the state. Key policy changes and appointments to senior positions require the approval of the government. Thus the Banking Department within the Ministry of Finance is charged with processing senior appointments. Based on a recommendation by the Finance Minister, the appointments are then made by the Prime Minister. The reason for making the appointments at the highest level of government is commonly believed to be the powerful patronage involved between politicians and bank officials.[106]

The government's influence on key policy decisions in nationalized banks has important consequences on the establishment of market discipline in state-owned banks. As long as the government exerts its influence over state-owned banks at the expense of minority shareholders, it will be difficult (if not impossible) to credibly impose market discipline. Moreover, the RBI plays a dual role as regulator and merchant bank for the government, which can lead to conflicts of interest.[107] Thus, the current institutional setting helps to maintain an element of stability in the sector by relieving banks from competitive pressures at the cost of a somewhat lower efficiency.

The interplay of political, economic and institutional factors also exerts an important influence on reforms in the banking sector. The fragmentation of the political landscape in India makes it more difficult to reach a consensus about reforms. Indeed, it is sometimes necessary to "buy off" coalition partners and special interest groups. The extent of the overall budget deficit makes this even more challenging. Besides making reforms more difficult, budget deficits mean that restraints in the banking sector are likely to continue, since a banking sector controlled by the government can be used as a captive source of finance.[108] The institutional setting of the banking sector and the resulting conflicts of interests exacerbate this. Since, to an extent, politicians can use the state-owned banks for patronage, they are less inclined to abolish these relationships.

On the economic side another important influencing factor for the reform process is the overall economic environment. The benign macroeconomic environment in India of the last years has certainly contributed to the stability of the banking sector. However, it does not bode well for fur-

[106] See Desai (1999), p. 36; ICRA (2004), p. 23.

[107] See ICRA (2004), p. 23; Sunder Ram (2001), p. 54.

[108] Some observers even regard the budget deficits in India as the main source of danger for the reform process. Manor (2005) for example argues that "the main threat to liberalization is not a U-turn, but fiscal indiscipline – budget deficits that result from overspending by ministers." Manor (2005), p. 102.

ther reforms. Indeed, the political-economy of reforms suggests that crisis is a more effective trigger for reforms than relatively prosperity.

2.4 Conclusion

The character of Indian banking has changed decisively several times since Independence. From the creation of the SBI in 1955 up until the second wave of nationalization in 1980, the degree of state involvement in the banking sector increased steadily. During the 1980s, the first efforts to reform the banking sector were enacted as the result of increasing inefficiencies in the sector. Yet these measures failed to avert the 1991 crisis. Since the crisis, India has followed a path of gradual reform, with the aim of increasing the stability of the banking sector and of fostering competition.

Two broad reform phases can be distinguished in the post-1991 reforms. At the beginning of the 1990s, the focus was on the creation of an efficient and productive banking sector in a competitive environment. Later, from the mid-1990s, the focus was on strengthening systemic safeguards and improving the structural environment.[109]

The Indian banking sector has come a long way since the start of the reforms in the early 1990s. But the reform process is not over yet. Further reforms cannot occur in isolation, but must take the overall political, economic and institutional setting into account. However, there are several impediments to further reforms. One important immediate factor for the slow pace of reforms is the fragmentation of the political landscape in India that makes it more challenging to find broad support for reforms. Closely related to the fragmentation of the political landscape are the high budget deficits. Under government control the banking sector can be a convenient tool to fund these deficits by for example requiring banks to buy government bonds. Finding alternative sources of financing or curbing the deficit will be necessary if the state disengages from direct involvement in the banking sector so that the high budget deficits in India serve as a strong disincentive for further reforms. Despite these difficulties, reforms have shown good progress in recent years. This can be attributed to a positive macroeconomic environment and consistently high growth rates; these have made it easier to implement reforms with distributive consequences.

Regardless of the difficulties to conduct further reforms, it is possible to evaluate the present situation and the progress made to date. While it is feasible to individually evaluate the reform progress of a country, it is

[109] See Indian Banks' Association (2003), p. 17; Mohan (2004), p. 853.

more instructive to include the experiences of a comparable country with a similar task of banking sector reform. In this respect, China is a good choice for comparison. Like India, it is currently liberalizing its banking sector, it is a large country with a fast-growing economy, and it faces structural issues such as high levels of state ownership and legacy NPLs. The next section therefore gives an overview of the development of the Chinese banking sector and addresses the issue of comparability with India.

3 The Chinese banking sector

Like the Indian banking sector, the banking sector in China is currently undergoing a profound transition.[1] Since China will be used to compare the progress and performance of reforms in India, this section attempts to give an overview of relevant aspects of the Chinese banking sector. The focus is on the development of the banking sector, its current structure and the major reforms initiated over the last years. In addition, relevant similarities and differences of the banking sectors of the two countries are discussed, as well as the possibilities and limitations of a comparison.

3.1 Development and structure of the banking sector

As in other countries, the development and the structure of the banking sector in China has been strongly influenced by the pre-dominant political philosophies. Since the foundation of the People's Republic of China in 1949, the banking sector has undergone several distinct policy changes. A watershed was been the opening up of the Chinese economy in 1979. Since then the banking sector has steadily evolved from a state-directed mono-banking system into a fairly open commercial banking system. The major changes and the current structure are described below.

3.1.1 Development of the banking sector

The major development phases since 1979 have been: the creation of a two-tier system between 1979 and 1985; the commercialization of the banking system through the foundation of new (policy) banks between 1985 and 1994; the build-up of infrastructure and regulation between 1995 to about 2002; and the preparation for the opening up of the banking sector between 2002 and 2006 after the accession to the World Trade Organiza-

[1] Throughout this thesis, "China" refers to the People's Republic of China; the special administrative zones Hong Kong and Macao are not included in the analysis.

tion (WTO). These phases and their implications are described below in more detail.

Until 1978: Mono-banking system

When the People's Republic of China (PRC) was declared in 1949, the mono-banking system of the Soviet Union was taken as a model for the banking system. The People's Bank of China (PBOC) stood at the center of a de-facto mono-banking system since it had the main responsibility for cash, credit and settlements. Even though other banks existed at the beginning of the 1950s, such as the Bank of China (BOC), the Bank of Communications, the Agricultural Bank of China (ABC) and rural cooperatives, they merely functioned as extensions of the PBOC, and were formally merged into the PBOC system in 1955.[2]

Under the central planning system, enterprises had two sources of funds: the state budget and the banking system. Companies received most of their funds through the official state budget. The remainder of the funds – primarily for working capital – were provided by the PBOC based on a national credit plan prepared by the State Planning Commission of the State Council. In turn, the enterprises had to settle their transactions through accounts with the banking sector. In addition, enterprises and public institutions had to deposit their cash with the PBOC. As the mono-bank, the PBOC combined central banking and commercial banking functions, and served as a tool for the implementation of the Five-Year Plans. The PBOC did not have any degree of freedom in its lending decisions – the size, term and interest rates of loans were all set administratively.[3] As pointed out by Anderson and Kegels (1998) "socialist banking is the monetary adjunct of the planning process. It allows for an accounting of real activities in monetary terms."[4]

Besides the PBOC, the People's Construction Bank of China (PCBC), established in 1954 as a successor to the Bank of Communications, provided funds in the form of non-repayable and interest-free grants for the creation of new enterprises or the extension of existing ones. The PCBC effectively acted as an agent for the Ministry of Finance, rather than a bank, since it merely distributed funds for fixed investment projects as part

[2] See Lo (2001), p. 16; Staude (2002), p. 5; Wolken (1990), p. 54; Yang (2004), p. 2.

[3] See Chen and Thomas (1999), p. 16; Lardy (1998), p. 60; Lo (2001), p. 16; Nanto and Sinha (2002), p. 472; Wolken (1990), p. 55. The only financial assets available pre-1979 were cash and bank deposits. See Nanto and Sinha (2002), p. 472.

[4] Anderson and Kegels (1998), p. 2.

of the overall economic plan. In addition to the PBOC and the PCBC, a network of rural credit cooperatives existed prior the opening of the Chinese economy. Overall, it can be concluded that prior to 1979 the banking system had little or no relevance for China's macroeconomic performance.[5]

1979-1985: Two-tier banking system

In 1979, China established a two-tier banking system. It founded three state-owned banks – the Agricultural Bank of China (ABC), the Bank of China (BOC) and the China Construction Bank (CCB).[6] The ABC was charged with the task of providing banking services to rural areas and townships. The BOC, which was separated from the PBOC, was supposed to act as an urban bank providing different banking services, while the CCB, as the successor of the People's Construction Bank, took responsibility for financing large capital intensive projects, especially in the construction sector. This was an important first step in creating a more diversified and specialized banking system.

In 1984, the Industrial and Commercial Bank of China (ICBC) was established and complemented the three other state-owned commercial banks by taking over the commercial banking functions and the branch network of the PBOC. The PBOC subsequently assumed the role of a central bank with responsibility for three main tasks: formulating and implementing monetary policy, regulating financial institutions and securities markets, and serving as the government's banker.[7]

To sum up, in the early years of the reforms the main focus was on breaking up the mono-bank system and establishing specialized intermediaries. Furthermore, for the first time banks had to incorporate profitability considerations in their operations.[8]

1985-1994: Commercialization of the banking system

Between 1985 and 1994, several important steps were taken to further commercialize the banking system. They included the replacement of direct grants with interest-bearing loans to harden the budget constraints of state-owned enterprises (SOEs), granting the PBOC formal responsibility

---

[5] See Girardin (1997), p. 21; Lardy (1998), p. 61f.; Lo (2001), p. 16; Wolken (1990), p. 55.

[6] In fact, the BOC and CCB were founded as separate entities with a new legal status since they were previously integrated into the PBOC mono-bank structure. See Lardy (1998), p. 62.

[7] See Chen and Thomas (1999), p. 17; Lardy (1998), p. 64; Lowinski and Terberger (2001), p. 5f.; Nanto and Sinha (2002), p. 472; Wolken (1990), p. 57.

[8] See Girardin (1997), p. 21.

over monetary policy and the supervision of the financial system in 1986, and the formulation of a credit plan that instituted an aggregate credit ceiling for each PBOC branch. Within these credit ceilings, the branches gained increasing autonomy to make credit decisions.[9]

Between 1988 and 1992, banking sector reforms were limited and experimental; the authorities had to focus on inflationary pressures. Reforms resulted in new loan products being offered by specialized banks and allowing the emergence of new financial intermediaries. In 1993 the State Council initiated further reform steps, including the transformation of the PBOC into a modern central bank with added responsibility for monetary policy, and the decision to separate policy and commercial lending. The latter was the basis for the transformation of state banks into commercial banks.[10]

In 1994, three policy banks were established in addition to the four large state-owned commercial banks: the State Development Bank, the China Export-Import Bank, and the China Agricultural Development Bank. This meant that the four state-owned commercial banks (SOCBs) could be released from their policy lending duties.[11]

1995-2002: Build up of infrastructure and regulation

A further important step toward the establishment of a more market-based banking sector was the enactment of the Commercial Banking Law of 1995. This law required the four SOCBs to operate as commercial entities with responsibility for profits and losses. This, along with the creation of the policy banks, marked an important step toward ensuring that loans were extended on economic and not political grounds. The Commercial Banking Law also required banks to focus on efficiency and liquidity in their operations, as well as to make inquiries into the creditworthiness of their customers. In addition, it mandated that banks should maintain an 8% equity ratio and introduced a classification system for non-performing loans.[12]

---

[9] See Qian and Weingast (1996), p. 17; Shirai (2002b), p. 21; World Bank (1996a), p. 27.

[10] See Girardin (1997), p. 22; Lo (2001), p. 20; World Bank (1996a), p. 27.

[11] See Chen and Thomas (1999), p. 17; Lo (2001), p. 20; Lowinski and Terberger (2001), p. 9; Nanto and Sinha (2002), p. 472f. In China, the state-owned banks are commonly referred to as "State-owned commercial banks", whereas in India they are commonly called "Public Sector Banks".

[12] See Lowinski and Terberger (2001), p. 10; Nanto and Sinha (2002), p. 472f.; World Bank (1996a), p. 27.

Enacting the 8% equity ratio in the Commercial Banking Law was however not sufficient. With an NPL of over 20%, the capital base of the Big Four banks was largely eroded, so that massive recapitalizations were needed. As a result in 1998, the equivalent of over USD 30 billion were injected in the form of special government bonds into the four SOCBs.[13] In 1999, the government established four Asset Management Companies (AMCs) whose task is to take over NPLs from the Big Four banks. The AMCs then try to either sell or collect the bad loans. Overall, the AMCs purchased RMB 1.4 trillion of NPLs, equivalent to roughly 16% of the total assets of the Big Four banks.[14]

Starting in the second half of the 1990s, the state-owned commercial banks saw an increase in competition through the establishment of new commercial banks. Most of the shares in these banks were owned by public authorities, but some were owned by individuals. The China Minsheng Bank entered the market in 1996 as the first non-state commercial bank. Other new commercial banks included the Shenzhen Development Bank, the Guangdong Development Bank, and Everbright Bank. Some of the new banks were the result of merging urban credit cooperatives into city commercial banks.[15]

2002-2006: Opening of the banking sector

Accession to the WTO required China to successively open up its banking sector between 2002 and 2006 in terms of business reach and geography. Until 2002, foreign banks had only been allowed to serve foreign companies and foreign individuals. This was extended to Chinese domestic companies in 2005, with the commitment to lift all restrictions in 2006 so that services can be offered to Chinese individuals as well. In geographic terms, the liberalization is proceeding in a phased manner; 2006 is the deadline for lifting all geographic restrictions on foreign banks' business in China.[16]

---

[13] See Mo (1999), pp. 106-108 for an overview of the mechanics of the recapitalization.

[14] See Mo (1999), p. 93; Pei and Shirai (2004), pp. 10-12; Staude (2002), p. 10.

[15] See Hope and Hu (2006), p. 38; Lardy (1998), p. 70; Nanto and Sinha (2002), p. 473f.

[16] See Deutsche Bank Research (2004), p. 2; Economist Intelligence Unit (2006), p. 17f.; Woetzel (2003), p. 17f.; Wong and Wong (2001), p. 19. While the WTO agreements grant foreign banks more freedom to conduct business in China, taking advantage of these freedoms is more difficult since the working-capital requirements will be increased six-fold to USD 72 million. See Economist Intelligence Unit (2006), p. 18.

3.1.2 Structure of the banking sector

The historical changes described above have also influenced the structure of the banking sector. Today, the banking sector in China is composed of a variety of different institutions. At the core of the sector are the four large state-owned commercial banks – the ABC, BOC, CCB and ICBC ("Big Four") – and the three policy banks – the Agricultural Development Bank of China, the Export-Import Bank of China, and the China Development Bank. In addition, there are over 120 domestic commercial banks, around 36,000 credit cooperatives[17], about 200 foreign banks, and a diverse set of non-bank financial institutions.[18] These institutions and their importance are briefly described below.

By far the largest players in the Chinese banking sector are the four SOCBs that were established in the early 1980s. After the establishment of policy banks in 1994, their business focus shifted from policy lending to commercial lending. Despite falling market shares, the four SOCBs still accounted for about 60% of assets in the banking system at the end of 2004, and they continue to be the most important providers of finance for SOEs. The fact that SOEs in the past were not subject to hard-budget constraints partly explains the low profitability and high NPL levels of the SOCBs. The three policy banks were established in 1994 to relieve the SOCBs of their policy lending responsibilities. Their business focus is on agricultural development, infrastructure and foreign trade, with a special emphasis on the poorer regions in Central and Western China. Together they hold about 10% of overall bank assets, which shows the continued importance of state-directed lending.[19]

Besides the Big Four and the policy banks, there are currently about 120 additional commercial banks collectively accounting for about 18% of total banking assets. This group can be further divided into shareholding or joint-stock commercial banks, and city commercial banks. Currently, there are 11 shareholding banks that are incorporated as joint-stock limited companies under the PRCs Company Law. These are still mostly state-

[17] The number of Chinese credit cooperatives varies greatly in the literature. While Garcia-Herrero and Santabarbara (2004) put the number at 36,0000, Shirai (2002b) estimates about 45,000, while Nanto and Sinha (2002) arrive at an even higher figure of 75,000 credit cooperatives. The discrepancies are probably due to the merging of urban credit cooperatives into city commercial banks in the late 1990s. See Bowers, Gibb and Wong (2003), p. 102.

[18] See Garcia-Herrero and Santabarbara (2004), p. 13; Nanto and Sinha (2002), p. 474; Shirai (2002b), p. 20.

[19] See Deutsche Bank Research (2004), p. 4; Garcia-Herrero and Santabarbara (2004), p. 14.

owned. They include the Bank of Communications, China Minsheng Bank, China Everbright Bank, Shenzhen Development Bank and the Shanghai Pudong Development Bank. Unlike the four SOCBs, their business focus is on the small and medium enterprise market. In terms of services offered and geographic reach they face few restrictions. City commercial banks, unlike joint-stock commercial banks, are not allowed to operate at the regional or national level and are mostly confined to the city where they are located. They were created in the mid-1990s by consolidating urban credit cooperatives. In general, local enterprises or governments hold their capital.[20]

The cooperative sector in China is divided into rural and urban credit cooperatives that account for about 10% of banking assets. In recent years, the number of urban cooperatives has significantly declined as they have been merged into the city commercial banks. However, rural cooperatives are still important for the extension of credit to the agricultural sector, individuals and small- and medium enterprises. Nevertheless, they are burdened by NPLs that are estimated to be as high as 50%. The credit cooperatives are collectively owned and as such subject to state control. As a result, their lending decisions are often influenced by local political considerations.[21]

Several types of non-banking financial companies emerged in China after the mid-1980s. Most notable among these are trust and investment companies, asset-management companies whose purpose is to manage the NPLs that were transferred from the balance sheets of the Big Four banks, securities companies, leasing companies and insurance companies. NBFCs are mostly engaged in lending activities – together they hold about 1% of banking assets. However, this does not fully reflect their importance as alternative providers of finance and for the development of the stock market.[22]

Foreign banks play a limited role in the Chinese banking sector. About 200 foreign institutions currently operate in China, accounting for about 1% of total banking assets. However, the WTO-related opening of China's banking sector will most likely lead to an increase of the role of foreign banks in China over the coming years.[23]

---

[20] See Chen and Thomas (1999), p. 18; Deutsche Bank Research (2004), p. 4f; Garcia-Herrero and Santabarbara (2004), p. 14.

[21] See Deutsche Bank Research (2004), p. 5; Garcia-Herrero and Santabarbara (2004), p. 15.

[22] See Deutsche Bank Research (2004), p. 6; Lardy (1998), p. 71.

[23] See Deutsche Bank Research (2004), p. 5; Garcia-Herrero and Santabarbara (2004), p. 15; Hope and Hu (2006), p. 9.

Despite the liberalization that has been enacted, the SOCBs continue to dominate the sector. This is due to a combination of factors, including their historical ties to the largest enterprises, the advantages of having an extensive branch network, and privileged access to the top policymakers in the country.

3.2 Major reform areas and status of the sector

The overview given in the previous section showed that the Chinese banking sector has undergone major changes since the early 1980s. In this section, the major reform areas are discussed in more detail to allow a more subtle view of the changes and challenges in the Chinese banking sector. The Chinese state-owned banks suffer from several major, inter-related problems that require reforms in key areas. These include the management of NPLs, recapitalization of banks, the upgrading of the supervisory system and regulatory environment, the liberalization of interest rates, the reduction of reserve requirements, the lowering of directed credit and the partial privatization of banks.

The profitability of Chinese banks has deteriorated over the past decade. While reported profitability was in line with international banks in the mid-1980s, by the mid-1990s it was below comparable banks in most markets. This trend has not reversed since this point. Between 2000 and 2002 the return on assets of Chinese banks stood at a mere 0.1%. By 2004 the figure had increased to 0.4%, compared to a 1.2% return for global banking institutions. The return on equity in 2004 was closer to international standards – 11% for the SOCBs versus 16% for global banks – but this reflected the lower capital basis of Chinese banks. In addition, there are reasons to believe that the true state of Chinese banks is worse than that reported. The most important factors include that Chinese banks often overstate interest income by capitalizing interest payments on NPLs; the provisioning for NPLs is inadequate; Chinese banks do not have to pay insurance premiums since a deposit insurance system does not exist; and the investments of SOCBs in trust-and-investment companies are often not consolidated so that losses are not reported on the banks' balance sheets.[24]

Given the low profitability and the high level of NPLs, the capital adequacy ratios of the large SOCBs have also deteriorated. While the unweighted capital to risk-adjusted assets ratio (CRAR) for the four SOCBs stood at 13.2% in 1985, it had declined to 2.8% by the end of 1997. In Au-

[24] See Anderson (2005), p. 11; Anderson (2006), p. 250; International Monetary Fund (2005), p. 200f.; Lardy (1998), pp. 101-105.

gust 1998, RMB 270 billion (USD 32.5 billion) was injected into the SOCBs to raise their capital. Despite transferring bad loans of the Big Four to AMCs and recapitalizing two of the SOCBs in preparation for their stock market listing, the ratio of bank capital to assets deteriorated from 5.3% to 4.1% between 2000 and 2004. In total, the three recapitalizations between 1998 and 2003 amounted to about USD 250 billion and were equivalent to 30% of banks' loan portfolio.[25]

A further major reform task was to bring the capital level of China's banks into line with international standards. As a first step, the PBOC informed the commercial banks in 1994 that they would have to fulfill the Basel Capital Standards. In 1995, the minimum 8% capital adequacy ratio was included in the PRC's Commercial Banking Law that came into effect in the same year. However, the PBOC neither issued guidelines on how to calculate capital adequacy nor enforced the rules. A significant step towards international best practice and the modernization of the capital adequacy rules was the adoption of a risk-based, five category loan classification system in 2002, which banks had to implement until the beginning of 2004. Furthermore, Capital Adequacy Procedures were promulgated in 2004 that included precise mechanisms for calculating capital based on the Basel I standards and including some aspects of Basel II.[26]

Prior to the enactment of far-reaching economic reforms in the late 1970s, the Chinese mono-banking system collected savings and channeled them into investment projects based on quotas set by the central government. Banks merely executed government policies and consequently had no need to build up skills to evaluate loan holders or manage risks. The deteriorating performance of large SOEs led to the build-up of a large stock of NPLs. Since 1997, the level of NPLs of China's SOCBs did not decrease significantly, despite several recapitalization attempts and a strong growth in loans. The development of NPLs from 1997 to 1999 was noteworthy because the transfer of loans to AMCs had virtually no effect in lowering

[25] See Anderson (2006), p. 246; Holland and Lague (2004), p. 26; International Monetary Fund (2005), p. 194; Lardy (2000), pp. 8-12; Mo (1999), p. 32. The official CRAR figures probably overstate the true level since the amount of non-performing loans that can be written-off is restricted. See Lardy (2000), p. 8f. In 2005, a further USD 15 billion were used to recapitalize ICBC in preparation for its stock market listing. See Hope and Hu (2006), p. 40.

[26] See DeSombre and Chen (2004), p. 12; Garcia-Herrero and Santabarbara (2004), p. 22f.; Lardy (1998), p. 93; Shirai (2002b), p. 25. Before the adoption of the loan classification system the quantity of provisions for NPLs was linked to the volume of outstanding loans and not their quality. As a consequence, Chinese banks did not have to increase their provisions as the quality of their loan portfolio declined. See Lardy (1998), p. 97.

the NPL level. At the end of 2004, it still stood at about 16% of total loans (Figure 9). However, these numbers do not take into account the NPLs transferred to AMCs. Considering the overall financial system, including the AMCs, the NPL level at the end of 2005 stood at an estimated 30% of GDP, down from about 39% in 2004. Some analysts put the number even higher, at 50% of GDP. This means that the banking system of the PRC is technically insolvent.[27]

Attempts to stabilize banks and upgrade the capital adequacy rules were accompanied by other regulatory efforts. For example, the first capital adequacy regulations were followed by other prudential rules, such as limits on the loan-to-deposit ratios and asset-to-liquid-liabilities ratios. In addition, attempts were made to enhance information disclosure. Thus, for example, listed banks have to go through an auditing process and must publish more comprehensive financial information. A further important step was the creation of the China Banking Regulatory Commission (CBRC) in 2003. It took over from the PBOC the task of regulating and supervising the banking sector. Current main objectives of the CBRC are the reduction of NPLs and the upgrading of financial institutions' indicators to international standards.[28]

[27] See Chen and Thomas (1999), p. 19; Deutsche Bank Research (2004), p. 10; Garcia-Herrero and Santabarbara (2004), p. 17; International Monetary Fund (2005), p. 196; Pei and Shirai (2004), p. 7; Setser (2006), p. 18. The four Asset Management Companies were founded in 1999 to deal with the NPL problem. They bought NPLs at face value from the banks in exchange for equity positions in the borrowing firms, and have tried to recover as much as possible from the loans various means including auctions, liquidation, sale of equity, or securitization. The AMCs finance themselves through the issuance of government-backed bonds. See Lardy (2000), p. 12.

[28] See Deutsche Bank Research (2004), p. 8; Garcia-Herrero and Santabarbara (2004), p. 22f.; Shirai (2002b), p. 25.

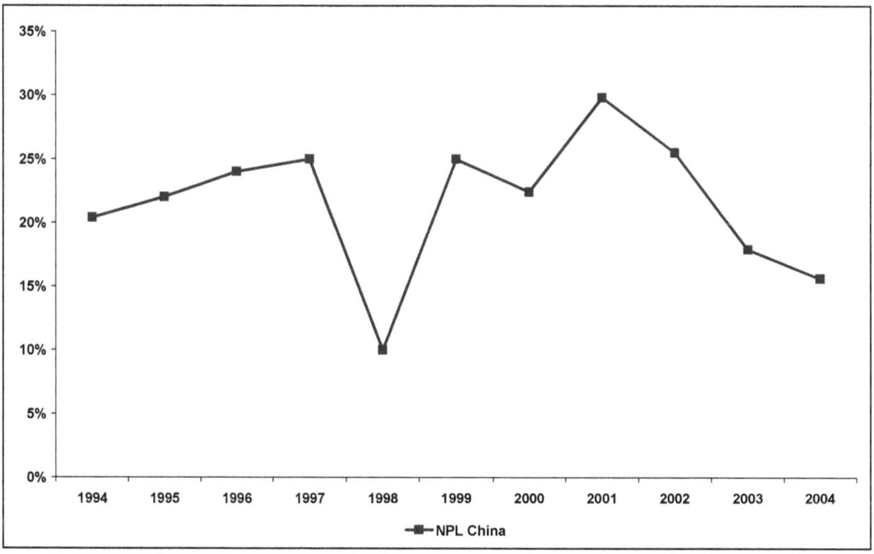

Fig. 9. NPL level of China's SOCBs as percent of total loans[29]

Besides attempts to stabilize the banking system and upgrade the supervisory system, significant steps have also been taken in the areas of interest rate liberalization, reserve requirements and directed credit.

In the late 1980s, Chinese banks gained the flexibility to adjust interest rates for lending within a certain range around the administered rate. Deposit rates, however, continued to be fixed. As part of the austerity program in 1989, interest rates were once again set centrally.[30] In 1993, some flexibility was re-introduced on the lending side. The PBOC set a lending rate ceiling of 20% of the basis rate and a floor of 10% for commercial banks; the ceiling rates were set higher for credit cooperatives. The ceiling interest rate for commercial bank lending was lowered to 10% in 1996 so that both the ceiling and floor rate stood at 10% of the basis rate.[31]

---

[29] See Hope and Hu (2006), p. 45; International Monetary Fund (2005), p. 196; Lardy (1998), p. 119 and 122; Pei and Shirai (2004), p. 7. Note: NPLs shown are gross of provisions. Some analysts estimate significantly higher NPL levels. See for example Setser (2006), p. 11.

[30] See Shirai (2002a), p. 21; Shirai (2002b), p. 23.

[31] See Shirai (2002b), p. 23. Between 1993 and 1995 real interest rates were actually negative since deposit and lending rates were set below the inflation rate. The government however subsidized the difference between the inflation rate and the deposit rate, so that the effective real interest rates stood at 0%. See Shirai (2002a), p. 23.

In 1998 and 1999 attempts were made to increase the flow of credit to small- and medium sized enterprises. This involved first increasing the interest ceiling on loans to these enterprises to 20% in 1998, and then to 30% in the following year. From 2002, banks received more flexibility in setting their interest rates on loans by being able to charge up to 1.3 times the central lending rate. This was raised to 1.7 times the central lending rate in 2004. This provided incentives for banks to upgrade their credit-evaluation skills. While substantial progress has been made in making lending rates more flexible, deposit rates continue to be regulated and fixed. By contrast, interest rates on foreign currency loans and deposits above USD 3 million have been fully liberalized. In addition, the PBOC instructed the China Association of Banks, a national level non-governmental organization, with setting the interest rates on foreign currency deposits below USD 3 million. More flexibility was also introduced in setting interest rates in the wholesale market and by lifting the ceiling on inter-bank rates.[32]

Significant improvements have also been made in the area of reserve requirements. In 1992, the reserve requirement in China was increased from 13% to 20%. It was lowered to 8% in 1998 and to 6% in 1999. To discourage banks from amassing liquid assets, the remuneration of excess reserves was also lowered.[33]

Progress has also been made in the area of directed credit. Here, several reform steps have been taken. Prior to the reforms, the allocation of credit was based on the credit plan that outlined a lower limit for the level of loans to be extended as well as the allocation of these funds to specific sectors. In 1986, the PBOC formulated a credit plan that would set an aggregate credit ceiling on every PBOC branch, thus giving more autonomy to the branches to collaborate with local governments in their credit decisions. The credit plan for working capital loans and fixed investment loans was replaced in 1998 with an indicative, non-binding target. In addition to setting up policy banks, this has helped banks to extend loans based on commercial considerations within the framework of the existing regulations. Yet government bodies still have some influence over credit decisions: for example, the Commercial Banking Law mandates that state banks have to provide credit for projects approved by the state council.[34]

---

[32] See Barnett (2004), p. 49; Garcia-Herrero and Santabarbara (2004), p. 19; Shirai (2002a), p. 23; Shirai (2002b), p. 23.

[33] See Garcia-Herrero and Santabarbara (2004), p. 19; Shirai (2002a), p. 23.

[34] See Mo (1999), p. 99; Shirai (2002a), p. 21; Shirai (2002b), p. 24. Nonetheless, a significant bias towards providing credit to state-owned enterprises and against private sector undertakings remains. For a discussion see Huang (2006), pp. 289-297.

Besides the attempts to strengthen and liberalize the domestic banking sector, entry barriers for foreign investors have also been lowered. Foreign investors can now take stakes of up to 20% in a Chinese bank. While this is a rise of five percentage points compared to the previous level, the maximum cumulative stake for foreigners in a single bank continues to stand at 25%.[35]

Closely connected to this are the partial privatizations of state-owned banks. The first partial privatizations of Big Four banks were the global initial public offerings of the China Construction Bank in October 2005 and of the Bank of China in June 2006. In addition, foreign investors have taken ownership stakes in second-tier banks. The first of these acquisitions was HSBC's purchase of an 8% stake of the Bank of Shanghai, a local joint-stock commercial bank, which took place in December 2001.[36]

For China, the legacy of state-led development has led to serious difficulties for the pursuit of banking sector reforms. After all, a mono-banking system combined with a command economy is arguably the most far-reaching form of government intervention possible in a banking sector. The resulting structural issues – such as the dominating role of first one, and later a handful of banking institutions – represent a major challenge for the transition process. Reforming these banks is extremely difficult since the changes affect virtually the entire economy. Moreover, the mono-bank did not work as a commercial bank, but as an administrative unit for the distribution of funds in line with economic plans. Skills such as the evaluation of credit proposals or risk management know-how were not necessary in such a system and had to be build up after liberalization. This helps to explain the extent and the persistence of NPLs in China, as well as the insufficient capital base and low profitability of banks. Again, these problems are aggravated by the fact that they are concentrated in a small number of banks holding a large percentage of overall assets.

Despite these challenges, China has made progress in reforming the banking sector over recent years, and especially so after WTO accession. But a significant reform agenda remains. This includes further upgrading of the regulatory system, disengagement of the state, management of NPLs, and further liberalization of interest rates. There are similarities here with India, although the reform context and the political and economic system differ. Many of the necessary reforms in China – such as recapitalization of banks, management of NPLs, privatization, entry of new banks – are shared with India. Thus it would appear to be useful to look at the ex-

[35] See Anderson (2005), p. 9; Choi and Kan (2004), p. 11; Kynge (2003), p. 15.
[36] See Bremner (2005), p. 26; Bremner (2006), p. 1.

periences with banking sector reforms in both countries. The next section further investigates the issue of comparability.

3.3 Similarities and differences to the Indian banking sector

Comparisons of China and India abound in the media. These often focus on the economic rise of the two countries.[37] Long (2005) for example points out that

"comparisons between the two are inevitable. Both are poor, largely agricultural, countries that have made great strides in reducing poverty, especially since embarking on radical, liberalizing economic reform. But India and China, always very different civilizations, have followed very different paths to growth. Under reform they have converged somewhat in the past two decades, but will remain distinctive."[38]

For the purpose of this thesis the relevant question is whether the different political, economic and institutional environments allow a comparison of reforms in the banking sector. In this section the focus is on the comparability of the reform experiences in the banking sector; a broader discussion of the different conditions for the transformation follows in section 5.5.

Perhaps the most obvious difference between India and China is the political system. While India is a democracy, China is a one-party autocracy ruled by the Chinese Communist Party. Differences in the political system influence the reform process in the areas of speed and the depth of reforms. The general assumption is that China is able to push through reforms faster than democratic India. However, this is not necessarily always

[37] See for example Business Week (2005) "China & India"; Huang and Khanna (2003) "Can India overtake China?"; The Economist (2005b) "The tiger in front – A survey of India and China". Henley (2004) points out that "China is a natural comparator for India for obvious geopolitical, economic and demographic reasons. They both have populations in excess of one billion – China with 1.27 billion and India with 1.03 billion people in 2001. [...] on a purchasing power parity (PPP) basis, they are respectively the second and fourth largest economies in the world." Henley (2004), p. 1041.

[38] Long (2005), p. 3.

the case: the Chinese leadership has often followed a trial and error approach to reforms as well.[39] Besides affecting the ability to pursue reforms, the different political systems influence the institutional framework of the two countries in general, and the judicial system in particular. The Chinese legal system is reliant on informal relations and often described as a "semi-legal system" by Western standards. More importantly however, the Chinese Communist Party's claim of absolute power means that it *de facto* stands above the law. By contrast, India's legal system was based on British Common Law and is fairly well developed, but suffers from a lack of resources that may lead to delays in law enforcement.[40] Nonetheless, these differences should not overly affect the comparability, since both countries have to upgrade their institutional infrastructure to meet the requirements of a market-based banking sector. While their respective institutional legacy may lead to different reform paths, the general institutional foundations for a well-functioning banking sector are to a large extent independent of these differences.

On the economic side, there are historical similarities between India and China. During the 1950s and 1960s, both countries followed development strategies that were based on the concepts of self-reliance, import-substitution and state-led development. Both focused on state enterprises in heavy industries to achieve their respective goals, which led to a neglect of the agricultural sector. Economic liberalization in both countries was triggered after the failure of their previous development strategies. Despite different outcomes of the reforms, there are similarities between the two during this phase as well: both have followed a gradual path to reforms, have made relatively little progress in changing the ownership structure of the state sector, and take a cautious stance toward the liberalization of the capital account.[41]

An important difference between the two is their exchange rate system: China's Renminbi is narrowly pegged to a basket of currencies, whereas

[39] See Manor (2005), p. 105; Mukherji (2005), p. 61; The Economist (2005a), p. 11f. Cases in point for the trial and error approach are the gradual and cautious establishment of special economic zones in China during the early reform stages, or the "percolation model" by which reform measures are first tried out in selected localities before they are rolled out at the national level. See Heberer and Schubert (2006), p. 16; Seitz (2000), pp. 245-247.

[40] See Chow (1997), p. 322; Chow (2004), p. 145; Desai (2003), p. 3; Jalan (2005), pp. 64-67; Wu (2006), p. 44.

[41] See Bhalla (1998), p. 152; Mukherji (2005), p. 61; Swamy (2005b), p. 78f.

the value of the Indian Rupee can float relatively freely.[42] With the interest rate and the exchange rate, China administers two key prices in the economy. This has significant implications for the banking sector as the Chinese central bank has to build up foreign exchange reserves to maintain the fixed exchange rate when capital flows into the economy, which leads to an increase of the monetary base. The subsequent monetary expansion can lead to inflationary pressures as well as to an increase in bank lending. Since interest rates also cannot fluctuate freely, administrative controls are needed to restrain credit expansion.[43] Despite these differences, key reform tasks in the banking sectors in India and China are independent of the prevailing exchange rate system – such as lowering non-performing loans, building an institutional infrastructure or privatizing banks. Therefore, while its important to appreciate the different exchange rate system, this does not limit the comparability with regard to the banking sector.

In the banking sector the two countries face similar problems stemming from their prior development strategies. In line with the paradigm of state-led development, the state controlled large parts of the banking system in both countries. Domestic savings were the main source of financing for economic growth and the banking sector has traditionally played an important role in the development strategies by channeling domestic savings to investment projects. This legacy is still present in both countries today. In 2004, state-owned banks in India and China still controlled about 75-85% of total assets in the banking sector.[44] Policy-lending is also still common in both countries. In India, banks have to extend 40% of loans to priority sectors, whereas in China a disproportionate share of loans goes to state-owned enterprises.[45]

Overall, the financial systems of both countries can be characterized as "bank-based" as opposed to "market-based" due to the predominance of banks. However, while China had a mono-bank system, India continued to have a variety of banking institutions and even some private-sector banks. Despite attempts to provide banking services to the population in rural areas, both countries face a dualism between the well-covered urban areas

---

[42] The peg of the Renminbi to a basket of currencies was introduced in July 2005. Between January 1994 and July 2005, the Renminbi was *de-facto* fixed to the US-Dollar. See Economist Intelligence Unit (2006), p. 9.

[43] See DeRosa (2005), p. 51f.; Dorn (2006), p. 2; Goldstein (2006), p. 260; Kohli (2001), p. 7; Prasad and Rajan (2006), p. 5; Rajan (2006), p. 272.

[44] See Garcia-Herrero, Gavila and Santabarbara (2005), p. 40; Reserve Bank of India (2005a).

[45] See Huang (2006), p. 289.

and poorly-covered rural areas.[46] Furthermore, the legacy of state-led development leaves especially state-owned banks with similar problems. In both countries, banks were at the beginning of the reforms burdened by non-performing loans from state-owned enterprises; as shown above, over 20% of the loan portfolio was considered non-performing at the beginning of the 1990s in both countries. Banks had excessive staff levels and were effectively shielded from competition – which made them vulnerable to the opening of the banking sector.

Despite differences in the political, economic and institutional systems, India and China today face comparable problems in their banking sectors. At the beginning of economic reforms, protected state banks dominated a sector in which the respective governments took many business decisions. This has resulted in a variety of common problems such as the need to upgrade regulations, reduce non-performing loans and privatize state-owned banks, where the two countries can learn from each other. While the general conditions in India and China are different, the similarity of the challenges faced in the banking sector are sufficient to warrant a deeper analysis. In fact, as noted by Saez (2001), "China and India's case is of particular importance because they offer insight into other low-income countries that have yet to initiate substantial financial liberalization."[47]

3.4 Conclusion

The Chinese banking sector has undergone significant changes over the last 25 years. After the abolishment of the mono-banking system and the establishment of a two-tier banking system, the country made significant progress towards the creation of a market-based banking system. It is, however, noteworthy that major progress in reforming the banking sector has only been made after accession to the WTO, which resulted in commitments to open up the banking sector. Reforming the banking sector also started noticeably later than reforms in other parts of the economy. These deviations from the pattern of reforms in other sectors signals both the special importance of the banking sector as an intermediary with close connections to enterprises and households, and the extent of the problems in the banking sector.

Despite progress made over the last decades, the Chinese state still plays an important role in the banking sector – both directly through ownership of banks and indirectly through various restrictions. There are still impor-

[46] See Tsai (2005), p. 123.
[47] Saez (2001), p. 235.

tant areas where further reform is required. These include the recapitalization of SOCBs, the lowering of NPLs, the introduction of prudential norms in line with international standards and the privatization of state-owned banks. The need to provide further capital to the SOCBs and the high level of NPLs in particular are evidence of the fundamental structural problems of the Chinese banking sector. These have not been solved despite an extremely favorable macroeconomic environment with strong credit growth and ample opportunities for profit through the asymmetric liberalization of interest rates.

The reform agendas in China and India contain similar elements. Both countries can learn from their respective experiences with banking sector liberalization. As stated above, comparability between the two countries is sufficient to allow a meaningful analysis. Despite the difficulties of enacting further reforms in both countries, the current status of reforms in India and China can be evaluated. The financial liberalization literature has dealt with the question of reforming state-dominated financial systems in detail and can thus provide a theoretical basis for an evaluation of the progress made. As a basis for this, the following section gives a detailed overview of the financial liberalization literature and its recommendations for countries wanting to liberalize their banking sectors.

4 Banking sector functions and coordination

Since the seminal works of McKinnon (1973) and Shaw (1973), there has been a considerable body of literature covering the topic of financial liberalization and the importance of the financial sector for the overall economy. A recurring recommendation in these studies is that the direct involvement of the government in the banking sector should be reduced in order to allow the sector to perform its functions better.

The following section begins with an overview of the functions of a banking sector. The discussion then moves on to present the two possible coordination mechanisms – state or market – and the rationales for their usage. Special emphasis is given to the financial liberalization literature in which possible forms of state involvement in the banking sector and the likely effects of the removal of these policies is discussed. The section closes with a discussion of empirical studies on the effects of banking sector liberalization.

4.1 Functions of the banking sector

The banking sector serves three important functions in an economy. First, it ensures the orderly flow of funds between economic agents through the provision of payment services. Second, it mobilizes resources in the form of savings by offering attractive investment opportunities. And third, it pools savings and allocates them in the form of loans to investment projects.[1] The banking sector thus acts as an intermediary between savers and investors in an economy and as a result enables the decentralization of economic decisions in a market economy. However, the banking sector has more importance than its role as an intermediary might suggest, since the

[1] The literature frequently mentions further functions of the banking system such as exercising corporate control or risk management (see for example Levine (1997), p. 691). These services of the banking system however have to be seen in connection to the allocation function and are therefore not explicitly discussed.

mobilization of savings and the allocation of capital can positively influence economic growth.[2]

In the following sections, the focus is on the mobilization and allocation functions of the banking sector, and their influence on economic growth. As in other studies focusing on the effects of the banking sector on growth, the provision of payment services is not discussed.[3]

4.1.1 Mobilization of resources

Households can use their disposable income either for consumption or for saving.[4] Savings can either be accumulated by households themselves or through the banking sector. The mobilization of savings through the organized banking sector has certain advantages for the providers and users of capital such as size transformation, maturity transformation and liquidity enhancement.[5]

Size transformation is achieved through the provision of small-denomination instruments that help to overcome the mismatch between the suppliers and users of capital. The suppliers of capital generally consist of a multitude of savers that save comparatively small amounts; the users of

---

[2] See Allen and Gale (2000), p. 3; Jaffe and Levonian (2001), p. 163, Lane (1994), p. 233; Megginson (2005), p. 1932; Quispe-Agnoli and McQuerry (2001), p. 2; Shirai (2002c), p. 4; World Bank (2001), p. 313. Theoretically, both banks and securities markets can provide the mobilization and allocation function. In the case of transition and developing countries, however, the banking system will play the dominant role because capital markets lack sufficient depth and banks provide better protection of small investors. See Berglof and Bolton (2002), p. 92; Lane (1994), p. 233; Quispe-Agnoli and McQuerry (2001), p. 2.

[3] See, for example, the studies by de Gregorio and Guidotti (1995), King and Levine (1993), Levine (1997) or Wachtel (2001) that do not focus on the effect of the payment system.

[4] Total domestic savings in a closed economy is the sum of the savings from households, enterprises and the state. For the mobilization of resources, savings from households are the most relevant, since in most cases the state produces negative savings (i.e. budget deficits) and enterprises often use their savings (i.e. retained earnings) as a source of internal financing. See Schmidt-Hebbel and Serven (1997), p. 56; World Bank (1989), p. 28f.

[5] These functions can in theory also be performed by the informal financial sector. However, the informal sector lacks the legal enforcement mechanisms of the formal banking sector, and so a close bond between borrower and lender is necessary. This in turn restricts the reach and reduces the overall economic benefits of the informal sector. See Krahnen and Schmidt (1994), pp. 36-38 for an overview of the characteristics of the informal financial sector.

capital generally need larger amounts of financing that an individual saver cannot provide. Size transformation enables the creation of small denomination instruments so that households have the opportunity to hold diversified portfolios, increase asset liquidity and invest in firms with an efficient scale. The provision of a set of attractive investment vehicles can accordingly support the mobilization of resources.[6]

Banks also provide *maturity transformation*. As well as different capital requirements, suppliers and users of capital often have different time horizons. While most private savers have a short- to medium-term horizon, after which they want to use their funds, investment projects can run over more extended periods. Here, again, banks facilitate the mobilization of savings by offering instruments with the maturities wanted by savers and borrowers. This has positive effects on the mobilization of resources through the organized banking sector. In addition banks, in their role as intermediaries, relieve savers from the task of finding and screening investors, and thus help them to deploy their savings more efficiently.[7]

Providers and users of capital also have different *liquidity* preferences. Savers prefer to hold liquid instruments that they can sell at short notice if they need funds. In contrast, the users of capital need long-term fixed commitments. Without this commitment, they are unable to invest in long-term projects. Banks are in a position to accommodate both types of liquidity preferences, which in turn helps to mobilize savings.[8]

Thus the banking sector encourages the mobilization of savings by offering attractive saving instruments that help to overcome liquidity, time and size constraints.

4.1.2 Allocation of resources

Yet the mobilization of savings alone is not sufficient to generate positive effects for the economy. It is equally important to bring the savings to productive use. Besides mobilizing sufficient savings, the banking sector has to ensure efficient allocation.

There are at least three ways in which banks can improve the allocation of resources. First, banks have a comparative advantage in screening fund-seekers and monitoring investment projects, which lowers the cost of intermediation. Second, as discussed above, banks transform claims of different maturities (i.e., from short-term savings to long-term loans) and

---

[6] See Achleitner (2000), p. 24f.; Levine (1997), p. 698f.; Wachtel (2003), p. 35.

[7] See Achleitner (2000), p. 25; Wachtel (2003), p. 35.

[8] See Achleitner (2000), p. 26; Wachtel (2003), p. 35.

consequently help to increase the liquidity in the market. Third, the banking sector provides risk management services, which makes it possible to fund high-risk, high-return projects.[9]

The efficient allocation of capital is however not only influenced by the services of monitoring, screening and risk management that the banking sector provides. The real interest rate is also an important factor in the efficient allocation of capital. A market-based real interest rate will prevent capital being allocated to projects that destroy value. Excluding these low-return projects increases the overall economic efficiency of the projects funded.[10] Stiglitz and Weiss (1981), however, argue that a market-based real interest rate does not necessarily improve the allocation of credit in markets with information asymmetries because banks react to the adverse selection problem in these markets by rationing credit. This lowers the overall economic welfare since some projects with positive returns do not get funding.[11] One possible solution to this problem is to set risk-adjusted interest rates.

A further way in which banks indirectly help to improve the allocation of resources is by reducing the fragmentation of financial markets. The setting of market-based real interest rates and the wide availability of banking services both help to reduce the attractiveness of fragmented curb markets. The organized financial sector has economies of scale in the allocation of savings to investment projects. Thus the overall efficiency of capital allocation is improved when funds flow through the formal banking sector.[12]

Allocating capital to the highest value use while limiting the risk of loss through moral hazard, adverse selection or transaction costs, is likely to have a positive effect on economic growth. Banks serve as the primary transmission channel for this allocation process. So it can be assumed that there is a positive relationship between the deepening of the banking sector and growth. This is discussed in the next section.

4.1.3 Fostering economic growth

Mobilizing savings and allocating them to the highest value use are of overall importance for the economy. However, this does not imply that is naturally causes economic growth. It is necessary to explore this relationship in more depth. Insights can be gained from the two main schools of

[9] See Achleitner (2000), pp. 24-26; Wachtel (2001), p. 339.

[10] See Deckert (1996), p. 25f.

[11] See Stiglitz and Weiss (1981), p. 408f.

[12] See Balassa (1990), p. 59; Loayza and Ranciere (2006), p. 1052; Lynch (1996), p. 5.

economic growth theory: the neoclassical and the endogenous growth theory.

Neoclassical growth theory dates back to the seminal work of Solow (1956). In its most basic version, it is based on a production function in which output is a function of capital, labor and the level of technology. Several predictions can be derived from this.[13] First, the steady state level of income per person is a positive function of the saving rate and a negative function of the rate of population growth. An increase in the saving rate will consequently increase the steady-state level of income per person. Second, in steady state the growth rate of income per person is a positive function of the rate of technological progress, and is thus independent of both the saving rate and the rate of population growth. Third, the capital-to-income ratio in steady state is constant since capital and income grow at the same rate.[14]

The standard neoclassical model explains the growth rate of an economy by population and productivity growth. Since both are exogenous to the model, macroeconomic policies do not influence the long-term growth rate. For this reason, the neoclassical model is not well-suited to explain the effect of policy changes such as liberalization on growth. A further implication is a significant reduction of the importance of financial intermediaries. An increase in the saving rate will lead to an increased level of income, but not to an increased growth rate of income. Consequently, even if banks contribute to an increase in the saving rate, this will have no influence on the rate of growth in an economy.[15]

These shortcomings have prompted the development of models that avoid the assumption of exogenous progress in technology in explaining growth. The main difference between this new approach – the endogenous growth theory – and the neoclassical model is that it treats growth as an endogenous outcome from an economic system and not merely as a result of outside forces such as exogenous technological progress. Another difference between the two approaches is that the endogenous growth theory does not require the assumption of exogenous technological progress as a driver of growth. Thus, while in the neoclassical model savings only have a temporary effect on growth and the economy eventually approaches a

[13] Only those predictions relevant to the functions of the banking sector are discussed here. For a complete overview, see Mankiw (1995), p. 277.

[14] See Mankiw (1995), p. 277.

[15] See Auerbach and Siddiki (2004), p. 234; Organization for Economic Cooperation and Development (2003), p. 5.

steady state, in the endogenous growth model savings can lead to permanent growth.[16]

A further difference between the two approaches is that the endogenous growth model assumes constant returns to scale, which is contrary to the generally assumed diminishing returns to scale. This apparent problem is overcome by assuming positive externalities from the creation of knowledge that cannot be kept perfectly secret. These spillover effects are used to explain the existence of constant returns: the benefits from increases in productivity are not only reaped by one company, but from the industry as a whole. In such an environment, increased growth can result from increased investment. The assumption of spillover effects from investment in the endogenous model also helps to establish a relationship between the functions of a banking sector and economic growth. This is because policies that influence the rate of saving and investment have an effect on the steady state rate of growth. As discussed in the previous two sections, a banking sector facilitates the mobilization of savings and the allocation of these savings between competing uses in an uncertain environment. Exerting the financial functions of savings mobilization and capital allocation affects two channels to growth: capital accumulation and technological innovation. Since a major determinant of long-term economic growth is the rate of capital accumulation, a well-functioning financial sector is a potential enabler for long-term growth, so that a causal relationship between finance and growth can be established.[17]

The question arises under which coordination mechanism – state or market as the two theoretical extremes – the sector can best perform its functions. In the next section, first different arguments for the involvement of the state in the financial sector are presented and the effects of such involvement discussed. Following this, arguments for a market-based banking sector are discussed in the context of the financial liberalization hypothesis, which argues the case for a market-oriented banking sector.

4.2 State involvement in the banking sector

After the Second World War, economists and governments alike advocated government ownership of enterprises in order to circumvent possible inequities or imperfections in the markets. As a result, many countries na-

[16] See Mankiw (1995), p. 296f.; Romer (1994), p. 3.

[17] See Auerbach and Siddiki (2004), p. 234; Greenwood and Jovanovic (1990), p. 1078f.; Lane (1994), p. 234; Levine (1997), p. 691; Romer (1986), p. 1003; Roubini and Sala-i-Martin (1992), p. 5.

tionalized "strategic" sectors of their economies – including banks. Another strategy besides outright nationalization of banks was the imposition of restrictions and regulations. The underlying rationale for these policies was the desire to achieve higher investment and saving ratios in a controlled financial sector.[18]

Thus there are different rationales and measures for state involvement in the banking sector. The next section first explores reasons for state involvement in the banking sector and then discusses different instruments of state involvement.

4.2.1 Reasons for state involvement

Broadly speaking, proponents of a controlled banking sector hope to achieve three types of goals through state ownership of banks or restrictions on their operations. These goals – economic, developmental and political – are explored in the following section.

4.2.1.1 Economic goals

Enhancing economic efficiency in the light of market failures is one of the key reasons for state involvement in the economy. This also holds true for the banking sector.[19]

Market failures occur where the conditions for the proper functioning of markets are not fulfilled. This results in welfare losses for consumers or producers. The most frequent types of market failures are natural monopolies, external effects, ruinous competition, and information asymmetries. In a natural monopoly, economies of scale persist through the whole range of possible outputs so that only one company will survive. External effects distort the allocative function of prices. In the case of a positive external effect, the beneficiary does not have to pay for the effect; in the case of a negative external effect, losses are not compensated.[20] Ruinous competition is the result of a distorted allocation mechanism in an industry combined with high exit barriers: the result is too much competition, which is problematic if some companies are also active in other industries and use the funds generated in that industry to cross-subsidize their products or ser-

[18] See Beck (2006), p. 13; Denizer, Desai and Gueorguiev (1998), p. 2; Shleifer (1998), p. 133f.

[19] See Megginson (2005), p. 1933.

[20] Public goods are an extreme case of external effects since nobody can be excluded from their consumption. An individual will thus not be willing to pay for them. See Schmidt (1999), p. 38.

vices. In this situation it is not necessarily the most efficient company that survives. In the case of asymmetric information, one side has privileged knowledge about decision relevant factors of a transaction and can use this information to its advantage. Information asymmetries can lead to adverse selection and moral hazard. Adverse selection problems arise because of uncertainty about decision-related variables before a contract is closed: as a result, the party that is most likely to produce an undesirable outcome is selected. In the case of a bank, borrowers with high risk, high return projects are most eager to get a loan because they are less likely to pay it back. After closing the contract, privileged information concerning fulfillment of the contract or the engagement in undesirable activities leads to moral hazard. For example, after having received a loan, a borrower might invest the money in a high risk venture, which is undesirable for the bank. If the project fails the bank bears most of the loss; on the other hand, it has no upside if the project succeeds.[21]

How relevant are these four types of market failures for the banking sector? Natural monopolies are no particular concern, since branch-based banking exhibits decreasing economies of scale. External effects exist to some extent in the financial sector. Examples are the provision of a stable currency or a well-functioning banking system, which both have positive repercussions on overall economic activity. But since the currency is provided by a central bank and banks also profit from a stable banking system, external effects should not play an important role for market failure. Ruinous competition in the banking sector is most likely to happen in the case of government involvement. When the government explicitly or implicitly guarantees the survival of banks, they will have an incentive to engage in price competition to drive competitors out of the market. This ruinous competition is however the result of a failed intervention and thus constitutes a case of state failure, rather than market failure. Natural monopolies, external effects or ruinous competition are thus not of major concern in the banking sector.

By contrast, information asymmetries are prevalent in various forms between shareholders, depositors, borrowers and banks' management. These information asymmetries can seriously undermine the stability and well-functioning of a banking system and – from an economic point of view – justify government involvement. They therefore warrant closer examination.

---

[21] See Aschinger (2001), p. 64f.; Besley (1994), p. 29; Döring (2003), p. 97; Fees (1997), p. 639; Feld and Kirchgässner (2003), p. 260; Mishkin (1996), p. 30f.; Schmidt (1999), pp. 36-40; Sheshinski and López-Calva (1999), p. 5.

Information asymmetries arise from the principal-agent relationship between a bank and its depositors. Depositors provide the funds a bank can use to award loans. However, since the depositors have limited or no information concerning the riskiness of loans, an information asymmetry exists that can lead to moral hazard. This is exacerbated by the moral hazard between banks and borrowers since borrowers may divert funds from the intended usage. To reduce these information asymmetries, banks have an incentive to provide depositors with additional information ("signaling"). Furthermore, given the "first come, first served" nature of withdrawals, the depositors themselves have incentives to monitor the bank.[22] However, depending on the overall perceived riskiness of the banking system, depositors might be inclined not to deposit their funds at all. There are two possible solutions to overcome such a situation: confidence can be restored either by outright ownership of banks by the government or by the introduction of deposit insurance.

Stiglitz and Weiss (1981) demonstrate that information asymmetries between bank and borrower over the riskiness of a project can lead to credit rationing. The reason is that charging higher interest rates can increase the riskiness of a bank's loan portfolio, since higher average interest rates make safer projects unprofitable. Thus despite excess demand for credit in the market, banks will not make further loans because the higher risk projects could crowd out lower risk projects.[23]

Apart from information asymmetries there are a multitude of other imperfections in the financial markets which may warrant government action. They include the major difference between the social and the private cost of bank failure, the public good nature of banks' solvency, negative externalities from bad banks on the overall confidence in the sector, and the discrepancy between the private and the social benefits of loans.[24]

It is unlikely that the conditions for the proper functioning of markets are fulfilled in any economy. This explains why governments play an important role even in the most developed economies. Since market failures – especially those related to asymmetric information – are much more preva-

---

[22] See Aschinger (2001), p. 66. As pointed out by Diamond and Dybvig (1983), the loans a bank hands out are illiquid – they are longer-term commitments that cannot be readily called if a bank needs cash for withdrawals. While liquidity transformation is one of the main purposes of banks, it also makes them vulnerable to bank runs since they only hold a fraction of their assets in cash. See Diamond and Dybvig (1983), p. 403.

[23] See Stiglitz and Weiss (1981), p. 393f.

[24] See Arestis, Nissanke and Stein (2003), p. 6; Yeyati, Micco and Panizza (2004), pp. 6-9.

lent in developing countries, a higher degree of state involvement may be necessary to guarantee a proper functioning of the markets. Thus there are convincing arguments for state involvement in the banking sector on economic grounds. Government intervention to counter market failure can range from increased supervision of banks and tighter disclosure standards to outright ownership of banks. As a consequence it is necessary to define the appropriate role of government in the banking sector that has both the possibility of market and state failure.[25]

4.2.1.2 Developmental goals

Another argument for government involvement in the banking sector is that it supports the development of the domestic economy. This development view dates at least back to Gerschenkron (1962), who stressed the necessity of financial development for economic growth. The starting point for Gerschenkron's analysis was a comparison of industrializing countries in the second half of the 19th century. He noticed that in some countries like Germany banks had played a vital role in channeling savings into industry. In other countries, most notably Russia, banks were not able to play an important role in development since economic institutions were not sufficiently developed. This led to a shortage of capital for large scale projects. Gerschenkron argued that where banks are not able to fulfill their economic role, governments could use state-owned banks to provide the stability and safety needed for financial and economic development. This was the case in Russia during the 1890s, where the government had to fulfill many of the functions of commercial banks.[26]

In the developmental view, the main argument for owning banks is that the government can collect savings from households and channel them into long-term strategic projects. Failures of private capital markets can be overcome, which allows a faster pace of development than with private financing. Furthermore, the government can provide funding to projects with low financial but high social returns, which presumably would not get sufficient financing from private banks.[27]

---

[25] See Ahrens (1998), p. 24f.; Stiglitz and Bhattacharya (1999), p. 96; Stiglitz (2004), p. 21; Wachtel (2001), p. 354. A more in-depth discussion of market failures and their effect on the liberalization of the banking sector follows in section 6.3.3.

[26] See Gerschenkron (1962), p. 22.

[27] See Denizer, Desai and Gueorguiev (1998), p. 5; La Porta, Lopez de Silanes and Schleifer (2002), p. 267; Megginson (2005), p. 1933; Yeyati, Micco and Panizza (2004), p. 8.

Another positive effect of public sector banks may be the creation of a branch network in less privileged regions. The provision of branch-banking services in these regions can help mobilize savings and give local firms access to credit, which contributes to economic growth.[28] In fact, these developmental goals do not necessarily require the state ownership of banks: they can also be achieved by means of regulations such as credit quotas for certain sectors and incentives to open branches in rural areas. In recent years, microfinance institutions have also attempted to serve these clients.

There is some overlap between the development view and the economic arguments for state involvement in the banking sector. In both approaches the private sector alone is considered insufficient to ensure a well-functioning banking system. The difference between the two approaches is that, according to the economic view, state involvement restores the efficiency of the market, while the developmental view advocates active intervention in the banking sector as part of the overall development strategy of a country.

4.2.1.3 Political goals

The political goals for state involvement in the banking sector are closely connected to the development goals discussed in the previous section. While the development view stresses government involvement in order to achieve social objectives, the political view emphasizes political objectives as the main motivation for intervention. In this view governments take control over banks to provide direct or indirect benefits for their supporters. Such political goals can be achieved either through outright ownership or through regulations.[29]

Besides financing politically desirable projects, state-owned banks can also be an easy source of money for the government to finance budget deficits. This can be achieved through reserve requirements, provision of credit to the government at artificially low rates, or by demanding that banks hold government bonds.[30]

---

[28] See Arun and Turner (2002c), p. 93.

[29] See La Porta, Lopez de Silanes and Schleifer (2002), p. 266f.

[30] See Denizer, Desai and Gueorguiev (1998), p. 2; Giovanni and de Melo (1993), p. 954. These instruments are discussed in more detail in section 4.2.2. China is a prime example for the use of banks to achieve political goals. Since the Chinese government was neither prepared to let large state-owned enterprise fail nor to provide further direct subsidies, the state-owned banks had to extend loans to keep these firms in operation. See Broadman (2001), p. 17; Lardy (1998), p. 38.

Another motive for political intervention in the banking sector can be the creation of a politically desirable infrastructure, such as a branch network.[31] Again, while the means are the same as in the developmental view, the underlying motivation is different. In the developmental view, a branch network is used as a development tool by providing banking services and credit to underserved parts of the economy; in the political view it is interpreted as a tool for patronage that can be employed for providing credit to political supporters, for example.

Megginson (2005) points out some other politically motivated reasons for state involvement in the banking sector. These include the desire to maintain control over the national financial system, ideological reasons such as punishing capitalists, the disenfranchisement of unpopular groups, or – in the case of many former colonies – a counter-reaction to former foreign dominance.[32]

Most of the politically motivated goals – such as the financing of firms or establishment of a branch network – could also be achieved by regulation or persuasion. This leaves the question of what the advantages of ownership are for a government. La Porta, Lopez de Silanes and Schleifer (2002) argue that the main advantage of ownership is that it gives the government the option to choose projects, while implementation can be delegated to the private sector. In countries with relatively poorly developed financial systems and property rights that are difficult to enforce, the benefits of political control over banks are probably the highest: here, state-owned banks have less competition for funds from private banks.[33]

Using banks to achieve political goals will most likely lead to inefficiencies. While the economic and developmental views of state involvement in the banking sector were concerned with increasing overall welfare, the political view only tends to increase the welfare of special-interest groups. Based on welfare arguments, political goals are thus not viable reasons for state involvement in the banking sector.

Besides outright ownership of banks – the most visible form of state intervention – a wide array of other instruments exists. These are discussed in the following section.

[31] See Schmidt (1999), p. 41.

[32] See Megginson (2005), p. 1933.

[33] See La Porta, Lopez de Silanes and Schleifer (2002), p. 266f.

4.2.2 Instruments of state involvement

There is a large array of financial restraints and competitive restrictions that governments can use to intervene in a banking sector. Before discussing these policies, it is important to note that not all forms of government intervention constitute repressionist policies. As has been discussed, there are cases in which government involvement can enhance the functioning of markets. Financial repression or financial restraints on the other hand are policies that inhibit the operation of the banking sector at its full potential.[34] In the classical McKinnon-Shaw framework they refer to "[...] distortions of financial prices including interest rates and foreign exchange rates and by other means [that reduce] the real rate of growth and the real size of the financial system relative to nonfinancial magnitudes."[35] In this section, first measures of financial repression and then other competitive restrictions in the banking sector are discussed.

Financial repression can take various forms. Three frequently-used policies are statutory pre-emptions, regulated interest rates, and directed credit programs.

Statutory pre-emptions can take the form of reserve and liquidity requirements. Reserve requirements oblige banks to deposit a certain percentage of deposits at the central bank. While this is common practice in many countries, it becomes a repressive policy if the amount of funds pre-empted is above the level required to ensure an orderly functioning of the monetary policy. Liquidity requirements are similar in nature and oblige banks to keep a certain percentage of deposits in government bonds or other approved securities. Statutory pre-emptions result in an under-supply of credit by taking liquidity out of the market and in an artificial demand for government securities.[36]

Interest rate controls take several forms. Frequently controls include ceilings, floors and fixed rates on both deposits and loans.[37] These controls constitute either incentives or disincentives for investment or saving. The controls on the lending side are especially important since they can affect the riskiness of the loan portfolio. Fixed lending rates or floors on the lending rate tend to crowd out "low-risk, low-return" projects that become unprofitable with higher financing costs. A ceiling on the lending rate can result in a *de-facto* subsidy for "high-risk, high-return" projects, if banks lack

---

[34] See Wachtel (2001), p. 336.

[35] Shaw (1973), p. 3.

[36] See Demetriades and Luintel (1997), pp. 311-314; Denizer, Desai and Gueorguiev (1998), p. 3 and p. 10f.; Joshi and Little (1997), p. 112 and p. 125.

[37] See Demetriades and Luintel (1997), p. 314.

credit evaluation skills. This can lead to inadequately low financing costs for high-risk ventures because the interest rate does not fully reflect the risk level.

Under a *directed credit program*, a certain portion of bank credit is allocated to specific sectors in the economy. In the case of India, for example, 40% of the total credit of domestic banks has to go to priority sectors such as agriculture, small-scale industries, small transport operators or the export sector. The rationale for directed credit programs is that banks might not otherwise allocate funds to projects with high social but low economic returns; the resulting lack of credit for certain sectors thus requires government intervention.[38]

The results of statutory pre-emptions and regulated interest rates are a forced low return on assets and high levels of reserve money. This helps to finance budget deficits. But it also leads to disincentives to save because of low real interest rates while at the same time creating demand for credit due to relatively low lending rates. Excess demand for credit permits the government to allocate it among competing users – for example via a directed credit program. To prevent capital from leaving the country in such an environment, governments have to institute capital controls on foreign exchange; otherwise the domestic restrictions could easily be circumvented.[39]

As a result of these interventions, banks become quasi-fiscal entities and are no longer autonomous profit-seeking enterprises. The problem is that these interferences can undermine the solidity of the sector and lead to a vicious cycle in which repressive policies can make further repression necessary. For example, an increase in the pre-emption of funds from the banking system can cause an erosion of banks' capital base and the build up of non-performing loans. This makes banks more vulnerable to shocks and may prompt the government to provide opportunities for banks' to earn profits through limits on competition or the imposition of ceilings on deposit rates.[40]

Competitive restrictions are closely related to the repressive policies described above. Both are politically motivated restrictions imposed on the banking sector. The difference between the two is that financial repression refers to restrictions on the use of funds, while competitive restrictions limit competition in the banking system. Two major forms of competitive

---

[38] See Ganesan (2003), p. 14; Shirai (2002c), p. 18; Stiglitz (1994), p. 42.

[39] See Caprio, Hanson and Honohan (2001), p. 5f.; Denizer, Desai and Gueorguiev (1998), p. 3; Giovanni and de Melo (1993), p. 954.

[40] See Honohan (1997), p. 7 and p. 11.

restrictions in the banking sector are entry and branch restrictions. Through restrictions on the entry of new domestic or foreign banks, the incumbent banks are protected. This results in a lower competitive intensity at the expense of consumers. Branch restrictions limit a bank's ability to open new branches. They come in various forms. Banks can face a cap on the number of branches in the country, the maximum number of new branches that can be opened during a year can be limited, or branches can be restricted to certain areas. These restrictions also reduce competition, which again benefits incumbents at the expense of consumers.[41]

Many development economists favored the measures of financial repression and competitive restrictions outlined above. Their arguments were that by intervening in the market mechanism, interest rate usury could be prevented and the cost of servicing the budget deficit be reduced. In addition, it was believed that governments are more efficient than banks in identifying socially desirable investments.[42]

The potential benefits of financial restraints are that governments – especially the governments of capital-scarce countries – can use capital to promote economic development. This is in line with the development argument for state intervention discussed above. There are three potential channels through which financial restraints can have a positive effect on growth. First, credit can be channeled into investment projects in certain priority sectors that otherwise might not receive the necessary financing. Second, interest rate ceilings may have beneficial effects by reducing moral hazard and adverse selection through improving the average quality of the pool of loan applicants. Third, regulations that set artificially low interest rates increase firm equity through a lower cost of capital.[43]

Two examples for the beneficial effects of an active government role in the banking sector are South Korea and Taiwan. Both started their economic take-off in the 1960s with highly regulated financial systems, which they did not start liberalizing until well into the 1980s. Early in their economic take-off, both countries raised real interest rates for deposits to levels that were only mildly negative or positive in order to mobilize savings. The savings mobilized in this way could then by allocated through directed credit.[44]

---

[41] See Shirai (2002c), pp. 19-21.

[42] See Roubini and Sala-i-Martin (1992), p. 7.

[43] See Arestis and Demetriades (1997), p. 793; Denizer, Desai and Gueorguiev (1998), p. 2; Stiglitz (1994), pp. 39-42. Lower financing costs will all else equal increase profits, which will through higher retained earnings increase equity.

[44] See Park (2004), p. 35; Rodrik (1995), p. 56 and p. 74; Rodrik (2004), p. 6. Another example for successful involvement in the financial sector is Japan, where

Financial restraints and competitive restrictions constitute measures under which a government can intervene in the financial sector. They may be connected to the economic, developmental and political arguments for state involvement in the financial sector. However, despite the positive case examples of South Korea and Taiwan, the idea that a government can positively intervene in the financial sector to enhance the outcome of the market process is contested by the financial liberalization literature. Here, it is claimed that state involvement is detrimental to the performance of the banking sector. A closer examination of these arguments follows in the next section.

4.3 The financial liberalization hypothesis

Up until the beginning of the 1970s it was a widely accepted tenet in development economics that the state should play an active role in the banking sector through regulations and ownership of banks. This view began to change after the publication of the seminal works of McKinnon (1973) and Shaw (1973), who argued that interest rate regulations and other restrictions adversely affect saving and investment and have a negative effect on economic growth.

Central for the understanding of the McKinnon-Shaw paradigm are the differing assumptions on the relationship between money and real capital. Both neoclassical theory and Keynesian theory assume a substitutive role between the two and thus recommend lowering the real interest rate to support the formation of capital.[45] The works of McKinnon (1973) and Shaw (1973) mark a deviation from the previously assumed trade-off between money and real capital. The starting point for their arguments are the shortcomings of the financial sectors in some developing countries where government-imposed restrictions have led to shallow finance. The McKinnon-Shaw framework assumes a fragmented economy[46] characterized by financial repression, where interest rates and exchange rates are distorted through a set of formal regulations and informal controls imposed

in the 1950s and 1960s the government was actively involved in pricing and allocating credit. See Arestis and Demetriades (1997), p. 791.

[45] See Deckert (1996), p. 11.

[46] McKinnon (1973) defines a fragmented economy as one where "[...] firms and households are so isolated that they face different effective prices for land, labor, capital, and produced commodities and do not have access to the same technologies." McKinnon (1973), p. 5.

by the government. Due to these restrictions, banks and capital markets are underdeveloped and the financial sector remains below its full potential. Financial deepening – i.e. increases of financial depth as measured by the stock of liquid liabilities in an economy – occurs outside the organized financial sector in curb markets.[47]

Financial repression has according to the proponents of financial liberalization several adverse effects on the quality and the quantity of investment in an economy. First, investment decisions may not be based on economic criteria but rather on personal ties to the relevant decision-making bodies. Second, interest rates are often set at artificially low rates to reduce the cost of capital for favored debtors. This leads to a crowding out of high-yielding investment and discourages savings due to low real interest rates. Third, due to the low or even negative real interest rates, instead of using the financial sector for saving, less efficient self-investment occurs.[48]

The essential elements of the models by McKinnon and Shaw are the same. In terms of savings and investments, they assume that savings are a positive function of both the real rate of interest and the real rate of output growth, and that investments are a negative function of the real loan rate and a positive function of the growth rate of the economy. In terms of government intervention, both McKinnon and Shaw assume a non-price rationing of loans in combination with an administratively fixed nominal interest rate that holds the real rate below its equilibrium level.[49]

The effects of interest rate ceilings are illustrated in Figure 10. If the government limits the real deposit rate with a ceiling to a level of r_1, which is below the equilibrium interest rate of r_e, the level of saving is equal to I_1. The level of saving at the administered interest rate is below the equilibrium level of I_0 and the demand for credit that stands at I_2. The effect of this disequilibrium is two-fold. First, since the demand for credit exceeds saving, credit is rationed and some otherwise profitable projects do not receive funding. As a result overall welfare is reduced. Second, if there is no ceiling on lending rates, banks can set the lending rate at r_2, which increases their net-interest margin by $r_2 - r_1$.[50] An increase of the deposit rate would in such a situation increase savings and reduce the demand for loans. Due to higher savings, more capital would be available for productive investments, which has positive effects on growth. Furthermore, the

47 See King and Levine (1993), p. 718; McKinnon (1973), p. 68f.; Shaw (1973), p. 3.

48 See McKinnon (1973), p. 68f and p. 73; Shaw (1973), p. 85f.

49 See McKinnon (1973), pp. 71-77; Shaw (1973), pp. 81-87.

50 See Auerbach and Siddiki (2004), p. 248f.

excess spread for the bank ($r_2 - r_1$) would be reduced and thus benefit banks' customers.

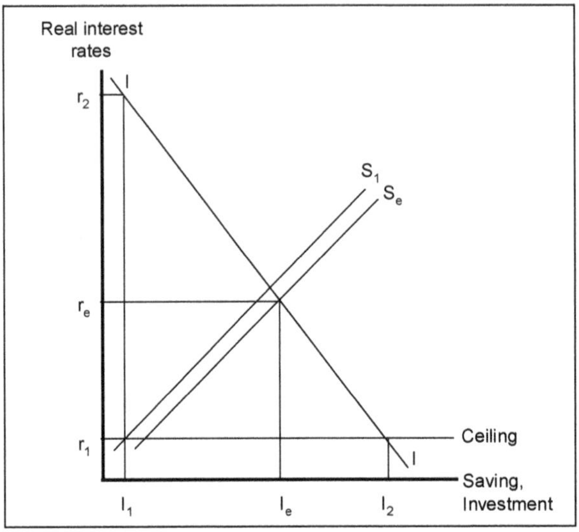

Fig. 10. Effects of interest rate ceilings in the McKinnon-Shaw model[51]

As a result of repressionist policies, banks do not necessarily allocate credit on the basis of the economic fundamentals of the projects. Instead they base their decisions on political pressure, the status of the borrower, the size of the loan, or the covert benefits to the loan officers. Due to the artificial low interest rate on loans, previously unprofitable projects become profitable and more firms enter the credit market. As a result adverse selection may occur, lowering social welfare.[52]

McKinnon and Shaw point out that interest rate ceilings in particular have at least six distinct distorting effects in such an environment. First, low interest rates cause a shift to current consumption since they provide disincentives for saving. Second, potential lenders may resort to low-yielding self-investment instead of providing the funds for more high-yielding investments in the form of savings that can be intermediated by banks. This also means that borrowers have to rely more on self-finance, since the amount of loans from the organized banking sector falls. Third, favored borrowers will tend to over-invest in capital-intensive projects. Fourth, as mentioned above, low-yielding interest rates attract borrowers with projects that would otherwise not receive funding, which lowers the

[51] Adapted from Auerbach and Siddiki (2004), p. 248.
[52] See Shaw (1973), p. 85f.

overall return on capital. Fifth, the setting of interest rates between different classes of borrowers contains an element of cross-subsidization, which provides disincentives for certain classes of borrowers to fulfill their banking needs through the organized banking sector. And sixth, access to foreign capital may be cut off or, if allowed, may be unproductive due to the restrictions in place.[53]

The general tenet of the McKinnon-Shaw framework is that financial repression adversely affects the functioning of the financial sector. From the discussion above and Figure 10, several implications can be derived. First, raising the real interest rate provides incentives to increase savings, which in turn leads to an increase of the available capital in an economy. Second, the removal of repressionist policies such as interest rate ceilings or directed credit increases the efficiency of capital allocation. And finally, increased availability of capital combined with a more efficient deployment, positively affects the growth rate.

The policy recommendation in the McKinnon-Shaw framework is either to raise the nominal interest rate and reduce the rate of inflation or to abolish the interest rate ceilings in order to achieve equilibrium in the market. Higher real interest rates provide incentives to increase savings and to provide those savings through the organized financial sector instead of fragmented curb markets or self-investment. This improves the allocation of savings. The higher savings rate then serves as the basis for the accumulation of capital. The increase in the savings rate and the investment rate should, as discussed in the context of the endogenous growth model, contribute positively to economic growth. Closely connected to this is the recommendation to reduce the non-price allocation mechanisms such as directed credit programs.[54] Overall, then, the McKinnon-Shaw school makes a case for a market-determined banking sector.

Of course, these recommendations are not undisputed. There have been at least two important lines of criticism. First, depending on the structure of the official and unofficial financial markets in a country, raising the interest rate might not in fact yield the desired effect of increasing savings

[53] See Fry (1997), p. 755; McKinnon (1991), p. 11f. McKinnon and Shaw reach similar conclusions with different explanations. While McKinnon introduces the complementarity hypothesis between money and real capital, Shaw uses the debt intermediation view. See McKinnon (1973), p. 3; Shaw (1973), p. 47f.

[54] See Balassa (1990), p. 58f.; Das (2003), p. 346; Deckert (1996), p. 13; Gemech and Struthers (2003), p. 3; McKinnon (1973), pp. 59-61; Shaw (1973), pp. 81-86. Figure 10 showed that despite an increase of the interest rate, the volume of loans should increase.

and investment if the increase in savings through the official financial system merely happens at the expense of curb markets. Second, higher interest rates may increase adverse selection and moral hazard problems in credit markets. This may raise the probability of a banking crisis, since higher interest rates provide incentives to increase risk-taking. Consequently, interest rate restrictions may in fact improve the stability of the banking sector.[55]

Thus the question whether financial liberalization has beneficial effects on savings and investments becomes an empirical one. A review of empirical studies on these issues follows in the next section.

4.4 Evaluation of financial liberalization

Financial sector liberalization should not be carried out for its own sake. As with any policy choice, pursuing this strategy is only worthwhile, if the benefits exceed the costs. Financial repression can be regarded as a tax the government imposes on the financial sector, as well as on the providers and users of funds.[56] Lifting the "repression tax" should have positive effects on the development of the financial sector and its stakeholders. Besides a lower quasi-tax, liberalization should help the sector to better perform its functions of mobilizing savings and allocating capital. The positive effects should accrue to both the financial sector and the overall economy. However, financial liberalization may not always be beneficial: in recent years there has been increasing evidence linking financial liberalization with financial crises.

The next section examines the evidence for the welfare-enhancing effect of financial liberalization according to the functions of a banking sector. It also looks at possible downsides. Wherever available, studies that cover the Indian or Chinese banking sector are included.

4.4.1 Financial liberalization, savings and capital formation

In the McKinnon-Shaw framework, financial liberalization has positive effects on both saving and capital formation. Removing interest rate restric-

---

[55] See Demetriades and Luintel (2001), p. 461; Stiglitz (1994), p. 39.

[56] The size of this tax can be substantial, as a study by Giovanni and de Melo (1993) found. The average revenue from financial repression across a sample of 24 countries was equivalent to about two percent of GDP or nine percent of total government revenue. See Giovanni and de Melo (1993), p. 962.

tions – especially the ceilings on deposit rates – should increase the overall quantity of savings (or at least the savings that are intermediated through the formal banking system). The lowering of statutory pre-emptions and an increased quantity of savings should increase the amount of capital available for productive investments. And if directed credit policies are abolished, a more efficient allocation of investments should be possible.

However, the empirical evidence is mixed. Schmidt-Hebbel and Serven (2002) investigate the relationship between financial liberalization and saving. They find a positive and significant relationship between the degree of financial liberalization and saving, but do not test for causality. Therefore it is not possible to state if countries with a liberalized financial system save more or if countries with a higher saving rate are more inclined to liberalize their financial system.[57]

A different approach is taken by Bandiera et al. (2000). They use an index of financial reforms to assess the impact of financial liberalization on private savings in eight developing countries over a 25-year period. They find no evidence that financial liberalization increases savings. Indeed, more often the opposite appears to be the case.[58]

Applying the approach of Bandiera et al. (2000) to India, Nair (2005) comes to a similar conclusion. The reason for this outcome is probably that even though financial liberalization improves saving opportunities, the increased availability of credit may have resulted in a shift from saving to consumption.[59]

Evidently the support for the hypothesis that financial liberalization positively influences saving is weak. This may be because of the multitude of saving motives – ranging from building reserves for unforeseen events, over the smoothing of consumption over the life-cycle to pay for consumption in the future.[60] Many of these motives – such as precautionary or insurance motives – are largely independent of the effects of changes in the real interest rate. In addition, a government-controlled banking system may have a higher degree of stability because of the explicit government-backing, which can positively influence the level of savings through in-

[57] See Schmidt-Hebbel and Serven (2002), p. 12.

[58] See Bandiera et al. (2000), p. 239 and p. 257. The composition of the index is discussed in section 6.3.2.

[59] See Nair (2005), p. 18.

[60] Browning and Lusardi (1996) provide a comprehensive overview and discussion of saving motives. Modigliani and Cao (2004) try to explain the level of Chinese saving by the life-cycle hypothesis. They argue that the two main drivers of the saving rate in China are income growth and demographic changes caused by the one-child policy. See Modigliani and Cao (2004), pp. 165-168.

creased confidence. Therefore, as the empirical evidence shows, the effects of financial liberalization on savings are ambiguous and can even be negative.

A second hypothesized effect of financial liberalization is that it increases the availability of capital in an economy, and improves the efficiency of its usage.

Through an increased availability of capital, financial liberalization might help to reduce the financing constraints of firms. Laeven (2003) tests this relationship with panel data for firms in 13 developing countries from 1989 to 1998 using an index of financial liberalization. His findings are that financial liberalization affects small and large firms differently. While the financing constraints of small firms are reduced after liberalization, those of large firms increase. A probable reason is that larger firms have better access to directed credit prior to liberalization.[61]

The efficient allocation of capital to the highest value use may also be affected by financial liberalization. Using a summary index of capital allocation efficiency for twelve developing countries including India, Galindo, Schiantarelli and Weiss (2003) find evidence that financial liberalization, as measured by different indicators relating to the start of banking sector reform, improved the allocation of investment funds.[62] Abiad, Oomes and Ueda (2004) come to a similar conclusion in their examination of the link between financial liberalization and access to credit. They establish a link between both factors that results in a reduced variation of expected returns across firms, which is positively associated with allocative efficiency.[63]

Guha-Khasnobis and Bhaduri (2000), however, cannot find evidence for more efficient allocation of capital following financial liberalization in India. For the 1989 to 1998 period they examine whether debt and equity capital flowed to more efficient firms after liberalization. They conclude that in India there was no significant rise in the efficiency of investment allocation in the early post-liberalization period. A possible reason for this

---

[61] See Laeven (2003), p. 5 and p. 25. The financial liberalization index used by Laeven is described in section 6.3.2.

[62] See Galindo, Schiantarelli and Weiss (2003), p. 25. The efficiency of capital allocation is measured by the sales per unit of capital and the operating profits per unit of capital. Financial liberalization is measured by two dummy variables. The first is a summary variable that includes interest rate deregulation, reduction of entry barriers, reduction of reserve requirements, reduction of credit controls, privatization of state banks, and strengthening of prudential regulations. The second is a dummy variable that is set to one in the year after the removal of the main restrictions on interest rates and credit allocation. See Galindo, Schiantarelli and Weiss (2003), p. 7 and p. 13f.

[63] See Abiad, Oomes and Ueda (2004), p. 27.

may be the misallocation of funds after liberalization in 1991, when funds were not channeled to the most productive investments.[64]

Misra (2003) also examines the allocative efficiency – defined as the elasticity of output with respect to credit – of the Indian banking system. The allocative efficiency is studied for 23 Indian states for the time periods 1981-1992 and 1993-2001. The finding is that the allocative efficiency almost doubled in the post-reform period. However, there were marked differences between sectors: while the allocative efficiency significantly improved in the service sector, it deteriorated in agriculture and industry in most states.[65]

These studies largely support the hypothesized positive effect of financial liberalization on capital formation and efficiency. It should be kept in mind, however, that the evidence presented is not unambiguous: the effects appear to be dependent on country factors and the methodologies used.

4.4.2 Financial liberalization, financial development and growth

Financial development refers to the size and composition of the financial system of a country. Typical indicators of financial development include the size of the formal financial system, measured by the ratio of liquid liabilities to GDP (financial depth) or the relative shares of deposit banks vis-à-vis the central bank in extending credit.[66] Financial liberalization and financial development are closely connected. Financial policies such as interest rate restrictions or reserve requirements may adversely affect the development of the financial system. If these restrictions are removed during the process of liberalization, this may help develop the financial sector (Figure 11). A more developed financial system may in turn be able to spur growth through higher capital accumulation and improved efficiency, which in turn might positively affect financial development through an increased demand for financial services. These relationships have been subject to intense debate in the literature in recent years.[67]

---

[64] See Guha-Khasnobis and Bhaduri (2000), p. 345.

[65] See Misra (2003), p. 161 and p. 175.

[66] See King and Levine (1993), p. 718.

[67] See Arestis et al. (2002), pp. 110-112; Levine (1997), p. 691; Mavrotas and Kelly (1999), p. 4; Shan and Morris (2002), p. 156. The relationship may also work in the other direction: more repressive policies may impede financial development, which in turn may negatively affect capital accumulation and capital efficiency.

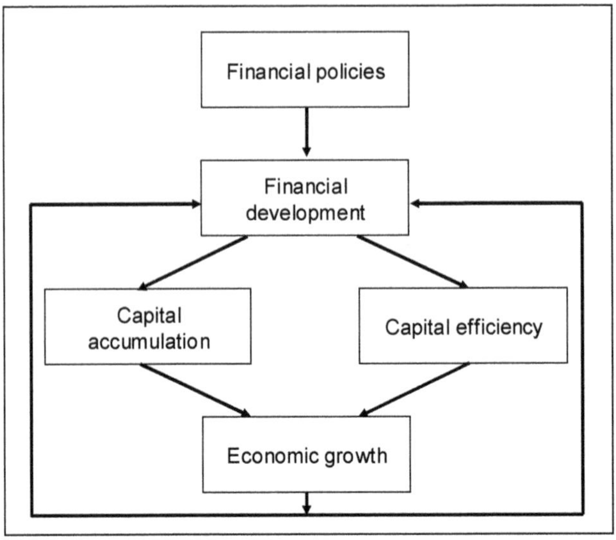

Fig. 11. Relationship between financial liberalization, financial development and growth[68]

Arestis et al. (2002) tested the effects of financial policies such as interest rate restrictions and statutory pre-emptions in six countries including India. They find that financial policies have a direct effect on financial development. This effect varies across countries. In most countries, financial liberalization contributes positively to financial development. There are however exceptions where financial restraints have positive effects on the development of the financial sector, which may be the result of market imperfections.[69]

A seminal work on the relationship between the development of the financial sector and growth is that of King and Levine (1993). In their study they found that financial development positively influences the rate of economic growth, physical capital accumulation and economic efficiency even after accounting for country-specific factors and policy differences. They also found a positive correlation between the average level of financial sector development between 1960 and 1989 and the average annual rate of real per capita GDP growth after controlling for initial conditions. They conclude that there is a causal relationship that runs from finance to growth.[70]

---

[68] Author's presentation based on Levine (1997), p. 691 and Shan and Morris (2002), p. 156.

[69] See Arestis et al. (2002), p. 119.

[70] See King and Levine (1993), p. 719f.

Roubini and Sala-i-Martin (1992) take a different research approach. They explore the negative effects of financial repression – defined by negative real interest rates – on economic growth in a cross-country growth regression. After controlling for other determinants of growth, they conclude that the financial underdevelopment associated with financial repression will result in lower economic growth. This adverse effect on growth depends on the degree of financial repression. While a relatively low degree of financial repression will only have a moderate effect on economic growth, high levels of financial repression have a significant negative effect.[71]

Rajan and Zingales (1998) instead explore whether firms that have a higher dependency on external finance develop better in countries with higher levels of financial development. Their findings suggest a positive link between financial development and growth. Specifically, they find that the ex-ante development of the financial sector positively influences the ex-post growth of sectors that depend on external finance.[72]

A positive correlation between financial development – defined as the ratio of bank credit to the private sector as a percentage of GDP – and long-term growth is found by de Gregorio and Guidotti (1995) in a study of about 100 countries for the 1960-1985 period. They find that the main channel from financial development to growth is the efficiency, and not the volume, of investment. However, this growth-enhancing effect varies across countries and time. Most notably, in Latin America the relationship was negative, which might be due to financial liberalization in an unregulated environment.[73]

Further evidence for a positive link between financial development and growth comes from Calderón and Liu (2003), who conducted a panel analysis on pooled data from 109 industrialized and developing countries for the 1960-1994 time period. They find evidence that financial development causes economic growth and that the growth-enhancing effect of financial development is more pronounced in developing countries. Concerning the channels through which financial development contributes to growth, they find positive effects from both faster capital accumulation and improved total factor productivity.[74]

Sylla (2000) takes a historical perspective on the relationship between financial development and growth. His argument is that the economic leaders of the past four centuries including the Dutch Republic in the 17th

[71] See Roubini and Sala-i-Martin (1992), pp. 25-27.
[72] See Rajan and Zingales (1998), pp. 559-561.
[73] See de Gregorio and Guidotti (1995), p. 445.
[74] See Calderón and Liu (2003), p. 323 and p. 331.

century, Great Britain in the 18th century and the United States of America in the 19th century developed a strong financial system before they emerged as economic leaders. In other words, financial development preceded economic growth.[75]

However, the positive effect of financial development on growth is not confirmed by all studies. In a study of 95 countries, Ram (1999) focuses on the correlations between financial development as measured by liquid liabilities to GDP and economic growth. In just 39 of the 95 countries could a positive correlation be established – the remaining countries exhibited a negative correlation between financial development and growth. The conclusion from this study is that financial development does not have a significant positive effect on growth.[76]

A similar conclusion is reached by Demetriades and Hussein (1996) who measure financial development as the ratio of bank deposit liabilities to nominal GDP, and the ratio of bank claims on the private sector to nominal GDP. In their study of 16 developing countries, they find little support for the hypothesis that finance leads economic development. However, they are able to show that there is a bi-directional relationship between the two.[77]

Shan and Morris (2002) examine 19 OECD countries and China. They define financial development by the level of credit and by financial efficiency as measured by the interest rate spread. They test for causality between different indicators of financial development and growth – such as total credit and economic growth – as well as total credit and productivity growth. In most of the countries they look at they could not find a causal relationship between the measures of financial development and growth for the 1985 to 1998 period.[78]

For India, Bhattacharya and Sivasubramanian (2003) examine the relationship between financial development as measured by M3 and economic growth. For the 1970-1971 to 1998-1999 period they find a one-way causal relationship that runs from M3 to GDP growth.[79]

In another study in the Indian context, Bell and Rosseau (2001) investigate if financial intermediaries have played a significant and leading role

---

[75] See Sylla (2000), p. 2.

[76] See Ram (1999), p. 168f.

[77] See Demetriades and Hussein (1996), p. 395 and p. 406.

[78] See Shan and Morris (2002), p. 153f. and p. 166.

[79] See Bhattacharya and Sivasubramanian (2003), p. 929. The results should be interpreted with caution: M3 is not always regarded as a reliable indicator for financial development as it is influenced by factors other than financial depth. See de Gregorio and Guidotti (1995), p. 438.

in India's economic development. They try to evaluate the strength and direction between indicators of formal financial intermediation and macroeconomic indicators. Their finding is that investment, aggregate output and structural change in India's industry were enabled by the financial sector, rather than by increased public sector spending. Specifically, they find that the financial sector played an important role in promoting capital accumulation and leading the shift in output from agriculture to industry. There is, however, no evidence that the financial sector contributed to an increase in total factor productivity. Their main conclusion is that a positive link between financial development and economic growth exists even in a highly-regulated environment.[80]

For China, Aziz and Duenwald (2002) investigate the relationship between bank credit and economic growth. They cannot find a statistically significant influence of credit on growth, which they attribute to the relatively large share of credit going to less productive SOEs.[81] Further evidence of the negative impact of credit going to the state sector in China is also found in another study by Boyreau-Debray (2003). The author also finds that financial development as represented by the ratio of deposits to GDP has no statistically significant influence on economic growth.[82] A further study by Chang (2002) uses Granger causality tests for the period between 1987 and 1999 in China; it, too, finds no relationship between financial development and growth.[83]

The majority of the studies discussed above find that financial policies affect financial development, which in turn influences economic growth through capital accumulation and the efficiency of capital usage. However, not all studies agree and so one may conclude that the predictions of the financial liberalization hypothesis are not valid in all settings. This appears to be the case especially for China, where the continued extension of loans to less efficient SOEs is a possible reason that the relationship does not hold.[84]

---

[80] See Bell and Rosseau (2001), pp. 153-155 and p. 173. It is important to note that Bell and Rosseau (2001) do not investigate alternative policies, so it is not possible to make conclusions about the effects of different policy regimes on economic growth. See Bell and Rosseau (2001), p. 155.

[81] See Aziz and Duenwald (2002), p. 11.

[82] See Boyreau-Debray (2003), p. 20.

[83] See Chang (2002), p. 872. Granger causality tests are described in more detail in section 7.2.2.2.

[84] It is also worth remembering that "finance cannot create opportunities. It only makes it easier to exploit them [...]." Rajan and Zingales (2003b), p. 112.

4.4.3 Financial liberalization and banking sector performance

The two previous sections have dealt with the effects of financial liberalization on macroeconomic variables. In addition, financial liberalization is likely to affect the sector level as well: the lowering of restrictions can alter the competitive dynamics of the banking sector. Liberalization can lead to a more flexible and competitive environment in which banks have to increase their performance in terms of efficiency and productivity to survive.

However, it is difficult to establish a clear cause-and-effect relationship between liberalization and bank performance. There are overlapping effects on the revenue and cost side. On the cost side, banks are likely to face increasing interest costs as competition for deposits augments, while it may be easier for them to either reduce costs by closing branches or passing costs on to their clients. On the revenue side, greater competition in the lending business is likely to lead to lower margins, while at the same time banks may have opportunities to increase revenues by expanding their business into new areas.[85]

An important policy change at the sector level is the deregulation of branching restrictions. Jayaratna and Strahan (1996) investigate the effects of this in the United States. They find evidence that the competition-enhancing effect of deregulation has led to an increase in the growth rate through increases in the quality of banks' loan portfolios, but not through an increase in the volume of loans.[86]

In a study of the effects of liberalization in the Pakistani banking sector in the early 1990s, Bonaccorsi di Patti and Hardy (2005) find positive effects on the profit productivity of banks, whereas the cost productivity has not improved significantly. In terms of average efficiency, new domestic banks were found to be more efficient than foreign banks that in turn outperformed state-owned banks.[87]

For the Indian banking sector, most studies find positive effects of liberalization on the banking sector. For example, Ataullah, Cockerill and Hang (2004) conclude that the efficiency of the banking sector improved after liberalization in 1991.[88] In a study of Indian Public Sector Banks, Ganesan (2001) finds that the liberalization of the banking sector has increased the profitability of PSBs as measured by ROA. The main factor for the im-

---

[85] See Ataullah, Cockerill and Hang (2004), p. 1916; Galindo, Micco and Ordonez (2002), p. 7f.; Humphrey and Pulley (1997), p. 91.

[86] See Jayaratna and Strahan (1996), p. 641f.

[87] See Bonaccorsi di Patti and Hardy (2005), p. 2402.

[88] See Ataullah, Cockerill and Hang (2004), p. 1924.

proved profitability was an easing of the priority sector lending requirements.[89]

An important competition-enhancing factor in a financial liberalization program is the opening up of the banking sector for new domestic and foreign entrants. Even if formerly state-owned banks are not privatized, entry liberalization and the subsequent increase in competition can have a positive effect on the performance of banks. This is shown by Bhaumik and Dimova (2004) for the Indian banking sector in the period between 1995 and 2001. Their conclusion is that the performance gap between public sector banks and foreign banks was closed due to increased competition after liberalization.[90]

Kumbhakar and Sarkar (2003) investigate the relationship between deregulation and productivity growth for the Indian banking sector between 1985 and 1996. For both public and private sector banks they find a higher productivity growth rate after liberalization in 1991. For public sector banks, however, the improvement is not statistically significant. Overall, they conclude that the decline in distortions has not led to the expected productivity increases. A possible reason – one that not only applies to India but to other developing countries with large state-owned banks – is that the incumbent banks are so dominant that they can insulate themselves to a certain degree from the necessary changes.[91]

Despite their limited scope, the above studies provide evidence that financial liberalization has performance-enhancing effects on the banking sector through increased efficiency and productivity. The two main driving factors appear to be an easing of restrictions and an increasing competitive intensity in the sector.

The studies cited in the previous three sections show that financial liberalization indeed influences the banking sector as well as the economy. Therefore, financial policies clearly matter. The positive effects of liberalization are especially pronounced with respect to the performance of the banking sector, the efficiency of capital allocation, financial development and economic growth. Whereas financial liberalization generally increases the efficiency with which capital is allocated, it does not lead to an increase of capital. For India and China these studies provide evidence that it is possible to positively influence the rate of growth through liberalization of the banking sector. Since the cited studies for the two countries have provided a mixed picture with respect to the liberalization results. This in-

[89] See Ganesan (2001), p. 36.

[90] See Bhaumik and Dimova (2004), p. 177.

[91] See Kumbhakar and Sarkar (2003), p. 405 and p. 421.

dicates that either the cause-effect relationships do not hold in the two countries, or more likely that the reforms are incomplete.

Nonetheless, the various studies have also shown that there is no general agreement on any of the investigated relationships. Therefore, the results are to a certain extent dependent on the context, the methodology and the operationalization of the variables.[92] Moreover, while the studies explore the effects of certain policy changes, they do not give advice on how to actually attain these results – i.e., on how to successfully manage the changes and on complementary reforms. This neglect is becoming more important in the light of recent evidence that financial liberalization may increase the likelihood of a banking crisis, which is discussed next.

4.4.4 Financial liberalization and financial crisis

Many of the cross-country studies cited in the previous sections establish a positive relationship between financial liberalization and the functions of a banking sector. However, these results may not hold for all countries at all times. Even though financial repression is generally regarded as negative in that it retards the development of the financial sector, it also shields the domestic financial sector from competition, which may increase its stability. Liberalizing the financial sector may therefore have a destabilizing effect, such as increased fragility of banks. Over the past years, there has been increasing evidence that financial liberalization can have severe negative effects in the form of financial and banking crises, whose likelihood increases after liberalization.

The classical article on financial crises in the aftermath of liberalization comes from Diaz-Alejandro (1985). This work describes the effects of financial liberalization in South American countries. According to Diaz-Alejandro, the "pessimum 'middle way': de facto public guarantees to depositors, lenders and borrowers, and no effective supervision and control (until it was too late) of the practices of financial intermediaries"[93] led to disastrous results of financial liberalization policies including widespread bankruptcies and government interventions to save failing banks.[94]

---

[92] Financial development is certainly a case in point. The various studies cited define financial development as liquid liabilities to GDP, the ratio of bank credit to the private sector as a percentage of GDP, M3, the ratio of bank deposit liabilities to nominal GDP, the ratio of bank claims on the private sector to nominal GDP and the level of credit.

[93] Diaz-Alejandro (1985), p. 17.

[94] See Diaz-Alejandro (1985), p. 1f.

These negative outcomes are not confined to South American countries. According to a survey by Kaminsky and Reinhart (1999) the likelihood of a banking crisis increases with liberalization of the financial sector. Of the total of 26 banking crises studied, 18 occurred in countries that had liberalized their financial sector less than five years earlier.[95] The most common immediate causes of a banking crisis after liberalization are, according to Caprio and Klingebiel (1997) general uncertainty, asymmetric information, and speculative bubbles led by excessive credit growth.[96]

In a study of 53 countries between 1980 to 1995, Demirgüc-Kunt and Detragiache (1998) come to the similar conclusion that the likelihood of a banking crisis increases in countries with a liberalized financial sector. They find that increased fragility of the banking sector occurs with a time lag of several years, so that it is not contingent on the start of the liberalization process. Overall, their conclusion is that financial liberalization leads to increased financial fragility, which is particularly dangerous in developing countries that are less likely to have established the institutions for supporting a well-functioning financial system.[97] In a further study, Eichengreen and Arteta (2002) show that financial crises are more likely when domestic financial markets are liberalized.[98]

Unlike bankruptcies in other industries, bank failures can have repercussions that are far larger than the direct negative effects of the loss of banks' profits and wages on GDP. Of particular importance are the indirect effects of a bank failure that arise from the possibility of contagion of the overall banking system. This contagion effect can be spread through bank runs, which can cause other bank failures and lead to a shutdown of the payments system. Bank crises associated with financial liberalization can thus result in significant output losses.[99]

As described above, there seems to be a relationship between the liberalization of the financial sector and the occurrence of banking crises. Identifying the root causes of the problems in the early stages of the liberalization process can help circumvent this. On the microeconomic level, Barton, Newell and Wilson (2003) identify weak credit evaluation skills combined with directed lending practices as the main factors explaining banking failures that lead to banking crisis in transition and developing countries that are liberalizing their banking system.[100]

---

[95] See Kaminsky and Reinhart (1999), p. 479f.

[96] See Caprio and Klingebiel (1997), p. 9.

[97] See Demirgüc-Kunt and Detragiache (1998), p. 6f.

[98] See Eichengreen and Arteta (2002), p. 67.

[99] See Blejer (1999), p. 388; Caprio and Klingebiel (1997), p. 4.

[100] See Barton, Newell and Wilson (2003), p. 58f.

Financial crises have a high economic and social cost. They can derail the transition process or severely damage the popular backing for reforms. Thus it is necessary to prevent a crisis from occurring by strengthening system safeguards. The policy implication is that strong regulation and supervision of banks should be established during liberalization. Additionally, countries that liberalize their financial system should make efforts to increase transparency, which is necessary to improve the flow of information. Along with strong regulation, this is needed to reduce the possibility of moral hazard that arises from explicit and implicit deposit insurance. Deposit insurance can lead to excessively risky lending and to the perception that the government will bail out banks should the overall reform program fail.[101]

The increased possibility of a banking crisis accompanying financial liberalization alters the cost-benefit calculations. Policy-makers have to weigh the possible short-run costs of a banking crisis against the benefits of financial liberalization that accrue over the long run. This has given rise to the view that some degree of financial regulation is preferable to premature liberalization where systemic safeguards are not yet in place. Also, a certain degree of political accountability is needed to reduce the risk of opportunistic defaults by banks.[102]

To sum up, financial liberalization can have both positive macroeconomic (through an increased mobilization and a more efficient allocation of resources) and microeconomic effects (through increased competition in the sector). Nonetheless, there is a substantial downside risk due to the danger of financial crisis, which can be mitigated to some extent by regulation and supervision. Overall, this requires a careful evaluation of the potential medium- to long-term benefits of liberalization and the costs in the short term.

In addition it is necessary to focus more on the process of liberalization and complementary reform steps. The academic literature has provided evidence on the risks and rewards of banking sector liberalization, and given some suggestions on ways to mitigate some of the potential costs. The necessary next step is to focus on the process of liberalization and give advice to policy makers regarding the necessary process elements for managing the transition to a liberalized banking sector.

---

[101] See Blejer (1999), p. 387f.; Caprio, Hanson and Honohan (2001), p. 16; Eichengreen and Arteta (2002), p. 72; Kaminsky and Reinhart (1999), p. 496; McKinnon and Pill (1997), pp. 191-193; Mehrez and Kaufmann (2000), p. 2f.

[102] See Demirgüc-Kunt and Detragiache (1998), p. 5; Loayza and Ranciere (2006), p. 1069; World Bank (2005), p. 182.

4.5 Conclusion

This chapter began with an overview of the functions performed by a banking sector in an economy: mobilizing savings, allocating these savings to investment projects and contributing to economic growth. It then discussed possible coordination mechanisms – i.e. state versus market. The three main rationales for state involvement in the banking sector are economic, developmental and political in nature. The proponents of financial liberalization challenge these views. On the evidence of empirical studies – and despite the potential problems with liberalization such as an increased risk of a banking crisis – it was shown that a market-based banking sector is likely to yield better economic outcomes.[103] Thus, the general policy recommendations are in line with the proponents of financial liberalization who argue that countries should abolish repressionist policies and privatize state owned banks. Countries with a state-run banking sector thus face the task of changing the prevailing coordination mechanism from state to market. Despite some evidence on the pre-conditions for financial liberalization and the necessary reform steps, a coherent blueprint on how to manage transition is still lacking.[104]

Similar problems have been faced by the countries of Central and Eastern Europe since the late 1980s. These countries have undergone the dual task of changing their political and their economic systems. Their experience managing change can offer insights for countries facing such a process – as will be discussed in the following section.

[103] See Fry (1997), p. 768; King and Levine (1993), p. 734f.; Wachtel (2001), pp. 357-359.

[104] See Deckert (1996), p. 3; Fry (1997), p. 768f.; Wachtel (2001), p. 357.

5 Management of transformation processes

Transformation studies attempt to explain the trigger, process and results of long-run systemic changes.[1] When the transformation in Central and Eastern Europe (CEE) started in 1989, only limited guidance existed on how to manage the transition from a command to a market economy.[2] Since then, numerous and often conflicting policy recommendations have been given on how to best manage such transformations. With the benefit of hindsight it is possible to evaluate the validity of these recommendations and assess the historical experience of the transition countries.

This section gives a brief overview of transformation studies. It attempts to identify phenotypical elements of the transformation of an economic system. These elements are then used in the next chapter to develop a framework for changing the coordination mechanism in the banking sector. Since the overall transformation process in an economy also influences the changes at the sector level, and because different countries have different transformation approaches, the transformation experiences of India and China are also briefly described; this makes it possible to put the two countries in a comparative perspective.

5.1 Classification of transformatory changes and applicability to India

The implications and "lessons-learned" from the transformation of former communist countries have been extensively discussed in the academic literature. Yet, to date there seems to be no general consensus on the definition of the term "transformation" and the constitutive elements of a trans-

[1] There is still some disagreement in the literature whether a general "transformation theory" exists. Because of the controversy, the rather general term "transformation studies" is used in this thesis to refer to a set of hypotheses describing the process of transition from a state-directed system to a market-based one. For a discussion see for example Pham-Phuong (2003a), Schulders (1998) and Solarz (1998).

[2] See Minsky (1991), p. 1.

formation. Therefore, before discussing the constitutive elements of a transformation in greater detail, two questions have to be answered. First, what distinguishes transformatory changes from other types of changes, namely a transition, evolutionary change and reforms? This distinction has important implications for the elements and the management of a transformation. Second, are the insights from transformation studies applicable to India, and more specifically to the Indian banking sector? This question is especially important since India is generally not included in the list of classical transformation countries. China, by contrast, is a frequently mentioned case example in the transformation literature.

5.1.1 Definition of transformatory changes

This section attempts to provide a definition of transformatory changes by contrasting them with three other forms of change: transition, evolutionary change, and reforms.

Dictionaries only slightly distinguish between the terms "transformation" and "transition": transformation is defined as "completely changing the appearance or character of something"[3] while the meaning of transition is "changing from one state or condition to another"[4]. However, the use of the two terms differs in the literature. This has implications on what can be deemed as a transformation, and which countries are actually undergoing one.

For Kloten (1991), the transformation of an economic system is triggered by political decisions and subsequent actions to replace characteristics of the current economic order so as to achieve a qualitative leap forward. The overall result is the substitution of the old economic order for a new one.[5] Like Kloten, Hermann-Pillath (1999) stresses that transformation is a change of the institutional order of the economic system that is initiated by the state.[6] Wagener (1996) defines transformation more generally as a reconfiguration of a political, economic or cultural order which, in the economic sphere, is triggered by a deliberate intervention in the market.[7]

Based on these definitions, transformation refers to an intentional change of the existing order, which should lead to a relative improvement compared to the previous situation. The focus is on the order of the sys-

[3] Oxford Advanced Learner's Dictionary (1989).
[4] Oxford Advanced Learner's Dictionary (1989).
[5] See Kloten (1991), p. 8f.
[6] See Hermann-Pillath (1999), p. 10.
[7] See Wagener (1996), p. 1.

tem: what are the constitutive elements of the new order and how do they compare to the old order? This differs somewhat from the term "transition", which emphasizes the process of change from the old to the new order.[8] This is for example expressed by Kolodko (2004b) who defines transition as a

> "[...] long-lasting, historical process of shifting from [a] centrally planned economy, based on the dominance of state property and bureaucratic control, to an open, free-market economy, based on market deregulation and the dominance of private property"[9].

Thus, both transformation and transition constitute necessary and complementary elements in explaining systemic changes: while the term transformation focuses on the characteristics of the beginning and ending order, transition focuses on explaining how to manage the process of moving from the old to the new order. Because the two terms are closely interrelated and refer to the same process, they are used interchangeably throughout this thesis.

The process of moving to a new, higher quality order is not confined to transformation. In the economic sphere, for example, "the invisible hand" can cause spontaneous changes that over time lead to a higher quality order. Therefore, it is necessary to make a distinction between transformatory and evolutionary change. The two distinguishing elements are the trigger and the management of change.

A transformation involves a fundamental change of the underlying economic, political or cultural order, which often entails a redistribution of relative power and wealth. If the uncertainty of the outcome is added, only a massive loss of confidence in the old system, such as a political or economic crisis, can trigger a transformation.[10] Consequently, a certain element of crisis is likely to prompt a transformation, which in turn makes it possible to assign a starting point. This is in contrast to evolutionary change, where a feeling that change is necessary might exist but there is no

---

[8] According to Lohmann (1997) the term "transformation" is more prevalent in the German and French literature while "transition" is predominantly used in the Anglo-Saxon literature. He explains this by a different understanding related to the change of the prevailing order: Germans and French equate a change of order to constitutional and legal changes, while to the Anglo-Saxon mind the change of order is associated with the process of change. See Lohmann (1997), p. 1 footnote.

[9] Kolodko (2004b), p. 2.

[10] See Kloten (1991), p. 9; Wagener (1996), p. 9.

crisis-like event that sets it off. Rather, the collective actions of decision-makers cause the change.

The management of transformatory and evolutionary changes will vary. Since the choice to transform the system is made deliberately, there are strong incentives to actively manage the process. As evolutionary change is not the result of a deliberate decision but the sum of often small changes in the collective actions of decision makers, the process is not actively administered or steered. The distinguishing characteristics of transformatory changes versus spontaneous evolutionary changes by markets are thus intention, active intervention, and direction-setting by the political or economic leadership.[11]

Active management of the change process is one of the necessary preconditions for a transformation. This holds true for a reform as well. The main difference between a transformation and a reform is the depth of change. In a reform, the underlying economic order is preserved, while a transformation involves the substitution of the underlying economic order with a new paradigm. For example, the change from a planned economy to a market economy is marked by a move from the fundamental characteristics of the socialist system to those of the capitalist system.[12] A reform only entails a partial change of the existing system and does not lead to a new order. Cases in point are the reform of the social security system or a monetary reform, which cause changes in a particular sub-system but leave the prevailing overall coordination mechanism largely untouched.[13] The transformation of an economic system can therefore be interpreted as the sum of several reforms that together cause a change of the fundamental aspects of the system.

Despite the lack of a generally accepted definition for an economic "transformation", it is possible to identify certain constitutive elements that distinguish transformation from other forms of changes. For the purpose of this thesis, a transformation is defined as a deliberately administered change of an economic system towards a free market economy that fun-

---

[11] See Pham-Phuong (2003a), p. 12; Wagener (1996), p. 8. This however does not preclude the possibility of revolutionary changes that are triggered by markets. The main difference is that these changes are not actively and directly managed.

[12] See Csaba (1993), p. 100; Kornai (2000), p. 29f.; Wagener (1996), p. 2; World Bank (1996b), p. 1. See Kornai (2000) for an overview of the defining characteristics of the socialist and capitalist system.

[13] See Csaba (1993), p. 100; Wagener (1996), p. 2. Csaba (1993) points out that "reforming a system means changing any element in order to preserve the underlying construct. Transformation starts at the point where substituting one construct for another becomes the issue." Csaba (1993), p. 100.

damentally alters the central coordination and allocation mechanism of the economic system.

5.1.2 Applicability to the banking sector and India

Transformation studies attempt to guide and explain systemic changes towards a market-based system. While this aspiration is universal in nature, the scope of theoretical studies on transformation is in reality rather narrow: the focus has predominantly been on Central and Eastern Europe, the former Soviet Union, China, Mongolia and Vietnam. India has generally not been included.[14] Research has also focused more on the overall macroeconomic environment and not on specific sectors of the economy. Therefore, the question arises of whether the insights from transformation studies are applicable to India and to the banking sector.

As discussed above, two defining criteria of a transformation are that it is an administered change toward a free market economy and that it has to be a change of the constitutive elements of the system. Thus, the central coordination and allocation mechanism of the economy has to undergo a fundamental change. India's economy prior to the reforms was characterized as a "mixed economy" in which far-reaching state-ownership and bureaucratic control co-existed with private enterprises. Under this strategy the state was supposed to take the "commanding heights" of the economy and mitigate the problems of capitalism by closely regulating economic activities. Private enterprises were controlled through far-reaching restrictions – a system known as the "license raj".[15] While the degree of state involvement in India was lower than in socialist countries, it was still considerably higher than in a free-market economy. India's reforms at the beginning of the 1990s aimed to introduce more market-based elements, so the reform process can be interpreted as a move towards a free-market economy. These reforms did not occur spontaneously, but were a deliberate response by the government of Narasimha Rao to the 1991 economic crisis. India's economic reforms thus fulfill the first criterion for a transformation: they were an administered change.

The next question is whether the reforms changed the fundamental elements of the system. India's economic system prior to the reforms was characterized by far-reaching restrictions on product and capital markets. Industrial licensing and import licensing were used to implement a policy

[14] See for example de Melo et al. (1997) or World Bank (1996b).

[15] See DeLong (2003), p. 185; Huang and Khanna (2003), p. 76; Kornai (2000), p. 34; Wagner (1997), p. 7 and p. 15; Williamson and Zagha (2002), p. 3.

of industrial development in which the bureaucracy had considerable control over allocation and production decisions of enterprises. The same applied to the allocation of capital. Nationalization of the largest public sector banks in 1969 and 1980 combined with high statutory preemptions and a closed capital account gave the government *de facto* control over the allocation of capital. The reforms of the 1990s had the goal of significantly reducing the government's influence in the economic sphere. They consequently led to a reduction of quantitative import restrictions, the virtual abolition of the "license raj" system, and a more market determined banking system.[16] Even though the old system has not been completely abolished, the fundamental features have been changed. Following the system specific attributes of socialist and capitalist systems by Kornai (2000) it can be seen that India changed in several important dimensions toward a more capitalist system. The changes include a significantly decreased role of bureaucratic coordination and of state-owned enterprises combined with a hardening of budget constraints.[17] Today, India is moving further towards a free market economy. The second criterion for a transformation – a change of the constitutive elements of the system – thus also applies to India.

The next question concerns the applicability of transformation studies to a sector, since the focus of the policy recommendations has been mainly on the level of the overall economy. A successful transformation program encompasses different policies such as institution building, privatization and liberalization. In addition, policymakers have to decide on the proper sequencing and timing of the reform steps. When designing a transformation program for a banking sector, policy makers are confronted with the same issues – albeit on a different level of analysis. Thus, while there are certainly differences in the design of the transformation strategy, the general insights of transformation studies are also applicable to a specific sector of the economy, in this case the banking sector. Furthermore, the individual sectors together make up the overall economy, so it is necessary to design sector-specific strategies.

[16] See Acharya (2002), p. 5f.; Forbes (2001), pp. 7-9; Majudmar (1998), p. 7; Wagner (1997), p. 16 and p. 30. The reforms of the 1980s however do not qualify as a transformation since there was no intention to change the prevailing coordination mechanism. Even so the reforms of the 1980s paved the way for the subsequent economic reforms of the 1990s, they are characterized as "pro-business" as opposed to "pro-market" reforms. The difference is that "pro-market" reforms aim at opening the economy and increase competition, while "pro-business" reforms favor the incumbents by giving them additional opportunities for generating profits. See Rodrik and Subramanian (2004), p. 4.

[17] See Kornai (2000), p. 29.

It can be concluded that the insights from transformation studies are applicable to the analyses in this thesis. The next section therefore explores their policy recommendations in more detail.

5.2 Initial policy recommendations for transition countries

Neither policymakers nor economists anticipated the radical changes in the CEE countries. When these countries started their transition to a market-based democracy, there were only few policy recommendations on how to manage the transition. In this vacuum, economic advisors and politicians turned to policy recommendations that had been given to other developing countries in general – and to countries in Latin America in particular. The most prominent collection of policy recommendations for Latin America at the time was the so-called Washington Consensus. This subsequently served as a blueprint for the reforms in the CEE countries. The following section first gives a brief overview of the policy recommendations of the Washington Consensus, before discussing further necessary elements for managing a transition successfully.

The Washington Consensus dates back to 1989, when it served as a framework to measure the status of policy reforms in Latin American countries. The policy recommendations comprise ten measures covering three broad areas: liberalization, privatization and stabilization.[18] Due to a lack of practical experience with managing the transformation to a market-based economic system, the policy prescriptions of the Washington Consensus were widely adopted in Central and Eastern Europe in the early 1990s.[19] However, this soon came under intense scrutiny. Criticism focused on two areas: the disregard of institutions, and the underestimation of the importance of structural change.[20]

The recommendations of the Washington Consensus were used in a relatively uniform way across the transition countries, without outlining

---

[18] The recommendations include a lowering of public deficits, redirection of expenditures, broadening of the tax base, interest rate liberalization, establishment of a competitive exchange rate, trade liberalization, creation of a level playing field for foreign direct investment, privatization of state-owned enterprises, deregulation of entry and exit barriers and the provision of property rights for the informal sector. See Williamson (1994), pp. 26-28, Williamson (2004), p. 3f.; Williamson (2005), p. 195f.

[19] See Ahrens (1999), p. 6; Rodrik (2000), p. 86; Solarz (1998), p. 8.

[20] A more in-depth overview of institution building and structural change follows in sections 5.3.4 and 5.3.5 respectively.

how to implement the policies and what sort of institutional framework was required. This neglect of institutions – in combination with a focus on stabilization policies in the early transformation literature – led to a seemingly universal applicability of the Washington Consensus, and to a limited view of the role of the state that did not extend much beyond providing macroeconomic stability and education. Since the emphasis was on rolling back the state and not on making it more effective, the institutional void further increased.[21]

Another factor that received insufficient attention was microeconomic restructuring. The need for restructuring stems from several important characteristics of transition countries, including concentrated ownership of firms and banks, incompatibility of the old production and distribution networks with those of a market economy, bias towards large-scale manufacturing, and low project evaluation and monitoring skills in banks. Additionally, the breakdown of complex production structures after the opening up of transition economies makes the restructuring of economic activities necessary to reduce the size of the output fall.[22]

The experiences in CEE showed that institution building is important to ensure the functioning of the market system, and structural changes in the economy are necessary to reduce the distortions from the breakdown of the old production system. These are both important components of a transition strategy. Thus, the main policy recommendations of stabilization, liberalization and privatization have to be complemented by institution building and structural change.[23] Even though there are certain overarching principles, the policy recommendations should take the initial conditions and country-specific factors into account. The main elements for managing the transformation process and the necessary pre-conditions are discussed in the next section.

---

[21] See Ahrens (1999), p. 8; Csaba (1997), p. 8; Hayami (2004), p. 56; Pham-Phuong (2003b), p. 7f Rodrik (2000), p. 86; Solarz (1998), p. 10; Wagener (2000), p. 2. A possible explanation for this neglect is the assumption of institutional neutrality in the neoclassical theory that is the basis of the Washington Consensus. See Pham-Phuong (2003b), p. 5.

[22] See Blanchard and Kremer (1997), p. 1122; Commander, Dutz and Stern (1999), p. 345 and p. 350f.; Kolodko (2004b), p. 4; Wyplosz (1999), p. 337.

[23] See Kolodko (2004b), p. 1.

5.3 Elements of transformation processes

For each of the process elements needed for a successful transformation, a wide array of differing and at times conflicting policy recommendations was given. With the benefit of hindsight, these recommendations can be evaluated based on the experiences in Central and Eastern Europe. In this section, the discussion focuses on the macro-level. This is necessary to apply the insights to the banking sector in the next chapter because the overall transformation strategy exerts a strong influence on the sector level. Since differences in the transformation processes between India and China might influence the evaluation, for every process step peculiarities of the situation in the two countries are presented.

5.3.1 Liberalization

In economic terms, liberalization refers to a reduction of state intervention in the market. As a tool of economic policy it can include a wide variety of changes, ranging from the deregulation of prices and wages to the reduction of trade barriers. The rationale for pursuing a liberalization strategy is to enhance competition in the respective markets, which is regarded as welfare-enhancing.[24]

In the transition countries the liberalization of internal and external markets was an important step towards the establishment of a market economy. But there were pitfalls. For example, there was a trade-off between the comprehensiveness of the initial price liberalization and the subsequent price appreciation. In the area of external liberalization, after an initial liberalization, protectionist measures were re-introduced in some countries to protect domestic industries which could not yet compete with foreign competitors. The liberalization strategies in CEE countries differed mainly in terms of the speed of liberalization: while most countries in central Europe and the Baltic region liberalized their markets early on in the transition, other countries like Bulgaria, Romania and most countries of the former Soviet Union opted for a more gradual approach.[25] These two liberalization strategies implicitly assume that state-control and market-

[24] See Ahrens (1994b), p. 25; Cornia and Popov (2001), p. 20. Cornia and Popov point out that to reap the benefits of liberalization, monopolistic, oligopolistic and free-riding behavior has to be avoided.

[25] See Ellman (1997), p. 28; European Bank for Reconstruction and Development (1999), p. 29f.

coordination are mutually exclusive, i.e. prices can either be set by the state or by the market, but not by both at the same time.

A completely different strategy for price liberalization was used in China. Here, liberalization followed a "dual-track" approach. Under dual-track liberalization two tracks are created: a plan track and a market track. In the plan track, economic agents have to produce a fixed amount of output at fixed plan prices. For the production of the output, they receive a fixed amount of inputs at fixed prices as laid out in the pre-existing plan. In the market track, economic agents can buy and sell goods at free market prices on condition that they fulfill their obligations under the plan track. The old system is at first maintained and the market is liberalized on the margins. In China, the dual-track approach was used to gradually increase the importance of the market. Since the increases of the quantities produced in the market track in China far exceeded the increases of the plan track, the relative importance of the plan track declined over time.[26]

Unlike in the CEE countries, the dual-track liberalization approach in China led to the establishment of market prices and institutionalized markets for resource allocations at the beginning of the reform process.[27] The advantage of this approach over the standard single-track liberalization approach is that it constitutes a mechanism to pursue reforms without losers. It is possible to achieve Pareto improvement[28] using standard single-track market liberalization when the conditions of profit maximization and perfect competition are met. However, it cannot be assured that the improvements will in fact occur. In contrast, the dual-track approach is independent of the initial conditions of supply and demand Pareto-improving. The only necessary pre-condition is the enforcement of the predefined plan. The Pareto-improving quality of dual-track liberalization stems from the provision of a credible mechanism to compensate reform losers in the form of the plan track. This is especially important in transition economies to avoid reform reversals by providing a form of temporary compensation to those who received subsidies under the old regime.[29]

---

[26] See Lau, Qian and Roland (2000), p. 121 and p. 138; Qian (1999a), p. 17. For example in agricultural goods, the market track accounted for less than 6% of output in 1978, but increased to 69% in 1990. The same happened in industrial goods such as coal or steel, albeit on a smaller scale. For example in steel, the share of the market track rose from 48% in 1981 to 70% in 1990. See Lau, Qian and Roland (2000), p. 138.

[27] See Qian (1999a), p. 17f.

[28] In a Pareto-optimum it is not possible for one economic agent to achieve an improvement without causing another economic agent to be worse off. See Fees (1997), p. 767.

[29] See Lau, Qian and Roland (2000), p. 121f.

Because of the special nature of India's mixed economy, in which the government took a prominent but not a dominant role, the overall liberalization did not have to be as far reaching as in transition countries. In India, the main liberalization thrust came from abolishing almost all licensing requirements and opening up sectors that were previously reserved for public enterprises in the early 1990s. Licensing continued only in five sectors, for health, security or environmental reasons.[30] India also dismantled some price controls that applied to certain essential commodities, including agricultural goods as well as energy.[31] However, price controls in India were not as far-reaching as in most former socialist countries, so the scope for liberalization was also smaller. Like most transition countries, India also followed a single-track liberalization approach.

5.3.2 Stabilization

Macroeconomic stability is generally regarded as an important precondition for a successful transformation. This importance was already recognized in the Washington Consensus, where three of the ten recommendations – fiscal discipline to reduce budget deficits, redirecting public expenditure, and broadening the tax base – aimed at achieving macroeconomic stability.

Stabilization can be interpreted in both a narrow and a broad sense. In the narrow sense, stabilization includes the restoration of an equilibrium price level, i.e. a reduction of the inflation rate so that prices reflect relative scarcities. In the broad sense, macroeconomic stabilization refers to the elimination of macroeconomic disequilibria, fiscal austerity and the balancing of total domestic demand with domestic production. Although it focuses on achieving macroeconomic equilibrium, stabilization does not require the total elimination of budget deficits. However, the linkage between budget deficits and money growth has to be cut.[32]

Macroeconomic stability can be interpreted as a public good that is both non-rival and non-excludable[33] and thus has to be provided by the government during the transition process and afterwards. Once achieved, macroeconomic stability can have positive repercussions on economic growth

[30] See Bajpai (1996), p. 10; Panagariya (2004), p. 23.

[31] See Economist Intelligence Unit (2005), p. 51f.

[32] See Ahrens (1994b), p. 24; Schrettl (1993), p. 211; Wyplosz (1999), p. 337.

[33] Non-rival goods are those where the use by one economic agent does not affect its availability to other economic agents. In the case of non-excludable goods it is prohibitively costly to restrict the access to the good. See Freebairn (1998), p. 72; Stiglitz (1994), p. 24.

due to an increased quantity and quality of investment.[34] From a political-economy perspective, stabilizations are especially difficult to implement since budget cuts entail distributional conflicts between different socio-economic groups that can lead to a "war of attrition" and as a consequence delay the stabilization. Where there is substantial disagreement about how to share the burden of stabilization between different groups in society, caused by the possibility that the burden can be shifted to other groups, each group has an incentive to outwait the others.[35]

These distributional conflicts affect the transition in India as well, especially since it is a federal state with a large number of different socio-economic groups. This helps to explain why the rising public deficits could not be brought under control (Figure 8). In turn inflation, which can be more easily influenced by the monetary authorities, never got out of hand even during the fiscal expansion in the 1980s. In recent years, the inflation rate in India has stabilized at a level of around 5% (Figure 12). Thus, in terms of stabilization, the main challenge for India is the consolidation of budget deficits.

Since China did not experience an economic crisis at the start of the reform program in the late 1970s, an initial stabilization program was not necessary. Throughout the reform period, China has gone through several boom-and-bust cycles, including a period of deflation following the Asian crisis that led the government to intervene in the form of ceilings on bank credit, prohibition of investments, price regulations and other administrative controls. However, due to the transfer of decision making authority to the sub-national level, central stabilization policies are increasingly difficult to pursue.[36]

---

[34] See Buiter, Lago and Rey (1999), p. 150.

[35] See Alesina and Drazen (1991), p. 1171.

[36] See Gang, Perkins and Sabin (1999), p. 68f.; World Bank (1996b), p. 34. One important factor that leads to inflationary pressures in China is the inflow of foreign exchange that results from the surplus in the current account and requires continuous sterilization by the PBOC. See Dorn (2006), p. 2.

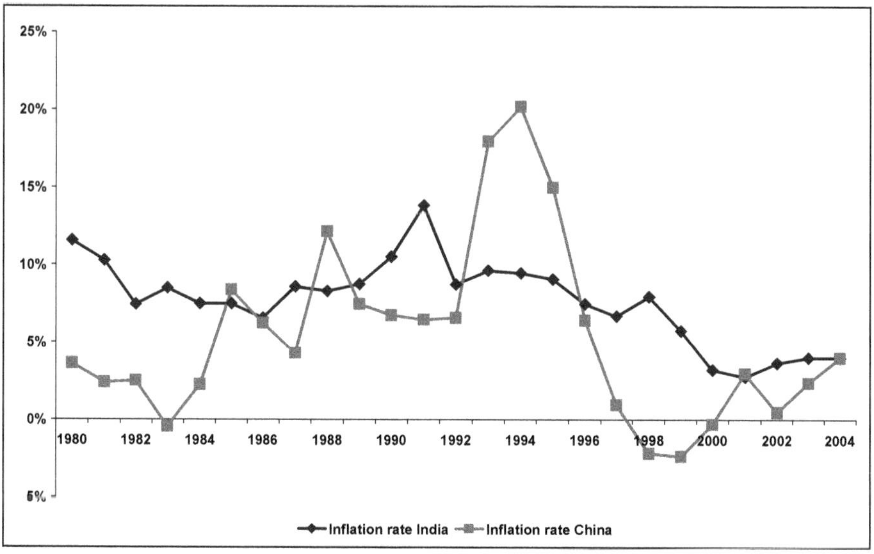

Fig. 12. Inflation rate (GDP deflator) in India and China[37]

5.3.3 Privatization

Privatization deals with the question of which goods and services should be provided by private enterprises rather than public ones.[38] If equitable concerns such as income distribution are neglected, the boundary between public and private sector can be drawn by the efficiency argument that a government should only provide goods or services if it can do it more efficiently than private firms.[39] While the theoretical argument for state ownership of companies is based on a market failure argument, privatization of SOEs in turn can be interpreted as a possible solution to the failings of state ownership, resulting from factors such as soft-budget constraints or the use of SOEs as a tool of political patronage. Given the problems associated with state ownership, privatization is seen as a way to introduce

[37] See Asian Development Bank (2006); International Monetary Fund (2006b).

[38] In the context of this thesis, privatization refers to the partial or full sale of state-owned property ("material privatization"). Questions related to the change of the legal entity of former state-owned firms into for example joint-stock companies ("corporatization" or "formal privatization") are not in the focus. See Balcerowicz (1995), p. 93.

[39] See Megginson and Netter (2001), p. 329; Schipke (1994), p. 172; Shleifer (1998), p. 133. Economic arguments for state involvement were discussed in section 4.2.1.1.

hard-budget constraints, prevent political rent-seeking and achieve an optimal usage of scarce resources.[40] However, especially in transition countries, those benefits could not always be achieved as privatization occurred in a largely unregulated environment, a strategy described by Stiglitz (1999) as a "privatize now, regulate later"[41] policy. This policy created strong incentives for vested interest groups to block later attempts to establish a regulatory framework. Furthermore, institutions to monitor managements' behavior such as liquid capital markets with high standards of corporate governance or strong banks were lacking in transition and developing countries alike, which further exacerbated the problems associated with the weak regulatory framework and the lack of competition.[42]

From the empirical experience of transition countries, some important lessons for a privatization strategy can be distilled. First, privatization is most likely to unfold its productivity-enhancing effects if the firm is controlled by outside owners. In firms that remain under insider control after privatization, no significant efficiency-enhancing effects could be found. Second, privatization strategies that started with the rapid privatization of small-scale enterprises were more successful than those in which large enterprises were sold first. Third, it is important to have a transparent sales process, which reduces the danger that insiders gain control over the newly privatized enterprise. Fourth, institutional factors are just as important as a change of ownership. These factors include a hardening of budget constraints, removal of entry barriers, and an effective legal and regulatory framework to ensure competition in the market.[43]

In the area of privatization, India differs from transition countries due to a comparatively low share of state ownership. As a result of the "mixed economy" approach, state ownership was limited to selected sectors. Therefore, the share of the public sector's industrial value added stands at a comparatively low 35%, and in terms of GDP at 7%. However, since the SOEs in India could at least until 1991 operate in a protected environment, they had limited incentives to invest in productivity-enhancing measures.

---

[40] See Guriev and Megginson (2006), p. 8; Megginson and Netter (2001), p. 329; Shleifer (1994), p. 99; Wagener (1997), p. 165.

[41] Stiglitz (1999), p. 44.

[42] See Parker and Kirkpatrick (2005), p. 527f.; Stiglitz (1999), p. 44.

[43] See Frydman et al. (1999), p. 1186f.; Guriev and Megginson (2006), p. 17; International Monetary Fund (2000b), p. 120; Megginson and Netter (2001), p. 364.

As a consequence both the labor and the capital productivity of Indian public companies is far below that of private companies.[44]

In order to give the private sector a greater role in the economy, India has lowered its involvement in SOEs through a strategy of "disinvestment". The focus of the disinvestment strategy has been to sell minority stakes while retaining management control. The main goal has been the mobilization of resources for the budget; improving the commercial orientation of SOEs has received little emphasis. However, the sale of minority stakes in public sector companies has until now remained well below expectations. Receipts between 1991 and 2005 have been more than 50% below target, which shows that investors were unwilling to invest in companies in which the government still had effective control over management decisions.[45] In addition, the current political power structure makes it difficult for the ruling Congress-led minority government to privatize profitable public sector enterprises.[46]

China followed a somewhat different privatization strategy to that of India or other transition countries. During the early stages of transition, China first attempted to create a non-state sector subject to market forces and gradually increase market incentives for SOEs. An important part of the reform process was the corporatization of SOEs, which included the restructuring of the internal governance system without relinquishing control. A more far-reaching privatization program was started in 1995 under the policy of 'grasping the large and letting go the small'. In this, the state retains control over the 500 to 1,000 largest firms, and as such over a considerable share of the state industrial firms. The privatization program consequently focused on small SOEs at the county level, while SOEs at the city level had to undergo restructuring.[47]

44 See Ahluwalia (2002), p. 83; McKinsey Global Institute (2001), p. 18; Pei (2006), p. 35.

45 According to Perotti (1995), a partial privatization constitutes a signaling mechanism that a government bears residual risk. This shows its commitment not to redistribute value through policy shifts. See Perotti (1995), p. 848. In the case of India, governance issues that are associated with government ownership appear to outweigh this signaling effect.

46 See Ahluwalia (2002), p. 83; Gupta (2005), p. 118. Makhija (2006) points out that in India politicians themselves constitute an important interest group against privatization, since the state-owned enterprises are used as vote banks and for political patronage. See Makhija (2006), p. 1950.

47 See Cao, Qian and Weingast (1999), p. 104f.; Ram Mohan (2004), p. 5 and p. 9. An important difference in the industrial structure between China and the CEE countries is that in China smaller SOEs are relatively more important than large

Since the Chinese privatization program mainly involves SOEs at the local level, it is largely decentralized. This constitutes a major deviation from the commonly found centralized privatization schemes. It also alters the cost-benefit analysis, because economic efficiency is not necessarily the only concern of a local government since even a loss-making firm may still be in a position to pay taxes and to maintain a sizable workforce. The major driving forces behind privatization in this particular setting were hardened budget constraints for local governments and SOEs. This again differs from the experience of other countries, where privatization was regarded as a way to introduce hard budget constraints.[48] These differences should be taken into account when evaluating the privatization strategies in India and China.

5.3.4 Institution building

Institutions comprise formal rules such as a constitution, laws or property rights, as well as informal constraints like sanctions, taboos or customs. Examples are a well-functioning legal system, an independent central bank, an antitrust agency, an efficient public administration, and an adequate social security system. Together, these rules and constraints structure political, economic and social interactions. Market participants benefit from institutions because they provide information, reduce risk and ensure a level playing field. The existence or non-existence of institutions determines transaction and production costs, and consequently the profitability of economic endeavors. Therefore they are one of the key factors for explaining wealth differences between countries.[49]

The experience of the transition countries with the Washington Consensus policies made it clear that the incentives created by privatization and liberalization of the economy would not work in the absence of proper institutions. To generate the desired results, a market has to be embedded into an institutional framework. For this reason even the most liberal market economies have a multitude of different institutions in areas such as

ones so that a privatization program that mainly involves small SOEs is of greater importance in China. See Cao, Qian and Weingast (1999), p. 107f.

[48] See Aivazian, Ge and Qiu (2005), p. 793; Cao, Qian and Weingast (1999), p. 106; Guo and Yao (2004), p. 23.

[49] See Ahrens (1994b), p. 25; Kolodko (2004a), p. 10f; North (1991), p. 97; Olson (1996), p. 19; World Bank (2002), p. 9.

goods, services, labor, asset and financial markets, which oversee and regulate the conduct of market participants.[50]

Institution building and institutional change are complex endeavors. The inherited institutions influence the expectations of the future and pose constraints on newly-established institutions. History and complex social processes influence the design of a new institutional framework, so that as a consequence there cannot be a single strategy for institutional reform. It is also impossible to simply copy institutions: they must develop in their own context. Thus an institution that works well in one country might flounder in another setting. Institution building is thus a time-consuming process that depends on the history of a country, the extent of social difference, and the general level of trust and social capital. When tailored to the specific circumstances of a country, institutions generate a three-fold benefit: they provide information concerning market conditions and participants, they reduce risk by defining and enforcing property rights, and they can influence the degree of competition in the marketplace.[51]

During the process of transition, the impetus for institutional change will most likely come from the government and the need to set general guidelines. However, this does not preclude that other actors initiate the process of institutional change, such as non-governmental organizations, companies or multilateral organizations. Building the institutions for a market economy entails redefining the economic role of the state, which has to retreat from direct intervention and focus instead on setting the general framework for economic activities.[52] In this context, Rodrik (2000) identifies five types of market-supporting institutions that are needed for a well-functioning market economy: property rights, regulatory institutions, institutions for macroeconomic stabilization, institutions for social insurance, and institutions for conflict management.[53]

[50] See Ellman (1997), p. 27; Rodrik (1999), pp. 2-4. The former Polish minister of finance, Grzegorz W. Kolodko, for example noted in this respect that "both the collapse in the early 1990s and the great transitional depression that followed proved beyond any doubt that the one-sided orientation towards liberalization and privatization, neglecting the importance of institution building for the efficient functioning and development of market economy, came at a heavy price for all of us". Kolodko (1999), p. 9.

[51] See Alesina (1997), p. 228; Engerer and Schrooten (2001), p. 4; Haynes and Husan (2002), p. 125; North (1991), p. 97; Raiser (2001), p. 237; Rodrik (1999), p. 8; World Bank (2002), p. 8.

[52] See Ahrens (1994b), p. 25; Küster (1996), p. 66; Shleifer (1994), p. 97; World Bank (2002), p. 11.

[53] See Rodrik (2000), p. 92.

Secure *property rights* are regarded as an important enabler for economic growth. In their absence, entrepreneurs do not have adequate control over the return on assets, which reduces the incentives for expansion and innovation. It is important to note that the key element of property rights is control rights as opposed to ownership rights.[54] *Regulatory institutions* are needed to ensure orderly conduct in product, labor and financial markets, and a level playing field. These institutions become more important with increasing degrees of freedom for market participants. *Institutions for macroeconomic stability* perform a stabilizing function in the economy, and include fiscal and monetary institutions. The central bank, as lender of last resort, plays an important role in this context since it provides safeguards against bank runs, which can trigger systemic banking crises. The institutions for *social insurance* ensure a certain legitimacy of a liberalized market economy, since they provide social stability and cohesion. These institutions comprise the basic forms of social security, such as pensions, health care and unemployment insurance. Closely connected to the institutions for social insurance are the *institutions for conflict management* which help different parts of society to agree on mutually-beneficial outcomes. They include the rule of law, the judicial system, free elections, representative political institutions, and independent trade unions, which ensure that a single group in society does not gain undue influence.[55]

In summary, effective institutions are the foundation of a well-functioning market economy that becomes more important as the scope of market transactions increases.[56] The difficulty in building institutions is that institutional arrangements are context-specific and thus cannot simply be transferred from another setting. Furthermore, they require changes in the mindset and practices of both government and private sector. Even if these challenges are managed successfully, the optimal institutional ar-

---

[54] The experiences of Russia and China are prime examples for this: in Russia formal property rights did not secure control rights so that privatized enterprises fell in the hands of a small oligarchy that used them for their purposes, while in China control rights without ownership rights in town and village enterprises were sufficient to significantly boost production. See Rodrik (2000), p. 92.

[55] See Rodrik (2000), pp. 92-97.

[56] Formal institutions have high fixed costs and low variable costs, while informal institutions have low fixed costs but high variable costs. Therefore, as the amount of market transactions increase, the average costs of using formal institutions will be lowered, which increases their attractiveness and importance. See Rodrik (2004), p. 29.

rangements changes over time and institutions have to be regularly readjusted.[57]

In the area of institution building, the starting point for India differs from the classical transition countries. At the beginning of the reforms, most market-supporting institutions were already in place. Private property continued to exist in India, so property rights were well defined. Regulatory institutions existed to manage the "licence-raj" system, which ensured that a certain basic foundation was in place. As previously mentioned, institutions for macroeconomic stability already existed in India. Basic forms of social insurance were also present in India at the start of the reforms. The same was true for institutions for conflict management – indeed, these are one of the cornerstones of Indian democracy. Overall, then, the necessary institutions were in place in India at the start of the 1991 reforms, even though their focus had to shift in some cases to accommodate a more market-oriented policy environment.

China had a more difficult institutional legacy than India, since most institutions either had to be adapted to a market economy or newly created. Like the rest of its reform program, the institutional changes in China occurred gradually, first introducing transitional institutions, then shifting to more Western-style institutions.[58] In terms of the market-based institutions discussed above, China still lags behind in most areas. Property rights are not defined clearly and are at times difficult to enforce, despite the fact that the protection of private property was included in the Constitution in 2004. Also, informal rules and arrangements are still prevalent so that regulatory institutions are not fully effective. Institutions for conflict management are, despite progress in the last years, not fully in place, since the rule of law is not fully established in China.[59] This, too, has negative repercussions on the enforcement of property rights and the effectiveness of legal institutions. However, it should be noted that some progress has been made in these areas following accession to the WTO. In terms of institutions for macroeconomic stability, the situation is more favorable since the central bank and the political leadership in China have so far managed the cyclical

[57] See Rodrik (2000), p. 94.

[58] See Qian (2003), p. 305; Ray (2002), p. 10. In addition, institutional change was not only brought forward by the central government, but also by local and regional governments that had considerable freedom within a broad frame defined by the central government. See Hermann-Pillath (1993), p. 217.

[59] See Allen, Qian and Qian (2005b), pp. 67-69; Economist Intelligence Unit (2006), p. 11; Gang, Perkins and Sabin (1999), p. 57. Nonetheless, the idea of the rule of law is gaining acceptance in China as can be seen by the 1999 Amendment to the Chinese Constitution that endorsed the rule of law. See Qian (1999b), p. 18; Zou (2006), p. 89.

fluctuations fairly well. Institutions for social insurance are also present in China today in a very basic form. Since SOEs have traditionally provided these services, their reach is declining significantly and coverage is thus significantly lower compared to the end of the 1970s. Thus there is a danger that the "iron rice bowl" – the provision of welfare benefits and job security – will be broken.[60]

5.3.5 Structural change

Structural changes involve the interaction between ownership, competition and performance. The two key elements are the reallocation of resources across activities and the restructuring of activities. Both elements aim at increasing productivity in a firm, a sector or an economy. The *reallocation* of resources involves closing down inefficient firms and redeploying the resources released to create new firms. The process of *restructuring* applies to firms that are economically viable in the long-term, but that need changes in operations or output mix. These changes generally require the shutting down of some activities within the firm so that resources are put to a more efficient use. Both reallocation of resources and restructuring of activities are equally important since transition involves the shrinking of some sectors through restructuring, and the expansion of other sectors through the entry of new firms. Since the industrial structure of most transition countries favored heavy industry, structural changes were necessary to make a shift in the industrial mix towards light industries and services. Besides providing larger choices for consumers, this should help to avoid continued rent-seeking by vested interest groups.[61]

The trigger for structural changes can come from the government, banks or new entrants. Since a large portion of capital stock is often state-owned at the beginning of a transition, the government is likely to play an important role. This can include direct measures such as changes in industrial policy and expenditure plans, as well as indirect measures like the establishment of a legal framework that regulates the entry and exit of firms. Banks also play an important role in restructuring efforts as important stakeholders in the enterprise sector. The ability of banks to act as agents of enterprise restructuring requires a credible hardening of budget constraints and a cutting of subsidies. Finally, structural changes can be triggered by market pressure through the entry of new domestic or foreign

[60] See Hughes (1998), p. 67f.; Woetzel (2006), p. 20f.

[61] See Ahrens (1994b), p. 24f.; Commander, Dutz and Stern (1999), p. 346f.; Roland (2000), p. 337; Schrettl (1993), p. 209.

competitors. Studies of transition countries indicate that increased competitive pressures are one of the major factors bringing about structural change.[62]

Several pre-conditions have to be met for structural change to be successful. First, the state needs to commit to hard budget constraints for firms and install a legal framework that addresses questions such as bankruptcy provisions and employee rights. Second, banks should not be burdened by legacy NPLs since this decreases their incentive to enforce budget constraints and monitor debtors. Third, entry barriers for domestic and foreign players alike should be lowered in order to be able to exert credible threats to incumbents.[63]

Even when these pre-conditions are in place, managing structural change creates a dilemma for policy-makers. The losses incurred from shutting down inefficient firms during the transition process will be immediate, while the benefits from reallocating resources and creating a better institutional framework for economic management will take time. As a consequence, reforms will be harder to implement since they come at an immediate cost for the population for example in the form of unemployment, while the benefits are delayed and uncertain.

India faced these issues of reallocation of resources and restructuring of firms at the beginning of its reform process. Major triggers for structural change were the lowering of government controls in the industrial sector, the reduction of import licensing, and a more liberal environment for foreign direct investment. The reallocation of resources in the industrial sector was somewhat limited by the fact that most reservations for small-scale industries remained in place. Furthermore, as already discussed in chapter 2, Indian banks were still burdened by legacy NPLs early in the transition process, so hard budget constraints could not always be enforced credibly.[64]

The main trigger for structural changes in China was the entry of new domestic and foreign firms. This was supported by the open-door policy for foreign trade and investment that started with the establishment of special economic zones in coastal provinces.[65] Likewise, as discussed in sec-

[62] See Carlin and Landesmann (1997), pp. 82-85; van Wijnbergen (1998), p. 5.

[63] See Carlin and Landesmann (1997), p. 83; Commander, Dutz and Stern (1999), p. 346.

[64] See Ahluwalia (2002), pp. 71-76. Through small scale reservations the production of about 800 different items is limited to factories where the combined investment in plant and machinery is below USD 250,000. See Ahluwalia (2002), p. 72.

[65] See Chow (2004), p. 131f.

tion 5.3.3, China tried to create a private sector subject to market forces, while the reallocation of resources through the closure of large SOEs was not an option since the leadership wanted to avoid massive job losses. While the structural changes in the Chinese economy have certainly proceeded quite far, they were as in India somewhat hindered by the lack of credible hard budget constraints and the legacy NPLs of the state banks.

5.4 Management of transition processes

Successful management of the transformation process does not merely depend on executing the five elements described above. The interaction between these elements is also important. Thus, a transformation strategy not only has to include the relevant policy changes, but also needs to outline the speed and the sequence of their implementation. These questions are addressed below.

5.4.1 Speed of reforms

The choice between "big bang" and gradual reforms has received considerable attention in the early transformation literature and in policy circles. The controversy centered around the question of whether it is viable to transform the legacy of the socialist system overnight or if a more long-term reform approach should be taken.[66]

A shock therapy through a big bang approach involves the simultaneous transformation of the economic order in the early stages of the transition. The rationale for this approach is to quickly and comprehensively implement reforms while there is a window of opportunity after a crisis of the old system because a delay of reforms would cause additional unnecessary uncertainty. The emphasis is typically on macro stabilization, price liberalization and the dismantling of the institutions of the old system. Proponents of gradual reforms, by contrast, focus on the development of laws and regulations and the necessary institutional framework. The rationale for this strategy is to build up public support for further reforms through an

[66] Cases in point are the intensely debated reform strategies in Poland and Hungary. While Poland opted for a big bang approach, Hungary chose a more gradual approach to reforms. See Dhanji (1991), p. 323.

appropriate sequencing of reforms – regarded as especially important given the adjustment costs.[67]

Both approaches have advantages and disadvantages. Shock therapy immediately puts general conditions into place, to which political and economic actors have to adhere. Proponents of this approach have pointed to three advantages over gradual reforms. First, it puts significant pressure on economic and political actors to change their way of thinking. Second, short-term adjustment costs may induce the government to reverse certain reforms – but a big bang approach significantly reduces the reversibility of reforms since the cost of taking back the reforms is likely to be higher than the short-term adjustment costs. Third, if the government does not have a prior track record of successful long-term reforms, gradual reforms may not be enough to signal its commitment to reform; here, shock therapy can improve the government's credibility. However, a major weakness of shock therapy is the lack of emphasis put on building institutions. Further limitations are that the irreversibility of reforms can never be fully assured, the burden the approach may put on public finances if income sources disappear before new ones can make up the shortfall. And finally there is a danger of political instability if large parts of the population are hurt by the reform package.[68]

Advocates of gradual reforms emphasize four advantages of this strategy. First, reforms can be reversed at relatively low costs.[69] Since policymakers are faced with uncertainty over the impact and outcome of reforms, they can use a trial-and-error approach, allowing unsuccessful reforms to be changed fairly easily. Second, the adjustment costs of gradual reforms occur over a longer period of time. The individual costs are spread out over a longer period of time and there is a chance that they might be lowered or totally avoided – which increases support for the reform package. Third, gradual reforms give industries in formerly closed economies a longer period in which they can increase their competitiveness. Fourth, a gradual approach allows the build up of the institutional framework during the transition period. [70]

---

[67] See Roland (1994), p. 29; Roland (2002), p. 29; Solarz (1998), p. 6; Svejnar (2002), p. 5; Wyplosz (1999), p. 324f.

[68] See Apolte (1992), p. 28; Funke (1993), p. 356; Roland (1994), p. 30f.; Solarz (1998), p. 6f.

[69] The advocates of shock therapy argue that irreversibility of reforms is an advantage. This shows that the advantages and disadvantages of the two approaches are dependant on the specific conditions in which the transformation takes place and the constraints of policymakers.

[70] See Roland (1994), p. 32; Solarz (1998), p. 7. This is similar to the "infant industry" argument, which calls for the protection of nascent and therefore still

Gradual reforms have potential limitations, too. A major constraint is the administrative capacity to manage the reform process. Managing a gradual reform process also requires the incorporation of feedback. If this feedback is not incorporated into further decision-making, a gradual approach may be useless. The same holds if the option to reverse reforms has no value. A gradual approach may also hinder companies' long-term planning, since the institutional framework might change constantly. This can lead to a random process where the current institutions adversely affect further institutional change.[71]

Besides adjustment costs, institution building and credibility, culture can be an equally important factor in the choice between shock therapy and a gradual approach. Schulders (1998), for example, points out that Asian countries have an emphasis on mutual consensus and long-term orientation, and there is thus cultural resistance to shock therapy.[72]

Both reform approaches have compelling theoretical arguments. In the CEE countries there was an initial enthusiasm for big bang reform programs that was reflected in the belief that the economic, legal, and institutional framework for a functioning market-economy could be established over an extremely short period of time, sometimes less than a year.[73] However, it soon became apparent that big bang reforms could not deliver the quick economic turnaround that was expected by policymakers. Gradual reform approaches alone are also unlikely to yield the expected results, since vested interest groups are given sufficient time to react to the new realities.

Ultimately, the question of shock therapy versus gradual reforms is a simplification of the real issues at hand. It is not possible either to conduct fully-fledged shock therapy or to implement several reforms one step at a time in a purely gradual manner. A transformation strategy will involve the specification and direct implementation of the major pillars of the new market-based system. The specific reforms within these pillars are then outlined and implemented in a more gradual manner.[74] Experience shows that "despite the facile recommendation that everything is important and everything should be done at once, choices are always necessary given the limitations on any government's time, focus, and resources".[75] Thus, since

uncompetitive local industries until they can effectively compete in the global marketplace.

[71] See Apolte (1992), p. 29; Funke (1993), p. 358; Roland (1994), p. 35.

[72] See Schulders (1998), p. 61.

[73] See Murrell (1995), p. 166.

[74] See Dhanji (1991), p. 327; Solarz (1998), p. 7.

[75] Stiglitz (1999), p. 43.

transformation is a long-term process, there will be a co-existence between the regulations of the old and the new system. During the transformation process, the elements of the old system will gradually give way to the new system so that the overall process will be gradual.[76]

India has followed a very gradual reform path since 1991. A likely reason for this choice is that India only suffered a relatively mild macroeconomic crisis, and did not have a strong executive that could push reforms through. India also shows the need to strike a balance between an overall gradual process with addressing certain issues quickly. A case in point is the initial stabilization program in the aftermath of the 1991 crisis, which in line with IMF requirements included expenditure reductions and a 19% devaluation of the rupee.[77]

The general perception of economic reforms in China is that they have followed a gradual path, as expressed by Deng's phrase "crossing the river by touching the stones". The Chinese leadership most often tackled problems in one or two sectors at a time. However, certain reforms such as the shift from collective agriculture to household farming were completed in less than five years. Thus elements of shock therapy were included in the overall gradual process.[78] A better description might in fact be "recurrent doses of shock therapy"[79] or "a series of small controlled explosions"[80] over a longer period of time. An additional feature of the Chinese reforms is that some reform initiatives were bottom-up as opposed to the general top-down reforms. This allowed the government to experiment with new policies without endangering the overall process, and to limit the costs of failure.[81]

5.4.2 Sequencing and timing of reforms

Since a transformation strategy will almost inevitably contain gradual reforms, the sequencing of the policy reforms as well as the timing of their implementation become important considerations. This, too, has been the subject of intense debate in the transformation literature. Sequencing is a major success factor in a transformation program: if not managed properly, it can make the transformation more difficult or even impossible. The dif-

[76] See Sulc (1994), p. 25.
[77] See Joshi and Little (1999), p. 10; Kapur and Ramamurti (2002), p. 2.
[78] See Gang, Perkins and Sabin (1999), p. 4, Yusuf (1994), p. 71.
[79] Gilley (2005), p. 37.
[80] Yusuf (1994), p. 71.
[81] See Chow (2004), p. 141; Ray (2002), p. 7.

ficulty in formulating a sequencing strategy is the dependence on initial conditions and the interdependence between the various reform measures.[82]

Despite the problems in drawing general conclusions, there seems to emerge a consensus from the experiences in transition and developing countries that institutional reforms as well as fiscal and monetary stabilization should be the first steps in a transformation program. The next steps should be price liberalization and reform of the domestic financial system. This should be followed by starting with the necessary structural changes in the economy. The start of privatization is conditional on reforms in the domestic financial system. At the beginning, the focus of privatizations should be on small-scale enterprises since these are more likely to adapt quickly to changing circumstances. Privatization should be followed by external liberalization, including trade liberalization and liberalization of the capital account.[83]

Once the sequence of reforms has been defined, it is important to decide on their timing. Transforming a country too fast is just as counterproductive as proceeding too slowly. The timing of reforms depends on the feasibility of their implementation. Major factors to be considered are the credibility of policy-makers, the acceptance of reforms by the economic and political actors, and the likelihood that the transition will be blocked by vested interests. These factors are dependent on the specific situation in each country: no rule of thumb for the optimal timing can be given. When formulating a transformation strategy, these questions should be taken into account under the general premise that it is necessary to create momentum for further reforms.[84]

---

[82] See Ahrens (1994a), p. 141; Dhanji (1991), p. 323; Funke (1993), p. 337; Kolodko (2004b), p. 2; Lindner and Bösswetter (1998), p. 16; Oberender, Fleischmann and Reiß (2003), p. 1. Rybczinski (1991) however remarks that there are certain common characteristics of transition countries that influence the sequencing of reforms. These include distorted prices, a dysfunctional banking system and the lack of an institutional infrastructure for a market economy. See Rybczinski (1991), p. 29.

[83] See Fischer and Gelb (1991), p. 102; Funke (1993), p. 340; Nsouli, Mounir and Funke (2002), pp. 13-23. While fewer reform steps are necessary in developing countries, their sequence is almost identical to that of transition economies. It should start with fiscal and monetary stabilization, followed by reforms of the domestic financial system and the implementation of structural changes, and finally trade reforms and the liberalization of the capital account. Adjusting and upgrading the institutional framework should – depending on the necessary adjustments – also start early. See Nsouli, Mounir and Funke (2002), pp. 11-23.

[84] See Ahrens (1994a), p. 160; Ghose (2000), p. 42; Lindner and Bösswetter (1998), p. 16.

In some areas India has deviated from the policy recommendations described above. The first step in the reform process was the necessary macroeconomic stabilization after the 1991 crisis. A variety of different reforms began soon afterwards. These included financial sector reforms, partial privatization, trade liberalization and the reduction of licensing requirements for industrial companies. Notable differences from the strategies above were the early start of privatization and trade liberalization. This was probably due to the specifics of India's political economy: privatizations were regarded more as a means to generate funds than to transfer ownership, and even though tariffs were lowered as part of trade liberalization, the overall level was still high by world standards (the result of the previously dominant policy of import substitution). Also, institution building was not necessary to the same extent as in transition countries. However, a shift from the control framework of the "licence-raj" system to a more liberal market-based framework was necessary.[85]

China, like India, has deviated from the general policy recommendations outlined above. At the beginning of the reform process the country did not suffer from an economic crisis. Therefore a stabilization program was not necessary. Institutional reforms were somewhat delayed and instituted on a case-by-case basis with pragmatic transitional institutions. Contrary to the general prescriptions, trade liberalization started fairly early in the process, although it was at first limited to special economic zones. The reform of the domestic financial system, structural changes and privatization started only some 15 years into the transformation process and even today are not fully complete. Overall, the transition sequence in China reflects the pragmatic Chinese approach to tackling the problems on a case-by-case basis and to first focusing on easier reforms, in order to build popular support.

5.5 Differences in transformation processes in India and China

As shown above, there are marked differences from country to country in the initial conditions, the scope of the transformation and the transformation strategy. For example, while most transition countries in CEE (including Russia) have undergone a double transformation of their political and economic systems, India – as a multi-party democracy – only has to trans-

[85] For example in 1995/1996 the average tariff level was about 40%. See Joshi and Little (1999), p. 22.

form its economic system. Likewise, China is as of now also undergoing only an economic transformation, while trying to preserve its political system. Different economic, political and institutional legacies as well as deliberate policy choices make the environment for a transformation distinct in India, China and the CEE countries. Since these factors also affect the comparability of the reform experiences, it is important to understand the major differences in terms of initial conditions and features of the transition. The discussion below follows and expands upon the framework provided by Balcerowicz (1995).[86] The focus is again on India and China, while the general experience of the CEE countries provides a perspective on the classical transition countries, which is helpful for contrasting the transformation experiences and identifying differences of India and China with respect to other regions of the world (for a summary see Table 1).[87]

The *political system* is an important distinguishing factor between the transformation processes in India, China and CEE. The transition countries in CEE are unique, in the sense that they have simultaneously conducted a political and an economic transition and that the political transition was carried out in most countries during the early stages of the process.[88] This is in stark contrast to India and China, who did not have to or did not want to change their political system. This led to a higher degree of political stability during the early stages of the transformation process.[89] India, as a multi-party democracy, has in a sense been more unstable than China: it experienced several post-election government changes during the transition process. While China's leadership also changed during the reform period, these changes occurred within the Communist Party, rather than following elections.

In terms of the *economic system* there are also important differences. The most visible is that China and CEE had socialist economies, while in India private and public ownership co-existed in a mixed economy. If the economic systems in China and CEE can be described as "destroyed" capitalism[90], the Indian system can be characterized as "regulated" capitalism. To guide their economies, India, China and the CEE countries all used five-year plans. India started with the first plan in 1951, which outlined important national economic policies such as import substitution. How-

[86] See Balcerowicz (1995), pp. 147-149.

[87] The CEE countries are also not a homogenous group. For simplification and illustration purposes the general features of their transformation experiences are grouped together here.

[88] See Kim and Pirttilä (2003), p. 7

[89] See Chow (2004), p. 140.

[90] See Balcerowicz (1995), p. 147.

ever, the five-year plans did not have the same reach as those of China or CEE due to the considerable share of private enterprises.[91]

Table 1. Overview of transformation processes in China, India and Eastern Europe

	China	India	Central and Eastern Europe
Initial conditions			
Political system			
In general	Communist party-state	Democracy	Communist party-state
Party system	Suppressed	Multi-party	Suppressed
Economic system			
In general	Socialist, i.e. 'destroyed' capitalism	Mixed, i.e.'regulated' capitalism	Socialist, i.e. 'destroyed' capitalism
Socio-economic structure	High share of agriculture	High share of agriculture	High share of socialist industry
Institutional legacy	Legal institutions as instruments of state control	Rule of law	Legal institutions as instruments of state control
Features of Transition			
Trigger	Dissatisfaction of political leadership with economic performance	Balance-of-payments crisis	Popular revolt against communist rule and lack of democracy
Scope	Only economic system	Only economic system	Both political and economic system
Sequence	First capitalism, then possibly mass democracy or political pluralism	Capitalism only	Mass democracy first or at least political pluralism - then capitalism
Speed	Periods of shock therapy within an overall gradual process	Rapid stabilization after crisis, gradual liberalization and privatization	Rapid shift from non-democratic to the pluralist political arrangements, speeed of economic reforms differs

Source: Adapted from Balcerowicz (1995), pp. 147-149.

There are also important differences in the intensity of central planning in China compared to CEE. Planning was far less entrenched in China. Thus while government agencies in the Soviet Union allocated about 60,000 commodities through their plans, the comparable figure in China in 1978 was about 1% of this amount.[92]

Another important factor affecting the transformation process in the economic sphere is the structure of the economy, and especially the degree of industrialization. On the eve of reforms in Russia in 1990, 13% of the workforce was employed in agriculture and 42% in industry, whereas in China in 1978, 71% of the workforce was working in agriculture and only 15% in the industrial sector. In Russia the state sector provided 90% of

[91] See Jalan (2005), p. 46f.

[92] See World Bank (1997a), p. 13. Another systematic difference of the planning system was that in China centralized decision-making was constrained because of administrative decentralization; in the Soviet Union, in contrast, the center had more far-reaching powers. See Qian (1999b), p. 28.

employment in 1990, while the comparable figure for China in 1978 was 19%.[93]

India is in this respect much closer to China than to the CEE countries. The share of employment in agriculture in 1980 was 68% and in industry 14%.[94] Pre-1991, the share of SOEs in employment in India stood at about 8.5%.[95] These structural differences in the economy can have a major influence on the transformation process. Sachs and Woo (1994), in a comparison of the reform experiences of China and CEE, argue that while China had to manage normal economic development (i.e. the transfer of workers from agriculture to industry) the CEE countries were faced with the much more difficult task of structural adjustment (i.e. the redeployment of labor and capital across industries). As a result it was much more difficult for Russia to achieve high growth rates.[96]

A further important initial condition affecting the transformation process is the *institutional legacy*. In the CEE countries, under central planning, legal institutions were instruments of state control and property rights were based on the identity of the owner in the sense that state property was more important than collective property, which in turn was more important than individual property.[97] Particularly in the CEE countries that have since joined the European Union, deliberate attempts have been made to upgrade the institutional framework to suit a market-based democracy.

China had an institutional legacy comparable to the CEE countries. Institutions for a market-based economy were lacking. However, the fact that China did not undergo a political transformation has had profound implications on the extent of the rule of law today. The Communist Party, for example, stands above the law in some respects, since laws cannot be written to restrict its power to rule China. As a result, the rule of men is often more

[93] See World Bank (1996b), p. 21.

[94] See Kochhar et al. (2006), p. 8. Data for 1990 is not available. Since the employment shares in 2000 stand at 59% for agriculture and 18% for industry, the respective shares for India should be around 64% for agriculture and 16% for industry assuming a linear shift. See Kochhar et al. (2006), p. 8. Interestingly, in India the share of agriculture in total employment has remained almost the same between 1901 and 1991, which illustrates the overall importance of this sector. See Roy (2002) p. 113.

[95] See World Bank (1995), p. 288f.

[96] See Sachs and Woo (1994), p. 103. It can however also be argued that China and not the CEE countries has faced the more difficult transition process. China actually has to manage a dual transition from a rural to an industrial economy, and from a planning system to a market-based economy. See Fan (2002), p. 3.

[97] See World Bank (1996b), p. 87f.

important than the rule of law.[98] The institutional legacies of China and CEE are in stark contrast to India. Here, there have always been property rights in the Western sense. This is due to the existence of a large private sector and the prevalence of the rule of law.[99]

After this brief overview of the political, economic and institutional legacies, the discussion now turns to some key features of the transition process. These include its trigger, scope, speed and sequence.

The *trigger* for reforms in many CEE countries was a popular revolt against the communist leadership and the lack of democracy. In addition, most countries in the region faced serious economic shortages. In China, by contrast, the start of the reforms in late 1978 was triggered by the political leadership, although the failure of the Cultural Revolution and its threat to the system of governance certainly provided a strong impetus. In India, the impetus for reforms was much weaker since the 1991 balance-of-payment crisis was a comparatively mild shock that never actually threatened the foundations of the Indian state.[100]

Another defining feature of the transformation processes is the overall *scope*. As already mentioned, India and China are similar in the respect that they are only transforming their economic system, while the CEE countries had the double task of transforming both political and economic systems.[101]

This also directly affects the broad *sequence* of reforms. In CEE, the political transformation preceded the economic transformation in most countries, while in China the economic transformation comes first in the sequence – and it is unclear if it is to be followed by political transformation. India, in contrast, is a democracy and so only has to manage an economic transformation.

The *speed* of reforms has also differed. The general pattern in CEE was to relatively quickly opt for more popular political participation. For the economic transformation, there have been examples of both shock therapy and gradualism. In India, after an initial stabilization of the economy after the 1991 crisis, most reforms in the areas of privatization and liberalization have proceeded gradually. The overall reform process in China was as discussed above also gradual, but contained elements of shock therapy.

[98] See Chow (2004), p. 145; Pei (2002), p. 96; Woetzel (2006), p. 18.

[99] See Huang and Khanna (2005), p. 167; Manor (2005), p. 98; Mukherji (2005), p. 64. The exception is the Emergency Rule of Indira Gandhi between 1975 and 1977 when elections and civil liberties were suspended.

[100] See Gilley (2005), p. 29; Mukherji (2005), p. 58; Ray (2002), p. 2.

[101] See Kim and Pirttilä (2003), p. 7

Thus the background for the transformations in CEE, India and China has differed significantly. This has implications for the transition process. In terms of initial conditions for the transition, there is a dichotomy between India and China: authoritarian regime versus multiparty democracy, socialist economic system versus mixed economy, and the rule of men versus the rule of law are just the most visible differences. Several areas of the transformation process are directly affected by these divergent initial conditions. For example, India has a significantly easier task in institution building than China.[102] Also, the extent of structural change necessary is lower in India because the private sector co-existed with the public sector, which resulted in lower distortions of the economy. Despite the differences, the two countries also share common problems, such as the task of privatizing state-owned enterprises and the need to develop a transformation strategy. Moreover, there are general similarities in the transformation process of India and China. The transformation is in both countries limited to the economy, so that the establishment of a market economy was the first step in the transformation sequence. With respect to the speed of reforms, both countries have opted for a gradual approach.

It can be concluded that despite the different initial conditions, the features of the transition are largely the same in India and China. While initial conditions –the political system and the institutional legacy being two of the most important ones – certainly shape policy makers' choices, they do not necessarily limit the comparison. Many economic policies in a transformation program are independent of these factors. However, it is certainly necessary to be aware of the key differences to be able to provide a meaningful comparative perspective on the transformation process. Without identifying and evaluating country-specific factors, it is impossible to come to general conclusions.

5.6 Conclusion

Transformation studies have evolved considerably over the past years. One of the key lessons learned is that the transformation of an economic system is more complex than was thought at the beginning of the 1990s, when

---

[102] For example as Gilley (2005) points out, India's task of implementing market-friendly policies is arguably significantly easier than China's task of building an institutional structure. See Gilley (2005), p. 44. Nonetheless, building institutions from scratch also has advantages since policy-makers for example face fewer restrictions from the institutional legacy.

there was a strong faith in the merits of the Washington Consensus and shock therapy in policy circles.

Managing a transformation needs to deal properly with five major inter-related elements. These must be implemented in the proper sequence. They are: liberalization, stabilization, privatization, institution building and structural change. Liberalization refers to the establishment of a market-determined price and allocation mechanism; the Chinese dual-track approach is generally considered an ingenious solution to this problem. Stabilization of an economy requires the reduction of the inflation rate and budget deficits, which is a necessary pre-condition to creating a sound economic foundation for transition. The recommendation to sell state-owned enterprises as a possible solution to government shortcomings is considered in the privatization process step. One of the most difficult parts of a transformation is institution building. At least five main institutions have to be either built up from scratch or adapted to a market system. These institutions are: property rights, regulatory institutions, institutions for macroeconomic stabilization, institutions for social insurance, and institutions for conflict management. Last but not least, it is necessary to manage structural changes in a transition economy, which involves the restructuring of firms as well as the reallocation of resources across firms and industries.

The inter-relations between the reform steps and the sequence of their implementation are also important considerations. Here the consensus is that a gradual management of economic transformation should start with stabilization and institution building, while the sale of state-owned enterprises should take place relatively late in the process, after the foundations for a market economy have been established.

How these general recommendations are implemented is affected by the initial conditions in the areas of the political, economic and institutional system of a country, as well as by deliberate decisions of policy makers regarding the scope, sequence and speed of the changes. India and China differ greatly in several of these dimensions, which has profound implications on the transformation experience. Perhaps the most visible example is the political system. The general assumption is that authoritarian China is able to pursue faster reforms than democratic India. However, the transformation experiences have also differed in other areas. Institution building is a case in point: India needed to make far less adjustments during the reform process because of a better developed legal framework.

These examples highlight the danger of overly simplistic generalizations of complex socio-economic processes. While there are certainly common elements to consider in a transformation strategy, these elements should be tailored to the specific circumstances of a country. A further complication arises when the general recommendations of transformation studies have to be applied to specific sectors of an economy. This may or may not require different or additional considerations. The banking sector is a case in point: due to its nature as an intermediary and the associated information asymmetries, this sector requires special attention in formulating a transformation strategy. This issue discussed in detail in the next section.

6 Framework for banking sector liberalization

The previous two sections have dealt with the main elements of transformation studies and the financial liberalization hypothesis. This section attempts to integrate these two approaches into a framework for the liberalization of the banking sector.

Integrating the two approaches yields clear benefits. While financial liberalization studies have emphasized the benefits of removing repressive policies, they have given little guidance on how to design the process. Transformation studies can help overcome this shortcoming since they have dealt extensively with questions surrounding system transformations. However, the main focus of transformation studies has been at the level of the overall economy, so the recommendations for transformation of the banking sector remain limited. It is therefore necessary to adapt the general policy recommendations to the banking sector. Since it is important for policy makers not only to design the process, but also to evaluate the status and progress of reforms, cause-and-effect relationships along the process elements and possible indicators to measure these relationships will also be discussed.

This chapter begins with a general overview of the issues and a look at some special considerations such as banks' need for a stable operating environment. Next, transformation studies and financial liberalization studies are integrated according to the process elements of transformation studies. Following this, the discussion turns to the measurement of the process and the impact at the sector and macroeconomic level.

6.1 Overview and special considerations

The discussion of studies testing the financial liberalization hypothesis (see section 4.4) has shown that, while financial liberalization may not always be beneficial, the majority of empirical studies support the conclusions of the financial liberalization school. The policy recommendation is to lower the role of the state in the financial sector through the removal of repressionist policies and the privatization of state-owned banks. Less clear, however, is how the change of the coordination mechanism from state to market can be managed best. Fry (1997) points out that

"since there is no question that financial repression inhibits growth, the debate should concentrate on the tricky problems of moving from the state of financial repression to a state of financial liberalisation. So far, the economics profession has failed to produce adequate blueprints for this crucial transition."[1]

Along similar lines, Wachtel (2001) argues that

"[...] there is ample empirical evidence to make a convincing case that financial sector development promotes economic growth. Although the academic literature strongly supports this conclusion, it provides little in the way of rigorous guidance about how to best develop the financial sector."[2]

Thus, although the literature describes the benefits of financial liberalization, a coherent blueprint of how to manage the transition from a state-directed to a market-based banking sector is still lacking. Even though it is presumptuous to believe that a general blueprint exists for every situation, it is worthwhile identifying best practice elements – particularly given the perils that arise during liberalization. As McKinnon (1991) noted, these dangers can resemble walking through a minefield.[3]

The task of transforming the banking sector is complicated by the fact that banks require a relatively stable environment for their operations. Banks need a fair amount of predictability to be able to evaluate projects and debtors. However, the transformation of the coordination mechanism is associated with rapid change and a high degree of uncertainty – a phenomenon best described as "transitional uncertainty". Thus, the needed stable environment is not present in a period of transformation. Transformatory changes pose a double challenge for banks. Besides adapting themselves to the changes, they also have to take a leading role in the transition process of the real economy. As discussed, in a period of transition, banks play an important role in hardening budget constraints of enterprises and in extending credit to newly-established enterprises.[4]

Various challenges have to be overcome for a successful liberalization of the banking sector. Guidance for successfully managing the process can be found in transformation studies. Transformation and financial liberalization studies have complementary elements. Both try to explain the

[1] Fry (1997), p. 768f.

[2] Wachtel (2001), p. 357.

[3] See McKinnon (1991), p. x.

[4] See Brandt and Li (2003), p. 387; Lago (2002), p. 4 and p. 9.

change from a system characterized by a high degree of state involvement to one that is more market-based. The common rationale is to overcome the limitations of state involvement with the goal of achieving a higher growth rate. While transformation studies attempt this for the economy as a whole, financial liberalization studies focus on the financial sector and can therefore be seen as an extension of the more general transformation studies. With their vast body of experience, transformation studies can help guide the liberalization of a banking sector on issues such as the necessary reform elements, sequencing and timing of reforms, and how to deal with impediments to change.

A framework for the liberalization of a banking sector can be derived from the recommendations of financial liberalization and transformation studies. The starting point is a state-dominated banking sector that is about to be liberalized. Before this can happen, certain basic requirements have to be in place (Figure 13). The different process elements for systemic changes can then be addressed. If the liberalization is not to be pursued in a big bang fashion, questions of speed, timing and sequencing of reforms become important, and the results of changes can be evaluated along several dimensions to see if the reforms are on track. Furthermore, goals for the transformation have to be defined to enable a measurement of the results.

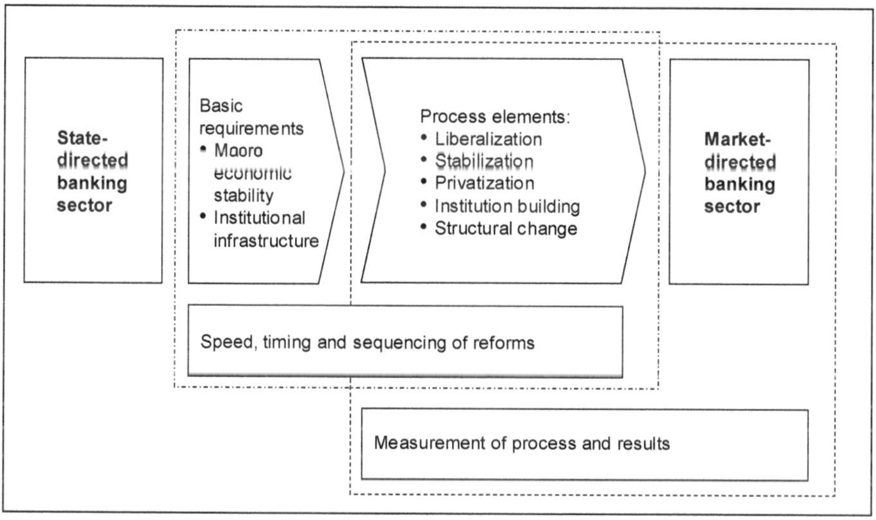

Fig. 13. Framework for banking sector liberalization[5]

[5] Author's presentation.

6.2 Transformation of the banking sector

This section attempts to integrate transformation and financial liberalization studies according to the process elements of transformation studies. It also addresses the basic requirements of transformation and speed and sequencing issues. Based on the key insights, general propositions for managing the process are derived and appear at the end of every sub-section.

6.2.1 Basic requirements for banking sector liberalization

Experience with financial liberalization over the past years suggests that two important pre-conditions exist that may help explain the successful experiences of some countries. These pre-conditions are macroeconomic stability and an adequate institutional infrastructure.[6]

Macroeconomic stability, as has been discussed, is an important element of any transformation program. A stable macroeconomic environment has a special importance for a successful liberalization of the banking sector since both inflationary pressures and budget deficits can have adverse effects on the performance of the banking sector.

One of the main factors making the government resort to repressive policies is the existence of budget deficits. Such deficits can induce the government to use the financial sector as a captive source of financing. Financing of the budget deficit can occur via high reserve requirements that provide funds, and via artificially low interest rates that keep the cost of financing down. Additionally, the effective burden of the debt can be lowered through a high inflation rate that effectively constitutes an "inflation tax". High inflation can result in a more difficult business environment for banks. It makes assessing and pricing the risks they take more difficult. Furthermore, large swings in the performance of the real economy, asset prices, exchange rates and inflation rates lead to significant problems for banks in correctly assessing and pricing the risks they take. Inflation not only affects investment but also saving activity, since it provides disincentives for financial vis-à-vis non-financial savings and against entering long-term saving contracts.[7]

Pursuing financial liberalization in an environment of high inflation rates and high budget deficits can destabilize an economy. Removing restrictions on the setting of the interest rate can cause the (real) interest rate to increase and fluctuate widely. A higher interest rate will make the fi-

[6] See Fry (1989), p. 26; Fry (1997), p. 759; McKinnon (1991), p. 4.

[7] See Beck (2006), p. 7; Funke (1993), p. 347; Koch (1998), p. 70.

nancing of the government deficit more expensive, which further increases the deficit. The higher financing needs of the government will result in a crowding out of enterprises and households from the limited financial resources. If the government then resorts to the central bank for additional financing, the monetary base will increase, leading to further inflationary pressure. Therefore financial liberalization will only be sustainable in an environment where the fiscal deficit is either under control or the government attempts to regain fiscal control in a credible fashion.[8]

Just as important as price stability and fiscal discipline is the existence of an appropriate institutional infrastructure. The banking sector requires a well-functioning legal system, an adequate system of prudential supervision, and regulation. Improving the supervisory system entails a fundamental shift from passive checks of compliance with lending guidelines to prudential checks of banks' risk management systems. This should help to lower the systemic dangers of a bank collapse, reduce information asymmetries and mark a first step in the shift from direct to indirect control.[9] Once these prerequisites are in place, the actual process of liberalization can begin.

Proposition 1:
Macroeconomic stability and a basic institutional framework that includes supervision and regulation of banks must be in place before beginning the liberalization of the banking sector.

6.2.2 Process elements for banking sector liberalization

As discussed in section 5.3, there are five essential process elements for transforming an economic system: liberalization, stabilization, privatization, institution building and structural change. So far, the discussion of these process elements has focused on the overall economy; now they have to be adapted to the transformation of a banking sector and integrated with the financial liberalization literature. The sections below present the policy recommendations and their rationale. They also discuss the necessary preconditions for conducting these policies. Again propositions for managing the process are presented at the end of every sub-section.

---

[8] See Deckert (1996), p. 36; Fry (1997), p. 759; Funke (1993), p. 347; McKinnon (1991), p. 4.

[9] See Bonin and Wachtel (1999), p. 94f.; Caprio, Atiyas and Hanson (1993), p. 12; Deckert (1996), p. 37; Fry (1989), p. 26; Fry (1997), p. 759.

6.2.2.1 Liberalization of price and volume restrictions

Liberalization in the banking sector is part of the internal liberalization of an economy. It involves the establishment of a market-determined price and allocation mechanism.[10] In the context of the banking sector, the price mechanism includes interest rates on deposits and loans,[11] while the allocation mechanism is concerned with the question of how funds flow from providers to users of capital. The two major impediments to a market-based allocation mechanism identified in the financial liberalization literature are statutory pre-emptions and directed credit rules. Liberalization of price and volume restrictions thus involves the three-fold task of deregulating interest-rates, lowering statutory pre-emptions, and removing directed credit policies.

The rationale for price liberalization is to restore the signaling function of prices. This should lead to a more efficient allocation of resources. For the banking sector, this refers to the efficient allocation of credit to investment projects. The generally proposed sequence for *interest rate liberalization* has the underlying rationale of liberalizing interest rates faster for financially more sophisticated entities that can adapt faster to the new environment. The recommendation is to first liberalize wholesale interest rates, then lending interest rates, and finally deposit interest rates.[12] This gives a certain element of stability, since it prevents excessively fierce competition over deposits. The necessary pre-conditions for interest rate liberalization are that the main economic players are subject to hard budget constraints to avoid an inefficient allocation of resources, a relatively stable inflation rate to prevent large fluctuations of the real interest rate, and a certain stability of banks to avert ruinous competition.[13]

The reform of *directed credit* programs is an important step in the restoration of the allocation mechanism. In this respect, the policy recommendations of financial liberalization and transformation studies alike appear to point toward a big bang liberalization, i.e. abolishing a non-market allocation mechanism as fast as possible. However, the experiences of transition countries show that this policy is not without pitfalls. Economic

---

[10] The removal of entry and exit barriers can be regarded as part of the liberalization of an economy as well. Here, these points are regarded as enablers for structural changes in a sector and are consequently described in section 6.2.2.5.

[11] Exchange rates are financial prices as well. However, since the focus is on the domestic banking sector, they are not included in the analysis.

[12] Wholesale interest rates are interest rates in the inter-bank market and those set by the central bank

[13] See Caprio, Atiyas and Hanson (1994), p. 434f.; Mehran and Laurens (1997), p. 33f.

agents need time to adjust. For example, most transition countries witnessed a prolonged output fall due to an overly fast abolishment of the old allocation mechanism.[14]

One possible solution is the Chinese dual-track approach, in which market liberalization occurs at the margins, while old contractual arrangements remain in place. However, dual-track liberalization in China was primarily applied to the agricultural and industrial sector. How, then, should it be applied to the banking sector?[15]

The central feature of dual-track liberalization is the coexistence of a plan track and a market track.[16] For a banking sector, a plan track would consist of a fixed amount of credit that banks have to provide at a predetermined interest rate. Under the market track, banks would have the possibility to lend their excess funds at the prevailing market interest rate. If the amount of credit under the plan track is set as an absolute volume target and not as a percentage of total credit, the plan track will – in an environment of growing credit demand – decrease in importance relative to the market track. Thus, the directed credit program slowly loses importance and is eventually phased out, while at the same time ensuring an adjustment period for economic agents. If market failures in the allocation of credit exist, a case can be made for leaving a residual nominal amount of credit for underserved sectors.[17]

Abolishing a directed credit program can result in abrupt portfolio changes as banks shift their credit portfolio away from priority sectors. This can be avoided by instituting "speed limits" for portfolio diversification and increasing supervision.[18] Under a dual-track approach, this problem can be mitigated as well, since the directed credit program is phased out slowly.

The third element of liberalization is the reduction of *reserve requirements*. The general policy recommendation is to reduce excess reserve requirements, since they constitute a distortionary tax on the banking system.[19] Consequently, they should only be used as an indirect tool of monetary policy. Since reserve requirements are a source of cheap funds

---

[14] See for example Roland (2001), pp. 44-46 for a discussion.

[15] Under the plan track, fixed quantities of goods at fixed prices are assigned to economic agents; under the market track, economic agents can do business at free-market prices provided that they have fulfilled their obligations under the plan track. The "dual-track" approach was discussed in detail in section 5.3.1.

[16] See Lau, Qian and Roland (2000), p. 121.

[17] The effects of market failure are discussed in more detail in section 6.3.3.

[18] See Caprio, Atiyas and Hanson (1994), p. 421.

[19] See Joshi and Little (1997), p. 125.

for the government, a pre-condition for their reduction is to bring the budget deficit under control. However, budget deficits should not serve as an excuse not to reduce statutory pre-emptions. One possible strategy to avoid this is to reduce them in a phased manner, thereby allowing the government to adjust its finances while at the same time preventing a build-up of excessive liquidity in the banking system, which could lead to inflationary pressures.

Proposition 2:
Interest rate liberalization should be pursued in a sequential manner by first liberalizing wholesale interest rates, then lending interest rates, and finally deposit interest rates.

Proposition 3:
A directed credit program should be phased out using a dual-track approach, with a fixed nominal volume target for credit on the plan track.

Proposition 4:
Statutory pre-emptions should exclusively serve monetary policy purposes. If their level is not commensurate for that purpose, they should be reduced in a phased manner.

6.2.2.2 Stabilization of banks

Stabilization is an important element of a transformation program for the overall economy and for the banking sector. Stabilizing banks becomes necessary for two reasons. First, banks in countries that are liberalizing their banking system are often burdened by legacies from the old economic system. These include high levels of often unrecognized NPLs due to directed credit to loss-making enterprises and a lack of risk-assessment capabilities. Closely connected to this is often a low level of bank capitalization. Second, a stabilization program for the overall economy will impact on banks' customers and thus may in the short term have adverse effects on the banks' business environment.

Banks play an active part in a stabilization program. They enforce hard budget constraints in the real sector – which is likely to affect their own performance as well. The imposition of hard budget constraints on enterprises to reduce subsidies is often associated with a build-up of bad loans in the banking sector. After the stabilization of the economy, these bad loans are no longer eroded by inflation. In fact, they may even increase due to positive real interest rates, which puts a further burden on companies and banks. The subsequent deterioration of banks' balance sheets can put significant pressure on the overall economy with the possibility of a credit crunch. A further possible effect of financial liberalization that makes stabilization of banks necessary is an increase in competition. This, in turn, reduces banks' profits and their net worth. The net worth of banks is an important factor in ensuring financial stability after financial liberalization. Loosening the ties between the government and banks will only be a credible policy if banks have a sufficient capital base and the financial means to operate independently. Sufficient financial strength is also a prerequisite for domestic banks to be able to compete with foreign banks – these may enter the market if entry barriers are lowered as part of liberalization.[20]

Consequently, the policy recommendation is to recapitalize banks and remove legacy NPLs from their books. To achieve this, the amount of bad loans and the capital needed first has to be estimated before fresh capital is injected into the bank. An especially important pre-condition in this respect is transparent accounting standards to correctly assess the amount of NPLs.[21]

There are at least three options for resolving legacy NPLs: they can be transferred from banks' balance sheets to a government agency or asset management company, they can be cancelled out against the loans of the enterprises[22], or they can remain on banks' balance sheets. If the latter option is chosen, efforts should be made to collect the outstanding loans, since this reduces the cost of bank restructuring and provides a signal to future borrowers that they are expected to honor their commitments. However, if the decision is taken to recapitalize banks, moral hazard and adverse selection problems arise, since a bailout provides incentives for banks to under-invest in risk-appraisal capabilities and to pursue excessively risky projects as the losses will be borne by the state.[23] Therefore, it should be conducted "once-and-for-all" and include credible threats as well as clearly defined terms and conditions for the provision of funds.

---

[20] See Balcerowicz and Gelb (1994), p. 37f.; Bonin and Wachtel (1999), p. 94f.; Buiter, Lago and Rey (1999), p. 157; Kaminsky and Schmukler (2002), p. 25.

[21] See Balcerowicz and Gelb (1994), p. 37f.; Sheng (1996), p. 46.

[22] This strategy has been advocated especially for economies in transition where both banks and enterprises are state-owned. Canceling the debt from banks' and enterprises' balance sheets would remove a burden from the old regime that has no effect on the value of state-owned assets. See Mitchell (2000), p. 64.

[23] See Balcerowicz and Gelb (1994), p. 38; Bonin and Wachtel (1999), p. 94 and p. 98; Buiter, Lago and Rey (1999), p. 159; Caprio, Atiyas and Hanson (1993), p. 22.

Proposition 5:
Resolve legacy non-performing loans via a "once-and-for-all" stabilization program and recapitalize banks to meet minimum capital standards.

6.2.2.3 Bank privatization

The financial liberalization literature puts relatively little emphasis on the question of privatization. A possible reason for this neglect is that financial repression was predominantly associated with interest rate controls, directed credit programs and statutory pre-emptions. Over the past years, interest in the topic has picked up. There has been increasing evidence that state-ownership of banks is associated with some of the same adverse effects as repressive policies, such as lower financial development.[24]

The same arguments that were discussed for SOEs in general apply also to the privatization of banks. In the banking sector, privatization of state-owned banks is regarded as one of the primary levers to achieve market-oriented banking. In light of the often inadequate systems of governance under state ownership, privatization is a way to enhance the performance of state-owned banks and avoid costly bailouts. A successful program of bank privatization should lead to entities that are both independent of the state and of insider control. This will most likely not only be efficiency-enhancing for the banking sector, but also increase the credibility of other reform measures.[25]

The experience of transition countries shows that bank privatization has proceeded more slowly than the privatization of firms. This divergence can be attributed to a variety of factors, including the high amounts of bad debts and opposition by employees and borrowers.[26] The general problem is that privatization of banks is only one necessary prerequisite to achieve market-oriented banking. To make privatization achieve the desired benefits, the state must disengage from direct governance of banks and develop a regulatory framework for indirect control. The establishment or upgrading of institutions to regulate and supervise the banking system has to go hand in hand with the formulation of a sales strategy. Another condition for successful bank privatization is that the privatized banks must be able to operate independently, so that the government's exit from direct intervention is credible. Thus it is essential to pursue a stabilization of banks

[24] See for example Barth, Caprio and Levine (2000), p. 7f.; Hawkins and Mihaljek (2001), p. 9; La Porta, Lopez de Silanes and Schleifer (2002), p. 267.

[25] See Bonin and Wachtel (1999), p. 93f.; Funke (1993), p. 353; Hawkins and Mihaljek (2001), p. 9; Williams and Nguyen (2005), p. 2148f.

[26] See Commander, Dutz and Stern (1999), p. 358.

through recapitalization, before banks are privatized, and to create institutions and regulations that prevent the government from interfering in the day-to-day operations.[27]

Based on empirical studies in transition countries, the most successful privatization method appears to have been the sale of state-owned banks to strategic partners – preferably foreign banks – in a transparent bidding process. Before the sale, legacy NPLs should be removed from the balance sheets and banks should be recapitalized to make the financial situation transparent. The know-how of foreign banks appears to be particularly performance-enhancing for banks in transition countries: studies have shown that the existence of a foreign owner had a positive effect on profit efficiency. In fact, privatized banks without a foreign owner did not show any efficiency improvements compared to the pre-privatization period. Furthermore, the experience in transition countries suggests that it is important that the government fully divests its holdings, since continued government involvement in the banks may impede the necessary restructuring efforts. This also makes the assurance that it will only act as a passive investor less credible.[28]

However, these policy recommendations are not undisputed. As pointed out by the World Bank (2001), many of today's advanced economies had – and on occasions still have – a modest share of state-owned banks during their economic take-off. State-owned banks may also be necessary to offer banking services to parts of the population that would otherwise not be covered by the formal banking sector as will be discussed in section 6.3.3 in more detail. In addition, most developing countries with a large share of state-owned banks do not have the institutional environment and regulatory capacity to quickly privatize their banks. Therefore, it is recommended that governments proceed carefully with bank privatization, ensuring that market incentives are in place.[29] A further argument against the large-scale sale of banks to foreigners is that it risks a popular backlash against "re-colonization" and may therefore be destabilizing for the overall political, economic and social environment.[30]

---

[27] See Bonin and Wachtel (1999), p. 93f.; Megginson (2005), p. 1961.

[28] See Bonin, Hasan and Wachtel (2005), p. 2172; Boubakri et al. (2005), p. 2018; Clarke, Cull and Shirley (2005), pp. 1914-1918; Hawkins and Mihaljek (2001), p. 11; Megginson (2005), p. 1961; Otchere (2005), p. 2090f. As previously discussed in section 5.3.3, the view that the government should fully divest its holdings is not undisputed since continued government ownership can serve as an incentive for the government to pursue policies that do not reduce the value of its holding.

[29] See World Bank (2001), p. 16f.

[30] See Parker and Kirkpatrick (2005), p. 531.

Overall, the issue of bank privatization shows the importance of balancing economic and political factors in economic policy-making. While bank privatization may, in the right institutional environment, lead to positive economic effects that benefit society as a whole, there can also be strong opposition to the sale of state banks. This must also be considered as part of a privatization strategy.[31]

Proposition 6:
Privatize state-owned banks when they are not needed to address market failure and the necessary pre-conditions are in place. Foreign banks should be allowed as strategic partners; they are able to quickly upgrade the skill level to international standards.

6.2.2.4 Institutional infrastructure of the banking sector

Institution building is perhaps the most neglected aspect of the policy recommendations that have been given to transition countries. This is stressed in the post-Washington Consensus literature, where high-quality institutions are extensively discussed and identified as the key prerequisite for a functioning market economy. In the financial liberalization literature, the question of institution building also received little attention until the link between financial crises and financial liberalization was established. One of the key factors used to explain this link was a lack of strong institutions. Thus, the necessity of creating resilient institutions to enhance the functioning of the market mechanism applies to the banking and financial sectors as well.

The task of building the institutions for market-oriented banking is difficult even in developed countries. Developing countries face additional challenges since they are exposed to a greater degree of volatility from for example more pronounced business cycles, which increases systemic risks, and have less regulatory capacity. During a transition process these problems are aggravated, since banks have greater incentives for risk-taking. At the same time the regulatory capacity may decline, since the private sector may try to recruit staff from the regulatory bodies. Thus the regulatory capacity declines when it is most needed. As a result, transition countries may need to impose an even tighter regulatory framework and more restrictions than developed countries.[32]

Building institutions is a time-intensive, gradual process. The existence of certain basic aspects of an institutional framework, such as bank super-

---

[31] Political-economy factors are discussed in more detail in section 6.2.4.

[32] See Stiglitz and Bhattacharya (1999), p. 106.

vision, is one of the pre-conditions for liberalizing the banking sector. Institution building must continue during the transition process. This is essential since the fundamental characteristics of the business environment change during transition. When the government is heavily involved in the banking sector and socializes the risks involved in financing projects, there is little demand or need for elements of a financial infrastructure such as accounting, auditing or legal systems. The process of financial liberalization leads to a reduction of government involvement, so market participants have to devote more resources to the evaluation and management of risks and market-supporting institutions have to be in place.[33]

Countries need certain institutions in place in order to have a well-functioning banking sector.[34] These are: capital adequacy standards to enhance the stability of banks; accounting and disclosure rules that promote transparency for outside stakeholders; a regulatory system to supervise market participants so that consumers are protected, competition is promoted and risk-taking is not threatening the stability of the overall system; and a deposit insurance system to protect consumers and prevents systemic crises triggered by bank runs.[35]

The international standard for *capital requirements* are outlined in the Basel capital accords. These call for an 8% equity ratio on risk-weighted assets. For developing and transition countries, higher capital requirements are often recommended. This is because the more volatile business environment increases the risk of default. For example, the World Bank (1997b) suggests capital requirements of 20% or more in countries with weak institutions in order to foster incentives for prudent banking.[36] Regulators have to strike a delicate balance since overly rigid capital adequacy ratios may lead to less prudent lending behavior to make up for the shortfall in profits caused by higher equity cushions. Similar problems arise when banks operate with a weak capital basis and may be tempted to place large bets to regain profitability.[37] Since a principal-agent relationship exists between bank managers and shareholders, bank managers will not necessarily always act in the best interest of shareholders. As a consequence,

[33] See Bandiera et al. (2000), p. 242.

[34] The institutions for the banking sector are embedded in the overall institutional framework of the economy. Therefore, institutions like a functioning legal system or well-defined property rights to have enforceable claims need to be in place as well. See Claessens (1996), p. 5; Stiglitz (1989a), p. 61.

[35] See Kormendi and Snyder (1996), p. 11; Rajan and Zingales (2003a), p. 18.

[36] See World Bank (1997b), p. 69.

[37] See Honohan and Stiglitz (2001), p. 42; Stiglitz and Bhattacharya (1999), p. 106.

banks need – besides capital adequacy standards – further rules concerning the recognition of income, the provisioning for bad loans, and portfolio concentration. [38] Thus, transparent accounting standards and a well-functioning supervisory system are complementary elements for capital standards.

Accounting standards are especially important for providing reliable information for both investors and supervisors. Standards concerning the recognition of non-performing loans are particularly important, as these may affect the stability of the banking system and the provision of credit for the overall economy. Rising NPLs can lead to a vicious cycle when banks try to hide losses by extending credit to firms that are unable to repay their loans. This increases the demand for loans, pushes up interest rates and leads to a decline in productive investments – which again increases the likelihood of loans becoming non-performing.[39] A commonly used method for accounting for loan quality is to rank loans by the probability of default as "substandard", "doubtful" and "loss". For each of these categories certain loan loss provisions have to be taken against the equity of the bank – e.g. 20% for substandard loans, 50% for doubtful loans, and 100% for loans classified as a loss.[40]

An adequate *supervisory system*, as mentioned above, is especially important in the context of financial liberalization. While the existence of a basic bank supervision system is a pre-condition for liberalization, the supervisory system will most likely need further upgrading during the liberalization process to manage the possible dangers that can arise from the removal of restrictions, the entry of new domestic and foreign banks into the market, and the possible deterioration of banks' loan portfolios. These forces intensify the pressure for banks competing for deposits and loans, which in the existence of deposit insurance or a lender of last resort can lead to undue risk-taking.[41]

Too much or too little supervision are both counterproductive. Its scope has to be clearly defined. The current consensus is that direct intervention through interest rate controls, credit allocation, or micro-monitoring of banks' decisions is not desirable. Instead, the imposition of minimum capital requirements is preferred, since adequate capital provides a cushion against losses and should restrict risk-taking by banks.[42]

---

[38] See Joshi and Little (1997), p. 116.

[39] See Fry (1989), p. 25; Honohan (1997), p. 19; Mishkin (1996), p. 56.

[40] See Freixas and Rochet (1998), p. 247; World Bank (2001), p. 94.

[41] See Honohan (1997), p. 6; Joshi and Little (1997), p. 116.

[42] See Joshi and Little (1997), p. 115.

A two-tier structure is generally proposed as a regulatory framework. The central bank, as the first tier, provides liquidity to the system and has a lender-of-last-resort function. An independent agency that grants licenses, defines the scope of banking activities and provides deposit insurance constitutes the second tier. It is important that this agency be sufficiently independent from political pressure so that it can act decisively if problems with one institution become apparent.[43]

Deposit insurance schemes are common in many countries today.[44] While deposit insurance is important for instilling confidence in the banking sector and preventing bank runs, it can lead to increased systemic risk due to moral hazard. With deposit insurance, depositors do not have an incentive to monitor the bank since their wealth is safe from bank failure. The bank, on the other hand, has an incentive to take on more risky projects, since it does not carry the downside risk of its business decisions due to the insurance. This in turn increases the likelihood of bank failures if deposit insurance is not accompanied by increased supervision over banks' portfolios or if the deposit insurance premium is not risk-adjusted. In general, however, the confidence-building effects of deposit insurance are believed to outweigh potential negative effects.[45]

To avoid banking failures, it should be a priority to rapidly develop the necessary institutions that ensure effective banking supervision and regulation as a priority. However, the creation of these institutions is only part of the task. More important is that they can exercise their regulatory powers by providing credible threats to the banking system.[46] Countries undergoing a transition must reduce their direct involvement in the banking sector and create institutions that provide an effective regulatory structure for market-oriented banking. As Bonin and Wachtel (1999) point out, "this apparent contradiction makes the task extremely difficult because there is a

---

[43] See Bonin and Wachtel (1999), p. 121; Honohan (1997), p. 19; Mishkin (1996), p. 56.

[44] In a database on the use of deposit insurance, a World Bank study found 68 countries with explicit deposit insurance in 2000. See Demirgüc-Kunt and Sobaci (2000), p. 9. Countries not having explicit deposit insurance systems are most likely having some form of implicit insurance due to banks that are considered "too big to fail" or public expectations that depositors will be shielded from losses by the government. See Diaz-Alejandro (1985), p. 13.

[45] See Aschinger (2001), p. 66; Bossone (2000), pp. 35-37; Diamond and Dybvig (1983), p. 417; Diaz-Alejandro (1985), p. 4f.; Freixas and Rochet (1998), p. 272; Hermes and Lensink (2000), p. 516; Lago (2002), p. 7.

[46] See Bonin and Wachtel (1999), p. 95.

great temptation to use the regulatory structure as a means of maintaining government influence or control over the activities of banks."[47]

Proposition 7:
Capital adequacy rules, transparent accounting standards, a supervisory system and deposit insurance are indispensable institutions for a market-based banking system and must be created during the transition process.

6.2.2.5 Structural change of the banking sector

Transformation studies point out the need for structural change in both the enterprise and the banking sector, if the economic structure is not market-oriented. In the industrial sector, structural change mostly refers to moving from heavy to light industries through the entry of new companies and the break-up of old conglomerates. Likewise, the levers for structural change in the banking sector are the reduction of the relative importance of state-owned banks through privatization, the break-up of banks, and entry of new banks.

There is a marked difference in the scope of structural change between transition countries and developing countries. While most developing countries have a two-tier banking system, the banking system in most transition countries was set up in the form of a "mono-bank" that performed the functions of both central bank and commercial banks. These mono-banks did not act as commercial entities but merely performed administrative tasks by taking in savings and channeling them into industrial companies according to plan priorities. There was no need for banks to evaluate the creditworthiness of borrowers or the riskiness of projects. However, while the need to restructure the banks was recognized in the transformation literature, the importance of strong banks in the transition process was underestimated.[48]

The banking sector in transition countries faces a double task in the context of structural change. First, since banks were typically state-owned and concentrated in a mono-bank, the banking sector itself has to undergo structural changes.[49] Second, the banking sector – or more broadly speaking the financial sector – is important for the management of the structural change of the rest of the economy since it can facilitate the reallocation of

---

[47] Bonin and Wachtel (1999), p. 118.
[48] See Ellman (1997), p. 27; World Bank (1996b), p. 98f.
[49] While the mono-bank cannot be found in all transition countries, a high degree of state ownership is as discussed in the previous section a characteristic that can be found in many countries of the world.

resources between sectors and enterprises. Banks, as providers of external finance, are typically important stakeholders in the process of enterprise restructuring since they are the major claimholders of companies. They can help determine the scale and pace of restructuring, provide additional funds and monitor the progress. This will harden the budget constraints of enterprises as well as improve corporate governance. Furthermore, if banks are actively involved in the process this may preclude undue interventions by the government.[50]

Two different approaches were proposed for banking sector restructuring in transition countries: the new entry and the rehabilitation approach. The new entry approach is based on the market entry of a relatively large number of new banks, either domestic or foreign. Existing state-owned banks are broken-up and privatized. If a privatization is not viable, a bank is liquidated. Estonia and Russia are examples of countries that followed this approach. The rehabilitation approach focuses on restoring the competitiveness of existing state-owned banks through their recapitalization and the build up of institutional skills. As with the new entry approach, the rehabilitated state-owned banks are privatized. Hungary and Poland are examples of countries pursuing this strategy. While the two approaches are in theory mutually exclusive, in practice many countries have included elements of both in their reform strategies. The final goal of structural changes will be to attain an efficient banking sector that is able to support the changes in the real economy.[51]

An important lever for forcing structural changes in the sector is the entry of new domestic and foreign competitors. The World Bank (2001) notes that "the very threat of entry has often been enough to galvanize the domestic banks into overhauling their cost structure and the range and quality of their services [...]".[52] In practice, the effects of the entry of foreign banks into developing countries are somewhat mixed. While foreign entry leads to increased competition and enhanced efficiency as measured by lower overhead costs and lower interest margins, for example,[53] it may also lead to a reallocation of loans towards more profitable or well-known firms and away from small- and mid-sized enterprises.[54] However, there is agreement on the necessary pre-conditions for making the entry of new banks beneficial. Besides transparent licensing requirements, there must be

---

[50] See Caprio, Atiyas and Hanson (1993), p. 22; Commander, Dutz and Stern (1999), p. 357; World Bank (1996b), p. 99.

[51] See Claessens (1996), p. 2; World Bank (1996b), p. 99.

[52] World Bank (2001), p. 20f.

[53] See Demirgüc-Kunt (2006), p. 27; Micco, Panizza and Yanez (2004), p. 6.

[54] See Detragiache, Tressel and Gupta (2006), p. 26; Gormley (2006), p. 27.

a certain degree of supervisory capacity, strengthened financial capabilities and sufficient net worth of the incumbent domestic banks. This will prevent undue risk-taking when new competitors enter the market.[55]

Proposition 8:
Entry barriers for both domestic and foreign banks should be lowered to enable structural change in the banking sector.

6.2.3 Speed, sequencing and timing of banking sector reforms

Simply implementing the different reform elements is not sufficient for the successful liberalization of a banking sector. The discussion has already shown that there are pre-conditions for certain reforms and interdependencies between others. Therefore, as for the overall transformation strategy, questions of speed, sequencing and timing are important aspects of a transformation program in the banking sector. Since the main arguments were already discussed in section 5.4, they are only covered briefly here.

6.2.3.1 Speed of reforms

There are two general choices for the speed of a financial liberalization program. These are the big bang and the gradual approach. The general arguments presented in section 5.4.1 – as well as the conclusion that the implementation of a transformation program in a big bang manner is not feasible – are also applicable to the banking sector.

One of the major arguments for a gradual process arises from the need to build strong and resilient institutions. Due to the inherent fragility of banks and the dangers of contagion, a gradual process of liberalization is preferable. This gives countries time to build appropriate system safeguards, such as market infrastructure, accounting standards and banking supervision.[56]

This recommendation is in line with historical experiences with financial liberalization. Latin American countries followed a strategy of rapid financial liberalization at the end of the 1970s and the beginning of the 1980s. However, many of these countries experienced severe financial crises, and the current recommendation is to implement financial liberalization programs in a more gradual manner. This allows for an adjustment pe-

[55] See Bonin and Wachtel (1999), p. 95; Caprio, Atiyas and Hanson (1994), p. 435; World Bank (2001), p. 21.
[56] See Barton, Newell and Wilson (2003), p. 27; Wyplosz (2001), p. 3.

riod during which the necessary supervisory and regulatory systems can be built up.[57]

Proposition 9:
Liberalization of the banking sector should be carried out a gradual manner.

6.2.3.2 Sequencing and timing of reforms

Some important themes for the sequencing and timing of reforms have already emerged from the discussion of the process elements of financial liberalization. First, financial liberalization includes elements that require time to implement – such as institution building – so that it is a gradual process. Second, the discussion of the process elements has shown that in most cases certain pre-conditions have to be fulfilled. Therefore, complementarities and interrelations between the various reform elements exist that require proper sequencing and timing.

In the context of the overall reform process the relevant question is if other reforms can be accomplished in the absence of banking sector reforms, and if there are certain reforms that are prerequisites for banking sector reforms. Financial reforms are regarded as an important part in any transformation program, since they directly affect stabilization and privatization – which are less likely to succeed if banks do not enforce hard budget constraints.[58] As discussed in section 5.4.2, there seems to be a consensus that banking sector reforms should be pursued towards the middle of the transition to a market economy. Institution building and attaining macroeconomic stability in particular are prerequisites to ensuring the banking sector can operate on a market-determined basis. In addition, banks need time to reorganize, streamline their operations, and clean up their balance sheets.[59]

Once a certain degree of stability and basic institutions are in place, the financial liberalization program can begin. The recommendation is to first stabilize banks through recapitalization and then to abolish controls on interest rates to ensure that they reflect relative prices. Interest-rate liberalization should start with wholesale rates, followed by lending rates, and fi-

[57] See Demirgüc-Kunt and Detragiache (1998), p. 36.

[58] See Funke (1993), p. 348.

[59] In developing countries the reform of the domestic financial system can start earlier than in transition countries because the scope of reforms is narrower. While reforms in developing countries are mostly about liberalization of financial markets, transition countries have to pursue more basic reforms that include for example the creation of institutions. See Funke (1993), p. 346f.

nally deposit rates. The second step is to reduce quantitative controls in the form of directed credit programs and statutory pre-emptions to give banks greater discretion over the use of their funds. The next steps in the reform sequence are the opening of entry barriers for domestic and foreign players and the reduction of government ownership of banks. Privatization of banks and structural changes through the lifting of entry barriers should come towards the end of the reform process due to the moral hazard associated with the increased competition in the sector. The liberalization of the external financial sector should – with the exception of the lifting of entry barriers for foreign competitors – come at the end of the overall reform program. It is important to keep in mind that the upgrading of the institutional framework in particular is an ongoing process that is likely to extend throughout the entire reform period.[60]

This sequence is broadly in line with the experiences from thirteen developing countries that have liberalized their banking sector analyzed by Laeven (2003). Usually these countries started with the deregulation of interest rates, followed by a reduction of reserve requirements. The next steps were the abolishment of credit controls and the lowering of entry barriers. Privatization and the introduction of prudential regulation came towards the end of the liberalization process.[61] The only important deviation from the policy recommendations outlined above is that the creation of prudential norms came toward the end of the liberalization program.

Proposition 10:
Banking sector liberalization should start when the basic institutions are in place and the macroeconomic environment is relatively stable. The reforms should start with a sequenced liberalization of interest rates, the lowering of statutory pre-emptions, and the abolishment of the directed credit program. If required, banks should be recapitalized. Afterwards, entry barriers for domestic and foreign competitors can be lowered and state-owned banks can be privatized.

6.2.4 Political-economy considerations for banking sector liberalization

Political-economy considerations are vital for managing the transition process in a banking sector – in fact, just as important as the reform ele-

[60] See Brownbridge and Kirkpatrick (2000), p. 12f.; Gibson and Tsakalotos (1994), p. 579; McKinnon (1991), pp. 6-8; Mehran and Laurens (1997), p. 34.

[61] See Laeven (2003), p. 18.

ments outlined above. Transforming a banking sector does not occur in isolation. It is closely connected to the situation in the enterprise sector and to the fiscal position of a country. A further complication is the influence of different interest groups – like savers, borrowers, bank employees – that are affected by the transformation of the banking sector. While there are certainly other political-economy factors that help to explain the transformation of a banking sector, this section focuses on the relationship between banking sector reforms, the enterprise sector and the fiscal situation, as well as the role of interest groups in the transition process.[62]

The banking sector serves as intermediary between providers and users of capital. To ensure the available capital is used efficiently, banks must identify the most promising projects and monitor the use of the funds, but also that companies – as the receivers of capital – adhere to hard budget constraints imposed on them. If they do not, the banking sector faces an increased likelihood that loans will become non-performing. This may not only make it necessary to extend further loans or government subsidies – it may also make a recapitalization of banks necessary, if the losses in the loan portfolio have depleted the capital base. There are two implications for the transition process in the banking sector. First, reforms in the banking sector have to be complemented by reforms in the enterprise sector. And second, the financial capabilities of a government to extend subsidies to enterprises or recapitalize banks affects the pace of banking sector reforms.

As discussed in section 6.2.2.1, hard budget constraints in the enterprise sector are an important pre-condition for a successful reform program. While hard-budget constraints are an important pre-condition for successful reforms, the extent of the available financial resources in a country also directly affects the speed of the transition process. The major effects are as follows. First, the extent of public debt influences the pace of privatization – the lower the public debt, the slower the privatization process, as sufficient funds are available to bail out loss-making enterprises or banks. Next, the higher the budget deficit, the more likely repressive policies such as interest rate controls and statutory pre-emptions will persist, as they lower the financing cost for the government. Third, where compensatory payments to reform losers or interest groups have to be made, the higher the

[62] For a summary of general political-economy factors affecting reforms see for example Williamson and Haggard (1994). Roland (2002) and Wagener (1993) provide an overview of political-economy factors in transition countries, while Denizer, Desai and Gueorguiev (1998) focus on the political-economy of financial repression, and Boehmer, Nash and Netter (2005) investigate political and economic factors for bank privatization.

public debt and deficits, the slower the reform pace. Fourth, the higher the public debt and deficits, the less likely is a "once-and-for-all" recapitalization because the necessary financial resources are lacking. Overall, all other things being equal, the higher the public debt and deficits, the slower the pace of banking sector reforms.[63]

But banking sector reforms and financial liberalization are not only influenced by the fiscal position or the situation in the corporate sector. They are also affected by interest groups. Since the seminal work by Olson (1965), the impact of interest groups has been a recurrent topic in the political-economy literature. As in all economic reform, reforms in the banking sector result in costs and benefits that are not equally shared by different groups in society. This leads to both anti- and pro-reform measures by different interest groups. All other things being equal, interest groups may have the following effects on the transition process in the banking sector. The likelihood of privatization decreases with the number of veto players such as coalition partners or trade unions. Also, interest groups that benefit from interest rate restrictions and directed credit program try to delay the liberalization process. The higher the rent from these restrictions, the fiercer the opposition and the less likely liberalization is.[64] Equally, the decision to liberalize market entry depends on the relative strength of incumbents compared to the outsiders who stand to benefit from it. An important factor in this respect is the degree of concentration in the market. In highly-concentrated oligopolistic markets, incumbents will be in a better position to organize their interests, which leads to higher barriers to entry. Even if the market structure is not oligopolistic, it can be assumed that incumbents are better organized and have closer ties to policy makers, which will delay the opening of the market. The dynamics between different interest groups also affects the speed of reforms. A delay in reforms can be caused if different interest groups are engaged in a "war of attrition", in which the group that gives in first, loses more. Also, uncertainty about the distributional consequences of reforms in the banking sector leads to a desire to stick with the status quo, and thus to reforms being delayed.[65]

While these effects are certainly not exhaustive and sometimes offset each other, they nevertheless help to explain the dynamics of the transition

---

[63] See Nsouli, Mounir and Funke (2002), p. 25; Opper (2004), p. 571; Roland (2002), p. 45.

[64] This can however be solved by using a dual-track liberalization approach in which pre-existing rents are preserved.

[65] See Abiad and Mody (2002), p. 12; Acemoglu and Robinson (2000), p. 126f.; Alesina and Drazen (1991), p. 1171; Fernandez and Rodrik (1992); Opper (2004), p. 569f.; Rajan and Zingales (2003a), p. 19f.; Zhang (2003), p. 70f.

process in the banking sector. They should thus form part of the liberalization strategy.

6.3 Measurement of process and results of banking sector liberalization

This section turns to the evaluation of the process and the results of liberalization. Since the liberalization of a banking sector stretches over a long period of time, it is important for policymakers to know precisely where a country stands in the process, and if the results are as initially expected.

The question to be asked is how the process and the results can be represented best in order to provide meaningful information for policymakers. Past studies have used a single indicator to either analyze the process or assign a starting date to financial liberalization. However, relying on a single indicator excludes important information and limits possible insights. Indicators by their very nature are snapshots of reality: the challenge here is to capture the broader aspects of reforms. One possible solution is the creation of an index that gives a broader picture of the progress of reforms.[66]

The discussion below first investigates potential indicators for the process and the results. Following this, the process indicators are integrated to an overall index. Finally, the impact of market failures on these indicators is discussed.

6.3.1 Identification of process and result indicators

The starting point for identifying possible process indicators is the requirement that values should be comparable across different sub-indicators, across countries and over time. Standardization is therefore necessary. One approach is to scale the numerical values, for example between 0 and 1. The necessary pre-conditions are to assign a range of values for every variable and to have data for every year. In reality, defining ranges for values is difficult.[67] An additional complication is that in some

---

[66] See Quispe-Agnoli and McQuerry (2001), p. 12.

[67] A case in point is the capital adequacy ratio. While the lower bound would be 0%, it is difficult to assign an upper bound. While 100% would be a theoretical upper bound, this is clearly not practical. The same problem arises with statutory pre-emptions, where it is difficult to separate the effects of monetary policy and appropriation of funds of the state.

countries data availability is limited. A more practical alternative is to categorize results. For example, Williamson and Mahar (1998) and Abiad and Mody (2002) use a four-scale classification system – fully repressed, partially repressed, largely liberalized and fully liberalized – to differentiate different policy regimes. The overall logic of the classification system is that under full repression the government virtually takes all relevant decisions, while under full liberalization, the government's role is negligible. In a partially repressed system, the government – while leaving some room for private economic agents – takes a majority of decisions. A largely liberalized system is one that is basically market-oriented, but where the government continues to play an important role in certain areas.[68]

Although this classification is to some extent subjective, the approach is practical as it is possible to apply the categorization to a wide range of variables and countries. Therefore, this thesis follows this four-scale classification methodology for the process indicators. Since most result indicators are quantitative in nature – such as the ROA or NPLs – no categorization is needed here. Working on this basis, possible process indicators for the respective transformation steps and result indicators are discussed according to the five main process elements described in section 6.2.2.

The three main policy areas for deregulating the banking sector are the liberalization of interest rates, the lowering of statutory pre-emptions and changes in the directed credit program. In the first area, a wide variety of different possible interest rate controls exist. Since it is difficult to fully account for all controls, general tendencies have to be considered.[69] Interest-rate controls can be categorized as follows: in a fully repressed system, the government sets all or almost all interest rates. In a partially repressed system, the government sets ceilings or floors. In a largely liberalized system, some interest rates are completely market determined. And in a fully liberalized system, virtually all interest rates are set by banks themselves.[70]

The results of interest-rate liberalization largely depend on the lifted restriction, the interest rate that would have prevailed in the absence of the restriction, and on the movement of interest rates after lifting the restrictions. In the McKinnon-Shaw models, the assumption is that both deposit and lending rates are set at artificially low levels. After the lifting of interest rate restrictions, both rates should increase. In addition, the increased competition for deposits and loans will lead to a narrowing of the spread

---

[68] See Williamson and Mahar (1998), p. 4.

[69] For example in 1989-1990 India had over 50 administered lending categories and a large number of stipulated interest rates that depended on loan size, usage and type of borrower. See Joshi and Little (1997), p. 130.

[70] For the classification see also Abiad and Mody (2002), p. 5 footnote 4.

between loans and deposits.[71] Result indicators for the relative movement of interest rates are (1) the fraction of lending rates divided by deposit rates, and (2) the net interest margin, i.e. the lending rate minus the deposit rate.[72]

Statutory pre-emptions can serve both as tools of monetary policy and as instruments of financial repression – if their amount exceeds the level that is necessary to pursue an orderly monetary policy. Since it is difficult to gauge the levels of reserve and liquidity requirements that are necessary for the pursuit of monetary policy, the degree of repression can only be approximated.[73]

One possible approach is to start from the effective reserve requirements, since they give an indication of the percentage of banks' funds that are pre-empted. The effective reserve requirements can be calculated from the IMF's International Financial Statistics using the following formula[74]:

$$\text{Effective reserve requirement} = \frac{(\text{reserve money}) - (\text{currency outside deposit money banks})}{(\text{money}) + (\text{quasi money}) - (\text{currency outside deposit money banks})}$$

Based on effective reserve requirements from developed and Asian countries to gauge the process,[75] it is assumed that in a fully repressed system the effective reserve requirements are above 15%; in a partially repressed system they are between 10 and 15%; in a largely liberalized system between 5 and 10%; and in a fully liberalized system below 5%.[76]

Lowering statutory pre-emptions should result in a shift in banks' use of funds. Since banks do not have to invest in government bonds, they can

---

[71] See Fry (1997), p. 755f.; McKinnon (1973), p. 69; Williamson and Mahar (1998), p. 48f.

[72] An overview of all process and result indicators can be found in Table 2 at the end of the section. In Table 3 the categorization of the process indicators is summarized.

[73] In the McKinnon-Shaw models the assumption is made that statutory pre-emptions reduce available funds for investments since they are used to finance government consumption. However, there are also models that assume that the funds from reserve requirements are channeled to development finance institutions that extend loans to projects in which banks would not invest. Under these circumstances and assuming that loan demand is not perfectly interest-rate elastic, it is possible to find a deposit-maximizing required reserve ratio. For a discussion see Fry (1995), pp. 133-150.

[74] See Williamson and Mahar (1998), p. 8. The formula using the line numbers of the International Financial Statistics is (14-14a)/(34+35-14a).

[75] See Table 15 in the appendix for an overview of the values.

[76] The possible caveats of this categorization are that a central bank may use an extremely high reserve requirement as a tool of monetary policy and that the categorizations are to some extent arbitrary.

distribute these funds as loans. Thus, banks' loan portfolios are likely to grow. However, on its own this measure is not sufficient – the loan volume can increase because of general market conditions. Better measures are the ratio of loans to deposits (credit-deposit ratio), or loans to assets. These measures give an indication of the changing use of funds on banks' balance sheets that are caused by the lowering of statutory pre-emptions. Since the two ratios are very similar in nature, only the credit-deposit ratio is used as a result indicator in this analysis.

Categorizing credit controls also includes a certain degree of subjectivity, as it is necessary to set percentage targets. Following the classification used by Demetriades and Luintel (1997), the following percentage targets are employed in this study as process indicators: a fully repressed system has over 40% directed credit and very detailed prescriptions for sector allocation and interest rates. In a partially repressed system, directed credit is between 20 and 40%, and detailed guidelines exist for its allocation. In a largely liberalized system, directed credit is below 20% and interest rates are largely market-based. And in a fully liberalized system, there is no directed credit program.[77]

Priority sector advances are commonly associated with eroding banks' profitability, due to a combination of low interest rates and low repayment rates.[78] Therefore, reducing credit to priority sectors should allow banks to reduce these income losses. A possible result indicator for the liberalization of directed credit is the ROA of banks.

To achieve stability of the system, banks must be resilient against internal and external shocks alike. In a market-based banking system, one of the main levers to achieve this stability is having an adequate capital basis, which provides a cushion against losses. This is recognized in the Basel Capital Accord, which requires banks to hold a minimum capital of 8% of risk-adjusted assets.[79] In repressed and closed banking systems, capital adequacy norms are generally not a concern since the government either implicitly or explicitly guarantees banks' survival. By contrast, banking regulators in developed countries have adopted detailed guidelines concerning the capitalization of banks.[80] Therefore, the status and enforcement

[77] See Demetriades and Luintel (1997), p. 314. This does not preclude that government-owned policy banks hand out subsidized credit to priority sectors.

[78] For example for the 1974-1999 period in India, Ganesan (2003) calculates sizeable income losses for banks due to directed credit. See Ganesan (2003), pp. 23-26.

[79] See Santos (2000), p. 17.

[80] See Rojas-Suarez (2001), pp. 2-4.

of capital adequacy norms can serve as an indicator for the progress made in creating the institutions for a more stable banking sector.

Accordingly, a fully repressed system is defined as one that does not follow internationally recognized prudential norms. In a partially repressed system, the implementation of Basel I is required for banks, but not fully implemented or enforced yet. In a largely liberalized system, the international capital standards are largely implemented and enforced. And a fully liberalized system enforces Basel I and moves toward the implementation of Basel II.[81]

Successful stabilization of the banking system should result in a lower risk of a banking crisis. Indicators that signal the absence of a banking crisis are therefore used to measure the results of stabilization. Commonly used indicators that signal distress in the banking system are nonperforming loans above five percent of total loans with a rising trend, return on assets of banks below 1%, and net interest margins below 200 basis points.[82] In this study, these are used as result indicators for stabilization. The four indicators – level of NPLs, trend of NPLs, ROA, and net interest margin – are treated as dummy variables, where 0 signals a higher probability of financial distress and 1 a lower probability.

The progress of privatization of state-owned banks can be measured using two different variables. First, it is possible to track the percentage of state-ownership in state-owned banks, i.e. the equity share held by the state. The pitfall of this approach is that it does not account for the *de facto* influence of the state.[83] A second option is to track the percentage of total assets that state-owned banks hold.[84] While this does not account for partial

---

[81] Since the Basel I standard was introduced in 1988, the standard has to be applied retrospectively. A possible pitfall of this approach is that countries are graded based on the guidelines of a standard that at the time did not exist.

[82] See Barton, Newell and Wilson (2003), pp. 53-55. The authors add high growth rates of the loan portfolio in relation to the growth rates of the real sector and capital adequacy ratios. The growth rate of the loan portfolio is not used in this analysis since the necessary sectoral data is not available. Capital adequacy ratios are not included as a result indicator since they are already used as a process indicator.

[83] For example if the government holds a "golden share", its ownership stake will be negligible while its influence over key business decisions such as a merger is significant.

[84] These two approaches resemble those used by La Porta, Lopez de Silanes and Schleifer (2002). The author's calculate the extent of state ownership for both approaches, and find that the two are highly correlated (above 90%). See La

privatization, it gives a better picture of the extent of state involvement in the banking sector. It is therefore the approach used in the present study. Again, the categorizations are to some extent subjective. For this study, state-owned banks are defined as banks where the government or a government agency holds more than 50% of voting rights or banks that are officially classified as state-owned.

To remove some of the subjectivity, the classification of the privatization process indicator is based on the extent of state-ownership under different policy regimes in selected countries.[85] The following categorizations are made: under a fully repressed system, state-owned banks hold more than 90% of assets of scheduled commercial banks; in a fully liberalized system, they hold less than 10% of total assets; in a partially repressed system, they hold 50-90% of assets; and in a partially liberalized system, between 10-50%.

Privatization of state-owned banks is associated with two effects that can be used as result indicators. First, private profit-seeking banks are regarded as more efficient than state-owned banks.[86] Therefore, following privatization, banks should be more profit-oriented, reflected in an increase in ROA. Second, state ownership of banks is associated with slower financial development, commonly measured by three different variables: commercial bank assets as a percentage of total bank assets, liquid liabilities as a percentage of GDP, and private credit as a percentage of GDP.[87]

The progress of reforms in institution building can be gauged by the extent to which the required institutions are in place. Among the most important institutions in a market-based banking system are accounting standards, capital adequacy requirements, a deposit insurance system, a supervisory framework, and a transparent licensing system. Integrating these institutions in a process indicator is not without problems, due to the qualitative nature of the evaluation. This is especially the case for transparent licensing, since regulators often have a certain degree of leeway in deciding which banks can enter the market. Consequently, this criterion is not included in the index. Capital adequacy requirements are also not included since they are already part of the process indicator for stabilization. Accounting standards, deposit insurance and the supervisory framework

Porta, Lopez de Silanes and Schleifer (2002), p. 269f. Therefore using the second indicator alone should not result in an undue loss of information.

[85] See Table 16 in the appendix for an overview of the countries.

[86] See Megginson (2005), pp. 1937-1941 for a discussion of the empirical evidence of the effects of state ownership of commercial banks.

[87] See La Porta, Lopez de Silanes and Schleifer (2002), p. 278 and p. 290.

are thus the three constituting elements used in the process indicator in this analysis.

For deposit insurance, the focus is on the existence of an explicit deposit insurance system in the country. In the index, an explicit deposit insurance system is taken as an indicator of a fully liberalized system. If no explicit deposit insurance system is present, the system is characterized as fully repressed. No further distinction is made between a partially repressed and a partially liberalized system.

Since it is outside the scope of this thesis to include all relevant accounting standards in the process indicator, the focus is on the recognition of NPLs because of their importance for the stability of the banking sector. The international standard is to recognize a loan as non-performing after one quarter of outstanding interest, which is indicative of a fully liberalized market-based system. On the other hand, the absence of a framework for recognizing NPLs is an indication of a fully repressed system.[88] A partially repressed system is defined as one where NPL standards exist, but are not enforced and compared to international best practice are very weak. In a largely liberalized system, an NPL classification system exists which is less stringent than the international best practice.

For the supervisory framework, the focus is on the independence and the powers of the bank regulator, and the scope of the legal and organizational arrangements. A fully repressed system has no independent bank regulator and the almost non-existent supervisory framework focuses on the compliance with government-imposed policies such as the distribution of directed credit. At the other end of the spectrum is a fully liberalized system where the supervisory agencies are independent and have far-reaching powers within the laws and regulations; the focus is more on the macro-management than the micro-management of the sector. A partly repressed system is taken to be one in which first attempts have been made to establish a regulatory and supervisory system, but the regulators are not always independent. In a partly liberalized system, most legal and organizational arrangements are established but they are not always applied.

There are several effects from upgrading the institutional framework. Better institutional standards are likely to increase the stability of the banking system. A possible effect is a lower level of NPLs.[89] A lower level of NPLs appears counterintuitive at first, because of the suggested tightening

[88] A case in point is the Chinese banking system where prior to the 1979 reforms banks handed out loans that were effectively grants; NPL recognition was consequently not an issue. See Lau (1999), p. 73f.

[89] Second-order effects of improved institutional quality are higher levels of investment and growth. See Aron (2000), p. 128f.

of accounting standards for the recognition of NPLs. However, in combination with deposit insurance, capital adequacy standards and a supervisory system, it is likely that banks will try to lower the level of NPLs in order to meet regulatory standards. For evaluating the progress with regard to NPLs, the same result criteria are used – 5% threshold and trend of NPLs – as for stabilization policies.

One of the main indicators of structural change in a banking sector is the lifting of entry barriers for new domestic and foreign banks. The following classifications are used for the process indicator. A fully repressed banking system is completely closed to new entrants. In a partially repressed system, entry guidelines exist but there are heavy restrictions on foreign players entering the market. In a largely liberalized system, the same restrictions apply to domestic and foreign players but foreign players may be subject to ownership caps when investing in domestic banks. A fully liberalized system is defined as one that offers a level playing field for the entry of both domestic and foreign players.[90]

Lowering the entry barriers can be interpreted as an option to enter the market. Thus, an increase in the number of banks can serve as a result indicator. However, simply looking at the number of banks might misrepresent the structural changes in the banking sector, if the new entrants remain small in comparison to the incumbents. Therefore, besides market shares, changes in the concentration of the sector have to be included. Common measures of concentration are the Herfindahl index and the M-concentration ratio.[91] Table 2 summarizes the proposed process and result indicators. Table 3 provides an overview of the classification of the variables for the process indicators and their attribution to different policy regimes. As already mentioned, the classification is to some extent subjective. Nevertheless it is the most feasible way to compare different countries and indicators.

---

[90] Taking changes of the entry regulations as the process indicator involves a certain degree of ambiguity since the effective changes depend on the implementation of the new regulation. Thus, there might be cases in which the entry is deregulated, but new competitors are nevertheless effectively barred from entering the sector through for example political pressure.

[91] The Herfindahl index is calculated by taking the sum of the squares of all banks, while the M-concentration ratio is the sum of the market shares of the largest banks, with "M" indicating the number of banks included. See International Monetary Fund (2002), p. 78.
Lifting of entry barriers can also affect interest rates. However, since the opening of the sector affects lending and deposit rates differently, it is not possible to specify the effects on the net interest margin ex-ante. See Chan and Hu (2000), p. 442.

Table 2. Overview of process and result indicators

	Indicators	
Process step	**Process**	**Results**
Liberalization		
Interest rate controls	Degree of interest rate setting by the government versus the market	(1) Lending rates/deposit rates (2) Net interest margin
Reserve requirements	Extent of effective reserve requirements	Credit-deposit ratio
Directed credit	Percentage of directed credit	Return on Assets
Stabilization	Status and enforcement of capital adequacy norms	Danger of financial distress: level of NPLs, trend of NPLs, ROA, net interest margin
Privatization	Assets of state-owned banks as percentage of total assets	(1) ROA (2) Financial development (2a) Commercial bank assets/total bank assets (2b) Liquid liabilities/GDP (2c) Private credit/GDP
Institution building	Development of accounting standards, deposit insurance and supervisory framework	(1) Level of NPLs (2) Trend of NPLs
Structural change	Degree of openness for new domestic and foreign players	(1) Market shares of bank groups (2) Concentration measures (2a) Herfindahl index (2b) M-concentration ratio

Table 3. Categorization of variables for the process indicators

	Liberalization					Institution building			
System	**Interest rate controls**	**Reserve requirements**	**Directed credit**	**Stabilization**	**Privatization**	**Deposit insurance**	**Accounting standards**	**Regulatory system**	**Structural change**
Full repression	Government sets all interest rates	Above 15%	Directed credit above 40%; very detailed prescriptions on deployment and interest rates	No international prudential norms applied	State-owned banks hold more than 90% of total assets	No explicit deposit insurance system	Accounting norms to recognize NPAs are either non-existent or not applied	No independent bank regulator; supervisory framework is almost non-existent - focus is on compliance with repressive policies	Banking system is closed to new entrants, or entry is limited to representative offices
Partially repressed	Interest rates vary within a band, or subject to a ceiling or floor	Between 10-15%	Directed credit between 20-40%; detailed guidelines	Basel I Standard not fully implemented or enforced	State-owned banks hold between 50-90% of assets	- - -	Very weak NPL rules (i.e. recognition of losses after only a year; roll over of bad loans possible)	Minimum supervisory and regulatory system is established, regulators are however not fully independent	Entry guidelines exists, heavy restrictions for foreign players
Largely liberalized	Some interest rates are completely market determined	Between 5-10%	Directed credit below 20%; interest rates for directed credit largely market determined	Basel I adopted and largely enforced	State-owned banks hold between 10-50% of assets	- - -	An accepted classification framework exists that is enforced; standards are however not yet best practice (f.ex. 90 day rule not applied)	Legal and organisational arrangements for regulation and supervision are established, but however not always applied	Ownership caps for foreigners (takeover not possible); licensening criteria are clearly formulated
Fully liberalized	Almost all interest rates market determined	Reserve requirements only as tools of monetary policy (below 5%)	No directed credit	Basel I fully implemented and enforced, significant progress in the adoption of Basel II standard	State-owned banks hold less than 10% of assets	Explicit deposit insurance system	Recognition of NPLs in line with international best practice	Independent supervisory agency with far-reaching powers (i.e. prompt-corrective action) acting within established regulations	Entry decisions based on transparent licensing process, if requirements are fulfilled free entry of domestic and foreign players

6.3.2 Construction of a liberalization index

The indicators discussed above focus on different individual aspects of the liberalization process. Integrating them into a single indicator provides a more holistic framework for evaluating the process. Financial liberalization is a multi-faceted process that can last several years. This makes it necessary for policy makers and economic agents alike to get an indication of where the process stands and what still remains to be done. An index of financial liberalization can help in this respect.

The literature contains several examples of financial liberalization indices covering different aspects of the liberalization process (Table 4). The focus is generally on variables that capture the progress of financial sector liberalization. An exception is the study of Quispe-Agnoli and McQuerry (2001), which focuses on variables that are proxies for liberalization results. Studies focusing on the liberalization process suffer from two shortcomings. First, some authors like Demetriades and Luintel (1997) and Kaminsky and Schmukler (2002) look at a very limited set of policy variables that mostly capture the reversal of repressive policies, such as the lowering of interest rate controls, credit allocation, or reserve requirements. However, just looking at the removal of repressionist policies does not take the complexity of the liberalization process into account – a process that requires further supporting elements, such as the creation of a regulatory structure. Second, some studies like Bandiera et al. (2000) and Laeven (2003) do not distinguish between the intensity of the policies. Instead, they assign binary values – typically 0 for repression and 1 for liberalization. The problem here is that many countries have in the past gradually liberalized their financial system by lifting restrictions over time. This cannot be accounted for using binary variables. Moreover, China is not included in any of the indices and India only infrequently, despite their rapidly growing economic importance.

Table 4. Overview of financial liberalization indices

Author(s)	Variables	Countries	Description
Demetriades/ Luintel (1997)	- Interest rate controls (fixed rate, ceiling or floor on deposit and lending rate) - Percentage of directed credit - Extent of statutory pre-emptions (reserve and liquidity ratio)	India	- Construction of an "Index of Financial Repression" from 1960 to 1991 - Variables are integrated using the method of principal components
Bandiera et al. (2000)	- Lowering of interest rate regulations - Reduction of reserve requirements - Lowering of directed credit rules - Privatization of state-owned banks - Strengthening of supervisory body - Liberalization of securities markets - Introduction of prudential regulation - International financial liberalization	Chile, Ghana, Indonesia, Korea, Malaysia, Mexico, Turkey, Zimbabwe	- Changes in the variables are captured with dummy variables (0 and 1) - Index is used to assess the impact of financial liberalization on financial savings from 1970-1994 - Variables are integrated using the method of principal components
Quispe-Agnoli/ McQuerry (2001)	- Average annual nominal interest rate - Commercial bank assets/total financial assets - Liquid liabilities/GDP - Private credit by commercial banks/GDP	Argentina, Brazil, Chile, Mexico and Peru	- Variables are used for an "Index of Banking Activity" that runs from 1980 to 2000 - Index measures changes in the activity, size and intermediation of the banking sector
Abiad/ Mody (2002)	- Credit controls - Interest rate controls - Entry barriers - Regulations and securites markets - Privatization - International financial transactions	35 countries (including India, excluding China)	- Variables are categorized as "fully repressed", "partially repressed", "partially liberalized" and "fully liberalized" - Index is used to test the existence of status-quo bias in financial reform
Kaminsky/ Schmuckler (2002)	- Liberalization of the capital account: regulations on offshore borrowing, multiple exchange rates, controls on capital outflows - Liberalization of domestic financial system: regulations on deposit and lending rates, allocation of credit, reserve requirements, foreign currency deposits - Liberalization of stock markets: acquisition of shares by foreigners, rules on repatriation of capital, interest and dividends	28 developed and developing countries (excluding India and China)	- Index runs from 1973 to 1999 - Each of the three areas is classified as "fully liberalized", "partially liberalized" and "repressed" - Index is used to make inferences about the occurrence of financial crises during times of financial liberalization
Laeven (2003)	- Deregulation of deposit and lending rates - Reduction of entry barriers for domestic and foreign banks - Reduction of reserve requirements - Reduction of credit controls and restrictions - Privatization of state-owned banks - Strenghtening of prudential regulations	Argentina, Brazil, Chile, India, Indonesia, Malaysia, Mexico, Pakistan, Peru, Philippines, Korea, Taiwan, Thailand	- Progress is captured with dummy variables that take a value of 1 in years without restrictions - Index runs from 1988 to 1998 and is used to measure the effect of financial liberalization on financing constraints of firms

Based on these observations, the financial liberalization index used in this thesis is constructed as follows. First, all five of the process elements identified are included to provide a holistic picture of the liberalization process. Second, the gradual nature of the process is accounted for by distinguishing between "fully repressed", "partly repressed", "partly liberalized", and "fully liberalized" systems. The different systems are assigned point scores: a fully repressed system receives 0 points, a partially repressed system 1 point, a largely liberalized one 2 points, and a fully liberalized one 3 points.[92] To remove some of the subjectivity in assigning point scores, the categorization guidelines from the previous section are employed (Table 3). Third, if more than one indicator exists for any one of

[92] This follows the approach of Abiad and Mody (2002). While the classification is to a certain extent subjective, it allows the comparison of different countries and policy environments.

the process elements – such as for the liberalization dimension, the average value of the sub-indicators is taken. Fourth, the five main process elements are equally weighted so that the overall index can have scores between 0 and 15 in any year.[93]

This index can be used to evaluate the process of financial liberalization – it comes close to what Bandiera et al. (2000) describe as the ideal index of financial liberalization by covering aspects of deregulation and institution building.[94] However, it does not take account of the effect of market failure on the indicators since it is possible that some state-intervention is needed to ensure a more efficient functioning of the financial sector. These issues are discussed in the next section.

6.3.3 Effects of market failure on indicators

The indicators discussed above are used to evaluate the progress of banking sector liberalization. The outcome will be interpreted in terms of absolute progress – i.e. how far liberalization has progressed in one country – and in relative terms – i.e. how far liberalization has progressed in comparison to another country. Yet these comparisons are only meaningful on the assumption that no market failures occur. Since it is unlikely that this assumption is fulfilled, it is necessary to adjust the process and result indicators to take market failures into account.[95]

In allocation theory, market failure refers to

> "[...] the failure of a more or less idealized system of price-market institutions to sustain 'desirable' activities or to estop [sic] 'undesirable' activities. The desirability of an activity, in turn, is evaluated relative to the solution values of some explicit or implicit maximum-welfare problem."[96]

As outlined in section 4.2.1.1, market failures occur where the conditions for the proper functioning of the market are not met. Due to monopoly power, information asymmetry, or external effects, the market will not

93 In addition, an index based on the method of principal components is constructed that includes all process elements.

94 See Bandiera et al. (2000), p. 242f.

95 For example, with respect to the process indicators, market failure can make it necessary not to achieve the full degree of liberalization. With respect to the result indicators, market failure can influence the assumed cause-effect relationships so that the expected results will not occur at all or not occur to the expected extent.

96 Bator (1958), p. 351.

provide efficient outcomes. This provides a rationale for government intervention to improve the market solution.[97] However, market failure is a necessary, but not a sufficient condition for state intervention. It is equally important that state intervention provides a better solution, since "[...] the deficiency of the 'visible hand' may be larger than that of the 'invisible' one."[98] Below, relevant market failures and their effect on the previously identified indicators are discussed.

The process indicator for liberalization comprises three different policies: interest rate restrictions, statutory pre-emptions, and directed credit. Interest rate restrictions are generally perceived to be an impediment to the proper functioning of the market mechanism and consequently do not constitute a market failure. The general policy recommendation as discussed above is to abolish them to enhance the efficiency of the market. Stiglitz (1994), however, points to the danger of excessive risk-taking by banks in an environment of fully liberalized interest rates. In the presence of explicit or implicit deposit insurance, banks can compete for funds on the basis of the highest interest rate, since the government guarantees the deposits. To pay for the interest rates on the deposits, banks have to take higher risks which in turn reduces the stability of the banking system.[99] While it is not implausible that liberalized interest rates induce banks to take higher risks that result in market failure as argued by Stiglitz, it is questionable whether interest rate restrictions on the deposit and/or lending side are the most efficient solution. Capital adequacy rules or net worth requirements are commonly used measures that provide disincentives for excessive risk-taking. If these policies are already in place, there should be no need for further restrictions on the interest rate. Therefore market failure is not accounted for in the process indicator for interest rate restrictions.

Statutory pre-emptions can either constitute a monetary policy instrument or a means of financial repression. In the context of monetary policy, reserve and liquidity requirements should be seen as tools that help the central bank to supply a stable monetary system, which is a public good. The possible uses of statutory pre-emptions can thus differ profoundly. It is not possible to distinguish between that part of statutory pre-emptions that is used for monetary policy and that which is used for pre-empting funds for the government, so the assumption is made that effective reserve requirements below 5% enable the central bank to carry out its monetary policy. The more developed countries with the exception of Japan have an

[97] See Freebairn (1998), p. 67.
[98] Balcerowicz (1995), p. 174.
[99] See Stiglitz (1994), p. 39.

effective reserve requirement well below 5%.[100] Consequently, a level of up to 5% is defined as fully liberalized for the purpose of this study. Since the 5% threshold is sufficient to provide the public good of a stable monetary system, no adjustments for market failure are needed for the process indicator.

The market failure argument for a directed credit program is that banks may not allocate credit to the projects with the highest returns. The total return of a project is the sum of the expected profits of the bank and the entrepreneur. Banks exclusively focus on the maximization of their expected return and, as a consequence, will not necessarily finance the projects with the highest total return. An additional problem is that small firms with insufficient collateral might not receive funding despite being innovative or delivering high returns.[101] The rationale for a directed credit program is thus to overcome credit rationing for projects that provide either high returns or high benefits from spillover effects.[102]

This problem can be especially pervasive in rural credit markets. Besley (1994) points out two features of rural credit markets in developing countries that may warrant directed credit for the agricultural sector. First, the lack of assets in rural markets that can serve as collateral, combined with poorly defined property rights, makes the appropriation of collateral in the event of default complicated for banks. Second, agricultural incomes are affected by weather shocks. Since these weather shocks are regional in nature, local banks cannot diversify this risk, which results in a significant increase of the loan portfolio's riskiness.[103]

The failure of banks to provide credit in these instances is an indication that the necessary condition for government intervention is met. The question then arises of whether government intervention can improve the outcome. This is by no means clear, since governments – as with setting inter-

---

[100] See Table 15 in the appendix.

[101] From banks' point of view, screening of projects would be a substitute to collateral. Banks however cannot recoup the cost of projects that were screened and rejected. Consequently, they will under-invest in project screening. See Manove, Padilla and Pagano (2001) for a discussion.

[102] See Joshi and Little (1997), p. 135; Stiglitz (1994), p. 30 and p. 42; Vittas (1991), p. 5. Stiglitz and Weiss (1981) show that credit rationing can occur if the profit maximizing interest rate for the bank is below the market clearing interest rate. See Stiglitz and Weiss (1981), p. 394.
Coco (2000) points out that the existence of collateral is only a necessary, but not a sufficient condition to overcome credit rationing. Factors such as the type of competition, the amount of collateral or the possibility to screen projects are also important. See Coco (2000), p. 209.

[103] See Besley (1994), p. 31f.

est rates – also face information problems. Credit rationing in private capital markets therefore does not necessarily constitute a rationale for the provision of credit by governments in all settings.[104] Based on countries' experiences with allocative controls, Vittas (1991) argues that their scope should be limited and accompanied by improvements in the legal and accounting systems.[105]

The potential problems with directed credit have to be weighed against the potential benefits. In countries like India or China, in which a large agricultural sector and small-scale industries compete for funds with large industrial enterprises, there might be scope for a directed credit program under the pre-condition of efficient delivery.[106] For India for example, Naastepad (2001) finds significant positive macroeconomic spillover effects from priority sector lending to agriculture and small-scale industries.[107] Consequently, there is an argument based on market failure in these countries to direct a certain percentage of bank credit to priority sectors.

How high should this percentage be, and what sectors should receive it? A starting point could be to reserve bank credit commensurate to the share of GDP of these sectors – for example 22% in the case of agriculture in India and 15% in China.[108] However, it would be necessary to adjust this percentage downward for the capital intensity of the sectors and the amount of capital that these sectors would receive in the absence of a directed credit program. Unfortunately this approach is impractical, since the amount of capital these sectors would receive in the absence of a directed credit program is hard to estimate.

A more feasible approach is to take the actual size-wise distribution of credit and assume that priority sector companies with credit amounts above a certain cut-off size would be able to receive credit on regular terms, since larger loans lower the per-unit fixed cost of evaluating the

---

[104] See Joshi and Little (1997), p. 126f.; Stiglitz (1989b), p. 202.

[105] See Vittas (1991), p. 6.

[106] Agriculture accounted for about 22% of GDP in India and 15% in China in 2003. See Deutsche Bank Research (2005), p. 3.

[107] See Naastepad (2001), p. 500. There are different reasons for credit rationing for small-scale industries and agriculture. As previously mentioned, the problem for small-scale industries is one of asymmetric information between borrower and lender, and lack of collateral. For agriculture the lack of collateral and the non-diversifiable exposure to (weather) shocks are the main issues. See Naastepad (2001), p. 479f.

[108] Setting the directed credit target based on the employed capital in the defined priority sectors is not feasible since the capital share might reflect credit rationing for certain sectors.

debtor. Thus the assumption is that companies in priority sectors that currently receive credit below a certain cut-off size would not receive this credit in the absence of a directed credit program. The percentage of credit that goes to these sectors would then be an indication of the necessary amount of directed credit. In India, where a breakdown of credit sizes is available, the share of credit below Rs 2 lakh (Rs 200,000) that goes to agriculture, artisans and small scale industries is about 6%. If the credit amount is increased to Rs 5 lakh, about 8% of total credit would go to priority sectors.[109] This is fairly close to the recommendation of the *Narasimham Committee*, which suggested a priority sector target of 10%.[110] Therefore, the 10% percentage goal is considered to be non-repressive for large, less developed economies.

The indicator for the process of stabilization is the application of capital adequacy standards. As discussed further above, the Basel Capital Accord recommends a CRAR level of 8%. Since the risk level in emerging markets is likely to be higher due to the higher vulnerability to exogenous shocks, the 8% threshold might not be sufficient. However, arguments abound in the literature about the need for a higher capital adequacy ratio in developing countries due to higher economic and financial volatility. Unfortunately there is little guidance on how they should actually be set.[111] A notable exception comes from the World Bank that suggests capital adequacy ratios of up to 20% for developing countries.[112] Thus, a range for capital adequacy standards for developing countries lies between 8 and 20%. Since it is difficult to specify precisely the "correct" capital adequacy level, it is assumed that in a fully liberalized system in a developing country, the capital adequacy standards should be above 8% to account for market failure. If the capital adequacy standards follow the international practice of 8%, the system is considered here "partially liberalized".

The efficiency of state-owned banks is commonly lower than that of private banks. This can be interpreted as a case of state failure to which privatization is advocated as a solution. There are, however, exceptions. Hawkins and Mihaljek (2001) point out that state-owned banks can play a useful role in serving poor customers and those living in remote areas of large countries. They can also extend credit to agriculture and small and

[109] See Reserve Bank of India (2004a), pp. 115-120. Rs 2 lakh are about 3,400 EUR and Rs 5 lakh about 8,500 EUR (based on an exchange rate of 58.54 Rs/EUR as of June 30th 2006).

[110] See Government of India (1998), p. 26.

[111] See Brownbridge and Kirkpatrick (2000), p. 15; Caprio, Atiyas and Hanson (1994), p. 422; Honohan (1997), p. 20; Rojas-Suarez (2001), p. 35.

[112] See World Bank (1997b), p. 69.

medium-sized enterprises. These rationales are essentially the same as those given for directed credit programs. Far-reaching financial liberalization does not eliminate the need to explicitly focus on these parts of the population, since liberalization has no built-in mechanism to induce banks to target less advantaged groups. India and China are both examples of countries with large rural populations and a high percentage of poor people; in these countries, state-owned banks may be in a position to overcome market failure by extending the reach of banking services.[113]

But state-owned banks are no panacea. In India, despite a policy of social banking, poorer households in rural areas have only limited access to formal sources of finance.[114] Furthermore, there are marked regional differences in the distribution of financial services, with households in poorer areas in India having lower access levels to formal sources of finance.[115] The same is true for China, were informal sources of finance remain a major source of credit, especially in rural areas, despite the development of a formal financial sector. While microfinance institutions can be an alternative provider of financial services to rural areas, most of these institutions cannot operate on a stand-alone basis; like self-help groups, they need linkage to banks.[116]

Thus there is a mixed picture regarding the privatization of state-owned banks. In the urban and semi-urban centers the affluent population could be served by private-sector banks, but state-owned banks are still needed to provide banking services to the rural areas as well as to the urban poor. Despite their mixed record in providing banking services to poorer parts of the population, there is still a need for state-owned banks to provide finan-

[113] See Hawkins and Mihaljek (2001), p. 15; Krahnen and Schmidt (1994), p. 80.

[114] For example, 70% of farmers with landholding below one acre do not have a bank account and 87% do not have access to formal credit and as a consequence have to resort to informal sources such as moneylenders. See Srivastava and Basu (2004), p. 9.

[115] See Srivastava and Basu (2004), p. 9f. This is highlighted by the distribution of bank branches in India (Figure 40). While the SBI and the other nationalized banks have 40% of their branches in rural areas, the Indian private sector banks with their much smaller branch network had only 18% of their branches in rural areas and the foreign banks none at all.

[116] See Srivastava and Basu (2004), p. 16. The linkages between banks, microfinance institutions and self-help groups are exemplified well by ICICI Bank's program in Tamil Nadu. See Prahalad (2005), pp. 302-312. For an overview of the importance of informal finance in India and China see Tsai (2005).

cial services – at least until private sector initiatives such as microfinance institutions take hold.[117]

If public-sector banks have a role in countering market failure, what share of the market should they have? The theoretical decision rule is that public sector banks should only cover those clients that cannot be profitably served by private sector banks, either because they are poor or live in remote areas. The share of bankable assets that these parts of the population hold should be used to approximate the necessary extent of state-owned banks. However, since these customers are often outside the formal banking system, this number cannot be estimated. An alternative approach is needed.

One alternative is to take the share of credit and deposits that is provided by state-owned banks in rural and semi-urban areas. In India, for example, private sector banks and foreign banks have only about 2,900 branches in these areas, compared to about 44,500 from state-owned banks.[118] It can be assumed that most of these areas cannot be profitably served by private banks, especially since state-owned banks already have a strong position in the market. Currently about 28% of total deposits and 19% of total credit in India are held by state-owned banks in these areas.[119] Depending on whether a deposit or a credit perspective is taken, the share of state-owned banks should be between 19% and 28%. For the calculations in this study, the average of these two values – 24% – is taken as the share of assets state-owned banks should hold for reasons of market failure. These numbers are based on data from India, but it is assumed that they mirror the situation in China, where there are similar problems of credit delivery to less privileged areas, as pointed out by Tsai (2005).[120]

Obviously, this is only a crude approximation since it assumes that banking services could not be offered profitably in those areas by private sector banks. It also assumes that all city-dwellers have access to the formal banking sector, which is most likely not the case. Furthermore, the "justified" share of state-ownership is likely to change in line with overall economic change. Yet, despite these limitations, the figure provides a first

[117] The endogenous growth theory provides a further argument for state-owned banks and more specifically branching requirements. Based on the endogenous growth theory, financial deepening can increase the growth rate of the economy. Therefore, the social return of providing banking services to underserved regions can exceed the private return of the respective bank so that branching requirements can help to reduce a market failure. See Sen and Vaidya (1997), p. 43 footnote 4.

[118] See Figure 40 in the appendix.

[119] See Table 17 in the appendix.

[120] See Tsai (2005), pp. 127-135.

approximation of the extent of state-ownership that is justified due to market failures.[121]

Strong institutions are necessary in both developed and developing countries to ensure the proper functioning of the banking system. Indeed, developing countries are likely to need stronger institutions because of the pervasiveness of market failures, which require extensive regulations.[122] The three relevant institutions in the context of the indicators discussed above are accounting standards with respect to NPLs, deposit insurance, and the supervisory system.

For accounting standards, the need to converge to international standards for the recognition of NPLs has been postulated. Since accounting standards are largely based on conventions, changes in the stringency of NPL recognition would not address market failure but merely change the yardstick for the evaluation of the business. Therefore, no adjustments will be made to the process indicator.

The process indicator for deposit insurance tests if the country has an explicit deposit insurance system or not – but the level of insurance is not taken into account. Like all insurance, deposit insurance can lead to moral hazard due to asymmetric information between the insured (the bank) and the insurer (the deposit insurance agency). Deposit insurance can induce banks to take higher risks, since it provides protection for depositors in the event of a crisis. This danger has to be weighted against the systemic risk of bank runs that may occur when depositors lose confidence in the solvency of a bank in a system without deposit insurance. Both cases are instances of market failure. In general, protection of depositors takes priority over the danger of increased risk-taking by banks, since this moral hazard can be mitigated by regulatory standards such as capital adequacy or net worth requirements that increase the costs to bank owners in the case of failure. Since it is possible to mitigate the effects, no explicit adjustments are made to the indicator to account for market failure from deposit insurance.

For the supervisory framework, the focus was on the existence of an independent supervisory agency with extensive powers to act within the established legal and organizational framework of bank supervision. Since a strong and independent supervisory body is a prerequisite for the proper

[121] Even if state-owned banks are regarded as a temporary second-best solution, they should be subjected to the same supervisory standards and prudential regulations as private-sector institutions to mitigate some of the downsides of state-ownership. See Hawkins and Mihaljek (2001), p. 15.

[122] See Rodrik (2000), p. 93.

functioning of the market mechanism in the banking sector, no adjustments for market failure need to be made.

The process of structural change in the banking sector is modeled by the possibility of entry for both domestic and foreign players. Structural changes are likely to increase competition in the banking sector, which is generally regarded as efficiency-enhancing. Increased competition can, however, also have a downside: it reduces profits, which in turn may lead to the decreased stability of banks and the increased risk of insolvency.[123] At the same time, in this context the failure of banks can also be interpreted as a sign of a healthy market process in which not every player in the market survives. To mitigate the downside, regulators can introduce safeguards such as capital adequacy requirements, deposit insurance, or net worth requirements. Decisions to limit entry into the banking sector are, if adequate safeguards are in place, mainly motivated by political arguments and not by market failure. Therefore no adjustments are made to the process indicator for structural change on market failure grounds.

Market failures should therefore be an important consideration during the process of financial liberalization, especially in developing countries such as India or China. The need for the provision of banking services through state-owned banks, a certain level of directed credit to provide funds for underserved parts of the economy, the need to have higher capital adequacy standards because of higher risks are the key considerations. Table 5 gives an overview of the indicators for the analysis, including the necessary adjustments for market failure.

Having identified possible indicators for the process and results, the discussion now turns to the overall effects of liberalization. In the next section, hypotheses are suggested on the effects of banking sector liberalization on the fulfillment of the functions of the banking sector and on macroeconomic aggregates.

---

[123] See Stiglitz (1994), p. 45f. Another argument against too much competition especially from foreign banks is a variation of the infant industry argument according to which small domestic banks may be at a disadvantage against large foreign banks. See Stiglitz (1994), p. 49.

Table 5. Effects of market failure on the indicators

Process step	Indicators: Process	Indicators: Results	Intervention necessary because of market failure? No	Yes	If yes, necessary changes
Liberalization					
Interest rate controls	Degree of interest rate setting by the government versus the market	(1) Lending rates/deposit rates (2) Net interest margin	×		
Reserve requirements	Extent of effective reserve requirements	Credit-deposit ratio	×		
Directed credit	Percentage of directed credit	Return on Assets		✓	10% directed credit in large, rural countries
Stabilization	Status and enforcement of capital adequacy norms	Danger of financial distress: level of NPLs, trend of NPLs, ROA, net interest margin		✓	Higher capital adequacy standards (>8%) because of higher risks
Privatization	Assets of state-owned banks as percentage of total assets	(1) ROA (2) Financial development (2a) Commercial bank assets/total bank assets (2b) Liquid liabilities/GDP (2c) Private credit/GDP		✓	About 25% state ownership in poor, large countries with large rural populations
Institution building	Development of accounting standards, deposit insurance and supervisory framework	(1) Level of NPLs (2) Trend of NPLs	×		
Structural change	Degree of openness for new domestic and foreign players	(1) Market shares of bank groups (2) Concentration measures (2a) Herfindahl index (2b) M-concentration ratio	×		

6.4 Macroeconomic effects of banking sector liberalization

In the previous sections, indicators for the process and results of banking sector liberalization were identified and the effects of market failure on these indicators discussed. While these indicators give an indication of the microeconomic performance of banks in areas such as profitability and stability, they do not indicate whether the banking sector can fulfill its macroeconomic functions better or worse. As discussed in section 4.1, the main functions of the banking sector are the mobilization of savings and the allocation of savings to investment projects. This should help to foster economic growth. This section identifies possible indicators for evaluating the effects of liberalization on these banking sector functions and develops hypotheses on their effects. The focus is on the assumptions of the standard McKinnon-Shaw framework presented in section 4.3. As such, this section directly summarizes the relevant cause-effect relationships and discusses potential indicators without delving into the theoretical foundations.

In the McKinnon-Shaw model, a main element of financial repression is artificially low deposit and lending rates to provide cheap credit to favored borrowers and the government. The resulting policy recommendation is to increase the real interest rate, which should increase the propensity to save. Positive effects on the savings rate can also come from increased competition in the banking system, which can result in the creation of more attractive savings instruments. A higher interest rate and more attractive savings instruments should increase the propensity to defer current consumption and increase savings, which can be measured by the ratio of saving to GDP.

However, an increase in the level of savings does not necessarily stem from an absolute increase in saving. It can also be the result of shifts in the structure of saving. Two likely effects must be controlled for. These are a shift from savings in the curb market to the organized banking sector, and a shift from physical savings to financial savings.

Hypothesis 1:
Liberalizing the banking sector increases the saving rate and the stock of savings.

Liberalizing the banking sector should have two effects on the allocation of capital to investment projects: an increase in the level of capital and an increase in the efficiency of capital allocation.

An increase in the level of capital is expected for two reasons. First, as discussed above, it is hypothesized that financial liberalization increases the amount of savings that are intermediated through the organized financial sector. Second, the lowering of statutory pre-emptions means that fewer funds are directed towards the financing of the budget deficit and more capital is available for investment projects. The increase of the level of capital can be measured by the level of private capital to GDP or credit to the private sector to GDP.

Hypothesis 2:
Liberalizing the banking sector increases the availability of capital.

Besides providing a higher level of credit, a liberalized banking sector is likely to be more efficient in allocating funds. This is the result of lower directed credit rules and increased competition. The rationale for priority sector credit is to provide funding for sectors with high social but low economic returns, and to support sectors that would otherwise not receive funding. Therefore, it can be assumed that after liberalization banks will gradually shift their lending portfolio away from priority sectors.

The second effect leading to an enhanced efficiency of capital allocation is increased competition in the aftermath of financial liberalization. With new competitors entering the sector and with banks under pressure from capital markets to improve results, there are strong incentives for management to actively look for the most promising investment opportunities and to upgrade their credit evaluation skills. Overall, these effects should lead to a more efficient allocation of investment funds as measured by the incremental capital-output ratio (ICOR).[124]

Hypothesis 3:
Liberalization of the banking sector increases the efficiency of capital allocation.

Reducing repressionist policies should help to increase the level of funds intermediated through the banking sector either through higher savings or by making informal curb markets less attractive. This increases financial development, which is in turn associated with economic growth. Standard measures of financial development are the ratio of liquid liabilities to GDP, and the share of deposit money bank assets of total financial assets. The ratio of liquid liabilities to GDP is a measure of financial depth that shows the size of the formal financial system. The share of deposit money banks' assets gives an indication of the importance of commercial banks, which allegedly provide better risk management and investment services than the central bank, for example.[125]

Hypothesis 4:
Banking sector liberalization positively influences financial development by increasing financial depth and the importance of deposit money banks.

---

[124] See World Bank (1989), p. 31. The ICOR is the investment ratio divided by the real growth rate; it is calculated as (Gross fixed capital formation$_1$ / GDP$_1$)/ (GDP$_1$ / GDP$_0$ -1). It measures the investment needed for an additional unit of GDP growth.

[125] See King and Levine (1993), p. 718; Wachtel (2001), p. 342.

Financial liberalization and the associated financial development are likely to contribute to higher economic growth. According to the endogenous growth theory, higher savings and investments should have a positive effect on economic growth, as discussed in section 4.1.3.

Hypothesis 5:
The liberalization of the banking sector causes through a higher level of financial development an increase in the growth rate.

To test these hypotheses, econometric tests are conducted, in which the liberalization process index serves as the independent variable. Since the macroeconomic variables under consideration are not only influenced by liberalization, further variables such as economic growth or GDP per capita are included in the analysis. This provides a clearer picture of the effects of banking sector liberalization on macroeconomic aggregates.

6.5 Conclusion

The aim of this chapter was to provide a comprehensive framework for the management of banking sector liberalization, based upon transformation studies and the financial liberalization literature. While the general transformation process elements are applicable to the banking sector, it is necessary to take the special nature of banks' business into account when formulating a transformation strategy. Important pre-conditions that arise from banks' role as intermediaries are the existence of a stable operating environment and of a certain institutional capacity for supervision.

Consequently, the framework for banking sector liberalization has been defined in accordance with the general recommendations and process steps for the overall economy, adjusting for the specific nature of a banking sector. A case in point is institution building. For the overall economy, it is necessary to build up an institutional framework. For the banking sector, however, more specialized institutions are necessary, such as a regulatory agency. The key insights from these recommendations have been summarized in a number of qualitative propositions for the management of the transformation process.

Managing these changes not only entails questions of speed and sequencing. Equally important are political economy factors. These can have a profound influence on the reform process. Interest groups and the fiscal situation of a country are two of the most important – they may influence a range of policy changes, including directed credit programs, privatization, and recapitalization of banks.

Although the propositions are certainly helpful in evaluating the broad outlines of banking sector liberalization in a country, they do not indicate where a country stands in the process, and what the results are so far. For this, indicators along the process steps have been identified and the cause-and-effect relationships discussed. The different process indicators were combined into an overall process index that allows an evaluation of the liberalization progress over time. In a further step, the possible influence of market failures on the liberalization program was discussed, as well as necessary adjustments.

Banking sector liberalization not only affects the banking sector, but also the rest of the economy. In a final step, the effects of banking sector liberalization on macroeconomic aggregates were therefore discussed and hypotheses on the expected results postulated.

In the next section, all of this – the propositions, process and result indicators, as well as the hypotheses on the macro-effects – are used to provide a comprehensive evaluation of the liberalization of the banking sectors in India and China.

7 Evaluation of banking sector liberalization in India and China

In this chapter, the framework and the identified indicators developed in the previous chapter are used to evaluate the liberalization of the banking sectors in India and China. The assessment begins with a qualitative evaluation according to the propositions for liberalizing a banking sector. This is followed by a quantitative evaluation of the process and the results at the sector level. Finally, the overall macroeconomic effects are tested (Table 6). The combined results provide a basis for the discussion of further reform steps in the following chapter.

Table 6. Overview of tests conducted in the chapter

Evaluation	Section	Description	Basis for evaluation	Categories
Qualitative	7.1	Discussion if the postulated propositions have been fulfilled	Propositions established in sections 6.2.1 to 6.2.3.2	Not fulfilled, partly fulfilled, fulfilled
Quantitative *Sector level*	7.2.1	Discussion of the status of the liberalization process and results along the transformation steps	Process and result indicators (overview in table 2 and 5)	Process indicators: fully repressed, partly repressed, partly liberalized, fully liberalized (table 3)
Macro level	7.2.2	Test of the hypotheses postulated in section 6.4 (1) India and China (1980-2004)	Liberalization index based on aggregated process indicators	Index values run from 0 to 1
		(2) India (1960-2004)	Liberalization index based on variables for interest rate controls, statutory pre-emptions and directed credit	Index values run from 0 to 1

7.1 Qualitative evaluation

The propositions derived from the reform experiences of transition and developing countries in section 6.2 form the basis for the qualitative evaluation of the liberalization process that follows. The fulfillment of the propositions is first discussed separately for India and China, then the two countries are compared. The focus in this section is merely on the fulfillment of the propositions and not on the absolute progress made. This is covered in the next section.

Proposition 1:
Macroeconomic stability and a basic institutional framework that includes supervision and regulation of banks must be in place before beginning the liberalization of the banking sector.

The trigger for the liberalization of the Indian economy was the balance-of-payment crisis in 1991. The worst imbalances in terms of inflation and the budget deficit were quickly brought under control, so that the first reforms in the banking sector in 1992/1993 were conducted in an environment of relative stability. India could insulate itself from the effects of the Asian crisis, so that the overall reform process since 1991 has taken place in a favorable macroeconomic environment.

In terms of its institutional framework, India has also fulfilled the precondition. The existence of private sector banks ensured that a supervisory capacity and a regulatory framework were in place.[1] This proposition is thus fulfilled in India.

The trigger for the gradual liberalization of the Chinese economy in 1978 was neither a political nor an economic crisis. Rather, the liberalization was caused by a general desire for market-oriented reforms resulting from the difficulty of managing a planning system, higher growth rates in neighboring economies, and necessary directional changes after the Cultural Revolution.[2] The general macroeconomic environment was very favorable at the outset of reforms, with GDP growth of almost 8% and inflation below 5% in 1980.[3]

At the same time, the institutional framework for supervision in China was insufficient because of the legacy of the mono-banking system. The mono-bank served as an administrative unit and not as a profit-oriented commercial bank, so a supervisory system and regulatory framework were not in place.[4] The first proposition is therefore only partially fulfilled in China.

---

[1] The overall institutional framework in India was fairly advanced as well at the start of the reforms in 1991. The basis of the Indian legal system is the British Common Law. While the enforcement of the law might at times be problematic due to a backlog of cases in the judicial system, the necessary elements were well in place.

[2] See Chow (2004), p. 128f.

[3] See International Monetary Fund (2006b); Kusic, Zhang and Cvijanovic (2003), p. 1.

[4] In China the overall institutional framework was also far less developed than in India especially due to the deficiencies of the legal system. The two primary reasons are that the traditional Chinese legal system is based on informal social rela-

Proposition 2:
Interest rate liberalization should be pursued in a sequential manner by first liberalizing wholesale interest rates, then lending interest rates, and finally deposit interest rates.

In India, the liberalization of interest rates followed the general prescription. Initial attempts to liberalize wholesale rates started in the late 1980s. After the start of the economic reforms in 1991, lending rates were liberalized before deposit rates. There was only a brief period of about a year between the initial liberalization of lending and deposit rates, so the adjustment period was fairly short. However, the proposition as such is fulfilled for India.

China also followed the general policy recommendation by first liberalizing wholesale rates, followed by lending rates. At the end of 2005, deposit rates were still largely set by the government. Even though the liberalization of interest rates has not come ended yet, the proposition is fulfilled since the general sequence has been followed.

Proposition 3:
A directed credit program should be phased out using a dual-track approach, with a fixed nominal volume target for credit on the plan track.

In India, despite the recommendation of the Narasimham Committee to lower the directed credit target to 10%, it continues to stand at 40% for domestic banks and 32% for foreign banks. While the overall target is unchanged, the burden has been somewhat lowered by enlarging the definition of priority sectors, increasing the interest rates on priority sector loans and enabling banks to make up the shortfall through contributions to the National Bank for Agriculture and Rural Development in the case of domestic banks and to the Small Industries Development Bank of India in the case of foreign banks.[5] India does not currently plan to abolish the directed credit program. Thus the proposition is not fulfilled.

The main instrument of directed credit in China was the credit plan that ensured that credit allocation was under control of various levels of government. Therefore, the abolishment of the credit plan in 1998 was a major

---

tions (*guanxi*) to ensure fulfillment of contracts so that by Western standards it may be considered a "semi-legal system", and that the Communist Party is *de-facto* above the law since it claims absolute power to rule China. See Chow (1997), p. 322 and Chow (2004), p. 145.

[5] See Reserve Bank of India (2005c), p. 16.

step in reducing the system of directed credit.[6] In legal terms, directed credit has been abolished in China; however, it is questionable whether it has also been abolished in practice. Thus, for example, state-owned enterprises still receive a disproportionate share of credit.[7]

This pattern is also found in other transition countries. However, longer established relationships between state-owned enterprises and state-owned banks only offer a partial explanation for China. A more important factor is that the state can still require banks to make loans – even to heavily-indebted state-owned enterprises – for specific profitable projects.[8] So the proposition is at best partially fulfilled for China: the program was not abolished in a dual-track manner and the state retains influence over credit allocation.

Proposition 4:
Statutory pre-emptions should exclusively serve monetary policy purposes. If their level is not commensurate for that purpose, they should be reduced in a phased manner.

In India, statutory pre-emptions have been gradually reduced. The RBI has the declared goal of bringing both the CRR and the SLR to their statutory minimum level of 3% and 25% respectively. This has almost been achieved: in 2005, the CRR stood just above the minimum level while the SLR was the statutory minimum of 25%. This progress is mirrored by the reduction in the effective reserve requirement – this stood at a high of 17% in 1989, but was reduced to 7% in 2004.[9] The proposition is therefore fulfilled.

China has no legal upper or lower limits for reserve and liquidity requirements. Therefore the effective reserve requirements have to be used to evaluate progress in this dimension. From 1985 – the first year, for which data is available for China – until 2004, the effective reserve requirements have been lowered from 33% to 17%. While this is certainly indicative of a reduction in a phased manner, it is questionable whether this level of reserve requirements serves exclusively as an instrument of monetary policy – especially since the level is far higher than in other Asian countries. Thus the high level of reserve requirements could either stem from a lack of indirect mechanisms of monetary policy in China or

[6] See Kusic, Zhang and Cvijanovic (2003), p. 9.

[7] See Allen, Qian and Qian (2005a), p. 16; Bai et al. (1999), p. 51; Lardy (2000), p. 35.

[8] See Lardy (2000), p. 40.

[9] See Table 15 in the appendix.

from the use of banks' resources to extract funds for the budget. Since it is not possible to rule out the latter possibility, the proposition is only partly fulfilled for China.

Proposition 5:
Resolve legacy non-performing loans via a "once-and-for-all" stabilization program and recapitalize banks to meet minimum capital standards.

During the 1990s, India embarked on a program of extensive bank recapitalizations. However, the stabilization program resulted in significant moral hazard, since several banks received more than four capital injections. Even though certain conditions for the capital injections were laid out in a Memorandum of Understanding between the management of the banks and the RBI, these conditions were not enforced, so no credible threats existed for underperforming banks.[10]

Chinese banks have also been recapitalized several times. This is especially the case for the Big Four banks, recapitalized three times between 1998 and 2005. The experience in China and India shows that the state-owned banks are deemed to be "too large to fail": government will provide fresh capital when needed. Bankruptcy is in such a situation not a credible threat. The proposition is therefore both in India and China not fulfilled.

Proposition 6:
Privatize state-owned banks when they are not needed to address market failure and the necessary pre-conditions are in place. Foreign banks should be allowed as strategic partners; they are able to quickly upgrade the skill level to international standards.

The environment for the privatization of state-owned banks in India was in place early on; some private sector banks continued to operate in India even after the two waves of nationalization, and the first efforts to upgrade the regulatory system started in the early 1990s. Hence it is not surprising that the government reduced its holdings in several state-owned banks

---

[10] The Working Group on Restructuring Weak Public Sector Banks pointed out that "although such failures to achieve agreed targets or to fulfill commitments were frequent, there never were any penalties for such failures. Banks reporting operating losses were, no doubt, barred from opening new branches, recruitment of staff and fresh capital expenditure without RBI approval, but these restrictions did not serve as a disciplining measure as, in any case, they were already overstaffed and were in no position to undertake branch expansion or to incur any major capital expenditure." Reserve Bank of India (1999), section 5.4.

early on in the reform process. The partial privatization of the SBI in 1993 marked the first in a series of disinvestments. However, the government still has the majority ownership position in all banks that were state-owned at the beginning of the reform process in 1991 and is so far determined to keep the public sector character of state-owned banks. Therefore the selling of equity stakes should be interpreted as a measure for raising capital, and not for relinquishing control. In addition, a 10% cap on voting rights limits participation by foreigners.[11] Even though state-owned banks may currently still be needed to offer banking services to parts of the population that live in rural areas or are poor, their current share of total assets and their overall size is not commensurate with this goal. The proposition is thus not fulfilled for India.

In China, the first partial privatization of a Big Four bank was the global listing of the China Construction Bank in late 2005, which was followed by the Bank of China in mid-2006. Foreign investors can take stakes of up to 20% in Chinese banks, with the overall ownership cap in Chinese banks for foreigners standing at 25%. Despite divesting its holdings, the government seems committed to retaining majority ownership of the large state-owned banks. The proposition is thus not fulfilled in China.

Proposition 7:
Capital adequacy rules, transparent accounting standards, a supervisory system and deposit insurance are indispensable institutions for a market-based banking system and must be created during the transition process.

Shortly after the start of banking sector reforms in 1992/93, the RBI issued guidelines to upgrade the institutional framework of the banking sector in India. Important features were the introduction of capital adequacy norms in line with international standards and more stringent accounting rules in the area of non-performing loans. The supervisory system was strengthened by the establishment of the Board of Financial Supervision in 1994, the introduction of the CAMEL indicator system, and the shift to off-site supervision. A deposit insurance system was already in place when the reforms began. Thus India tried early on to strengthen and upgrade the institutional infrastructure and systemic safeguards for a market-based banking system – the proposition is fulfilled.

China started upgrading the institutional infrastructure of the banking system relatively late in the liberalization process. Regulatory standards are also comparatively weakly enforced. Although, for example, capital adequacy standards or accounting standards were upgraded in the 1990s,

[11] See Shirai (2002c), p. 28.

they were not readily enforced – for reasons ranging from the weak financial situation of banks to insufficient regulatory capacity. A step forward in this direction was the establishment of the China Banking Regulatory Commission (CBRC) that took over the regulatory responsibilities from the PBOC in 2003 and whose main goals are to implement the Basel capital standards and reduce NPLs.[12] A formal deposit insurance system is as of 2005 not in place in China. Overall, the proposition is only partly fulfilled.

Proposition 8:
Entry barriers for both domestic and foreign banks should be lowered to enable structural change in the banking sector.

Entry barriers for new banks were lowered early on in the reform process in India. New private sector banks entered the market in 1993, while the market entry of foreign banks started a year later. There remain however some restrictions on the entry mode of foreign banks since they cannot acquire majority stakes in Indian private or public sector banks. Despite the opening up of the banking system to new competition, the structure of the system has not changed significantly, since state-owned banks only lost market share at a rate of about 1% a year. As of 2005, they remain the dominant players in the system. Major factors in this respect are their significant presence in rural and semi-urban areas as well as the size of their balance sheet, which allows them to participate in larger transactions. In selected niches of the market – such as in large cities – the new entrants have been able to gain significant ground, so the competitive intensity has increased. The proposition is therefore partly fulfilled for India.

Until its accession to the WTO in 2002, China proceeded very cautiously with the opening up of the banking system, in order to protect ailing state-owned banks from overly fierce competition. While some new private banks were allowed to enter the market, foreign banks were heavily restricted in terms of geography and business areas. This changed after 2002, when a phased opening of the banking system by 2006 was agreed upon. Caps for foreign ownership in domestic banks remain in place: in 2005 this was 25% overall and 20% for any single owner. The proposition is therefore only partly fulfilled.

[12] See Deutsche Bank Research (2004), p. 8.

Proposition 9:
Liberalization of the banking sector should be carried out a gradual manner.

In both India and China, gradualism is one of the central tenets of the overall reform process. The liberalization of both countries' banking sectors has followed a gradual approach. The proposition is therefore fulfilled in both countries.

Proposition 10:
Banking sector liberalization should start when the basic institutions are in place and the macroeconomic environment is relatively stable. The reforms should start with a sequenced liberalization of interest rates, the lowering of statutory pre-emptions, and the abolishment of the directed credit program. If required, banks should be recapitalized. Afterwards, entry barriers for domestic and foreign competitors can be lowered and state-owned banks can be privatized.

As shown above, India has mostly followed the proposed reform sequence, albeit with some important deviations. At the beginning of the reforms, a basic institutional infrastructure was in place and the macroeconomic imbalances after the 1991 crisis subsided fairly quickly. Also, India liberalized interest rates, lowered statutory pre-emptions, and recapitalized banks early on. Important deviations from the general sequence are that the directed credit program was not reduced and that entry barriers were lifted fairly early in the process. The proposition is therefore partly fulfilled.

Like India, China has mostly followed the proposed general reform sequence, with some deviations. It followed the recommendations concerning the sequencing of interest rate liberalization, recapitalization of banks, lifting of entry barriers and privatization of state-owned banks. However, the institutional framework for the banking sector was developed fairly late in the process, with the Commercial Banking Law becoming effective only in 1995, for example. Given China's more difficult institutional legacy (see section 5.5), it is no surprise that China has not proceeded farther. Furthermore, statutory pre-emptions are still fairly high in China. The proposition is therefore only partly fulfilled for China.

Overall, both India and China have followed the general propositions on how to transform a banking sector fairly well (see Table 7 for a summary).

Table 7. Fulfillment of propositions

#	Proposition	India	China
1	Pre-conditions	✓	(✓)
2	Interest rates	✓	✓
3	Directed credit	✗	(✓)
4	Statutory pre-emptions	✓	(✓)
5	Recapitalization	✗	✗
6	Privatization	✗	✗
7	Institutions	✓	(✓)
8	Entry barriers	(✓)	(✓)
9	Reform speed	✓	✓
10	Reform sequence	(✓)	(✓)

Legend: ✓ = proposition is fulfilled; (✓) = proposition is partly fulfilled;
✗ = proposition is not fulfilled.

It is noteworthy that despite the different political and economic backgrounds, there is a fairly high degree of similarity with respect to implementation of the propositions. The greatest deviations from the propositions can be found in the areas of bank recapitalization, privatization, and directed credit.

The extent to which the propositions have been followed in India and China can to some extent be explained by the political economy factors discussed in section 6.2.4.

First, the partial privatizations are – especially in India – a prime example of the interplay between interest groups and fiscal pressures. Especially during the 1990s, proceeds from the sale of state-owned enterprises and banks were regarded as important for eliminating budget deficits. Nonetheless, for a variety of reasons – ranging from job security to the need to keep strategic industries – there has also always been strong opposition from interest groups against the sale of state-owned property. In this scenario, one explanation for the early start of bank privatization are the fiscal pressures at the beginning of the reform. The incompleteness and gradual nature of the process are probably due to the influence of interest groups that gained influence after the macroeconomic situation had improved.[13]

A second factor is the influence of interest groups on policy making. This is apparent in the area of directed credit in India. The persistence of the 40% directed credit target for domestic banks can be explained by the opposition from the affected groups, including farmers and small store owners, which are a sizable part of the Indian electorate. Due to this opposition only minor and less visible changes, such as the inclusion of IT companies in the list of priority sectors, could be made.

A third factor is that, in both India and China, despite the lowering of entry barriers, market entry for foreign banks is still somewhat restricted with ownership caps on the purchase of domestic banks and restrictions on the number of branches. Possible motives are the protection of weaker domestic banks and opposition from domestic players. Opposition from the domestic banks themselves was an important factor, especially at the beginning of the reform process: state-owned banks were not in a position to compete with best-practice players, so they had an interest in keeping entry barriers in place.

These factors described above were probably more important impediments to reform than a "war of attrition" between different interest groups, or uncertainty about the distribution of gains and losses from the reforms.

The assumed cause-and-effect relationships do not hold in certain areas, such as the influence of budget deficits on the dismantling of repressive policies, the recapitalization of banks, and bank privatization. Despite relatively high budget deficits and debt levels, both India and China have made considerable progress in deregulating interest rates and lowering statutory pre-emptions.[14] One possible reason is that the long-term costs associated with these repressive policies were likely to have been perceived as higher than the fiscal impact of their removal. Yet it is important to note that, even though statutory pre-emptions in India have been low-

---

[13] This is also triggered by the current political environment with weak coalition governments that increasingly have to rely on single-state parties and are heavily influenced by vested interest groups. These weak governments are also particularly vulnerable to a loss of voter support. See Echeverri-Gent (2001), pp. 1-5; Jalan (2005), pp. 88-90.

[14] India has annual budget deficits of around 10% of GDP and government debt of around 65% of GDP (see Figure 8). China has relatively moderate official deficit and debt levels of 3-4% of GDP and about 40% of GDP respectively. However, China has relatively high contingent liabilities from the bad loans that are accumulated in the banking sector, which are estimated to stand at 30% of GDP. See Mukherji (2005), p. 64f.; The Economist (2004), p. 18f.

ered almost to their legal minimum, the SLR of 25% still constitutes a significant pre-emption of resources.

The extent of the budget deficit and public debt does not to appear to be the primary reason that no "once-and-for-all" recapitalization was pursued – the overall capital needed for the recapitalizations was relatively low. In India the recapitalization amounted to the equivalent of 2% of GDP, while China would have had sufficient foreign reserves to pay for a recapitalization. The reason may rather be the lack of transparency over the true financial situation of the banks, which made an estimation of the size of the required capital injection difficult. Besides this, it is unlikely that the governments in India and China had the political will to let large state-owned banks fail. The weak fiscal situation in both countries also had little influence on the privatization process. As discussed above, the opposition from interest groups appears to have been a more important factor than fiscal pressures.

It can be concluded that both India and China have faced strong impediments to fully implementing the general policy recommendations. Nonetheless, both countries have made considerable progress. The gradual liberalization process, combined with the limited degree of openness of the capital account, has ensured that both countries have been able to implement the reforms while avoiding disruptions in the form of banking crises.

7.2 Quantitative evaluation

The following quantitative evaluation of the reform results at the sector and macro level is structured according to the indicators identified in section 6.3 and the hypotheses from section 6.4.

7.2.1 Sector level

The evaluation of changes on the sector level follows the five process steps that were identified for the transformation of a banking sector. The status of the process and the results are discussed individually for each step. Since the historical developments of the Indian and the Chinese banking sectors have already been discussed in earlier chapters, the emphasis here is on key events influencing the evaluation of each process step. The evaluation is conducted for the period 1980 to 2005, so that the early Chinese reforms as well as the Indian reform experiences in the mid-1980s are included. At the end of this section, the relevant indicators are integrated to an overall process index.

Liberalization

Interest rate restrictions, statutory pre-emptions and the intensity of the directed credit program are the variables in the liberalization process step.

Interest rate restrictions in the Indian banking sector increased fairly steadily until reaching a peak in the early 1980s.[15] After the first deregulation attempts in the mid-1980s, the degree of interest rate controls was somewhat lowered, but then increased again at the end of the 1980s. Since the early 1990s, interest rate controls have been steadily dismantled, and today most interest rates in India are determined by the market and the system can be characterized as fully liberalized.

In China, too, a gradual liberalization of interest rates started in the mid-1980s when banks were allowed to adjust lending rates within a certain margin around the official rate. However, this partial liberalization was reversed at the end of the 1980s. The next liberalization attempt began in 1993 with the imposition of a lending rate ceiling that was gradually increased until 2004 to 1.7 times the central lending rate. Deposit rates continued to be set by the government until the end of 2005. Overall, the state continues to play an important role in the setting of interest rates in the Chinese banking sector, so that it is categorized as partially repressed.

Between 1980 and 2000, the liberalization of interest rates in India resulted in a decline in the net interest margin and the ratio of lending-to-deposit rates (Figure 14 and Figure 15) because of a relative increase of deposit rates to lending rates. The net interest margin in particular declined significantly in the immediate aftermath of liberalization between 1992 and 1994, from a very high level of about 8%. This is indicative of significant government interference.[16] After 2000 the net interest margin and the lending-to-deposit ratio increased again in India, the result of normal competitive forces affecting supply and demand.

---

[15] See Demetriades and Luintel (1997), p. 320.

[16] The net interest margins in Europe and the United States have been between 140 and 400 basis points over the last years. See International Monetary Fund (2006a), pp. 160-162.

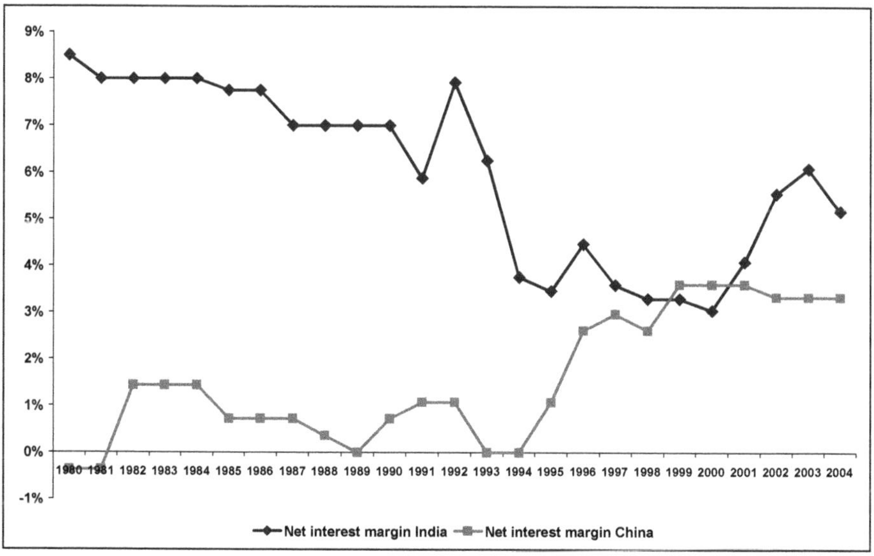

Fig. 14. Net interest margin India and China[17]

In China, the results of the partial interest rate liberalization differed significantly from India. At the outset of reforms in the early 1980s, the net interest margin was well below 2% and at times even negative, which shows that, like in India, the setting of interest rates was heavily influenced by the government. The possibility of charging ever higher lending rates after 1993, with deposit rates still set by the government, resulted in an increase of the net interest margin and the lending-to-deposit ratio. This outcome is due to the asymmetric partial liberalization in China and reflects the need to give state-owned banks opportunities to increase profits to bolster their capital base – a typical characteristic of a repressed system. Despite the low deposit rates, there is no immediate threat that the flow of savings to Chinese banks will decline, since Chinese savers have almost no opportunity to invest abroad because of the closed capital account.

[17] Author's calculation based on International Monetary Fund (2006b).

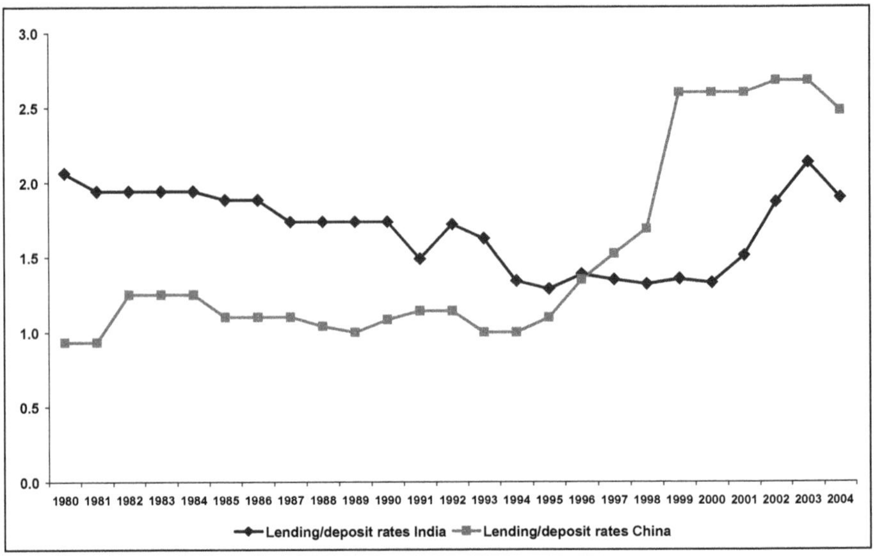

Fig. 15. Lending-to-deposit-rate ratio India and China[18]

The extent of *statutory pre-emptions* also changed significantly in the post-liberalization period in India. The CRR and SLR increased fairly steadily from 1960 until 1991, when the combined amount reached a peak of 53.5% (Figure 3). Starting in 1991, the combined statutory pre-emptions have been gradually lowered to a level of around 30% at the end of 2005. The degree of financial repression through statutory pre-emptions has been significantly reduced in line with these changes. This is mirrored in the lowering of the effective reserve requirements from 33% in 1980 to 7% in 2004. The overall system in India can be described as largely liberalized in this respect.

In China, the effective reserve requirements have been steadily lowered since the 1980s. However, the absolute level continued to stand at 17% in 2004, which is a sign of heavy government involvement in the banking sector – even though the high reserve requirements might be used to some extent as a monetary policy tool. Therefore, the system in China should be classified as fully repressed.[19]

Lower statutory pre-emptions give banks more funds to distribute as credit. One would expect a rise of the credit-deposit ratio in line with the

---

[18] Author's calculation based on International Monetary Fund (2006b).

[19] The difference to the evaluation compared to proposition 4 in section 7.1 stems from the fact that here the absolute level of reserve requirements is evaluated, whereas in the previous section the progress in the reduction ("reduction in a phased manner") was also included in the evaluation.

lowering of the reserve and liquidity requirements in India. However, in most of the 1991-2004 period, the ratio in India has been lower than at beginning of the 1980s (Figure 16), which indicates that banks have not used the additional funds to extend credit. Instead they have invested heavily in government securities, which offered opportunities for trading profits in an environment of falling interest rates.[20] Only after 2003 has the credit-deposit ratio increased significantly in India, coinciding with an increase in the interest rate level so that investing in government bonds is no longer financially attractive.[21]

In China, also, the credit-deposit ratio has not changed as would be expected by the decrease of the reserve requirements. Possible reasons for its decline are the attempts by the Chinese leadership to restrict credit growth to cool down the economy and the increasing in the overall savings rate.

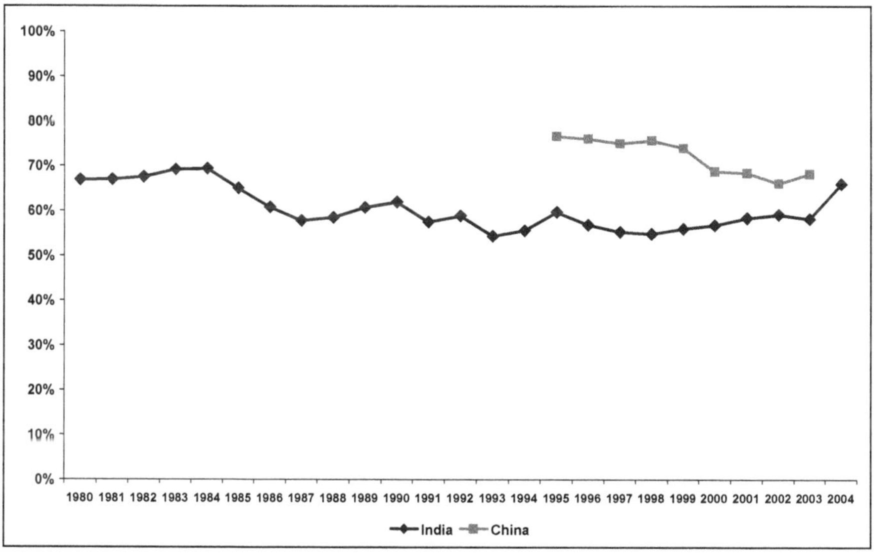

Fig. 16. Credit-deposit ratio India and China[22]

[20] See Reserve Bank of India (2005c), p. 73. An inverse relationship between interest rates and bond prices exists: lower interest rates result in higher bond prices.

[21] Another factor that may have affected the limited expansion of credit is that credit officers of PSBs may be charged with corruption if a borrower defaults. This leads to strong incentives not to extend credit even to profitable enterprises. See Banerjee and Duflo (2004), p. 6.

[22] See Garcia-Herrero and Santabarbara (2004), p. 43; Garcia-Herrero, Gavila and Santabarbara (2005), p. 40f.; Reserve Bank of India (2005c), p. 305.

Until the beginning of the 1980s, the intensity of the *directed credit program* in India increased steadily, with 40% of bank credit earmarked for priority sectors. The overall liberalization since 1991 has not changed the nominal percentage goals for directed credit, so that at the end of 2005 domestic banks had a 40% directed credit target and foreign banks a 32% target. Overall, the level of directed credit in India has been slightly below 40%, so that the overall program must be classified as partially repressed.[23] This also applies when taking market failure arguments into account, since the 40% target is significantly above the 10% that would be required by market failure.

In China, there were no explicit directed credit rules. Until the early 1980s, banks merely served as accounting units that channeled loans toward enterprises according to the overall plan.[24] In this respect, almost all credit was "directed credit". This changed somewhat in 1986, when the PBOC formulated a credit plan that set aggregate ceilings for every PBOC branch. The branches could then allocate the credit up to those ceilings. This marked the first, partial liberalization. A further step to a more liberalized system was the establishment of the policy banks in 1994. These took over the directed lending functions of the state-owned banks. Finally, in 1999 government interference in commercial lending was forbidden. Because a certain degree of *de facto* state influence over lending decisions still exists today, even in state-owned banks, the directed credit system in China can only be characterized as partially liberalized.

One indicator for measuring the result of the liberalization of the directed credit program is return on assets (ROA). However, this indicator should not be over interpreted since the ROA is affected by a wide variety of factors, ranging from the cost of deposits to overhead expenses. After an adjustment period in the aftermath of the balance-of-payment crisis, the ROA for the Indian banking sector has followed an upward trend (Figure 17).

[23] As discussed before, the directed credit program was somewhat eased by broadening the definition of priority sectors and decreasing the interest rate subsidies.

[24] See Wolken (1990), p. 55.

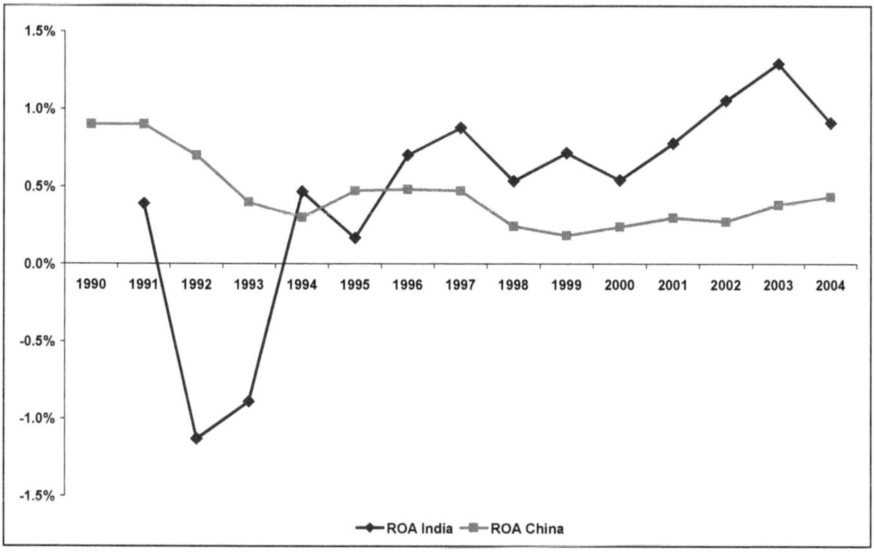

Fig. 17. ROA India and China[25]

This would not be expected given the high extent of directed credit.[26] In China, after a decline that started in the mid-1990s the ROA has improved somewhat since 2000, but the improvement remains at a relatively low level. Both countries show unusual results: the ROA in India has increased despite the influence of the directed credit program, while the easing of restrictions in China has not led to significant improvement. However, the ROA is not only influenced by the directed credit program, so that this indicator is not fully representative of the liberalization results.[27]

Integrating the three sub-indicators for liberalization – interest rate liberalization, directed credit, and reserve requirements – reveals that significant progress has been made in India. Today, India can be seen as largely liberalized in this dimension (Figure 18).

[25] See BankScope (2006); Garcia-Herrero and Santabarbara (2004), p. 42; Lardy (1998), p. 100; Reserve Bank of India (2005a).

[26] Private, state and foreign banks alike contributed to the ROA improvement (see Figure 41 in the appendix).

[27] Furthermore, it is important to keep in mind that the calculation of the ROA is based on accounting data. Differing accounting standards across countries may consequently limit the comparability to some extent. See Ferris et al. (2000), p. 8.

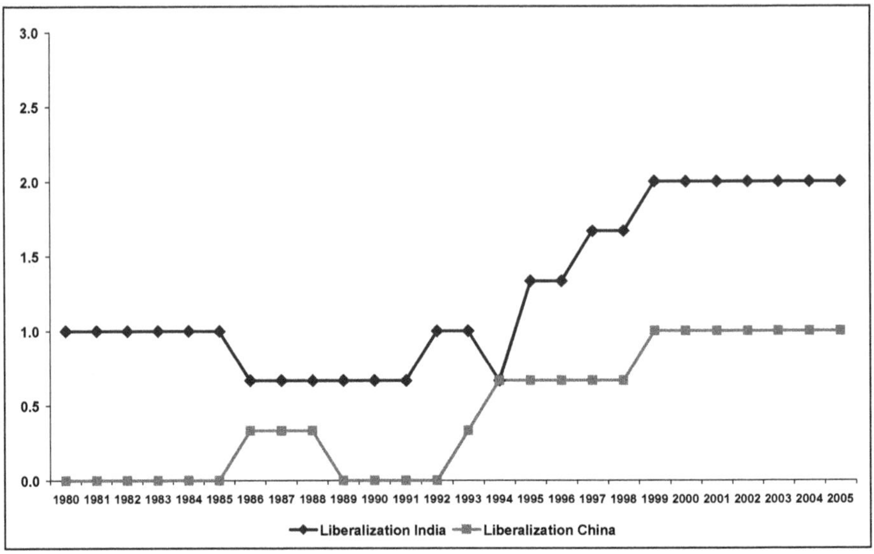

Fig. 18. Liberalization progress

China has also progressed quite far. However, because of the high effective reserve requirements and government setting of deposit rates, China is still partially repressed in this dimension.[28]

Stabilization

The proxy variable for measuring the stabilization of the banking sector is the development of prudential norms with respect to capital adequacy. In India, the RBI first introduced the Basel Capital Standards in 1992, allowing for a phased implementation up to 1996. The RBI further tightened the capital adequacy standards by increasing the required CRAR to 9% – one percentage point higher than that mandated by the Basel Standards. Since 1995, the CRAR has stayed consistently above 10% for the overall banking sector (Figure 19). There were plans to move towards the Basel II Standards by the end of 2005, but no significant move has been made.[29] In terms of prudential norms, the Indian banking sector can be characterized as largely liberalized. This evaluation does not change when taking market failure arguments into account. The capital adequacy standards are stricter

[28] The point scores for every year can be found in the appendix in Table 18 and Table 19. A summary of key events in the banking sectors in India and China can be found in Table 21.

[29] The phased implementation of the Basel II standards in India is not expected to start before April 2007. See Gopinath (2006), p. 1f.; Mohan (2006a), p. 3.

than those prescribed by the Basel Committee – this is necessary in the light of the higher risks in emerging markets.

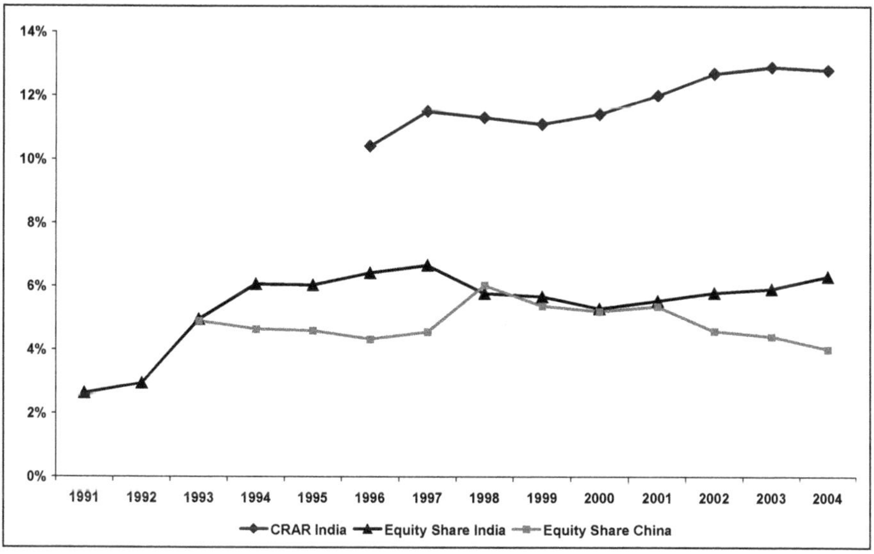

Fig. 19. CRAR and equity share India and China[30]

China has made considerably less progress in the area of prudential norms. Although the Basel Capital Standards were included in the Commercial Banking Law and made mandatory for all commercial banks in 1995, the requirements were not strongly enforced. Since longer continuous time series data on the CRAR is not readily available for China, the equity share has been used as a proxy indicator for the trend. Despite significant capital injections into the SOCBs, the ratio has declined over the last years and is probably insufficient for the level of risk in the system.[31] With its lack of enforcement and its banks' insufficient capital base, the Chinese system can be considered still partially repressed in terms of the prudential norms for capital adequacy.

Compared to other reforms, the stabilization process was initiated fairly late in both India and China. Indeed, it is still incomplete (Figure 20). Both countries are currently somewhat insulated from external shocks due to

[30] See BankScope Database (2006); Garcia-Herrero and Santabarbara (2004), p. 42; Reserve Bank of India (2004b), p. 85; Reserve Bank of India (2005c), p. 95.

[31] At least until 2004, the aggregate CRAR of the Big Four has been well below the mandated 8%. See for example Fitch Ratings (2005), p. 10; Morgan Stanley (2004), p. 33; Pei and Shirai (2004), p. 9.

their closed capital accounts. It is nonetheless important that they continue to upgrade their systemic safeguards and the capital base of their banks.

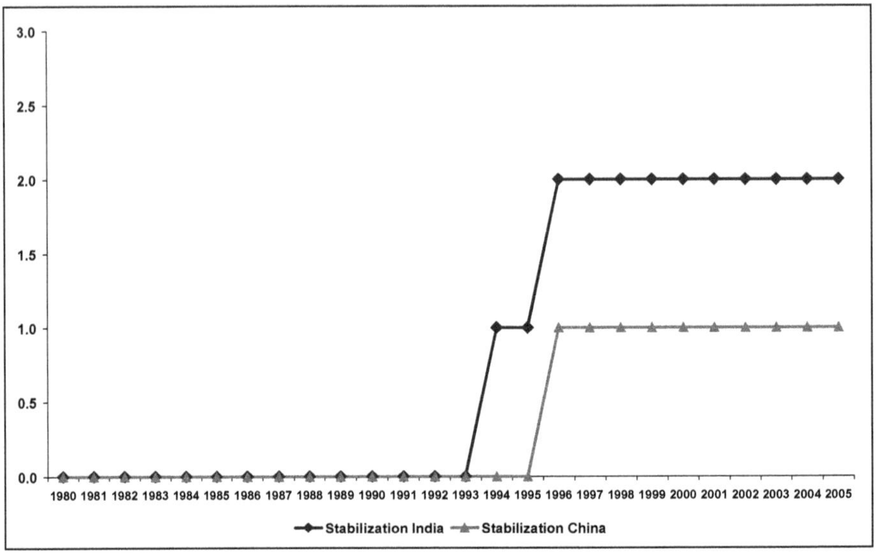

Fig. 20. Stabilization progress

Four indicators are used to measure the results of the stabilization of the banking sector. These indicators are signals of a banking crisis, and comprise a ROA below 1%, a level of NPLs above 5%, a rising trend of NPLs, and a net interest margin below 2%.[32] On the evidence of these four indicators, the stability of the banking systems in India and China has improved since the beginning of the 1990s. However, a considerable risk of financial distress remains (Figure 21). This is the result of the high level of NPLs in both countries, as well as the relatively low profitability as measured by the ROA. Despite the progress made, further efforts are required to reduce the threat of financial distress.

[32] See Barton, Newell and Wilson (2003), pp. 53-56.

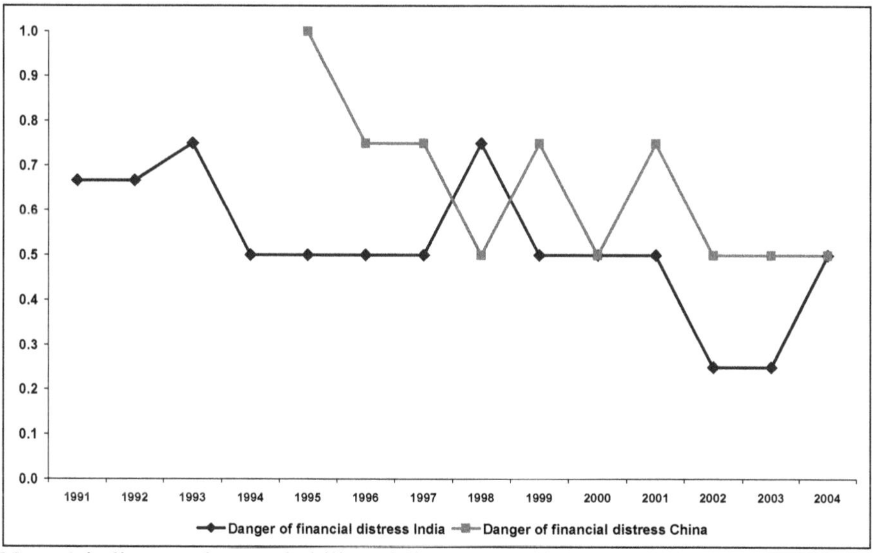

Note: 0 indicates a low probability of distress; 1 a high probability.

Fig. 21. Danger of financial distress

Privatization

The asset share of state-owned banks with respect to the overall formal banking sector measures the progress of privatization. Of course, this measure does not reflect privatization progress in terms of a change of ownership. However, it reveals the effects of a reduced role of the government in the banking sector, which can be caused either by ownership changes or a growing importance of private-sector banks. Thus, privatization in this context should be regarded as giving an increased role to the private sector.[33] Both India and China have seen a steady reduction of the asset share of state-owned banks since the mid-1990s (Figure 22).

[33] In addition, it is important to remember the distinction between ownership and control rights: partial private ownership of state-owned banks signal a change of ownership rights but not necessarily control rights if the state remains the dominant shareholder.

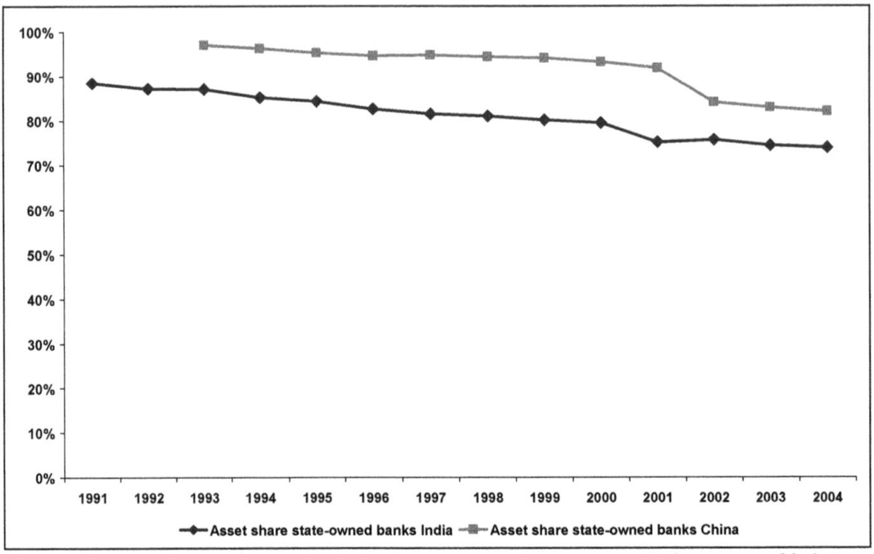

Note: (1) asset shares do not include the cooperative sector; (2) because of joint private-public ownership of most joint stock commercial banks in China, it is assumed that 50% of their market share counts towards the state sector.

Fig. 22. Asset share of state-owned banks India and China[34]

The level of state ownership has been reduced from 100% in China and about 90% in India to about 75% in both countries in 2004. This level is significantly above the 25% that would be warranted by market failure arguments. Thus despite the progress made, and even allowing for arguments relating to market failure, both countries are still partially repressed in this dimension. This is mirrored in the limited progress of the privatization process indicator (Figure 23).

The likely result of a decreased role of the state in the banking sector is an increase in efficiency. This can be measured by the ROA and faster financial development. As shown above (Figure 17), the ROA of the Indian banking sector has increased fairly steadily over the last years, as would be expected given the reduced share of state-owned banks, while the ROA of Chinese banks has fallen. However, it is interesting to note that despite the limited progress of privatization in India, the ROA of the state-owned banks has increased in line with the overall banking sector.[35] This is likely

[34] Author's calculation based on Garcia-Herrero, Gavila and Santabarbara (2005), p. 40 and Reserve Bank of India (2005a).

[35] See Figure 41 in the appendix. In addition, there are no significant differences in the returns of the different bank groups in India. This is a deviation from the general assumption that state-owned banks are less efficient than private ones.

to be due to the increased competition to which the state-owned banks have been subjected.

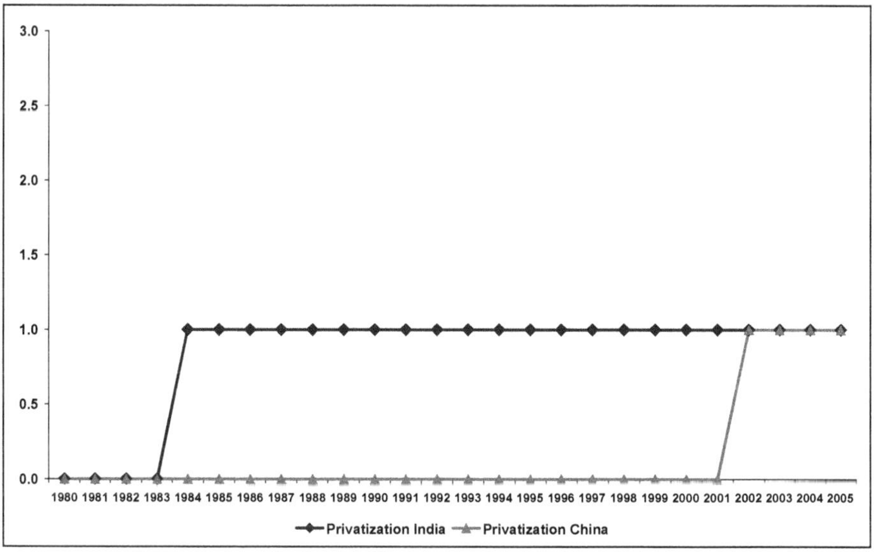

Fig. 23. Privatization progress

Progress has been made in both India and China in the field of financial development. This is measured by two indicators: liquid liabilities to GDP, and private credit to GDP (Figure 24). These indicators have relatively steadily increased in both countries. However, China witnessed a significantly faster increase than India, even though it started the reforms from a higher level and has not proceeded farther with reforms than India. Possible reasons for the significantly deeper financial system in China are the higher savings rate and the higher economic growth rate, which was to a large extent fueled by cheap credit.[36]

[36] Holz (2000) argues that the higher level of financial depth in China is the result of expansionary government policies. The NPLs and the implicit government guarantee of the banking system mean that a large share of the funds in the banking system is de-facto government debt. This means that financial depth may not lead to the same positive effects like in other countries because of the distorted underlying mechanisms so that the comparatively high level is somewhat misleading. See Holz (2000), p. 91.

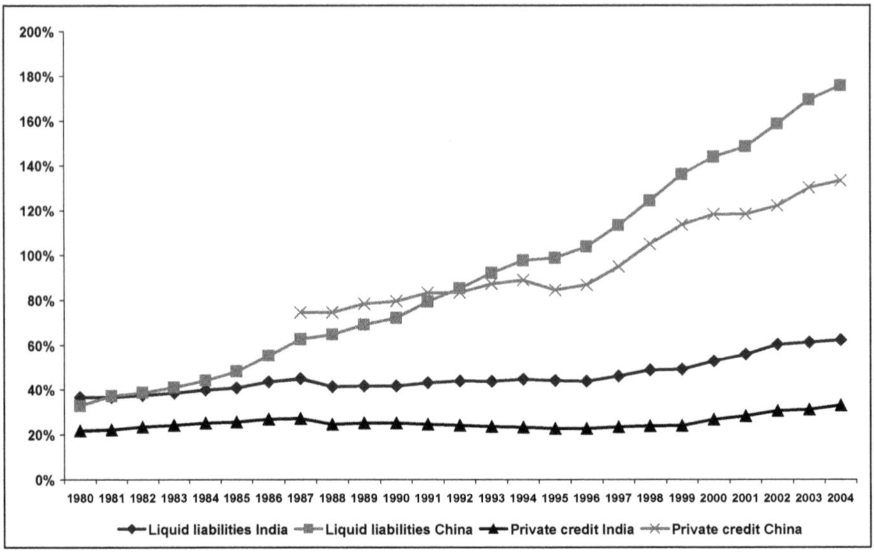

Fig. 24. Financial development indicators[37]

Institution building

Institution building requires policies towards deposit insurance, accounting for NPLs, and changes in the regulatory system.

Since India already had a deposit insurance system in place before 1980, no further adjustments were necessary during liberalization. This was not the case for the accounting rules concerning NPLs. Despite a tightening, they are still below international standards, and the system in this respect is only largely liberalized. Significant progress was made in terms of the regulatory system. The first attempts to construct a market-based regulatory system were started in 1992. Further progress was made with the foundation of the Board of Financial Supervision, whose task is the oversight of the banking sector. In 2002, the regulatory system was further upgraded to include measures for prompt corrective actions, for example. These expanded the regulators' options to intervene in case of difficulties. Overall, the supervisory system in India conforms largely to international standards today so that it can be characterized as fully liberalized. Overall, the three measures of institution building indicate that India has created the foundations for a market-based banking system over time. Figure 25 illustrates the gradual process of institution building in India, as well as the relatively high starting point.

[37] Author's calculation based on International Monetary Fund (2006b).

China has made far less progress in terms of institution building. It still does not have an explicit deposit insurance system, relying instead on implicit state guarantees. In terms of accounting standards for NPLs, China introduced a five-tier classification system only in 1998, and its stringency is below international standards. A further tightening of accounting standards occurred before WTO accession. Some progress has also been made in terms of the regulatory system. A first step towards creating the institutions for a market-based banking system was the introduction of prudential regulations in 1996, which were however not fully enforced. A further step was the establishment of the CBRC as an oversight body for the banking sector in 2003. Overall it can be concluded that, in terms of accounting standards and the supervisory system, China is moving in the direction of a market-based banking sector, but further progress is needed. In the light of these deficiencies and the lack of a deposit insurance system, the Chinese banking sector is rated as partially repressed in terms of institution building.

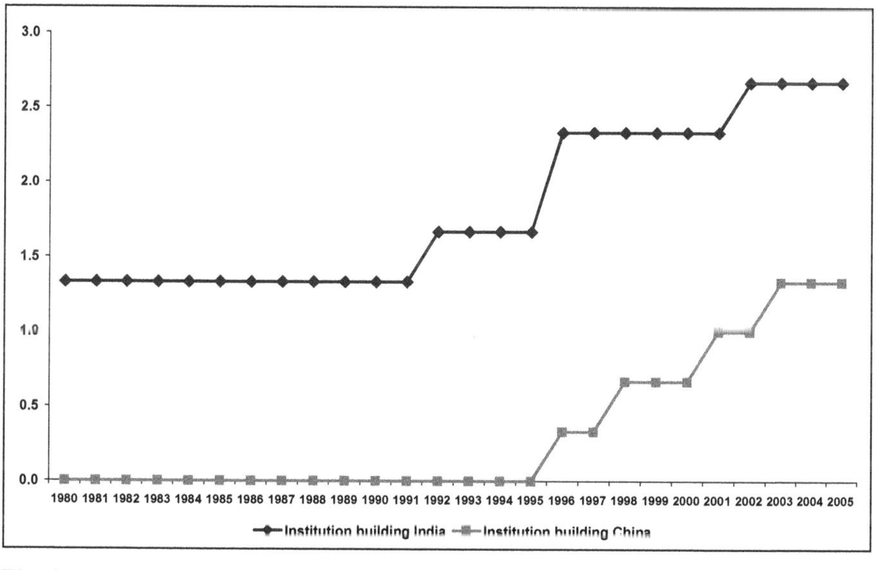

Fig. 25. Process institution building

The results of institution building are measured by an increased stability of the banking sector. As discussed above, both India and China have made some progress in this respect, but remain vulnerable to financial distress due to high NPLs and low profitability. This is particularly true for China, where despite rapid loan growth, recapitalizations, and a benign macro-environment, the level of NPLs is still over 15%. India, by contrast, has made considerable progress in the reduction of NPLs since 1993, partially attributable to the stronger institutional infrastructure (Figure 26).

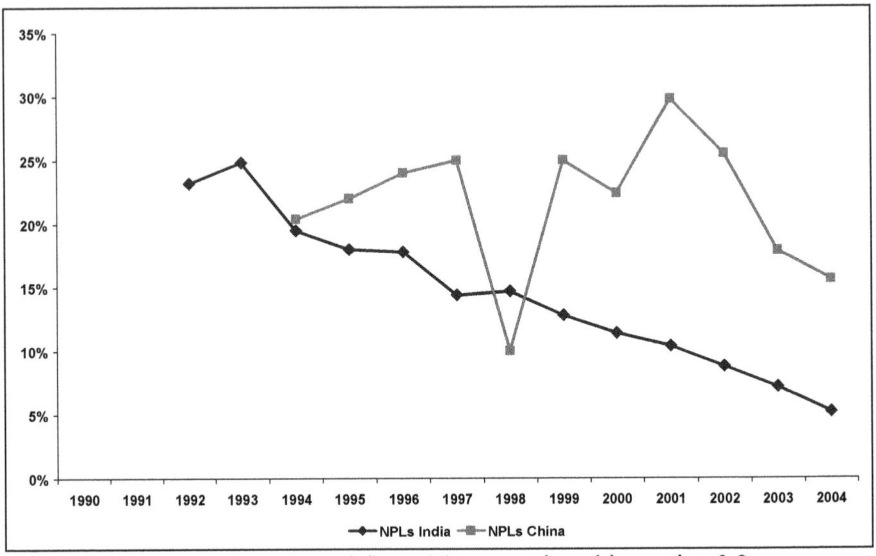

Note: (1) NPLs are gross of provisions; (2) as mentioned in section 3.2, some analysts estimate higher NPL levels for Chinese banks.

Fig. 26. NPLs India and China as percent of total loans[38]

Structural changes

The indicator for structural changes is the extent to which new domestic and foreign banks can enter the market. In India, the sector was effectively closed for new entrants prior to 1993. Entry barriers were dismantled for domestic banks in 1993 and for foreign banks in 1994. Restrictions remain on the entry mode for foreign banks, since they cannot take majority stakes in Indian banks.[39] Therefore this dimension can only be regarded as largely liberalized because of the remaining ownership caps.

A similar situation exists in China. From 1980 until 1994 the banking sector was effectively closed to foreign banks: they were only allowed to set up branches with a limited business scope in special economic zones. In 1994 the first law to regulate the entry of foreign banks became effective, but the operational scope of foreign banks was still heavily limited.

---

[38] See Hope and Hu (2006), p. 45; International Monetary Fund (2005), p. 196; Lardy (1998), p. 119 and 122; Muniappan (2002), p. 2f.; Pei and Shirai (2004), p. 7.

[39] The exception is the takeover of Indian private sector banks that the RBI declares as in need of restructuring. See Reserve Bank of India (2005b), p. 2.

This changed with WTO accession in 2002, when the Chinese market was opened up to foreign banks in a phased manner. However, as in India, there are still caps on the ownership of Chinese banks by foreigners. New domestic banks faced less stringent entry restrictions and could enter the market earlier than foreign banks – the China Minsheng Bank was the first non-state commercial bank to enter the market in 1996. Overall, the system can be characterized, as in India, as largely liberalized.

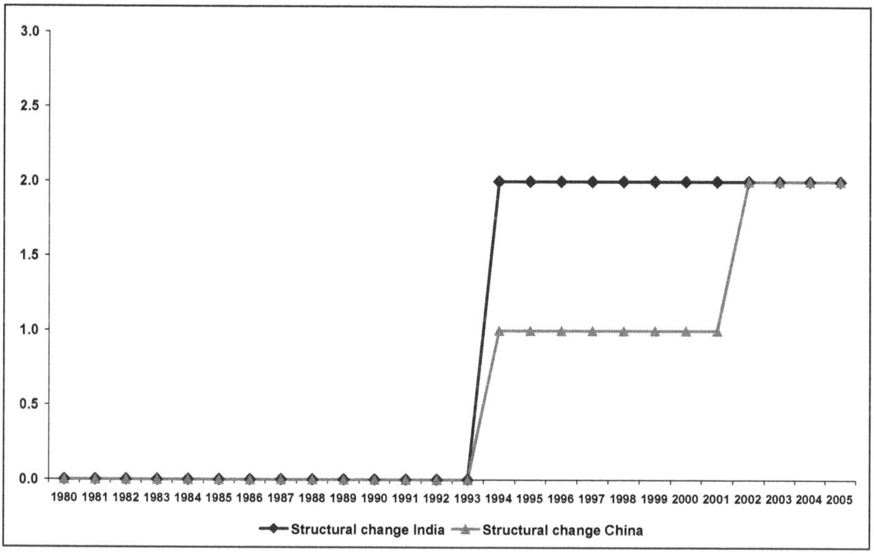

Fig. 27. Process structural change

The results of the deregulation are evaluated by means of two concentration measures: the M-4 concentration ratio for assets and the Herfindahl index.[40] Despite the lifting of entry barriers, concentration in India has not decreased significantly as measured by these indicators (Figure 28). Given the number of new banks – both private and foreign – that have entered the market, it is surprising that the market share of the state-owned banks has not eroded more quickly.[41] Possible reasons for their continuing dominance are their extensive branch network across India and their balance-sheet strength, which allows them to serve larger corporate clients. In line with

[40] The Herfindahl index can only be applied to India because of insufficient data for China.

[41] It should be noted, however, that one private sector bank – ICICI Bank – has been among the four largest banks in terms of assets since 2001. Nonetheless, the State Bank of India still accounts for over 50% of the assets of the four largest banks.

the relatively slow market share gains of the new entrants, the concentration in the banking sector has only declined slightly.

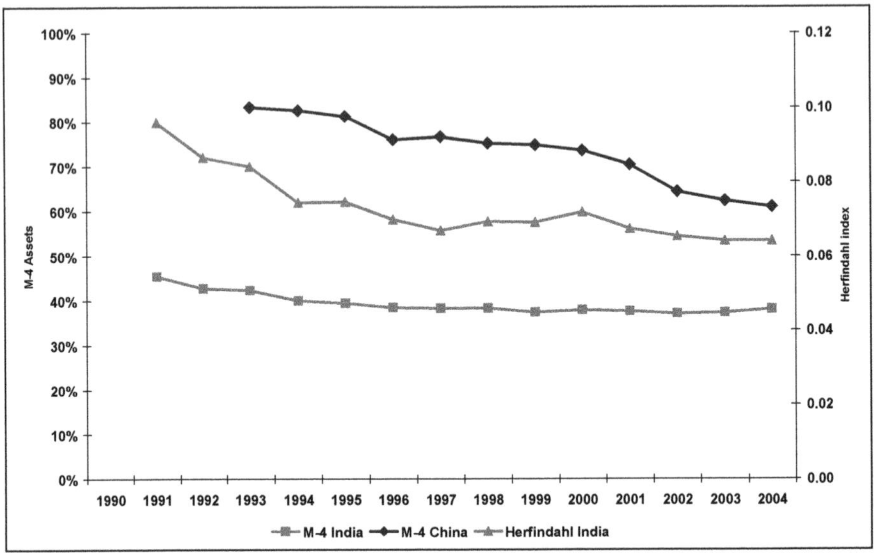

Fig. 28. M-4 concentration ratio and Herfindahl index assets[42]

The dominance of the largest banks in China is even higher than in India. This can be seen by the higher scores for the M-4 concentration index. As in India, the large state-owned banks have kept their dominant position despite the entry of new competitors. The only larger decline in concentration was in 2001, when the policy banks gained market share relative to the SOCBs. However, this is further evidence that new private sector and foreign banks have not so far been able to challenge the dominant position of the largest banks in the system.

Integrating the five categories into an overall process index shows that both India and China have made considerable progress in transforming their banking sectors (Figure 29, Figure 30 and Figure 31). Of the two, India has moved significantly farther in the establishment of a market-based banking sector. Since market failure had no significant effect on the evaluation, the point scores without market failure effects are reported here.[43] At the beginning of the 1980s, India had the better starting point due to lower restrictions on interest rates and directed credit. In addition, elements of an institutional framework were already in place and the pri-

[42] See Garcia-Herrero, Gavila and Santabarbara (2005), p. 40; Reserve Bank of India (2005a). Note: assets in cooperative banks excluded from calculations.

[43] The scores for the market failure index are reported in the appendix in Table 24.

vate sector had a small share of assets. From this basis India made considerable progress between the balance-of-payment crisis and the mid-1990s. Since then, however, the speed of reforms has slowed down considerably. Greatest progress has been made in the area of institution building, while least progress has been made in the area of privatization. Overall, India is about two-thirds of the way toward having a market-based banking sector.

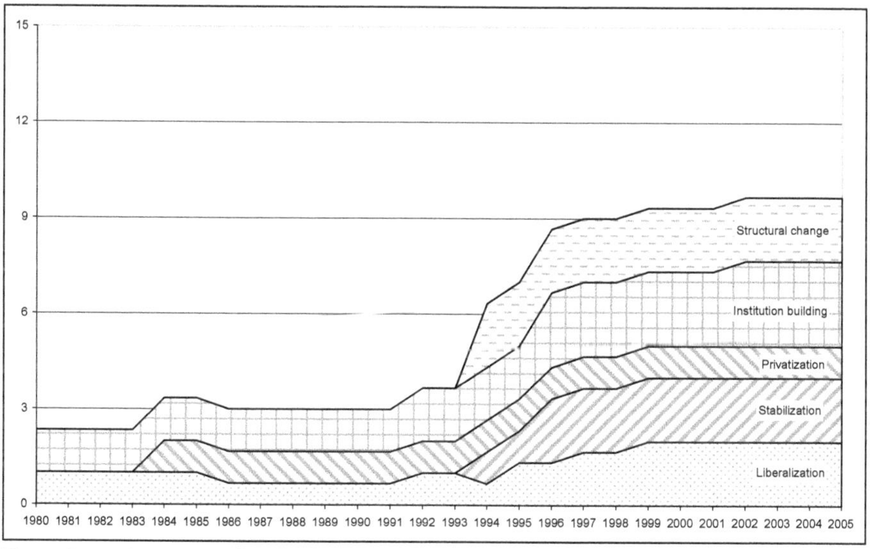

Note: the point scores for the index can be found in Table 18.

Fig. 29. Liberalization progress India

In China, the legacy of the mono-banking system that prevailed before 1980 meant a more difficult starting position. The liberalization progress started to accelerate in the mid-1990s with the creation of specialized banks and increased flexibility in the setting of lending and wholesale interest rates. During the late 1990s, liberalization in China proceeded fairly cautiously, since a spillover of instability from the Asian crisis was feared. The speed and depth of liberalization picked up in 2002, with China's WTO accession – this required a phased opening of the banking sector and thus the creation of a stronger institutional infrastructure and a more market-based banking sector. Overall, China is only mid-way through the liberalization process and still has some way to go until it reaches a fully liberalized banking system. With the exception of structural changes, where the largest advancements have been made, the progress has been fairly equal in all categories.

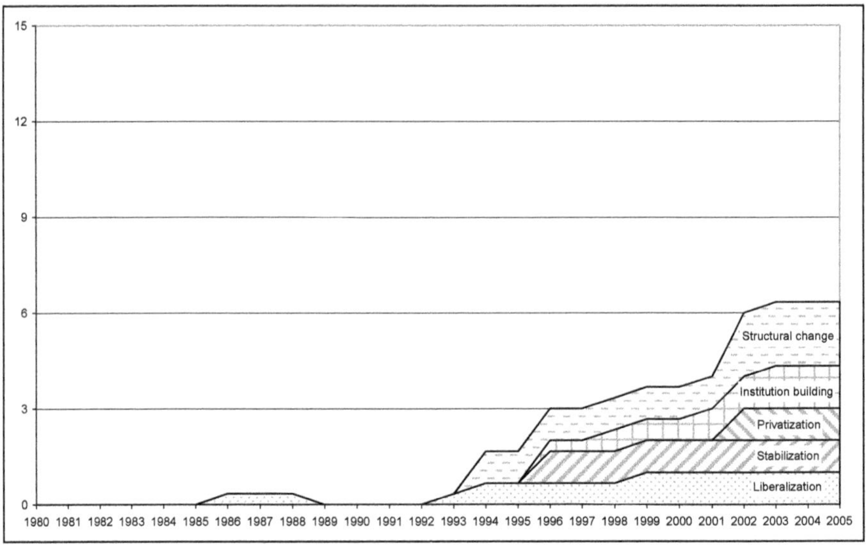

Note: the point scores for the index can be found in Table 19.

Fig. 30. Liberalization progress China

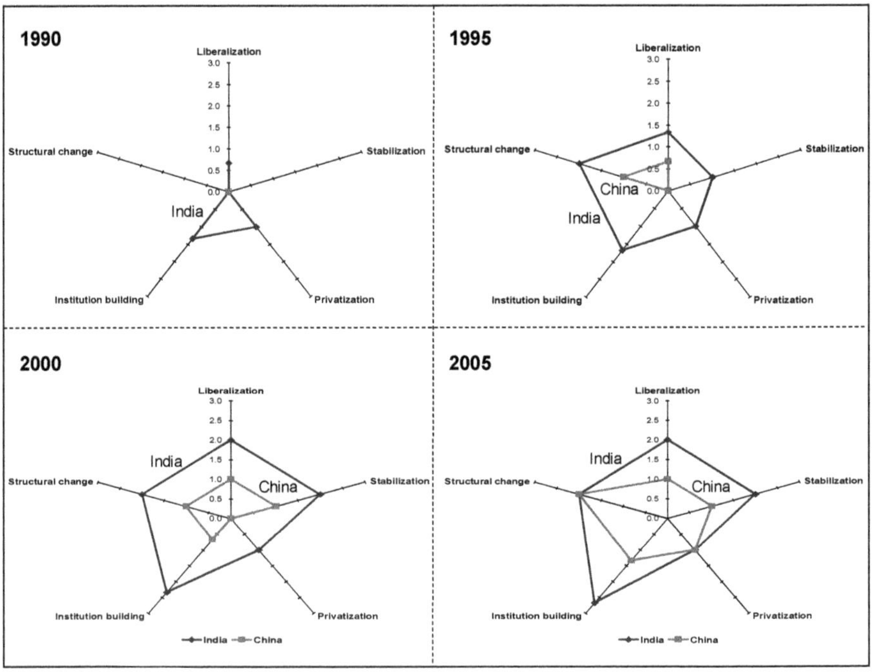

Fig. 31. Comparison of reform progress

The comparison of India and China over time shows that India has been well ahead of China with banking sector reforms over the last 15 years (Figure 31). Only between 2000 and 2005, i.e. during the time of the preparation for the accession to the WTO, has China been able to catch up with India in categories such as privatization or structural change.

Several initial conclusions can be drawn from the reform experiences in India and China. First, neither country experienced any major reform reversals, with the exception of some relatively minor setbacks in the mid-1980s in both countries. This is especially noteworthy because both countries have experienced several leadership changes and because the Asian crisis led to a tightening of government control in other countries in the region.

Second, reform progress in the banking sector depended partly on the development of the enterprise sector. There appears to be a link between the pace of reform in the enterprise sector and the banking sector due to the interdependencies between state-owned banks and state-owned enterprises. The legacy NPLs from state-owned enterprises made it difficult to introduce hard budget constraints early on in the reform process. Since the governments in India and China tried to avoid bankruptcies of large state-owned enterprises, banks had to extend further loans to these companies, which negatively affected the quality of their loan portfolios.[44] Under these circumstances it was not possible to credibly stabilize banks; and because banks did not operate fully according to commercial principles, privatization became more difficult. This also explains the late start of comprehensive banking sector reforms in China.

Third, while the gradual reform process in both countries helped to create a certain continuity and support for the reforms, the question is if there are any negative effects from the relatively slow pace of liberalization and the fact that it is still incomplete. Studies have shown that financial liberalization results in a higher risk of a banking crisis during the five years after liberalization, with this risk being higher in countries with weaker institutions and lower transparency.[45] The degree of vulnerability in the transition period thus crucially depends upon building up the necessary institutional infrastructure – including, for example, bank supervision and capital standards. Even though it is preferable to have these institutions in place before liberalization starts, a slower pace of liberalization can gain

[44] The distribution of bank loans in China shows that this pattern continues: private enterprises received only 27% of bank loans in 2003, but accounted for 52% of GDP. See McKinsey Global Institute (2006b), p. 11.

[45] See Llewellyn (2002), pp. 168-171; Mehrez and Kaufmann (2000), p. 2; Williamson and Mahar (1998), pp. 52-54.

time to create these institutions, reducing vulnerability to a crisis. In the light of these factors, the situation in China is especially worrisome, since it has not used the relatively long reform period to build up its institutional infrastructure sufficiently.

Fourth, despite the opening up of the market to domestic and foreign competitors, state-owned banks have managed to keep their dominant position in both countries, even after more than ten years of more or less unrestricted market entry. After dismantling the entry barriers, it was believed that state-owned banks would lose market share quickly, due to factors such as lower customer service standards and a lower degree of product sophistication. Yet this has not happened – many newly established banks still do not have the critical size in terms of assets and branch network to effectively compete with the incumbents. Until now, the loss of market share has been relatively limited. This might change when the new competitors reach a size that allows them to compete on an equal footing; this could then result in significant market share losses for the large state-owned banks in India and China.[46]

Fifth, despite differing political, economic and institutional backgrounds in India and China there is a remarkable degree of similarity between the reform processes. The political system in particular appears to have less influence on the reform process than expected. The general assumption in this respect is that China, with its one-party system, is in a position to pursue reforms faster than India with its multi-party democracy. The reform experiences in the banking sectors of India and China, however, provide some evidence that the political system is less important for the reform process than is commonly assumed.[47]

The result indicators show that the liberalization process led to a better sectoral performance. This is especially true for the Indian banking sector, where profitability and capital adequacy have increased steadily across all types of banks while NPLs have been significantly reduced. However, liberalization not only benefited banks through higher profits. Customers also benefited, as can be seen by the decreased net interest margin in India and

[46] Another factor is that foreign banks are according to China's WTO commitments barred from offering services to Chinese individuals until the end of 2006. See Deutsche Bank Research (2004), p. 2.

[47] As reported by Saez and Yang (2001), this not only appears to be the case in the banking sector but also in the electricity and telecommunications sector, where India has made more progress than China. See Saez and Yang (2001), p. 90. Other political-economy factors were discussed in the previous section. For a summary of statistical studies on the relationship between different political regimes and economic growth, see for example Przeworski and Limongi (1993).

increased choice after the entry of new banks. The Chinese banking sector still lags behind in terms of capital adequacy, profitability and NPLs, despite the overall progress made. This can in part be attributed to the later start of reforms, a more difficult legacy and less stringent implementation of certain institutional reforms.

Overall, liberalization has had positive effects on the banking sector. The question now arises of whether liberalization has also created spillover effects into other parts of the economy. This is explored in the next section.

7.2.2 Macroeconomic level

The previous section attempted to establish a link between the progress made in certain areas of liberalization and the results at the sector level. This section tries to go a step further – both in terms of methodology and the level of analysis – and test if the overall policy changes in the banking sector had a statistically significant effect on various macroeconomic variables. As some of the discussions of result indicators have shown, establishing causality can be difficult: a variety of factors can potentially influence the variables under investigation. Statistical analyses help overcome some of these problems. Before conducting the statistical tests, the econometric specifications for the tests are discussed, as well as the variables used in the calculations.

7.2.2.1 Econometric specification and data description

Two general methods exist for establishing a link between financial liberalization and macroeconomic variables: cross-country panel analysis, and time-series analysis.[48] Cross-country panel analysis has been the method of choice in many studies. It can be used to identify relationships between macroeconomic variables, including the relationship between financial liberalization, financial development and growth.[49]

In panel studies, explanatory variables – such as financial liberalization – are averaged out over longer time periods for each country and then used in a regression analysis to estimate the average influence of the variables on economic growth. However, there are serious objections to the use of panel data to evaluate economic policies. First, the methodology relies on the unrealistic assumption that every country in the sample has a stable

[48] See Arestis and Demetriades (1997), p. 784; Kennedy (2003), p. 301.

[49] See for example the studies by Galindo, Micco and Ordonez (2002), King and Levine (1993) and Roubini and Sala-i-Martin (1992).

growth path. Second, small and large countries are given equal weight in the regression. Third, the values for policy indicators in a country are likely to be correlated over time. Only the initial value or an average of initial values over a certain time period is included in the analysis, while the current value is excluded. Therefore, only a contemporaneous correlation between the policy variable and growth can be established, but no causality. Fourth, cross-section analysis does not account for different patterns of causality in different countries – it only gives a result that is valid on average. And fifth, cross-section analysis assumes homogeneity across countries in terms of general economic characteristics, the implementation of policies and institutions.[50]

It is possible to avoid these problems by focusing on a single country and analyzing the effects of policy changes on macroeconomic variables over time. Doing so, however, involves a trade-off between the insights from a country-case study and the ability to generalize the conclusions. This downside of time-series analysis is to a certain extent mitigated in this thesis by including China as a comparator country. Time-series analysis, however, requires some econometric issues to be dealt with in addition to the general requirements of regression analysis. The possible issues and necessary considerations for conducting a time-series analysis are discussed below.

Stationarity

A time series is stationary if its mean and variance do not change over time. "Nonstationarity" creates problems because it can cause spurious results in a regression and make standard inference procedures – such as R^2 or t-statistics – unreliable. A nonstationary variable can be made stationary by means of differencing, i.e. subtracting the value of the time series in the previous period from the current value.[51] Nonstationarity in a time series can be detected with unit root tests; in this thesis, the standard Dickey-Fuller test is used. If nonstationarity is present, the variable enters the regression in differenced form.

---

[50] See Arestis and Demetriades (1997), p. 784; Demetriades and Hussein (1996), p. 390f.; Hu (2002), p. 3; Quah (1993), p. 1.

[51] See Kennedy (2003), p. 325f. The number of differencing operations necessary to make the time series stationary is the order of integration. For example, a variable that requires one differencing operation to achieve stationarity is referred to as integrated of order one, which is expressed as "I(1)". See Kennedy (2003), p. 326.

Serial correlation

One of the assumptions of regression analysis is that the residuals are uncorrelated. If this assumption is violated, serial correlation is present.[52] The effect is that the deviations from the trend line in the regression are not random, but depend on values in previous periods. Incorporating error terms from previous periods would improve the forecast of current values. As a result, the standard errors of the coefficients are incorrect.[53] Besides visual inspection of the residuals, tests for serial correlation include the Durbin-Watson test and the Breusch-Godfrey Lagrange multiplier test. If serial correlation is detected, the regression is estimated with an autoregressive AR(p) model in which the residuals from past observations are integrated in the regression model.[54]

Multicollinearity

Multicollinearity refers to the correlation between independent variables in the regression. While low degrees of correlation between variables are not problematic, increasing correlation between variables has the effect of reducing the precision of the estimate of the coefficient and thus leads to an increase of the coefficient's standard error. This problem is apparent for policy variables such as statutory pre-emptions or the directed credit program: they cannot be included in the same equation because of their high correlation.[55] This problem is solved by using the unweighted summary index of financial liberalization and constructing a summary index using the method of principal components to combine the policy variables to a limited number of factors.[56]

Structural breaks

In an ordinary least square regression, structural breaks constitute a violation of the assumption of a linear relationship between the independent and the dependent variable. Possible remedies are the inclusion of dummy variables for the two periods, or splitting the data set and conducting separate analyses for the different time periods.[57] Since splitting the data set

---

[52] Serial correlation is also commonly referred to as autocorrelation.

[53] See Backhaus et al. (2003), p. 87f.

[54] For AR(p) models the Durbin-Watson test is no longer reliable. In this case, only the Breusch-Godfrey test is used.

[55] The policy variables under consideration are highly correlated as can be seen in Table 20.

[56] See Backhaus et al. (2003), p. 91; Demetriades and Luintel (1996b), p. 366; Mankiw (1995), p. 304f.

[57] See Backhaus et al. (2003), pp. 79-82.

would result in an insufficient number of observations for the statistical tests, dummy variables to account for the structural breaks are included in this study where needed.

Heteroskedasticity
Heteroskedasticity is a violation of the ordinary least square regression assumption of constant variance in the error terms. Under conditional heteroskedasticity, the value of the error term depends on the value of the independent variable, which leads to incorrect estimates of the standard error. Heteroskedasticity can be detected with the White heteroskedasticity test. A possible solution to the problem is to use White heteroskedasticity consistent standard errors.[58]

Endogeneity and simultaneity
Simultaneity in regression analysis can occur if the independent variables are not exogenous, but determined together with the dependent variable, making them endogenous to the model under consideration. An example is the correlation between investment and financial development: causality could run in both directions – i.e. from investment to financial development or from financial development to investment – or could be influenced by a third variable. A possible solution to the problems of simultaneity and endogeneity is the inclusion of instrumental variables such as political stability or human capital in the equation. However, these variables are likely to also be correlated with the macroeconomic variables under consideration, which makes it difficult to establish causality between endogenous variables. Therefore, the interpretation of the results may have to be limited to the correlations between different variables.[59]

Measurement errors and data quality
Besides problems with the application of the statistical tests, regression results can also be influenced by variables being measured inaccurately or misreported by governments. To deal with these issues, the general suggestion is to identify the variables that are particularly badly measured and isolate the least reliable findings.[60] Data quality is a particular problem in China. A case in point is the recent upward revision of GDP growth fig-

---

[58] See Backhaus et al. (2003), pp. 84-87; Platek (2002), p. 187f.
[59] See Mankiw (1995), p. 303f.; Temple (1999), p. 128f. In the former example of two-way causation the independent variable would be endogenous.
[60] See Temple (1999), p. 130.

ures.[61] To ensure comparability between the India and China, data from the Asian Development Bank, the IMF and the World Bank are used. However, the risk remains that the official statistics on which these international agencies base their reports exhibit measurement error. Possible issues with data quality will be discussed on a case-by-case basis where necessary.

The variables used in the regression analysis are based on the theoretical relationships mentioned above and the empirical literature. Following Levine and Renelt (1992), a distinction between four different types of variables can be made: the dependent variables, variables that are always included in the regression, the variable of interest, and variables identified as potentially important.[62] In the context of this thesis, the dependent variables are the macroeconomic aggregates such as saving or capital formation, for which the effect of financial liberalization is tested. The main variable of interest is the financial liberalization index, since the aim of the tests is to find out if financial liberalization has exerted a significant influence on the dependent variables. Explanatory variables that are always included in the regression are the log of GDP per capita, the GDP growth rate, and the interest rate: these have a potential influence on the dependent variable.[63] Other potentially important variables include dummy variables for structural breaks and the percentage share of financial and physical savings, for instance. A detailed description of the variables and their sources can be found in the appendix (Table 22).

The equation used to test the relationships between financial liberalization and the various macroeconomic variables has the following general form:

$$L_t = c + \lambda_1 LGDP_t + \lambda_2 RATE_t + \lambda_3 \Delta GDP_t + \lambda_4 INDEX_t + \lambda_5 VAR_t + \varepsilon_t$$

where L is the respective dependent variable, LGDP is the logarithm of real GDP per capita, RATE is depending on the tested macroeconomic variable either the lending or the deposit interest rate, ΔGDP is the growth

[61] See National Bureau of Statistics of China (2006). For a discussion of the limitations of Chinese economic indicators and the problems of China's statistical system, see Wu (2003).

[62] See Levine and Renelt (1992), p. 944.

[63] Note: (1) the logarithm of GDP per capita is used to account for the exponential nature of the time series; other variables that exhibit an exponential trend also enter the regression in their logarithmic form; (2) depending on the variable under consideration, either the interest rate for deposits or lending is included.

rate of GDP, INDEX is the summary index of financial liberalization, and VAR is a placeholder for additional variables that are included on an as-needed basis in the regression. C is the constant in the regression, λ denotes the regression coefficients and ε stands for the random error in the regression.

7.2.2.2 Results of statistical tests

To test the effect of banking sector liberalization at the macroeconomic level, the hypotheses postulated further above are tested for India and China. These hypotheses are related to the effects of removing repressionist policies on the saving ratio, capital formation and financial development. The tests are conducted with two indices: one is an unadjusted liberalization index, and the other is adjusted for market failure. Since the two indices are highly correlated with each other in both countries, only results for the unadjusted index are discussed and reported. Since some of the adjustments for market failure were explicitly based on Indian data, this should increase the confidence in the overall results. The values for the index that is adjusted for market failure can be found in the appendix. The same applies to the index that is constructed with the method of principal components. Since it is highly correlated with both the unadjusted index and the market failure index, the statistical tests are not conducted separately for this index. The index values can again be found in the appendix.[64]

The analyses are conducted for India and China for the period 1980 to 2004. The same analyses are conducted separately for the 1960-2004 period. This provides further insights into the long-term effects of financial liberalization. Since data for 1960-1980 is only available for India, the results cannot be put in a comparative perspective with China.

Hypothesis 1:
Liberalizing the banking sector increases the saving rate and the stock of savings.

The financial liberalization hypothesis predicts that a reduction of repressionist policies increases the incentive to save. This is tested by regressing saving to GDP, and bank deposits to GDP, against the process index of financial liberalization. This is done to account for the overall amount of saving and the savings intermediated through the banking sector.

[64] See Table 23 for the correlations between the different indices and Table 24 for the values of the indices.

Saving to GDP
For both India and China, GDP per capita and GDP growth enter the regression as expected with a positive value, while – surprisingly – the real deposit rate enters with a negative value (Table 8). Statistically significant at the 1% level are GDP per capita and the real deposit rate in India.[65] One possible explanation for the negative sign for the real deposit rate can be the positive correlation between deposit and lending interest rates: since saving to GDP includes saving of households, the public sector and private companies, the later two might be inclined to save less when interest rates rise, so as to avoid higher costs for loans.

The liberalization index enters as predicted by the financial liberalization hypothesis with a positive coefficient in the case of India, but with a negative one for China. However, the index is only statistically significant for India. In other words, in India saving has been influenced by liberalization.

Bank deposits to GDP
GDP per capita and the real deposit rate enter the regression as expected with positive values for the two countries, while the financial liberalization index enters with negative values, contrary to the predictions of the financial liberalization hypothesis. GDP growth enters with a negative coefficient for India and a positive one for China.

For China, GDP per capita is significant at the 1% level, while the financial liberalization index is not statistically significant. For India, the real deposit rate and the GDP growth are statistically significant, while the liberalization index is, as in China, not significant.

Overall, the main driving factors for saving appear to be the GDP per capita and the real deposit rate. Except for saving to GDP in India, liberalization has no statistically significant effect on saving and might even have the opposite effect – as can be judged by the negative coefficients of the liberalization index in the regressions. Therefore, the hypothesis that liberalization increases the level of savings has to be rejected. There is even weak evidence that the opposite may be true. A possible explanation is that in a liberalized banking sector there is less need to save since credit is more easily available if capital is needed. These results are confirmed by visual inspection of the development of saving over time (Figure 32): savings and deposits have shown an upward trend, irrespective of the prevailing policy environment.

[65] This means that they are different from 0 with a probability of more than 99%.

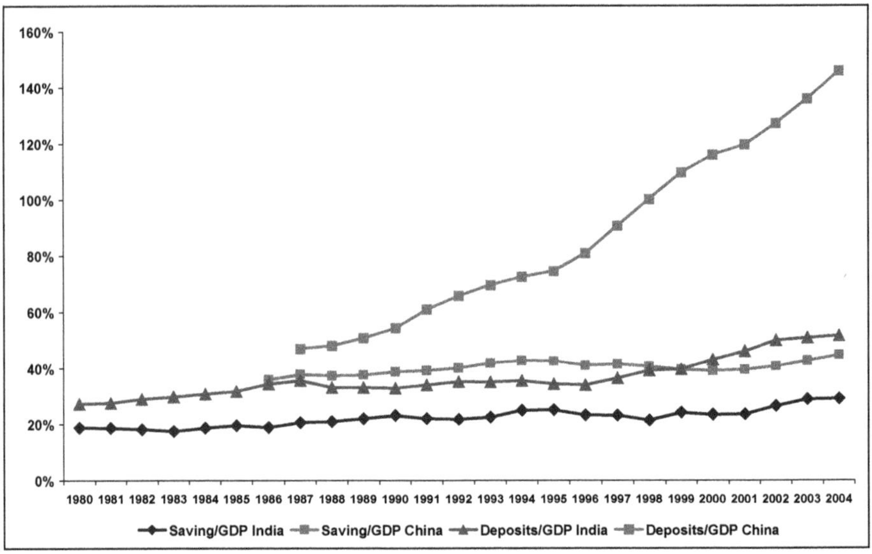

Fig. 32. Saving and deposits India and China[66]

Hypothesis 2:
Liberalizing the banking sector increases the availability of capital.
Closely connected to the previous hypothesis is the prediction that liberalization leads to an increased availability of capital. The indicators to test this hypothesis are the ratio of private credit to GDP and the gross fixed capital formation as a percentage of GDP.

Private credit to GDP
For both countries, GDP per capita has a positive coefficient as expected. This implies that demand for credit increases with increasing wealth. GDP growth has a negative coefficient. Surprisingly, the real lending rate enters with a positive coefficient in both countries. The liberalization index enters – contrary to the predictions of the financial liberalization hypothesis – with negative coefficients in both countries.

Statistically significant coefficients are the GDP per capita for both India and China. In the case of India, the real lending rate and the GDP growth are also statistically significant. The liberalization index is not statistically significant and enters with a negative sign. Therefore, financial liberalization does not appear to have an effect on the demand for private credit.

[66] See Asian Development Bank (2006); Government of India (2006); International Monetary Fund (2006b).

Gross fixed capital formation to GDP
GDP per capita enters as expected with a positive coefficient, whereas the real lending rate has a negative coefficient in both countries. Thus the expected positive relationship with capital formation holds in both countries. For GDP growth the picture again differs for India and China: the coefficient is as expected positive for China, but negative for India. The liberalization index enters with a negative coefficient for India, but with the expected positive coefficient for China. However, for both countries, the results are not statistically significant. No relationship between gross fixed capital formation and liberalization can therefore be established.

The results of the tests imply that financial liberalization does not have a statistically significant effect on either private credit or capital formation. Both private credit and gross fixed capital formation have shown a relatively steady upward trend since 1980 (Figure 33). The negative signs of the liberalization coefficients provide weak evidence that even the opposite relationship occurs, which would point to a more successful accumulation of capital in India and China when the banking system was more restrained. This might be the result of higher capital intensity in the early phases of the economic take-off. Again, the hypothesis has to be rejected.

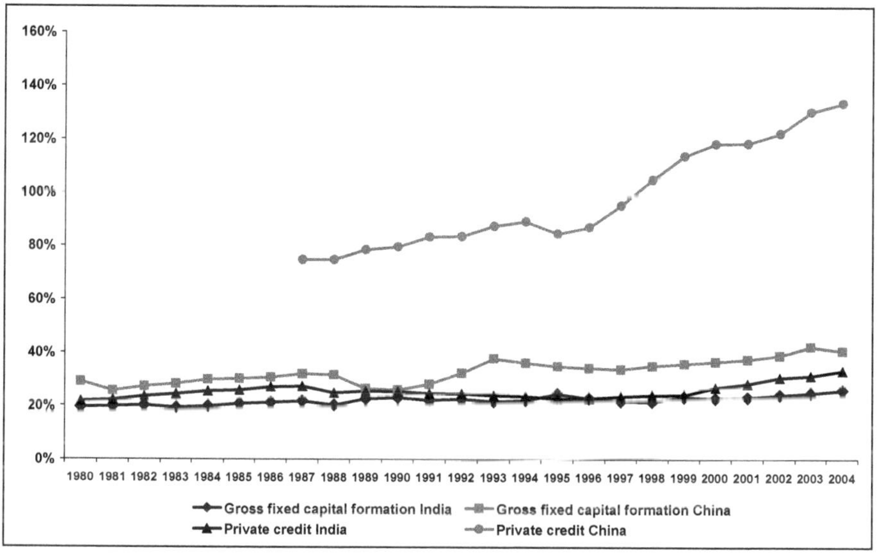

Fig. 33. Credit and capital formation India and China[67]

[67] Author's calculation based on International Monetary Fund (2006b).

Hypothesis 3:
Liberalization of the banking sector increases the efficiency of capital allocation.

The proxy for measuring the efficiency of capital allocation is the incremental capital-output ratio (ICOR) that measures the units of capital needed for an additional unit of GDP growth. If the financial liberalization hypothesis is correct, liberalization increases the efficiency with which capital is employed so that less capital is needed for an additional unit of GDP growth. Consequently, the ratio is expected to decrease in a more liberal banking sector.

For India, the real lending rate, GDP growth and the liberalization index enter the regression with negative values. This indicates a more efficient use of capital in India with increasing GDP growth, increasing interest rates and financial liberalization. However, since only the coefficients for the real lending rate and GDP growth are statistically significant, financial liberalization does not contribute in a significant manner to the increased efficiency of capital allocation. This becomes evident if one looks at the ICOR. This has fluctuated constantly between values of two and five since 1980 (Figure 34).

The extremely high value for 1991 is an outlier that can be explained by the low growth after the balance of payment crisis. It is interesting to note that the ICOR has not differed significantly between India and China since the early 1990s, despite a somewhat better developed banking system and lower investment rates in India.

Table 8. Results of statistical tests

Regressors	Dependent variable Log Saving India		Log Deposits India		Log Credit GDP India		Log Capital India		Delta Capital GDP India		Deposit Money India		Liquid Liabilities India	
	Coefficient	Std. Error	Coefficient	Std. Error	Coefficient	Std. Error	Coefficient	Std. Error	Coefficient	Std. Error	Coefficient	Std. Error	Coefficient	Std. Error
Intercept	-7.0135 ***	0.4601	-0.0338	0.2668	-0.6387 **	0.2793	-3.9202 ***	0.3565	22.8230 ***	3.2413	-5.4498 ***	0.9528	-0.1438	0.1098
GDP_CAPITA	0.5713 ***	0.0488	0.0129	0.0283	0.0651 **	0.0285	0.2506 ***	0.0364	---	---	0.5317 ***	0.0962	0.0190	0.0116
REAL_DEPOSIT	-2.2730 ***	0.6468	0.7421 *	0.3750	---	---	---	---	---	---	0.3433	0.3272	0.2339	0.1543
REAL_LENDING	---	---	---	---	1.1214 **	0.4687	-0.1637	0.5983	-113.8888 ***	35.4550	---	---	---	---
INDEX_INDIA	0.4955 **	0.2319	-0.1164	0.1345	-0.0865	0.1680	-0.0274	0.2145	-4.0614	12.8297	0.1706 *	0.0904	-0.0155	0.0553
GDP_GROWTH	0.3428	0.5404	-1.3030 ***	0.3133	-0.9777 **	0.3927	-0.0209	0.5014	-160.6157 ***	29.4556	---	---	-0.5650 ***	0.1289
AR(1)	---	---	---	---	---	---	---	---	---	---	0.7793	0.0942	---	---
Adjusted R^2	0.8820		0.4900		0.3332		0.6704		0.6257		0.9616		0.5213	
Observations	24		24		24		24		24		23		24	
Year	1981-2004		1981-2004		1981-2004		1981-2004		1981-2004		1982-2004		1981-2004	

Regressors	Dependent variable Log Saving China		Log Deposits China		Log Credit GDP China		Log Capital China		Delta Capital GDP China		Deposit Money China		Liquid Liabilities China	
	Coefficient	Std. Error	Coefficient	Std. Error	Coefficient	Std. Error	Coefficient	Std. Error	Coefficient	Std. Error	Coefficient	Std. Error	Coefficient	Std. Error
Intercept	-1.7473 ***	0.1714	-7.3252 ***	0.7890	-4.1630 ***	0.9248	-3.1615 ***	0.1737	7.4219 ***	0.3868	-0.3599 ***	0.0517	2.0913	5.6225
GDP_CAPITA	0.0950 ***	0.0198	0.8360 ***	0.0891	0.4852 ***	0.1062	0.2278 ***	0.0202	---	---	0.0383 ***	0.0071	0.1251	0.3042
REAL_DEPOSIT	-0.4734 *	0.2564	0.4807	0.2957	---	---	---	---	---	---	0.0291	0.0336	0.0848	0.2054
REAL_LENDING	---	---	---	---	0.0734	0.3632	-0.2247	0.2525	-1.0696	2.3947	---	---	---	---
INDEX_CHINA	-0.1365	0.2322	-0.0607	0.1783	-0.0386	0.2243	0.2368	0.3231	2.4381	2.7742	0.0013	0.0214	0.0216	0.1359
GDP_GROWTH	0.3613	0.3822	0.2854	0.4447	-0.2137	0.5086	1.6578 ***	0.3847	-38.5108 ***	3.6272	---	---	0.1385	0.2592
AR(1)	---	---	0.7221	0.2901	0.7262	0.2453	---	---	---	---	0.6488	0.1836	0.9827	0.0171
Adjusted R^2	0.6067		0.9899		0.9463		0.8841		0.8414		0.9333		0.9953	
Observations	19		17		17		24		24		19		23	
Year	1986-2004		1988-2004		1988-2004		1981-2004		1981-2004		1986-2004		1982-2004	

Note: * = significance at the 10% level, ** = significance at the 5% level, *** = significance at the 1% level

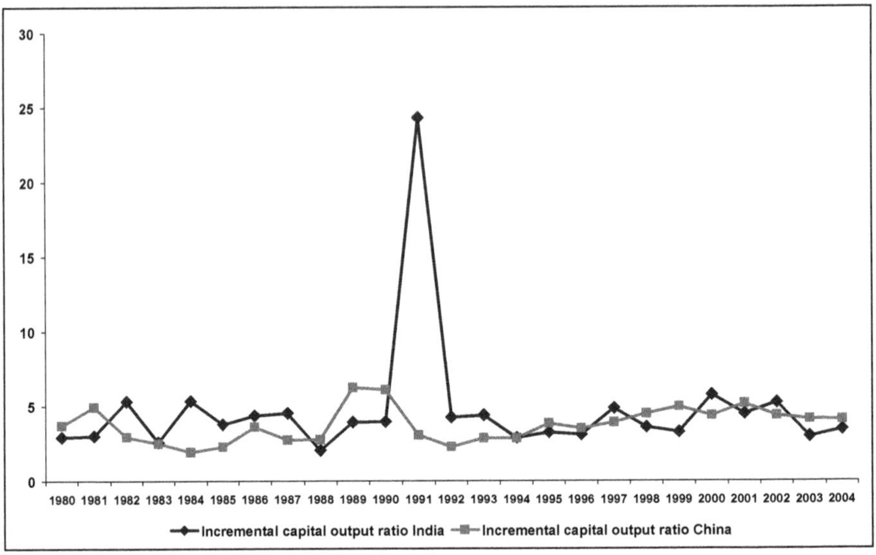

Fig. 34. Capital efficiency India and China[68]

For China, the coefficients for the real lending rate and GDP growth enter with negative values, while the liberalization index has a positive coefficient. However, only the GDP growth rate is statistically significant, while the liberalization index is not significant. As in India, capital efficiency in China appears to be driven mainly by GDP growth, while financial liberalization has little influence. The development of the ICOR in China shows that the values have fluctuated over time without a clear trend. It is especially striking that the efficiency of capital allocation declined between 1992 and 1998, which was also a time of progress in banking sector reforms. Nonetheless, since loan growth was also particularly strong in these years, this is an indication that the credit appraisal skills of banks were still insufficient.

As for the previous tests, the hypothesis that financial liberalization increases the efficiency of capital allocation has to be rejected. Possible reasons for this are lending to less efficient, state-owned enterprises that especially in China still receive a disproportionate share of credit as well as banks' insufficient credit evaluation skills.

Hypothesis 4:
Banking sector liberalization positively influences financial development by increasing financial depth and the importance of deposit money banks.

[68] Author's calculation based on International Monetary Fund (2006b).

The reduction of repressionist policies is commonly associated with improved financial development. Financial development is proxied by the ratio of liquid liabilities to GDP and the ratio of bank credit to bank and central bank credit. The ratio of liquid liabilities to GDP is a measure of financial depth that shows the size of the formal financial system. The ratio of bank credit to bank and central bank credit gives an indication of the importance of deposit banks, which provide better risk management and investment services than the central bank.[69]

Liquid liabilities
GDP per capita and the real deposit rate enter as expected with positive coefficients for India and China. The GDP growth rate has an unexpected negative sign in India, but a positive one in China. The liberalization index enters the regression in India with a negative sign, and in China with a positive one. The only statistically significant coefficient is GDP growth in India. The liberalization index is not statistically significant, so the hypothesis must be rejected.

Deposit money bank assets
All coefficients of the independent variables enter with positive signs in both countries. Statistically significant are the GDP per capita in both countries and the liberalization index in India. As predicted by the financial liberalization hypothesis, there is a statistical significant relationship between the importance of deposit money banks and banking sector liberalization in India.

Overall, it can be concluded that financial liberalization in India and China has not had a statistically significant impact on financial development. A more important factor was the increasing income level that brought more people into the formal banking system. Again, this result is mirrored by the development of the respective indicators of financial development over time (Figure 24). In both countries, the indicators increased fairly steadily since the late 1980s; it is therefore difficult to establish a relationship with the liberalization measures in either country.

Hypothesis 5:
The liberalization of the banking sector causes through a higher level of financial development an increase in the growth rate.

[69] See King and Levine (1993), p. 718; Wachtel (2001), p. 342.

Three possible channels of causality must be explored in order to test this hypothesis: (1) economic growth causes financial development, (2) financial development causes economic growth, and (3) there exists a two-way relationship between financial development and economic growth. As for the previous hypothesis, liquid liabilities to GDP and the share of deposit money bank assets are indicators for financial development.

Causality is tested with the Granger causality test. In this test, *x* causes *y* if the lagged values of *x* provide statistically significant information on future values of *y* and vice versa. If this is the case, the conclusion is that "*x* Granger causes *y*". When interpreting results from a Granger causality test, it is important to be aware that Granger causality does not necessarily imply a cause-and-effect relationship. Rather it is a measure of the information contained in one variable to explain the second variable.[70]

The Granger causality tests reveal a split picture. For China, Granger causality runs from financial development when defined as deposit money bank assets to economic growth (Table 9). In India, the causality runs from growth to financial development. For the second indicator – liquid liabilities – no statistically significant relationship in either direction could be established. The evidence is thus weak, at best, that financial development causes economic growth, as assumed by the financial liberalization hypothesis.

Table 9. Results of Granger causality tests India and China

	Causality runs from....		
GDP growth and ...	Growth → Financial Dev.	Financial Dev. → Growth	Two-way causality
Deposit money bank assets India	✓**	✗	✗
Liquid liabilities India	✗	✗	✗
Deposit money bank assets China	✗	✓*	✗
Liquid liabilities China	✗	✗	✗

Note: (1) * significance at the 10% level, ** significance at the 5% level, *** significance at the 1% level. (2) the test statistics can be found in Table 25 in the appendix.

[70] See Quantitative Micro Software (2004), p. 226f.

Looking at the overall results form the hypothesis tests, it can be concluded that financial liberalization has so far not had significant positive effects on the macroeconomic functions of the banking sector in either India or China. Analyzing the development of the various indicators such as saving, capital, and capital efficiency shows that they generally experienced a relatively steady upward trend during the period under consideration. Since in both countries the state dominated the banking sector heavily at least until the mid-1980s, the question arises of why financial repression did not have more negative effects. Based on these results, there appears to be – contrary to the McKinnon-Shaw school – no significant connection between the policy environment in the banking sector and the fulfillment of the macroeconomic functions of the sector. This also shows that the differences in the transformation processes between the two countries discussed in section 5.5 had no significant influence on the outcomes. Consequently, the results are not only valid for India or China, but for other countries as well.

The analysis has two potential pitfalls. First, the basis of the liberalization index used in the previous statistical analyses were the process elements suggested by transformation studies. By contrast, the early financial liberalization literature focused more narrowly on the removal of repressionist policies, including interest rate restrictions, statutory pre-emptions and directed credit programs; these are covered in the sub-index for liberalization and so only get a 20% weight in the index. Second, the tests were conducted for the period after 1980, when a more liberal banking system emerged in both India and China. The period before 1980 – when for example in India the influence of the state on the banking sector increased – is not covered. The inclusion of a longer time period with a different policy environment might thus lead to different conclusions.

To cross-check the validity of the results, the same analyses are conducted again using a narrower index of financial liberalization for a longer time period. This longer period allows for a more detailed examination of different policy regimes. Reliable data for 1960 to 1980 is only available for India, so China cannot be included in the analysis. The index for evaluating the effects for India from 1960 to 2005 consists of the policies towards interest rate controls, credit controls and effective reserve requirements. It is thus the sub-index for liberalization from the broader index. As before, the different policies are equally weighted. The index values can be found in Table 27 in the appendix.

As discussed in section 2.1, state involvement in the Indian banking sector was relatively low until the beginning of the 1960s. The role of the state increased until the mid-1980s, when first steps to ease regulations were taken. Prior to the crisis in 1991, state involvement increased again, before declining permanently in the 1990s. These policy changes are mirrored in the narrower liberalization index for India from 1960 to 2005 that clearly reflects increasing state influence between 1960 and 1990 as well as the liberalization progress from the early 1990s (Figure 35). The period between 1960 and 2005 therefore makes it possible to analyze the effects of different policy regimes on macroeconomic variables over time. The same hypotheses as before are tested. Since broader data is available for India than for China, additional variables such as household savings are included in the tests where they might help to refine the results.

As before, the effects of the policy changes on the saving ratio are explored first. A visual inspection shows that all three *saving* aggregates under investigation – household saving, overall saving, and bank deposits – have steadily increased in India since the 1960s (Figure 36).

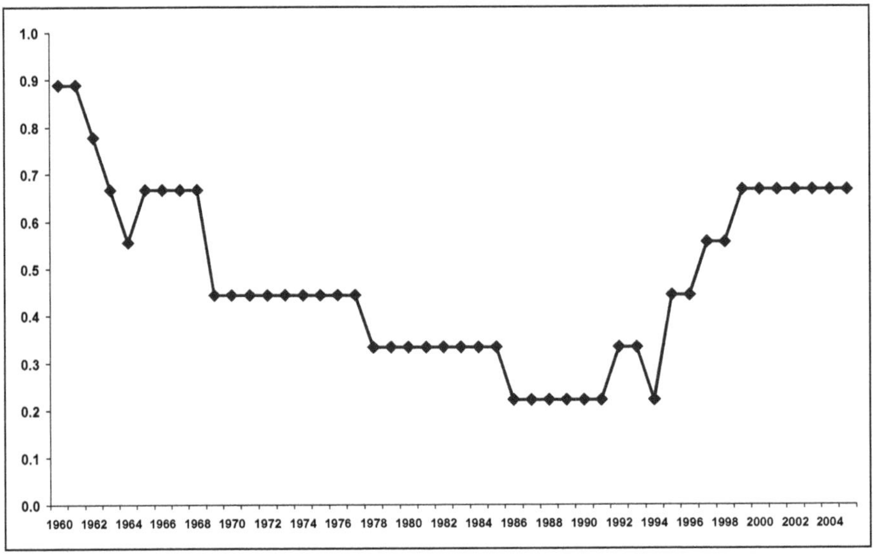

Fig. 35. Liberalization index India

Thus, the different policy regimes and the level of government involvement appear to have had an insignificant influence. This is confirmed by the statistical tests: again the removal of repressionist policies has no statistically significant effect on saving. The main influencing factor is GDP per capita, so that rising incomes appear to be the main driver of saving in India over time (Table 10).

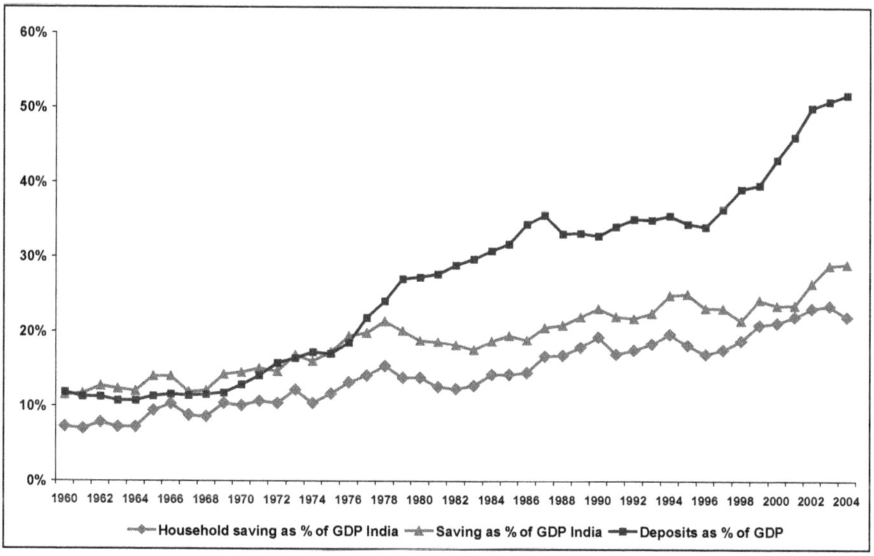

Fig. 36. Savings India[71]

Both *capital* and *private capital* have increased relatively steadily since the 1960s, while credit to GDP has developed somewhat differently: after rapid expansion until the mid-1980s, it declined and then increased again in the late 1990s (Figure 37).

The statistical tests show that liberalization had a significant positive influence on both capital and private capital. As for the previous tests for saving, GDP per capita also exerts a positive influence. Unlike the results for the 1980-2004 time period, the shifting policy regimes in the sector had an influence on the availability of capital. For the third indicator under investigation in this category – credit to GDP – no statistically significant influence of either repression or liberalization can be found.

[71] See Government of India (2006), table 15; International Monetary Fund (2006b).

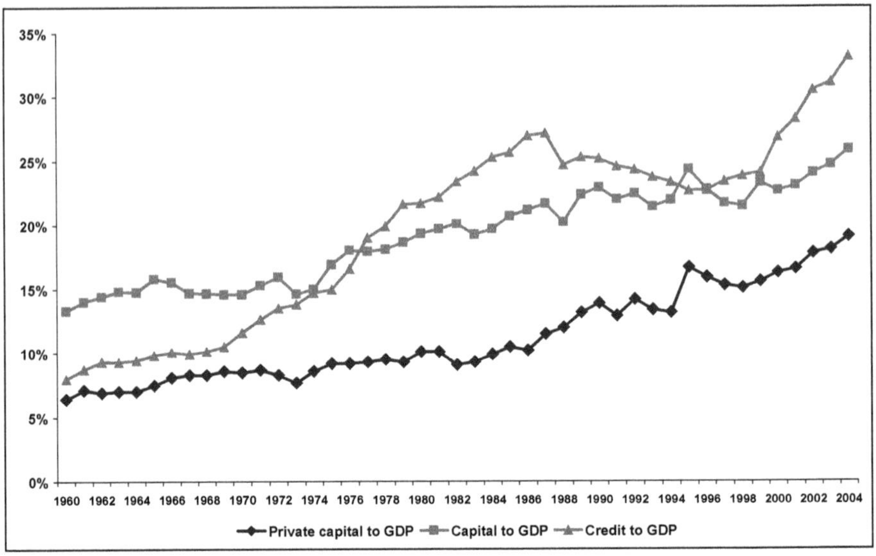

Fig. 37. Capital and credit India[72]

Capital efficiency has fluctuated widely in India over the last decades with no clear trend (Figure 38).[73] Because of this, it is not surprising that financial liberalization has no significant influence on capital efficiency in the statistical tests. Besides that GDP per capita enters again with a positive sign, while GDP growth has a negative influence on capital efficiency. However, the results should not be over-interpreted because of the low explanatory power as measured by the R^2. This points to the effects of boom-bust cycles in the economy on the efficiency with which capital is used.

[72] See International Monetary Fund (2006b).

[73] The outliers are the result of either low or negative growth without a significant reduction of investment activity.

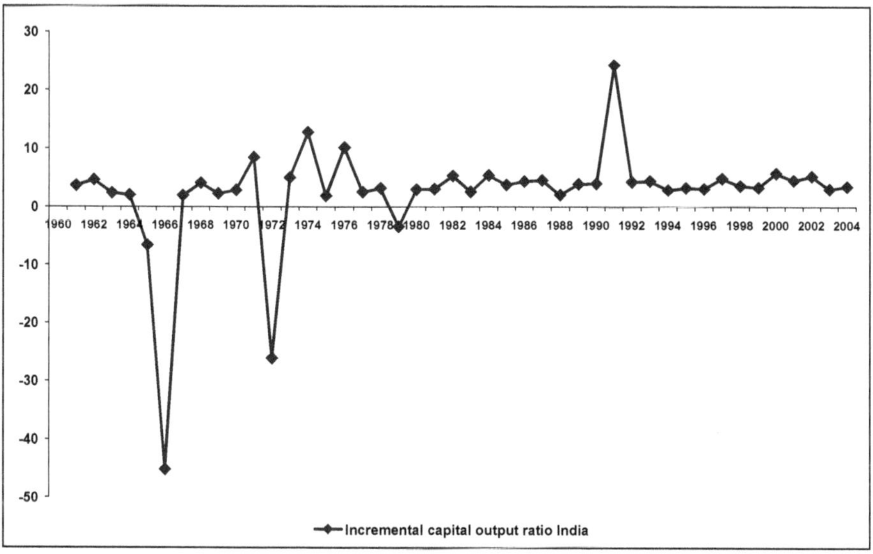

Fig. 38. Capital efficiency India[74]

The indicators of *financial development* have increased relatively steadily in India over time (Figure 39). Liquid liabilities to GDP increased from the mid-1970s, while deposit money bank assets increased until about 1980s, then declined and then increased again at the beginning of the 1990s.

The statistical tests show that financial liberalization has no significant influence on financial development. The main factors influencing the financial development indicators are GDP per capita, the real interest rate, and GDP growth. A likely reason for the lack of a relationship between financial liberalization and financial development is that state intervention in India increased the size and reach of the formal banking sector, which in turn helped it to increase the degree of monetization.

[74] Author's calculation based on International Monetary Fund (2006b).

Table 10. Results of statistical tests India 1960-2004

Regressors	Dependent variable Log Saving		Log Deposits		Log Saving Households		Log Credit GDP		Log Capital	
	Coefficient	Std. Error	Coefficient	Std. Error	Coefficient	Std. Error	Coefficient	Std. Error	Coefficient	Std. Error
Intercept	-7.3388 ***	1.6006	-1.1124 **	0.5199	-9.3699 ***	2.0521	-0.7534	0.4682	-5.6333 ***	1.1313
GDP_CAPITA	0.6090 ***	0.1692	0.1298 **	0.0571	0.7919 ***	0.2204	0.0904 *	0.0514	0.4242 ***	0.1205
REAL_BANKRATE	-0.3926	0.2560	-0.0486 *	0.1834	-0.2189	0.3567	-0.2818 *	0.1652	0.1467	0.1661
INDEX_LIB	0.0336	0.1136	-0.0742	0.1017	-0.0674	0.1599	-0.0500	0.0916	0.1657 **	0.0734
GDP_GROWTH	-0.5498 *	0.2796	-0.8599 ***	0.2395	-0.5233	0.3885	-0.6502 ***	0.2157	-0.2823	0.1827
DUMMY_1980	- - -	- - -	-0.0439 *	0.0245	- - -	- - -	-0.0473 **	0.0221	0.0202	0.0509
DUMMY_1991	-0.0163	0.0728	-0.0333	0.0305	0.0189	0.1000	-0.0171	0.0275	-0.0095	0.0474
SHARE_FINSAV	- - -	- - -	- - -	- - -	-0.0010	0.2249	- - -	- - -	- - -	- - -
AR(1)	0.8105	0.0887	- - -	- - -	0.7541	0.1013	- - -	- - -	0.8230	0.1034
Adjusted R^2	0.9246		0.2342		0.9196		0.2656		0.9430	
Observations	43		44		42		44		43	
Year	1962-2004		1961-2004		1962-2003		1961-2004		1962-2004	

Regressors	Dependent variable Log Private Capital		Delta Capital GDP		Deposit Money Banks		Liquid Liabilities	
	Coefficient	Std. Error	Coefficient	Std. Error	Coefficient	Std. Error	Coefficient	Std. Error
Intercept	-9.8458 ***	0.9814	-79.8740 *	46.6604	-2.8536 **	1.1454	-1.0314 **	0.4536
GDP_CAPITA	0.8100 ***	0.1071	8.5734 *	5.0770	0.2771 **	0.1152	0.1185 **	0.0498
REAL_BANKRATE	0.0150	0.2193	-71.1425 *	39.0262	-0.0913	0.0908	-0.1601	0.1600
INDEX_LIB	0.2911 ***	0.0992	-1.2408	21.6472	-0.0312	0.0398	-0.0714	0.0887
GDP_GROWTH	-0.0078	0.2409	46.2242	51.3419	-0.2123 *	0.1093	-0.8189 ***	0.2090
DUMMY_1980	-0.0009	0.0495	- - -	- - -	-0.0426	0.0269	-0.0267	0.0266
DUMMY_1991	0.0209	0.0549	- - -	- - -	0.0655 **	0.0267	-0.0305	0.0254
SHARE_FINSAV	- - -	- - -	- - -	- - -	- - -	- - -	- - -	- - -
AR(1)	0.5819	0.1412	- - -	- - -	0.9302	0.0421	- - -	- - -
Adjusted R^2	0.9686		0.0949		0.9765		0.2554	
Observations	43		44		43		44	
Year	1962-2004		1961-2004		1962-2004		1961-2004	

Note: * = significance at the 10% level, ** = significance at the 5% level, *** = significance at the 1% level

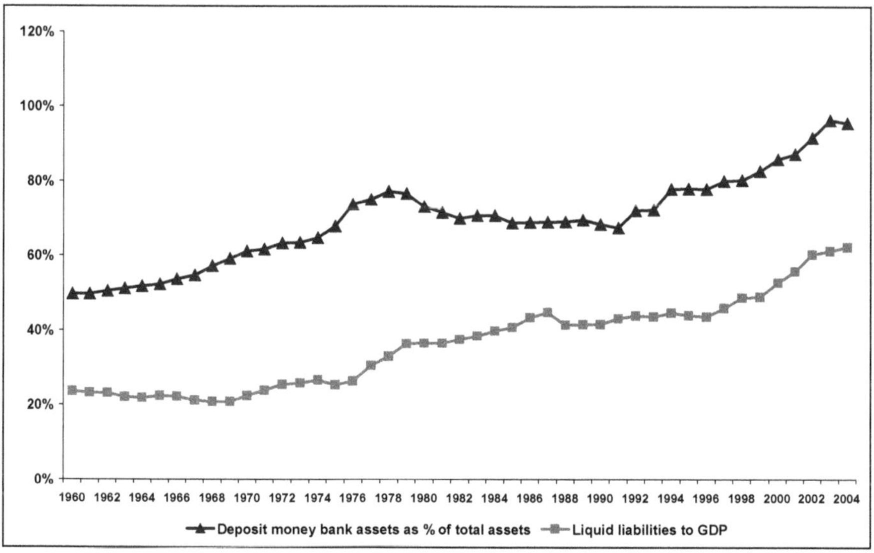

Fig. 39. Financial development ratios India 1960-2004[75]

As before, tests are conducted for Granger causality between *financial development* and *economic growth*. The outcome is that, for both indicators of financial development – the share of deposit money bank assets and liquid liabilities to GDP – causality in the Granger sense runs from financial development to economic growth (Table 11).

Table 11. Results of Granger causality test India

	Causality runs from....		
GDP growth and ...	Growth → Financial Dev.	Financial Dev. → Growth	Two-way causality
Deposit money bank assets India	✗	✓**	✗
Liquid liabilities India	✗	✓***	✗

Note: (1) * significance at the 10% level, ** significance at the 5% level, *** significance at the 1% level. (2) the test statistics can be found in Table 25 in the appendix.

The results of the Granger causality tests for 1960-2004 are clearly at odds with the previous results, which showed one-way causality running from growth to financial development. This indicates that the relationship

[75] Author's calculation based on International Monetary Fund (2006b).

between financial development and growth depends on the time period under consideration, and therefore might be spurious. The results of the tests should thus not be over-interpreted.

The overall results show that financial liberalization had no significant effects on the macro-variables under investigation (Table 12). While this is very clear for China, there is some evidence for India that financial liberalization had a positive influence on certain macroeconomic variables. However, the positive effects appear to depend on both the time period and the index used, since different variables are statistically significant.

Table 12. Summary of statistical tests

	Liberalization index (1980-2004)		Liberalization index (1960-2004)
Regressor	India	China	India
Saving	Positive	Not significant	Not significant
Deposits	Not significant	Not significant	Not significant
Saving Households	- - -	- - -	Not significant
Credit	Not significant	Not significant	Not significant
Capital	Not significant	Not significant	Positive
Private Capital	- - -	- - -	Positive
Delta Capital to GDP	Not significant	Not significant	Not significant
Deposit Money Bank Assets	Positive	- - -	Not significant
Liquid Liabilities	Not significant	Not significant	Not significant

Both India and China had highly restricted banking sectors until at least the mid-1980s. The results thus also imply that, besides the lack of positive effects from liberalization, financial repression had no significant negative effects on the functioning of the banking sector. This is supported by the analysis of the 1960 to 1990 period in India, when saving, capital and financial development increased despite growing levels of financial repression. Two questions must be asked as a result: how have the interventionist policies contributed to the banking sector's better than expected fulfillment of its functions? And why has liberalization not yielded more positive results?

The development background of the banking sectors in the two countries offers partial answers, which is exemplified well by the changes in India. In India in the 1960s, large parts of the rural population had no access to the formal banking sector. For example, in 1969 – the year of the first nationalizations of banks – less than 25% of the roughly 8,300 bank branches were located in rural areas. In line with the goal of branch expansion – one of the objectives of the nationalizations – the number of branches in India increased to more than 67,000 in 2004, of which almost 50% are in rural areas.[76] Larger parts of the population thus had the possibility of using formal sector banking institutions for savings and loans. This led to an increase of the macroeconomic importance of the banking sector – a development that was fueled by government intervention in a largely underdeveloped environment. This neither implies that the branch expansion was efficient in economic terms nor that it might not have occurred without the government's active role, but simply that the state-directed policy was helpful in accelerating the expansion of the formal banking sector in formerly under-served regions.

A further contributing factor to the development of the banking sector in a repressionist environment was the policy of extending subsidized credit to priority sectors. This increased the demand for credit and helped to build up the capital stock in previously under-served parts of the economy. Government intervention in the banking sector helped to achieve this expansion. But, again, this does not imply that capital was allocated efficiently or that banks would not have extended loans on their own. While these two factors help to explain why increasing financial repression did not have the expected negative effects, it does not shed light on the question of why liberalization has not led to more positive results.

Prior to the start of liberalization, both India and China had made significant progress in extending the reach of their formal banking sectors, which led to steady increases in saving and credit by integrating larger parts of the population into the system. The progress made in the years prior to liberalization also made further improvements after liberalization more difficult, since the low-hanging fruits had already been picked. Further expansion in terms of saving or capital was therefore difficult to achieve through a policy change such as liberalization, which clearly has no built-in mechanism for increasing available funds for saving or credit demand. As the statistical tests show, increases in income had a more important influence on these variables.

While further quantitative expansion of the banking sector was difficult after liberalization, an improvement in the quality of intermediation could have been expected. However, in both India and China the efficiency of capital allocation as measured by the ICOR did not improve – with potentially severe adverse effects for both countries. This is particularly important for India, due to the lower savings rate.

---

[76] See Reserve Bank of India (2004a), p. 1.

Possible explanations for the lack of improvement in the ICOR are the still insufficient credit evaluation skills and the continuing dominant position of state-owned banks in the two countries. State ownership of banks is associated with lower financial development, and this also helps to explain why liberalization has so far not resulted in more positive results at the macro level. Closely connected is the relatively limited competition from more sophisticated banks, which to some extent insulates the incumbents from improving the efficiency of credit allocation. Country-specific factors include the fact that in India, 40% of credit still goes to priority sectors, while in China, less efficient state-owned enterprises still receive a disproportionate share of credit.[77] For China, with its extremely high saving rate, the closed capital account also offers an explanation for why investment efficiency has not improved. Because of the closed capital account, savings have to be invested in the country, which can lead to over-investment and subsequently lower returns, especially at China's saving rate.[78]

7.3 Conclusion

In this chapter the banking sector reforms in India and China were evaluated in three ways. First, the reforms were evaluated qualitatively based on propositions on how to liberalize a banking sector; second, the performance at the industry level was analyzed across several dimensions; and third, it was tested if liberalization has had any significant effects on macroeconomic variables that are commonly associated with banking sector reforms.

The qualitative evaluation of the reforms showed that the general propositions were followed fairly well in both countries. Larger deviations occurred in the more "visible" reform areas – recapitalization, privatization, and directed credit – that affect large, well-organized interest groups. Of the different political economy factors discussed, interest groups had the largest impact on the reform process and as such had a greater importance

[77] Lal (2006) points out that the faster-growing and more efficient private sector in China is crowded out from credit by inefficient SOEs, which lowers the ICOR and the growth rate. See Lal (2006), p. 280.

[78] See Makin (2006), p. 313. This leads to a dilemma for Chinese policy makers: opening the capital account could enhance the efficiency of domestic investments and offer Chinese savers higher returns by investing abroad. However, given the fragile state of the Chinese banking system, a large capital outflow would significantly increase the risk of a banking crisis. See Lardy (2005), p. 46.

than the weak fiscal situation in the two countries, for example. This also shows the need to anticipate and incorporate the likely responses of interest groups into the transformation strategy and to design mechanisms to compensate reform losers. Also important is the credibility of the government. Credibility will not only help remove impediments to reform – it is also necessary for pursuing policies such as "one-time only" stabilizations of banks and enterprises.

At the sector level, reforms in most areas have proceeded quite far, with India being clearly ahead of China. Over the past years, the pace of reform has slowed somewhat in both countries, but this is only to be expected since the easier and more popular reforms are generally conducted first. Pursuing further reforms requires – besides the necessary political will – that political-economy factors are included in the reform strategy, as described above. On the result side, the reforms have contributed to a significantly improved performance of the sector as measured by indicators such as ROA or NPLs, especially in India. In China, the improvements have been rather small, since the burden of change is higher and reforms have not proceeded as far as in India. In both countries, private sector banks have not yet been able to take a significant share of the market and the concentration of the banking sector remains high. Improvements have been made in terms of stability in both India and China, but NPL level in China remains high given the favorable macroeconomic environment.

The evaluation of the reforms on the macro level found no significant link between financial liberalization and improvements in the areas of savings, credit and financial development. Especially for India, there is evidence that these macroeconomic variables increased under both a more repressive and a more liberal policy environment. Thus, while financial liberalization appears to have helped banks to perform more efficiently, there have not yet been any positive spillover effects to the economy in general. Hence the hypotheses from the financial liberalization literature on the macro effects of liberalization must be rejected.

The insignificant effect of liberalization on the macro variables is especially worrisome in the light of India's growth target and its ambition to catch up with China. Capital accumulation is the main factor explaining the growth differential between India and China.[79] This reveals the importance for India of increasing both saving and capital formation.

[79] See Morgan Stanley (2004), p. 10.

8 Policy recommendations and implications of research findings

This final chapter summarizes the major findings of the thesis and discusses policy recommendations for banking sector reforms. It also discusses some limitations of the research methodology and the possibility of generalizing the findings. It concludes with some with suggestions for further avenues of research.

8.1 Summary of goals and results

The goal of this thesis was to provide an in-depth evaluation of the transformatory changes of the Indian banking sector and to put them into a comparative perspective with the Chinese banking sector. The main findings are summarized below according to the initial research objectives.

Objective 1: *To review potential reasons for state involvement in a country's banking sector and the rationale for financial liberalization*
Potential reasons for state involvement in the banking sector can be grouped into three broad categories: economic, developmental and political. On economic grounds, market failures can justify state involvement. However, this is a necessary but not a sufficient condition, since the state must be in a position to provide a better outcome than the market. Developmental reasons for state involvement are closely related to arguments concerning market failure. For example, if projects in certain sectors such as agriculture do not receive financing because of a lack of collateral, requiring banks to provide funds would have a development objective, but also might mitigate market failure. The political reasons for state involvement also involve the provision of funds to projects that would otherwise not receive financing, whereas the motivation in this case does not stem from funding socially desirable projects as in the development view, but rather from supporting projects that are politically desirable, for example, as a tool of patronage.

There is a wide array of different instruments for intervening in the banking sector. While nationalizing banks is certainly the most visible form, others include restricting the setting of interest rates, statutory pre-emption of funds, and directed credit programs. When these instruments are not implemented with the specific aim of addressing market failure, they are likely to lead to welfare losses. This is due to their distorting effect on the market mechanism.

Financial liberalization can in this context be interpreted as a way to reduce the adverse effects of state involvement by allowing the banking sector to function according to market principles. This should help enhance the efficiency of the sector. It should also allow the banking system to perform its functions of mobilizing savings and allocating capital better – creating a positive impact on growth. But financial liberalization is not without pitfalls since there is no mechanism leading to an improved sector performance. Furthermore, studies have shown that the risk of a banking crisis increases after the liberalization of a banking sector. In addition, as the research results have shown, a certain extent of government involvement may actually be beneficial for countries.

Objective 2: *To review key policy recommendations of transformation studies in the context of the transformation of a banking sector*
Transformation studies have dealt extensively with the problem of changing the coordination mechanism of an economic system and how to manage the transition from a state-led to a market-based economy. The initial policy recommendations of transformation studies focused on the triad of liberalization, privatization and stabilization. The experiences of transition countries have shown that these elements are insufficient and need to be complemented by institution building and structural change. In addition, questions of sequencing, speed and timing of the reforms should receive greater emphasis because of the gradual nature of the process.

The main policy recommendations of transformation studies focus on the overall economy. But the general recommendations can also be adopted to the banking sector. Thus the price and allocation mechanism of banks has to be liberalized, banks have to be stabilized through capital injections, state-owned banks should be privatized, the sectoral structure that is often biased towards large state-owned banks needs to be adjusted, and institutions for a functioning banking sector should be established.

Objective 3: *To integrate transformation studies and financial liberalization studies to provide a framework for banking sector liberalization*
Transformation studies and financial liberalization studies are complementary: both are concerned with changing the coordination mechanism and creating a more market-based system. Whereas the financial liberalization literature advocates the reduction of state involvement through the removal of price and volume controls, but remains relatively silent on how to manage this change, transformation studies have dealt extensively with the process of changing a system and help to understand the scope and complexities of the liberalization process. Together, transformation and financial liberalization studies can provide a framework for managing the transition of a banking sector and give indications on the likely effects.

The framework described in chapter 6 (see Figure 13) attempts to integrate the two approaches. It starts with an outline of basic requirements for liberalization, followed by propositions along the process steps of transformation studies on best practices for reforms. These propositions are complemented by suggestions for the speed, timing and sequencing of the different reform elements. The framework is completed with indicators for measuring the process and the results of liberalization.

Objective 4: *To discuss the necessary extent of state involvement in the banking sector*
Market failure in the banking sector can make state intervention necessary. But the existence of market failure is a necessary, not a sufficient condition for intervention since it is important that the state ensures a more efficient outcome. One important source of market failure in banking is information asymmetries. These asymmetries can occur between banks, debtors and depositors. Yet most market failures arising from information asymmetries can be solved without direct intervention, but by ensuring that the necessary prudential regulations and adequate bank supervision are in place.

There are, however, cases in which state involvement may be needed to address market failure. State intervention might be justified, for example, in countries with large rural or poor areas, where profit-oriented banks would not be interested in establishing a presence. In these circumstances, state-owned banks can provide banking services to parts of the population that would otherwise be excluded from the formal banking system. Another justification for state intervention is the provision of credit to certain sectors that would otherwise not receive financing. And finally, government intervention is required in developing countries where more pronounced business cycles make higher capital adequacy requirements necessary, set and enforced by the state.

Objective 5: *To identify a set of indicators for evaluating banking sector reforms*
Three different sets of indicators for the evaluation of the process and effects of banking sector reforms were discussed. First, at the sector level, indicators for the process and the results of banking sector liberalization were identified in line with the findings of transformation studies. Possible causal relationships between the process and the results were discussed to enable a better evaluation of the results. The different process indicators were then integrated to an overall process index. Next, qualitative propositions on how to liberalize a banking sector were formulated on the basis of the experiences of transition and developing countries. This is especially important since qualitative propositions provide a good way of evaluating the multi-facetted liberalization process. Third, indicators for measuring the macro-level effects of liberalization were identified for each of the functions of a banking sector. This was done to explore the link between the liberalization of a banking sector and the macroeconomic performance of a country. These indicators and propositions are generic enough to be applicable to other countries.

Objective 6: *To compare and evaluate the status and effects of banking sector reforms in India and China*
The status of banking sector reforms in India and China was evaluated using the qualitative propositions and the identified indicators. Both countries have made considerable progress in liberalizing their banking sectors overall. Within this, India is clearly ahead of China. Interestingly, despite their different political, economic and institutional settings, the reform process in both countries is fairly similar. This reveals that the influence of political system on reforms may be lower than generally assumed. Also, both countries have so far made less progress in areas such as privatization, where there are strong interest groups who are against liberalization. But despite the difficulties of reform, and leadership changes in both countries, neither India nor China have experienced major reform reversals.

Liberalization has led to an improvement of the functioning of the banking sector in both countries. Here, again, India has generally achieved better results. This is partly due to the fact that banking sector reforms started earlier in India. There was also a less challenging institutional legacy, since India has always had a small share of private sector banks. China, on the other hand, followed a Soviet mono-bank model. Whereas performance at the sector level improved in both countries after liberalization, no link could be established between financial liberalization and better fulfillment of the macroeconomic functions of the banking sector.

Objective 7: *To discuss further necessary steps for banking sector reforms in India and China*
This objective will be covered in the next section.

The working hypothesis postulated at the beginning of this study was that India has made greater liberalization progress than China, but that the reforms are still incomplete which should limit the positive liberalization benefits on the level of the sector and the economy. The results have shown that India has indeed proceeded faster with banking sector reforms than China and that it also needs to make further progress. The assumed cause-effect relationships for both the sector and the economy have however not materialized: progress was better than expected on the sector level, whereas liberalization did not cause significant improvements of macroeconomic variables.

These research results have implications for the underlying theoretical foundations of this thesis. The general assumption of the McKinnon-Shaw school is that financial liberalization has a positive impact at the macro level by removing constraints on banks. The discussion of the empirical studies on this subject (see section 4.4) showed that this relationship does not hold in every setting. The research results provide further evidence that financial liberalization does not necessarily cause a significant increase of saving, capital or capital efficiency. Of course, this does not mean that liberalization leads to negative results – but rather that, at least on the macro level, the performance improvements are not as expected. The peculiarities of India and China, and the fact that some restraints have remained in place, may influence the transmission of liberalization effects. However, it is safe to assume that no country will fully meet the assumptions of the formal economic models. Therefore, this should not unduly constrict the validity of the research findings.

It is also important to incorporate the pre-reform regime in the evaluation. In India, the state-controlled banking sector was able to expand significantly under the auspices of the government. This had a positive impact at the macro level, so the positive adjustment effect of liberalization was necessarily smaller. The positive development in the pre-liberalization regime also shows that, irrespective of the choice of greater or lesser levels of state influence, it is possible to achieve positive outcomes. This suggests that how the system is managed is more important than the system itself. For example, a well managed banking sector with a high degree of state involvement might be preferable to a weak liberal sector with inconsistent regulatory policies. The banking sectors in India and China were able to perform their functions of mobilizing saving and allocating capital despite high degrees of financial repression. This is clearly at odds with the arguments of the financial liberalization school.

While financial restraints have not affected the fulfillment of the banking sector functions negatively on the macro level in India and China, this does not hold true for the effects on banks themselves. Indicators such as ROA, NPLs or capital levels show the fragile footing of banks in India and China in the pre-reform period. In many respects, the policies that led to a positive macro-performance caused a deterioration of the fundamentals on the micro level. An example is directed credit with subsidized interest rates in India despite higher default risks from borrowers in priority sectors. The result was a lower profitability coupled with higher NPLs.

In China, these effects were even more pronounced in the pre-reform period, since the mono-bank served as an instrument for channeling funds from savers toward enterprises without considering profitability or repayment. State ownership of banks exacerbated these problems in both countries. In addition to the general incentive problems associated with state ownership, both countries regarded banks as tools to achieve development goals and not as commercial entities. Combined, these factors led to significant distortions, that resulted in major adjustment costs during the reform period.

Certainly, some of the factors leading to this "macro-micro mismatch" – meaning a good fulfillment of the macroeconomic functions combined with a poor sectoral performance – are peculiar to India and China. The Chinese mono-bank system is the most obvious example. Nonetheless, state ownership of banks in combination with price and allocation controls are likely to lead to a mediocre sectoral performance in other settings too. Consequently, the effects of liberalization on the performance of banks needs to receive more attention, since the main liberalization effects are likely to come from this area.

8.2 Policy recommendations

These research results have implications for policy makers in India and China. This section presents some recommendations for the future reform process in the Indian and Chinese banking sectors.

India has proceeded quite far with banking sector reforms in most areas, but has not yet fully completed the transition to a market-based banking system. In addition, there is a need for further complementary reforms in the enterprise and the fiscal sector.

The first of these is a significant reduction of the directed credit program. Today, the directed credit program is one of the last relicts of the pre-reform banking sector. In line with earlier recommendations by the *Narasimham Committee*, the level of directed credit should be reduced from 40% to 10%. This is also the level that is approximately warranted by market failure, as has been discussed. To ensure a smooth transition, the amount of directed credit should be reduced in a dual-track manner in which the percentage goal of 40% is replaced with a fixed rupee target. If the current trend of credit growth persists, this should result in a phased reduction of the percentage of directed credit. In addition to this gradual phasing out, temporary mechanisms such as credit guarantees could be created to ensure that credit flows to priority sectors. Reducing the amount of directed credit will also have a signaling effect for other reforms. Fry (1995), for example, argues that "abandoning directed credit programs must constitute one of the first steps of any sensible financial development program. If the government is too weak to take this step, it may well be too weak to implement any well-conceived macroeconomic policy."[1]

The second reform needed is a lowering of the minimum level of the SLR. After the initiation of banking sector reforms, the SLR has been quickly reduced to its legal minimum. Pre-emption of resources through the SLR is still considerable, since the legal minimum stands at 25% of net demand and time liabilities. Combined with the CRR that stands at about 5%, 30% of deposits have to be invested in government-approved securities. For monetary policy purposes, a lower amount would be sufficient. The RBI has only made minimal changes to the CRR in order to counter inflationary pressures in the last years. As a result, the current level of pre-emptions serves as a captive source of government bonds. The legal minimum of the SLR should therefore be lowered significantly so that more funds are available for credit.

Third, a level playing field must be created with respect to foreign banks. Foreign banks have both advantages and disadvantages compared to domestic players. Currently, foreign banks have the advantage of lower priority sector lending requirements (32%, compared to 40% for domestic banks) and less strict requirements regarding setting up branches in rural and semi-urban areas. At the same time, they are restricted as to the number of branches they can open in a single year, and there are restrictions on the ownership of domestic banks.

Leveling of the playing field should include aligning directed credit requirements and branch regulations. To achieve planning security, mandatory dates for taking of equity stakes in Indian banks should be included in

[1] Fry (1995), p. 469.

the "Roadmap for the Presence of Foreign Banks". This would help to appease domestic opposition and prevent cherry-picking by foreign banks. Overall, the sector would benefit from further investments by foreign banks and from the transfer of expertise.

The fourth area where reform is needed is in the privatization of public sector banks. The current level of assets controlled by PSBs is significantly above the 25% that would be necessary to cover rural areas and disadvantaged parts of the population. Despite political obstacles, the Indian government should reduce its stake in the banking sector by privatizing PSBs. This would also be in the interests of the ultimate owners – the Indian people. Since the PSBs have lost market share steadily over past years, the current "do nothing" strategy not only amounts to a desirable reduction of the role of the government in the banking sector. It also is likely to cause an erosion of the value of the PSBs because of their weaker relative position.

Fifth, complementary fiscal and enterprise reforms must be implemented.. As has been discussed, there is a close relationship between the banking sector, the enterprise sector, and the fiscal situation of a country. In particular, India should press ahead with fiscal reforms so as to reduce the budget deficit. This is an important pre-condition for further reforms in the banking sector, such as the reduction of statutory pre-emptions, currently used as a captive source of funds for the government. This should also help to create incentives for saving, which is important since the lower saving rate in comparison to China is one of the major factors behind the lower growth rate of the Indian economy.[2]

Despite beginning the reform process earlier, China has had to face the problem of its difficult institutional legacy and could therefore not proceed as fast, and as far, as India. In certain areas, China could learn from the Indian reform experiences. The major recommendations for further reforms are given below.

First, the NPL level should be reduced significantly. Despite progress in recent years, the extent of NPLs in the Chinese banking sector is still extremely high. This is even more worrisome given the strong growth in loans over recent years and the benign macro environment. It is relatively safe to assume that, in a downturn, NPLs would again increase significantly – as has happened in other Asian countries in the aftermath of the

[2] See Morgan Stanley (2004), p. 24f.; Mukherji (2005), p. 66. Also large public sector borrowing from domestic banks may impede financial development. For a discussion on the relationship between fiscal policy and financial development, see Hauner (2006).

Asian crisis. Since a large share of the NPLs of the state-owned commercial banks stem from loans extended to support state-owned enterprises, they are in fact to a large extent government debt.[3] Thus solving the problem of NPLs requires a joint effort on the part of banks and the government. Important first steps towards this goal are estimating the level of bad loans accurately and making a credible commitment going forward to re-capitalizing the banks once and once only.

Second, more stringent enforcement and further upgrading of the regulatory framework are needed. This is a pre-condition for the sustained reduction of NPLs and the improvement of the systemic stability of the banking sector. A certain amount of progress has been made in this respect, the foundation of the CBRC being one of the most prominent examples. However, further efforts are needed to bring the institutional framework up to international standards. One important area is the capital adequacy requirement that should be tightened further to exceed the 8% Basel Standard. It is however not only necessary to enact new rules and regulations; the enforcement is also important. China must strive to extend the positive example of the CBRC to other areas of the banking sector.

Third, there must be further privatization of state-owned banks. The partial privatizations that started in 2005 must continue. Although the Big Four banks have lost market share over the last years, they and thus the government, still dominate the banking landscape. There are, of course, market failure arguments for the provision of banking services, especially to the Western regions of China. However, just one of the four SOCBs would probably be sufficient to fulfill this task. The government should divest its holdings in the other three banks and instead provide the legal and institutional framework for a market-based banking sector. This would also lend credibility to other reform measures. As Anderson (2006) argues, "[...] privatization is the only long-term method of making structural reforms 'stick' and ensuring macroeconomic stability."[4]

Fourth, interest rates should be further liberalized. Interest rates in China are still largely determined by the government, which has negative implications for savers and the overall economy. Deposit rates in China are set at relatively low levels. Since Chinese savers cannot invest abroad and the stock market is still under-developed, the largest part of savings flows into the banking system. The artificial low interest rates paid on the deposits

---

[3] See Fan (2002), p. 12, Lal (2006), p. 280. Cutting the link between state-owned banks and state-owned enterprises with bad loans is an important step in escaping what Li (2001) calls the "trap of financial repression". See Li (2001), pp. 83-85.

[4] Anderson (2006), p. 248.

constitute a transfer of wealth from savers to banks, companies and the government. Lending rates are also comparatively low in China, so projects that would have a negative net present value at market interest rates appear to be viable investments due to the lower cost of capital. This can ultimately lead to the build-up of non-performing loans.[5] Therefore, further deregulating lending and deposit rates will benefit savers, banks and the economy alike: this should be one of the main priorities for further reforms.

Fifth, complementary reforms in the enterprise sector are essential. There is a close link between the banking sector and the enterprise sector. This is particularly so in China, where the government still owns the largest banks and some of the largest enterprises. Historically, this linkage has been extensively used to channel loans from banks toward enterprises, which has resulted in today's large stock of NPLs. For further reforms in the banking sector, it is thus necessary to reform the largest SOEs and put them on a viable commercial basis. After an adjustment phase, this will also benefit the banks, since stronger borrowers increase banks' stability. The ability to operate on a commercial basis is also an important precondition for bank privatization.

The scope of the recommendations for India and China show the need for an impetus for second-generation reforms. This is especially challenging since the triggers for the transformatory changes were crises – in India, the balance-of-payments crisis, in China, the failings of the Cultural Revolution. The leaders of both countries now need to find ways to generate momentum for further reforms in the absence of such triggers. They also need to manage the interconnections between the banking sector, the enterprise sector and the general economic situation. Weak state-owned enterprises in China and fiscal deficits in India create barriers to change in the banking sector. Further liberalization requires addressing these issues.

[5] Nominal lending rates in China have between 1999 and 2004 been below 6%, which is lower than the yields on US Treasury security that are commonly used as benchmarks for risk-free investments. See International Monetary Fund (2006b).

8.3 Limitations of research approach

This thesis has attempted to provide a multi-faceted assessment of banking sector reforms. However, it is not possible to grasp the full complexity of the real world: trade-offs and simplifications have been necessary. The most important of these are discussed below.

First, even though the index-based evaluation of liberalization used here is preferable to other approaches by providing a multi-facetted view of the process, it also has certain limitations. Even a broad aggregate index provides an incomplete picture of reality since it is not able to capture the full breadth of existing policies. Aspects such as the definition of priority sectors, interest rate restrictions on priority sector loans or changes in the role of the regulator could not be included in the index, although they certainly have an impact on the sectoral performance. The policy variables entered the index with equal weights. This is a simplification since different policy changes will in practice most likely not have a similar level of importance in practice. In an attempt to address this problem, a liberalization index was created using the method of principal components to give different weights to different policies. However, this method is purely statistical and does not take into account the importance of different policies in reality.

Second, this thesis is a country case study. This provides an in-depth evaluation of one country, but lacks comparability due to country-specific factors. An attempt has been made to strike a balance here by including data from China – a country that, like India, is in transition. India and China have had similar reform experiences, which make a comparison meaningful; nevertheless, this does not imply that it is possible to fully generalize the results.

Third, the availability and reliability of data are problems faced by all empirical studies. In this respect, the current study is no exception. The most desirable data has not always been available, and approximations and proxy variables have been resorted to. Where this was not possible, the variable in question was excluded. Even where data was available, its reliability was sometimes questionable. For example, experience shows that NPL figures are often understated and their true extent only becomes apparent in a crisis. This applies to accounting information as much as to macroeconomic variables. These problems are certainly more pronounced for China than for India, which should be kept in mind when drawing conclusions from the results.

Besides the general limitations, there are issues pertaining to India and China that may have influenced the research results and the ability to generalize the results. One is the sheer size of India and China, their low income levels and the huge regional disparities compared to smaller or richer countries. Both India and China have a pronounced urban-rural divide with large parts of the population living in the less-developed countryside, which is more expensive to serve for banks. While this dichotomy might not always affect the results, using aggregate statistical figures is clearly a simplification. In addition, low income levels especially in the countryside reduce the possibility of a profitable coverage with formal banking services. As a result, informal finance remains important in both countries. Smaller or richer countries do not face this problem, which to some extent limits the comparability of the results.

Another factor peculiar to India and China is that their capital account is not fully liberalized. As a result, their citizens cannot save abroad and are bound to banks operating in their own countries. This means that local banks have a quasi-monopoly on domestic savings. In India, this has led to a disproportionately large share of physical savings in the form of gold, which may influence the comparability of the results. In China, the closed capital account in combination with the fixed exchange rate leads to a perpetuation of state influence in the banking sector, since the government has to sterilize the excess liquidity from the capital inflows.

Despite these limitations, the results presented here have broad implications. Even if comparability is limited, the results are valid for two of the most important emerging markets in the world who represent about 40% of the world's population, which warrants attention in its own right.

8.4 Perspectives for future research

A doctoral thesis can seldom cover all relevant aspects of a topic. Moreover, new issues may emerge during the course of the research. This thesis is no exception and so several areas remain that warrant further investigation.

First, more country case studies of liberalization experiences are needed, as opposed to cross-country regressions. Cross-country regressions have serious limitations for policy analysis, since all countries receive the same weight in the regression. For a more in-depth understanding of the underlying processes, country case studies are more appropriate. This thesis has been an attempt to do this for India and China; other researchers have focused among others on countries in Asia or South America.[6] Further in-depth studies of individual countries' experiences will yield valuable new

[6] See for example Demetriades and Luintel (1996a), Demetriades and Luintel (2001) and Diaz-Alejandro (1985).

insights into how the challenges of transforming a banking sector can be mastered. The liberalization index and the propositions investigated here are a first step to providing a common reference frame for this exercise. The developed liberalization index is generic enough to be applied to other countries or regions, and consequently allows a broad comparison of liberalization experiences.

Second, this thesis has also attempted to incorporate the impact of market failure. Here, there is scope for refinement, both regarding which market failures are considered and the methodology used to gauge their effect on the indicators. Market failures are an important issue in enacting public policy, which makes their operationalization critical for policy makers.

Third, future studies need to focus more on sectoral recommendations as opposed to the overall economy. Transformation studies have provided a helpful framework for evaluating the liberalization process. However, as has been shown, it is necessary to adjust the general recommendations to the peculiarities of the banking sector. The banking sector is a special case due to its role as an intermediary; but other sectors in the economy – such as utilities, for example – also need a tailored transformation strategy. This should also help to advance the state-of-the-art of transformation studies.

Fourth, another area worth investigating are the micro effects of liberalization and the interactions with the macroeconomic functions of the banking sector. The review of empirical studies in section 4.4 found that studies investigating the macro-level effects of liberalization by far outnumber studies focusing on the micro level. Yet the research results for India and China have shown that the effects of repression and liberalization are far more pronounced on the micro than on the macro level. Furthermore, during the times of repression the banking sector was able to fulfill its macro-economic functions despite a lackluster performance on the micro level, whereas improved sectoral performance after liberalization did not exert a significant effect on the macro level.

Micro-level barriers to financial development should also be investigated. For example, the amount of lending depends partially on the ability of the creditor to seize collateral.[7] This in turn depends on factors such as the definition of property rights, the enforceability of property rights and the enforcement costs. If any of these factors is not well-defined, the amount of credit extended may be negatively affected and economic development will suffer as a result. India is a case in point. While property rights are relatively well-defined, they are difficult to enforce despite the recent establishment of special debt recovery tribunals. This may induce banks to extend less credit, despite liberalization. Exploring these ques-

[7] See Rajan and Zingales (2003b), p. 31.

tions will help reach a better understanding of the effect of financial liberalization at both the sector and the macroeconomic level, and thus lead to better policy recommendations.

Finally, the optimal management of the banking sector during the process of economic development warrants further investigation. The research results have shown that financial liberalization has had no significant effect on economic growth in India: growth acceleration happened well before the liberalization of the banking sector. Furthermore, developments since 1960 in India have shown that increases in the amount of savings and capital were possible in a largely repressed system, and indeed liberalization has not led to significant improvements. While this is not sufficient evidence to refute the validity of the McKinnon-Shaw school's approach, it marks an important deviation from the generally expected cause-and-effect relationships. This finding is highly important, given that recommendations argue for further liberalization in order to accelerate the growth rate of the economy.[8] The findings presented here raise the question of what the optimal level of state involvement in the banking sector during economic development should be. It would be presumptuous to assume that a general blueprint for the management of liberalization exists. However, this investigation helps to bridge the dichotomy between the state and the market. This would represent a move away from economic orthodoxies and towards a less doctrinaire economic and development policy.

[8] See for example McKinsey Global Institute (2006a); Organization for Economic Cooperation and Development (2005).

Appendix

Table 13. Recapitalization of nationalized banks

Bank	up to 1992-93	1993-94	1994-95*	1995-96	1996-97	1997-98	1998-99	1999-2001	Total
Allahabad Bank	171.33	90.00	101.61	160.00					522.94
Andhra Bank	89.00	150.00			165.00				404.00
Bank of Baroda	163.00	400.00							563.00
Bank of India	455.00	635.00	348.22						1,438.22
Bank of Maharashtra	182.08	150.00		80.00					412.08
Canara Bank	112.50	365.00				600.00			1,077.50
Central Bank of India	175.74	490.00			500.00				1,165.74
Corporation Bank	65.40	45.00							110.40
Dena Bank	145.63	130.00	72.28						347.91
Indian Bank	194.00	220.00	180.94			1,750.00	100.00		2,444.94
Indian Overseas Bank	357.00	705.00	132.74						1,194.74
Oriental Bank of Commerce	76.90	50.00							126.90
Punjab and Sind Bank	205.61	160.00		72.00	150.00				587.61
Punjab National Bank	165.00	415.00							580.00
Syndicate Bank	148.50	680.00	88.79	172.00					1,089.29
UCO Bank	492.00	535.00		110.00	54.00	350.00	200.00		1,741.00
Union Bank of India	132.00	200.00							332.00
United Bank of India	360.19	215.00		256.00	338.00		100.00		1,269.19
Vijaya Bank	125.72	65.00			302.00				492.72
Total Capital Subscribed	**3,816.60**	**5,700.00**	**924.58**	**850.00**	**1,509.00**	**2,700.00**	**400.00**	**0.00**	**15,900.18**

Note: * = capital contributed as tier-II; recapitalization amounts are Rs. Crore.[1]

[1] See Reserve Bank of India (2001b), p. 26.

Table 14. Government ownership shares of Public Sector Banks

	Bank	Major Shareholder	1991	1992	1993	1994	1995	1996	1997	1998	1999	2000	2001	2002	2003	2004
Nationalized Banks	Allahabad Bank	GOI	100	100	100	100	100	100	100	100	100	100	100	71	71	71
	Andhra Bank	GOI	100	100	100	100	100	100	100	100	100	67	67	63	63	63
	Bank of Baroda	GOI	100	100	100	100	100	66	66	66	66	66	66	67	67	67
	Bank of India	GOI	100	100	100	100	100	100	70	70	70	70	70	70	70	70
	Bank of Maharashtra	GOI	100	100	100	100	100	100	100	100	100	100	100	77	77	77
	Canara Bank	GOI	100	100	100	100	100	100	100	100	100	100	100	73	73	73
	Central Bank of India	GOI	100	100	100	100	100	100	100	100	100	100	100	100	100	100
	Corporation Bank	GOI	100	100	100	100	100	100	68	68	68	68	57	57	57	57
	Dena Bank	GOI	100	100	100	100	100	71	71	71	71	71	71	71	71	51
	Indian Bank	GOI	100	100	100	100	100	100	100	100	100	100	100	100	100	100
	Indian Overseas Bank	GOI	100	100	100	100	100	100	100	100	100	100	75	61	61	61
	Oriental Bank of Commerce	GOI	100	100	100	67	67	67	67	67	67	67	67	67	67	67
	Punjab and Sind Bank	GOI	100	100	100	100	100	100	100	100	100	100	100	100	100	100
	Punjab National Bank	GOI	100	100	100	100	100	100	100	100	100	100	80	80	80	58
	Syndicate Bank	GOI	100	100	100	100	100	100	100	100	74	74	74	74	74	74
	UCO Bank	GOI	100	100	100	100	100	100	100	100	100	100	100	75	75	75
	Union Bank of India	GOI	100	100	100	100	100	100	100	100	100	100	100	61	61	61
	United Bank of India	GOI	100	100	100	100	100	100	100	100	100	100	100	100	100	100
	Vijaya Bank	GOI	100	100	100	100	100	100	100	100	100	70	70	54	54	54
SBI Banks	State Bank of Bikaner and Jaipur	SBI	100	100	100	100	100	100	75	75	75	75	75	75	75	76
	State Bank of Hyderabad	SBI	100	100	100	100	100	100	100	100	100	100	99	99	98	100
	State Bank of India	RBI	100	100	66	66	66	66	60	60	60	60	60	60	60	60
	State Bank of Indore	SBI	100	100	100	100	98	98	98	98	98	98	98	98	98	98
	State Bank of Mysore	SBI	100	100	100	100	89	89	92	92	92	92	92	92	92	94
	State Bank of Patiala	SBI	100	100	100	100	100	100	100	100	100	100	100	100	100	100
	State Bank of Saurashtra	SBI	100	100	100	100	100	100	100	100	100	100	100	100	100	100
	State Bank of Travancore	SBI	100	100	100	100	97	97	97	75	75	75	75	75	75	79

Note: GOI = Government of India; RBI = Reserve Bank of India; SBI = State Bank of India. Sources: Mohan (2004), p. 861; Reserve Bank of India (2001b), p. 85f.; Reserve Bank of India (2005c), p. 297; Shirai (2002c), p. 26f.

Table 15. Effective reserve requirements in selected countries[2]

			Asian emerging countries			Developed countries		
Year	**India**	**China**	**Thailand**	**Korea**	**Malaysia**	**USA**	**UK**	**Japan**
1980	13%	NA	6%	13%	8%	3%	3%	3%
1981	13%	NA	5%	6%	8%	3%	2%	2%
1982	13%	NA	5%	7%	8%	3%	2%	2%
1983	12%	NA	4%	6%	8%	2%	2%	2%
1984	12%	NA	3%	5%	8%	2%	2%	3%
1985	15%	33%	4%	4%	7%	2%	2%	2%
1986	16%	31%	4%	4%	6%	3%	2%	2%
1987	16%	27%	4%	8%	6%	2%	1%	2%
1988	17%	25%	4%	10%	6%	2%	1%	2%
1989	17%	28%	3%	13%	8%	2%	1%	2%
1990	16%	31%	3%	11%	11%	2%	1%	2%
1991	16%	31%	4%	11%	11%	2%	1%	2%
1992	15%	24%	4%	11%	29%	2%	2%	2%
1993	15%	25%	3%	11%	12%	2%	2%	2%
1994	16%	25%	3%	10%	16%	2%	2%	1%
1995	15%	24%	4%	10%	18%	2%	1%	1%
1996	12%	27%	5%	6%	22%	2%	1%	2%
1997	11%	26%	5%	4%	25%	2%	1%	2%
1998	11%	22%	4%	3%	7%	1%	1%	2%
1999	9%	20%	7%	3%	7%	2%	1%	6%
2000	8%	19%	6%	3%	6%	1%	1%	2%
2001	8%	18%	6%	3%	5%	1%	1%	4%
2002	6%	17%	5%	4%	6%	1%	1%	5%
2003	6%	17%	8%	4%	5%	1%	1%	6%
2004	7%	17%	9%	3%	5%	1%	1%	7%

[2] Author's calculation based on IMF International Financial Statistics.

Table 16. Government ownership of banks in selected countries[3]

Country	Liberalized	Largely liberalized	Partly repressed	Repressed
Argentina			61%	
Australia		21%		
Bangladesh			100%	
Brazil			23%	
Britain	0%			
Canada	0%			
Chile	20%			
Colombia		52%		
Egypt			86%	
France		22%		
Germany		37%		
Hong Kong	0%			
India			95%	
Indonesia				43%
Israel			82%	
Italy			28%	
Japan		0%		
Korea		22%		
Malaysia		10%		
Mexico		36%		
Morocco			42%	
New Zealand	0%			
Pakistan			80%	
Peru		24%		
Philippines		34%		
Singapore	5%			
South Africa	0%			
Sri Lanka			69%	
Taiwan				100%
Thailand		22%		
Turkey			56%	
United States	0%			
Venezuela			53%	
Average	3%	26%	65%	71%

Note: (1) Percentage values refer to percentage of state ownership in the top-10 banks in which the government owns more than 50% of the shares; (2) percentage values are for 1995, while the classification of the policy regime is for 1996.

[3] Author's presentation based on data from La Porta, Lopez de Silanes and Schleifer (2002), pp. 272-274 and Williamson and Mahar (1998), p. 5f.

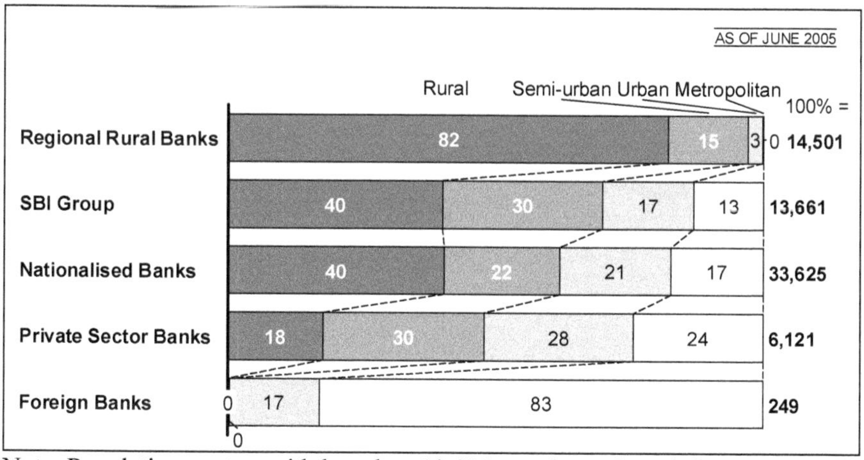

Note: Population centers with less than 10,000 people are "rural, from 10,000 to 100,000 people "semi-urban", from 100,000 to 1,000,000 people "urban" center, and above 1,000,000 "metropolitan". See Reserve Bank of India (2004a), p. iv.

Fig. 40. Distribution of bank branches[4]

Table 17. Deposit and credit share in rural and semi-urban areas[5]

Bank Group	Data	Rural	Semi-urban	Urban	Metro-politan	Grand Total
Nationalised Banks	Offices	13,624	7,222	7,233	6,141	34,220
	Deposits	101,220	127,285	184,493	339,444	752,441
	Credit	43,652	45,692	81,089	237,672	408,105
SBI	Offices	5,465	4,033	2,378	1,823	13,699
	Deposits	45,824	95,852	90,230	128,904	360,809
	Credit	19,469	38,122	45,089	105,786	208,465
Foreign banks	Offices	0	0	28	180	208
	Deposits	0	0	1,979	70,725	72,705
	Credit	0	0	807	62,808	63,615
Regional Rural Banks	Offices	11,914	2,229	497	23	14,663
	Deposits	37,712	13,434	4,620	144	55,909
	Credit	18,265	5,917	1,772	66	26,020
Private Sector Banks	Offices	1,104	1,768	1,567	1,416	5,855
	Deposits	10,327	31,647	48,974	178,462	269,409
	Credit	3,634	10,435	21,580	138,458	174,107

[4] Author's presentation based on Reserve Bank of India (2005c), p. 303.
[5] Author's calculation based on Reserve Bank of India (2004a), p. 25f.

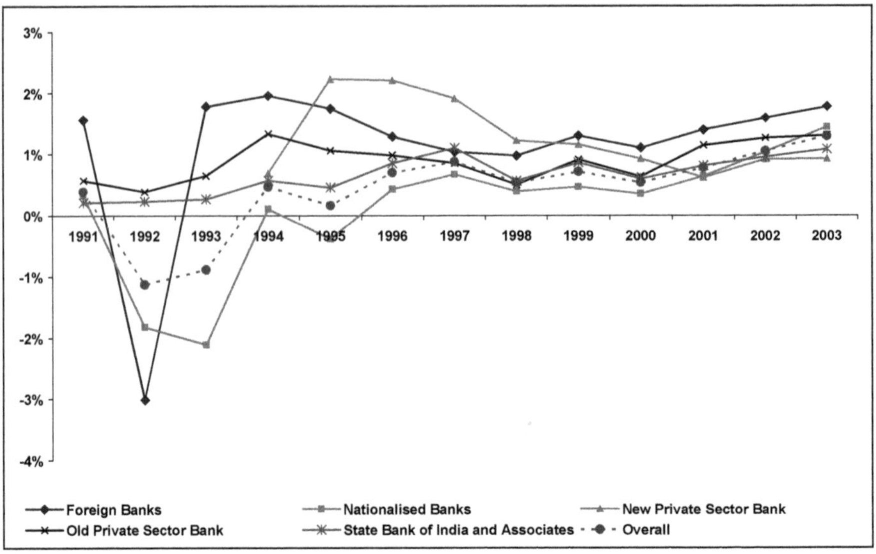

Fig. 41. ROA of bank groups India[6]

[6] Author's calculation based on Reserve Bank of India (2005a).

Table 18. Values for process index India

	Liberalization			Stabilization	Privatization	Institution building			Structural change	
Year	Interest rate controls	Credit controls	Reserve requirements	Prudential norms	Privatization	Accounting standards	Regulatory system	Deposit insurance	Entry barriers	Sum India
1980	1	1	1	0	0	1	0	3	0	2.3
1981	1	1	1	0	0	1	0	3	0	2.3
1982	1	1	1	0	0	1	0	3	0	2.3
1983	1	1	1	0	0	1	0	3	0	2.3
1984	1	1	1	0	1	1	0	3	0	3.3
1985	1	1	1	0	1	1	0	3	0	3.3
1986	1	1	0	0	1	1	0	3	0	3.0
1987	1	1	0	0	1	1	0	3	0	3.0
1988	1	1	0	0	1	1	0	3	0	3.0
1989	1	1	0	0	1	1	0	3	0	3.0
1990	1	1	0	0	1	1	0	3	0	3.0
1991	1	1	0	0	1	1	0	3	0	3.0
1992	1	1	1	0	1	1	1	3	0	3.7
1993	1	1	1	0	1	1	1	3	0	3.7
1994	1	1	0	1	1	1	1	3	2	6.3
1995	2	1	1	1	1	1	1	3	2	7.0
1996	2	1	1	2	1	2	2	3	2	8.7
1997	3	1	1	2	1	2	2	3	2	9.0
1998	3	1	1	2	1	2	2	3	2	9.0
1999	3	1	2	2	1	2	2	3	2	9.3
2000	3	1	2	2	1	2	2	3	2	9.3
2001	3	1	2	2	1	2	2	3	2	9.3
2002	3	1	2	2	1	2	3	3	2	9.7
2003	3	1	2	2	1	2	3	3	2	9.7
2004	3	1	2	2	1	2	3	3	2	9.7
2005	3	1	2	2	1	2	3	3	2	9.7

Note: 0 = fully repressed; 1 = partially repressed; 2 = largely liberalized; 3 = fully liberalized.

Table 19. Values for process index China

	Liberalization			Stabilization	Privatization	Institution building			Structural change	
Year	Interest rate controls	Credit controls	Reserve requirements	Prudential norms	Privatization	Accounting standards	Regulatory system	Deposit insurance	Entry barriers	Sum China
1980	0	0	0	0	0	0	0	0	0	0.0
1981	0	0	0	0	0	0	0	0	0	0.0
1982	0	0	0	0	0	0	0	0	0	0.0
1983	0	0	0	0	0	0	0	0	0	0.0
1984	0	0	0	0	0	0	0	0	0	0.0
1985	0	0	0	0	0	0	0	0	0	0.0
1986	1	0	0	0	0	0	0	0	0	0.3
1987	1	0	0	0	0	0	0	0	0	0.3
1988	1	0	0	0	0	0	0	0	0	0.3
1989	0	0	0	0	0	0	0	0	0	0.0
1990	0	0	0	0	0	0	0	0	0	0.0
1991	0	0	0	0	0	0	0	0	0	0.0
1992	0	0	0	0	0	0	0	0	0	0.0
1993	1	0	0	0	0	0	0	0	0	0.3
1994	1	1	0	0	0	0	0	0	1	1.7
1995	1	1	0	0	0	0	0	0	1	1.7
1996	1	1	0	1	0	0	1	0	1	3.0
1997	1	1	0	1	0	0	1	0	1	3.0
1998	1	1	0	1	0	1	1	0	1	3.3
1999	1	2	0	1	0	1	1	0	1	3.7
2000	1	2	0	1	0	1	1	0	1	3.7
2001	1	2	0	1	0	2	1	0	1	4.0
2002	1	2	0	1	1	2	1	0	2	6.0
2003	1	2	0	1	1	2	2	0	2	6.3
2004	1	2	0	1	1	2	2	0	2	6.3
2005	1	2	0	1	1	2	2	0	2	6.3

Note: 0 = fully repressed; 1 = partially repressed; 2 = largely liberalized; 3 = fully liberalized.

Table 20. Correlation matrix India and China

Correlation matrix India

		Interest rate controls	Credit controls	Reserve requirements	Prudential norms	Privatization	Accounting standards	Regulatory system	Deposit insurance	Entry barriers
Interest rate controls	Pearson Correlation	1	a	.787**	.960**	.352	.959**	.920**	a	.891**
	Sig. (2-tailed)		.	.000	.000	.078	.000	.000	.	.000
	N	26	26	26	26	26	26	25	26	26
Credit controls	Pearson Correlation	a	a	a	a	a	a	a	a	a
	Sig. (2-tailed)	.	.	.	.	.	.	.	.	.
	N	26	26	26	26	26	26	26	26	26
Reserve requirements	Pearson Correlation	.787**	a	1	.718**	.000	.754**	.781**	a	.631**
	Sig. (2-tailed)	.000	.		.000	1.000	.000	.000	.	.001
	N	26	26	26	26	26	26	26	26	26
Prudential norms	Pearson Correlation	.960**	a	.718**	1	.380	.962**	.935**	a	.964**
	Sig. (2-tailed)	.000	.	.000		.055	.000	.000	.	.000
	N	26	26	26	26	26	26	26	26	26
Privatization	Pearson Correlation	.352	a	.000	.380	1	.337	.402*	a	.395*
	Sig. (2-tailed)	.078	.	1.000	.055		.092	.042	.	.046
	N	26	26	26	26	26	26	26	26	26
Accounting standards	Pearson Correlation	.959**	a	.754**	.962**	.337	1	.917**	a	.854**
	Sig. (2-tailed)	.000	.	.000	.000	.092		.000	.	.000
	N	26	26	26	26	26	26	26	26	26
Regulatory system	Pearson Correlation	.920**	a	.781**	.935**	.402*	.917**	1	a	.884**
	Sig. (2-tailed)	.000	.	.000	.000	.042	.000		.	.000
	N	26	26	26	26	26	26	26	26	26
Deposit insurance	Pearson Correlation	a	a	a	a	a	a	a	a	a
	Sig. (2-tailed)	.	.	.	.	.	.	.	.	.
	N	26	26	26	26	26	26	26	26	26
Entry barriers	Pearson Correlation	.891**	a	.631**	.964**	.395*	.854**	.884**	a	1
	Sig. (2-tailed)	.000	.	.001	.000	.046	.000	.000	.	
	N	26	26	26	26	26	26	26	26	26

** Correlation is significant at the 0.01 level (2-tailed).

* Correlation is significant at the 0.05 level (2-tailed).

a. Cannot be computed because at least one of the variables is constant.

Correlation matrix China

		Interest rate controls	Credit controls	Reserve requirements	Prudential norms	Privatization	Accounting standards	Regulatory system	Deposit insurance	Entry barriers
Interest rate controls	Pearson Correlation	1	,674**	.[a]	,625**	,337	,496**	,570**	.[a]	,659**
	Sig. (2-tailed)	.	,000	.	,001	,092	,010	,002	.	,000
	N	26	26	26	26	26	26	26	26	26
Credit controls	Pearson Correlation	,674**	1	.[a]	,894**	,631**	,873**	,873**	.[a]	,931**
	Sig. (2-tailed)	,000	.	.	,000	,001	,000	,000	.	,000
	N	26	26	26	26	26	26	26	26	26
Reserve requirements	Pearson Correlation	.[a]	.[a]	.[a]	.[a]	.[a]	.[a]	.[a]	.[a]	.[a]
	Sig. (2-tailed)	.	.	.	.	.	.	.	.	.
	N	26	26	26	26	26	26	26	26	26
Prudential norms	Pearson Correlation	,625**	,894**	.[a]	1	,539**	,794**	,912**	.[a]	,841**
	Sig. (2-tailed)	,001	,000	.	.	,004	,000	,000	.	,000
	N	26	26	26	26	26	26	26	26	26
Privatization	Pearson Correlation	,337	,631**	.[a]	,539**	1	,803**	,769**	.[a]	,800**
	Sig. (2-tailed)	,092	,001	.	,004	.	,000	,000	.	,000
	N	26	26	26	26	26	26	26	26	26
Accounting standards	Pearson Correlation	,496**	,873**	.[a]	,794**	,803**	1	,870**	.[a]	,851**
	Sig. (2-tailed)	,010	,000	.	,000	,000	.	,000	.	,000
	N	26	26	26	26	26	26	26	26	26
Regulatory system	Pearson Correlation	,570**	,873**	.[a]	,912**	,769**	,870**	1	.[a]	,902**
	Sig. (2-tailed)	,002	,000	.	,000	,000	,000	.	.	,000
	N	26	26	26	26	26	26	26	26	26
Deposit insurance	Pearson Correlation	.[a]	.[a]	.[a]	.[a]	.[a]	.[a]	.[a]	.[a]	.[a]
	Sig. (2-tailed)	.	.	.	.	.	.	.	.	.
	N	26	26	26	26	26	26	26	26	26
Entry barriers	Pearson Correlation	,659**	,931**	.[a]	,841**	,800**	,851**	,902**	.[a]	1
	Sig. (2-tailed)	,000	,000	.	,000	,000	,000	,000	.	.
	N	26	26	26	26	26	26	26	26	26

** Correlation is significant at the 0.01 level (2-tailed).

a Cannot be computed because at least one of the variables is constant.

Table 21. Key events in the banking sectors in India and China

Year	Liberalization	Stabilization	Privatization	Institution Building	Structural Change
Pre-1980	India 1969: Priority sector lending introduced		India 1955: State Bank of India founded India 1969: nationalization of 14 banks	China 1979: ABC, BOC and CCB founded as separate entities from the mono-bank	
1980	India CRR at 10% (statutory minimum at 3%)		India Nationalization of six private banks		China Foreign banks allowed to re-enter the PRC after the 1979 reforms by setting up representative offices
1981					
1982					
1983					
1984				China PBOC assumes the role of central bank China ICBC created to take over PBOC's commercial banking functions	
1985	India Priority sector lending raised to 40% (from 33%)				China Foreign banks allowed to set up branches with limited operational scope in the SEZ in southern China
1986	China Banks in the late 1980s allowed to adjust lending rates within a certain margin below and above the administered rate China PBC took responsibility for formulating a credit plan that set an aggregate credit ceiling on each PBC branch			China PBOC made explicitly responsible for monetary policy and supervision of financial system	
1987					
1988	India Unification of ceiling lending rates and ranges in minimum rates India CRR raised to 11% China Reserve requirement stands at 13%				
1989	India CRR raised to 15% (maximum legal limit) India Maximum interest rate on call money liberalized China Austerity program of 1989 reversed the interest rate liberalization process				
1990					
1991		India Start of recapitalization of nationalized banks (lasts until 1999)			
1992	China Reserve requirement raised to 20%			India Introduction of Basel Capital Standards (phased in until 1996) and tightening of NPL recognition	India Banks receive greater flexibility in opening, transfering or closing branches
1993	India CRR lowered to 14% China PBC reimposed a lending rate ceiling at 20% of the basic rate and floor at 10% for commercial banks		India Amendment of SBI Act and partial privatization of SBI (33% of equity)	India Establishment of Debt Recovery Tribunals	India RBI issues guidelines for the establishment of new private sector banks
1994	India Minimum lending rate for loans above Rs 200,000 abolished China Policy banks assume government-directed lending functions of the four SOCBs		India Amendment of Banking Regulation Act allows PSBs to offer up to 49% of their equity to the public	India Establishment of Board of Financial Supervision China Establishment of policy banks to free SOCBs from policy lending requirements	India New foreign banks start operations in India; an individual shareholder can hold up to 10% of a bank China First national banking law regulating the entry and scope of foreign banks becomes effective

Year	Liberalization	Stabilization	Privatization	Institution Building	Structural Change
1995	India Interest rates for deposits with maturity above 2 years liberalized			China Commercial Banking Law enacted, including requirement to introduce capital adequacy rules in all commercial banks	India Banks receive complete discretion to open branches subject to certain conditions such as fulfillment of capital adequacy standards
1996	India Interest rate for deposits with maturity above 1 year liberalized India CRR lowered to 11% China PBC sets lending rate ceiling and floor both at 10% for commercial banks China Ceiling on interbank interest rates lifted				China The first non-state commercial bank - Minsheng Bank - is founded
1997	India Lending rates on priority sector loans above Rs 200,000 liberalized India SLR lowered to statutory minimum of 25%				
1998	India Interest rates on priority sector loans below Rs 200,000 liberalized India Interest rate for deposits with maturity above 15 days liberalized China Elimination of credit quotas for SOCBs China Lending interest rate ceiling for commercial bank loans to SMEs raised to 20% China Reserve requirement lowered from 20% to 8%	China Recapitalization of Big Four Banks			
1999	China Lending interest rate ceiling for commercial bank loans to SMEs raised to 30% China Government interference in commercial lending forbidden China Reserve requirement lowered from 8% to 6%	China Creation of Asset Management Companies and transfer of bad loans from SOCBs to AMCs		India Adoption of CAMEL framework	
2000					China Start of creation and listing of Joint Stock Commercial Banks
2001					
2002	China Banks allowed to charge up 1.3 times the central lending rate			China Tightening of loan classification and provisioning standards	China Start of phased opening of the banking sector until 2006 in line with WTO-requirements
2003	China Reserve requirement raised to 7%	China Capital injection of USD 45 bn into two SOCBs (BOC and CCB)		China Creation of CBRC	China Foreign banks authorized to operate in the wholesale market in domestic currency
2004	China Banks allowed to charge up 1.7 times the central lending rate China Reserve requirement increased to 7.5%			China Further tightening of loan classification system	
2005		China ICBC receives USD 15 bn recapitalization	China IPO of China Construction Bank		India RBI Roadmap: until 2009, foreign banks may acquire up to 74% of private banks in need of restructuring
2006			China IPO of Bank of China		China From late 2006, foreign banks will be allowed to operate in the retail market in domestic currency without geographic or business restrictions

Sources: Arun and Turner (2002a), p. 184f.; Bhide, Prasad and Ghosh (2001), p. 7; Bremner (2005), p. 26; Chen and Thomas (1999), p. 17; Garcia-Herrero and Santabarbara (2004), pp. 19-25; Hanson (2001a), p. 3 and p. 27; Hope and Hu (2006), p. 37; Kumbhakar and Sarkar (2003), p. 407; Lardy (2000), p. 8f.; Leung, Rigby and Young (2003), p. 22; Shirai (2002c), pp. 21-23.

Table 22. Overview of variables

Variable	Units and Measurement	Data sources
Index_India	Liberalization process index for India running from 1980 to 2005	---
Index_China	Liberalization process index for China running from 1980 to 2005	---
Index_lib	Liberalization process index for India running from 1960 to 2005	---
GDP_capita	Real GDP per capita in prices of 2000 calculated as (GDP in year 2000 in local currency)*(GDP volume indexed to 2000) / Population	GDP IFS line 99B..ZF; GDP volume IFS line 99BVPZF; population IFS line 99Z..ZF
GDP_growth	Growth rate GDP based on deflated GDP volume ((GDP t1)/(GDP t0)-1)	GDP volume IFS line 99BVPZF
real_deposit	Real deposit rate calculated as (nominal deposit rate) ./. (inflation rate)	Deposit rate China IFS line 60L..ZF; inflation rate calculated from GDP deflator IFS line 99BIPZF
real_lending	Real lending rate calculated as (nominal lending rate) ./. (inflation rate)	Lending rate IFS line 60P..ZF; inflation rate calculated from GDP deflator IFS line 99BIPZF
real_bankrate	Real bank rate calculated as (nominal bank rate) ./. (inflation rate)	Bank rate IFS line 60..ZF; inflation rate calculated from GDP deflator IFS line 99BIPZF
dummy_1980	Time dummy: 0 from 1960 to 1980; 1 afterwards	---
dummy_1991	Time dummy: 0 from 1980 to 1991; 1 afterwards	---
share_finsav_India	Share financial saving as percent of financial and physical saving	Central Statistical Organization GOI statement 10
saving	Gross domestic saving (sum of household, private corporate and public sector) to GDP	Economic Survey GOI table 15 for India; ADB Key Indicators 2005 line 62 for China
deposits_GDP	Sum of demand, time and saving deposits in deposit money banks to GDP. Calculated using the following deflation method: {(0.5)*[Ft/P + Ft-1/P]}/[GDPt/P] where F is the sum of deposits, and P is the CPI	Demand deposits IFS line 24..ZF; time and savings deposits IFS line 25..ZF; GDP in local currency IFS line 99B..ZF; CPI IFS line 64..ZF
saving_household	Household saving to GDP	Economic Survey GOI table 15
capital	Gross fixed capital formation to GDP	Gross fixed capital formation IFS line 93E..ZF; GDP in local currency IFS line 99B..ZF
private_capital	Gross fixed capital formation of private sector to GDP	Economic Survey GOI table 15
credit_GDP	Credit to private sector by deposit money banks to GDP. Calculated using the following deflation method: {(0.5)*[Ft/P + Ft-1/P]}/[GDPt/P] where F is credit to the private sector, and P is the CPI	Credit to private sector IFS line 22D..ZF; GDP in local currency line 99B..ZF; CPI line 64. ZF
delta_capital_GDP	Incremental capital output ratio calculated as (gross fixed capital formation/GDP)/(growth rate GDP)	Gross fixed capital formation IFS line 93E..ZF; GDP in local currency IFS line 99B..ZF
dep_money	Deposit money bank claims on domestic nonfinancial real sector to total financial assets. Sum of claims by deposit money banks on central government and private sector divided by value of numerator plus claims of monetary authorities on central government	Claims by deposit money banks on central government IFS line 22A..ZF and claims on private sector IFS line 22D..ZF; claims of monetary authorities on central government IFS line 12A..ZF
liquid	Liquid liabilities to GDP. Calculated using the following deflation method: {(0.5)*[Ft/P + Ft 1/P]}/[GDPt/P] where F is liquid liablities, and P is the CPI	Liquid liabilities (money + quasi-money) IFS lines 34..ZF and 35..ZF; GDP in local currency line 99B..ZF; CPI line 64..ZF

Note: (1) values from IFS based on electronic version per July 2006 (2) deflation method adapted from World Bank's Financial Development and Structure Database except for use of year-end CPI values instead of the average CPI due to data availability.

Table 23. Correlations between different indices

		Standardized index India	Unadjusted index India	Index Market Failure India	Index Factor Analysis India
Standardized index India	Pearson Correlation	1	1,000**	,998**	,993**
	Sig. (2-tailed)	.	,000	,000	,000
	N	26	26	26	26
Unadjusted index India	Pearson Correlation	1,000**	1	,999**	,992**
	Sig. (2-tailed)	,000	.	,000	,000
	N	26	26	26	26
Index Market Failure India	Pearson Correlation	,998**	,999**	1	,987**
	Sig. (2-tailed)	,000	,000	.	,000
	N	26	26	26	26
Index Factor Analysis India	Pearson Correlation	,993**	,992**	,987**	1
	Sig. (2-tailed)	,000	,000	,000	.
	N	26	26	26	26

**. Correlation is significant at the 0.01 level (2-tailed).

Table 24. Overview of indices

	India				China			
Year	Unadjusted	Standardized	Market Failure	Factor Analysis	Unadjusted	Standardized	Market Failure	Factor Analysis
1980	2.33	0.16	0.17	-0.91	0.00	0.00	0.00	-0.87
1981	2.33	0.16	0.17	-0.91	0.00	0.00	0.00	-0.87
1982	2.33	0.16	0.17	-0.91	0.00	0.00	0.00	-0.87
1983	2.33	0.16	0.17	-0.91	0.00	0.00	0.00	-0.87
1984	3.33	0.22	0.27	-0.98	0.00	0.00	0.00	-0.87
1985	3.33	0.22	0.27	-0.98	0.00	0.00	0.00	-0.87
1986	3.00	0.20	0.24	-0.86	0.33	0.02	0.02	-0.81
1987	3.00	0.20	0.24	-0.86	0.33	0.02	0.02	-0.81
1988	3.00	0.20	0.24	-0.86	0.33	0.02	0.02	-0.81
1989	3.00	0.20	0.24	-0.86	0.00	0.00	0.00	-0.87
1990	3.00	0.20	0.24	-0.86	0.00	0.00	0.00	-0.87
1991	3.00	0.20	0.24	-0.86	0.00	0.00	0.00	-0.87
1992	3.67	0.24	0.29	-0.74	0.00	0.00	0.00	-0.87
1993	3.67	0.24	0.29	-0.74	0.33	0.02	0.02	-0.81
1994	6.33	0.42	0.47	0.42	1.67	0.11	0.12	-0.05
1995	7.00	0.47	0.51	0.35	1.67	0.11	0.12	-0.05
1996	8.67	0.58	0.62	1.08	3.00	0.20	0.21	0.51
1997	9.00	0.60	0.64	1.14	3.00	0.20	0.21	0.51
1998	9.00	0.60	0.64	1.14	3.33	0.22	0.23	0.68
1999	9.33	0.62	0.67	1.02	3.67	0.24	0.27	1.08
2000	9.33	0.62	0.67	1.02	3.67	0.24	0.27	1.08
2001	9.33	0.62	0.67	1.02	4.00	0.27	0.29	1.25
2002	9.67	0.64	0.69	1.26	6.00	0.40	0.46	1.53
2003	9.67	0.64	0.69	1.26	6.33	0.42	0.48	1.77
2004	9.67	0.64	0.69	1.26	6.33	0.42	0.48	1.77
2005	9.67	0.64	0.69	1.26	6.33	0.42	0.48	1.77

Notes: (1) The standardized index is calculated by dividing the unadjusted values by 15, which is the maximum score a country can achieve. The values are standardized between 0 and 1; (2) the market failure index is standardized between 0 and 1; (3) the factor analysis index values were calculated with the principal components method and are the values for the first rotated factor that explains 65.8% of the total variance of the individual scores.

Table 25. Values for Granger causality tests India and China

Null Hypothesis	F-Statistic	Probability
GDP_GROWTH_INDIA does not Granger cause DEP_MONEY_INDIA	4.01831	0.03408 **
DEP_MONEY_INDIA does not Granger cause GDP_GROWTH_INDIA	0.53217	0.74772
GDP_GROWTH_INDIA does not Granger cause LIQUID_INDIA	0.55381	0.73307
LIQUID_INDIA does not Granger cause GDP_GROWTH_INDIA	0.51345	0.76044
GDP_GROWTH_CHINA does not Granger cause DEP_MONEY_CHINA	2.45037	0.20292
DEP_MONEY_CHINA does not Granger cause GDP_GROWTH_CHINA	4.96041	0.07297 *
LIQUID_CHINA does not Granger cause GDP_GROWTH_CHINA	0.96875	0.48495
GDP_GROWTH_CHINA does not Granger cause LIQUID_CHINA	0.45660	0.79913

Note: (1) Time period for test is 1980-2005 with 5 lags with the exception of DEP_MONEY_CHINA where data is only available from 1985; (2) * denotes significance at the 10% level; ** at the 5% level; *** at the 1% level.

Table 26. Values for Granger causality test India

Null Hypothesis	F-Statistic	Probability
GDP_GROWTH does not Granger cause DEP_MONEY	0.2739	0.92368
DEP_MONEY does not Granger cause GDP_GROWTH	3.38071	0.01582 **
GDP_GROWTH does not Granger cause LIQUID	1.736	0.1579
LIQUID does not Granger cause GDP_GROWTH	7.53617	0.00012 ***

Note: (1) Time period for test is 1960-2005 with 5 lags; (2) * denotes significance at the 10% level; ** at the 5% level; *** at the 1% level.

Table 27. Values for liberalization index India

Year	Liberalization: Interest rate controls	Credit controls	Reserve requirements	Average value	Standardized index
1960	3	3	2	2.7	0.889
1961	3	3	2	2.7	0.889
1962	3	2	2	2.3	0.778
1963	2	2	2	2.0	0.667
1964	1	2	2	1.7	0.556
1965	2	2	2	2.0	0.667
1966	2	2	2	2.0	0.667
1967	2	2	2	2.0	0.667
1968	2	2	2	2.0	0.667
1969	1	1	2	1.3	0.444
1970	1	1	2	1.3	0.444
1971	1	1	2	1.3	0.444
1972	1	1	2	1.3	0.444
1973	1	1	2	1.3	0.444
1974	1	1	2	1.3	0.444
1975	1	1	2	1.3	0.444
1976	1	1	2	1.3	0.444
1977	1	1	2	1.3	0.444
1978	1	1	1	1.0	0.333
1979	1	1	1	1.0	0.333
1980	1	1	1	1.0	0.333
1981	1	1	1	1.0	0.333
1982	1	1	1	1.0	0.333
1983	1	1	1	1.0	0.333
1984	1	1	1	1.0	0.333
1985	1	1	1	1.0	0.333
1986	1	1	0	0.7	0.222
1987	1	1	0	0.7	0.222
1988	1	1	0	0.7	0.222
1989	1	1	0	0.7	0.222
1990	1	1	0	0.7	0.222
1991	1	1	0	0.7	0.222
1992	1	1	1	1.0	0.333
1993	1	1	1	1.0	0.333
1994	1	1	0	0.7	0.222
1995	2	1	1	1.3	0.444
1996	2	1	1	1.3	0.444
1997	3	1	1	1.7	0.556
1998	3	1	1	1.7	0.556
1999	3	1	2	2.0	0.667
2000	3	1	2	2.0	0.667
2001	3	1	2	2.0	0.667
2002	3	1	2	2.0	0.667
2003	3	1	2	2.0	0.667
2004	3	1	2	2.0	0.667
2005	3	1	2	2.0	0.667

Notes: (1) Values for 1980-2005 are equivalent to the respective categories in the overall process index (Table 18); (2) values for reserve requirements assigned according to the effective reserve requirements like for the overall process index; (3) values for interest rate controls for 1960-1979 are based on Demetriades and Luintel (1997), p. 320 with average values for interest rate restrictions above 0.67 indicating a largely repressed system; (4) values for directed credit program for 1960-1979 are based on the directed credit dummy in Demetriades and Luintel (1997), p. 320.

References

Abiad, Abdul/ Mody, Ashoka (2002) Status Quo Bias in Financial Reform. IMF Working Paper: pp 1-38

Abiad, Abdul et al. (2004) The Quality Effect: Does Financial Liberalization Improve the Allocation of Capital? IMF Working Paper, WP/04/112: pp 1-34

Acemoglu, Daron/ Robinson, James A. (2000) Political Losers as a Barrier to Economic Development. The American Economic Review, 90 (2): pp 126-130

Acharya, Shankar (2002) India: Crisis, Reforms and Growth in the Nineties. Working Paper Stanford University, No. 139: pp 1-40

Achleitner, Ann-Kristin (2000) Handbuch Investment Banking. Wiesbaden

Ahluwalia, Montek S. (2002) Economic reforms in India since 1991: Has Gradualism worked? Journal of Economic Perspectives, 16 (3): pp 67-88

Ahrens, Joachim (1994a) Der russische Systemwandel - Reform und Transformation des (post)sowjetischen Wirtschaftssystems. Diss., Göttingen

Ahrens, Joachim (1994b) The Transition to A Market Economy: Are there Useful Lessons from History? In: Schipke, A./ Taylor, A.M. (ed): The Economics of Transformation - Theory and Practice in the New Market Economies. Heidelberg, pp 17-46

Ahrens, Joachim (1998) Economic Development, the State, and the Importance of Governance in East Asia. Economic Systems, 22 (1): pp 23-51

Ahrens, Joachim (1999) Toward a Post-Washington Consensus: The Importance of Governance Structures in Less Developed Countries and Economies in Transition. Journal for Institutional Innovation, Development & Transition, 3: pp 1-38

Aivazian, Varouj A. et al. (2005) Can corporatization improve the performance of state-owned enterprises even without privatization? Journal of Corporate Finance, 11 (5): pp 791-808

Alesina, Alberto (1997) The Political Economy of High and Low Growth. In: Pleskovic, Boris/ Stiglitz, Joseph E. (ed.), Paper prepared for the Annual World Bank Conference on Development Economics 1997, Washington D.C., pp 217-237

Alesina, Alberto/ Drazen, Allan (1991) Why are Stabilizations Delayed? The American Economic Review, 81 (5): pp 1170-1188

Allen, Franklin/ Gale, Douglas (2000) Comparing Financial Systems. Cambridge (MA)/London (England)

Allen, Franklin et al. (2005a) China's Financial System: Past, Present, and Future. Working Paper: pp 1-103

Allen, Franklin et al. (2005b) Law, finance, and economic growth in China. Journal of Financial Economics, 77: pp 57-116
Anderson, Jonathan (2005) The Great Chinese Bank Sale. Far Eastern Economic Review, 168 (8): pp 7-12
Anderson, Jonathan (2006) Five Persistent Myths About China's Banking System. Cato Journal, 26 (2): pp 243-250
Anderson, R.W./ Kegels, C. (1998) Transition Banking: Financial Development of Central and Eastern Europe. Oxford
Apolte, Thomas (1992) Politische Ökonomie der Systemtransformation - Gruppeninteressen und Interessenkonflikte im Transformationsprozeß. Hamburg
Arestis, Philip/ Demetriades, Panicos O. (1997) Financial Development and Economic Growth: Assessing the Evidence. The Economic Journal, 107: pp 783-799
Arestis, Philip et al. (2002) The impact of financial liberalization policies on financial development: evidence from developing countries. International Journal of Finance and Economics, 7 (2): pp 109-122
Arestis, Philip et al. (2003) Finance and Development: Institutional and Policy Alternatives to Financial Liberalization Theory. Working Paper Levy Economics Institute, No. 377: pp 1-24
Aron, Janine (2000) Growth and Institutions: A Review of the Evidence. The World Bank Research Observer, 15 (1): pp 99-135
Arun, T.G./ Turner, J.D. (2002a) Financial liberalisation in India. Journal of International Banking Regulation, 4 (2): pp 183-188
Arun, T.G./ Turner, J.D. (2002b) Financial Sector Reforms in Developing Countries: The Indian Experience. World Economy, 25 (3): pp 429-445
Arun, T.G./ Turner, J.D. (2002c) Public Sector Banks in India: Rationale and Prerequisites for Reform. Annals of Public and Cooperative Economics, 73 (1): pp 89-109
Aschinger, Gerhard (2001) Währungs- und Finanzkrisen - Entstehung, Analyse und Beurteilung aktueller Krisen. München
Asian Development Bank (2006) Key Indicators 2005. <www.adb.org/statistics>, Accessed: April 2006
Ataullah, Ali et al. (2004) Financial liberalisation and bank efficiency: a comparative analysis of India and Pakistan. Applied Economics, 36 (17): pp 1915-1924
Auerbach, Paul/ Siddiki, Jalal Uddin (2004) Financial Liberalisation and Economic Development: An Assessment. Journal of Economic Surveys, 18 (3): pp 231-265
Aziz, Jahangir/ Duenwald, Christoph (2002) Growth-Financial Intermediation Nexus in China. IMF Working Paper, No. 02/194: pp 1-16
Backhaus, Klaus et al. (2003) Multivariate Analysemethoden - Eine anwendungsorientierte Einführung. Berlin et al.
Bai, Chong-En et al. (1999) Anonymous Banking and Financial Repression: How Does China's Reform Limit the Government's Predation without Reducing Its Revenue? Working Paper Stanford University: pp 1-54

Bajpai, Nirupam (1996) Economic Crisis, Structural Reforms and the Prospects of Growth in India. HIID Discussion Paper, Harvard University, No. 530: pp 1-21

Balassa, Bela (1990) Financial Liberalization in Developing Countries. Studies in Comparative International Development, 25 (4): pp 56-70

Balcerowicz, Leszek (1995) Socialism, Capitalism, Transformation. Budapest/London/New York

Balcerowicz, Leszek/ Gelb, Alan (1994) Macropolicies in Transition to a Market Economy: A Three-Year Perspective. In: Bruno, Michael/ Pleskovic, Boris (ed.), Paper prepared for the Annual World Bank Conference on Development Economics 1994, Washington D.C., pp 21-44

Bandiera, Oriana et al. (2000) Does Financial Reform Raise or Reduce Saving? The Review of Economics and Statistics, 82 (2): pp 239-263

Banerjee, Abhijit V./ Duflo, Esther (2004) What do banks (not) do? MIT Working Paper: pp 1-7

BankScope (2006) BankScope Database. Accessed: July 2006

BankScope Database (2006) Accessed: July 2006

Barnett, Steven (2004) Banking Sector Developments. In: Prasad, Eswar S. (ed): China's Growth and Integration into the World Economy: Prospects and Challenges (IMF Occasional Paper No. 232). Washington D.C., pp 43-50

Barth, James R. et al. (2000) Banking systems around the globe: do regulation and ownership affect performance and stability? World Bank Policy Research Working Paper, No. 2325: pp 1-60

Barton, Dominic et al. (2003) Dangerous Markets: Managing in Financial Crises. New York et al.

Basel Committee on Banking Supervision (1997) Core Principles for Effective Banking Supervision. Basel

Basu, Priya (2005) Introduction. In: Basu, Priya (ed): India's Financial Sector - Recent Reforms, Future Challenges. New Delhi, pp 1-22

Basu, Priya/ Srivastava, Pradeep (2005) Improving Access to Finance for India's Rural Poor. In: Basu, Priya (ed): India's Financial Sector - Recent Reforms, Future Challenges. New Delhi, pp 138-175

Bator, Francis M. (1958) The Anatomy of Market Failure. Quarterly Journal of Economics, 72 (3): pp 351-379

Beck, Thorsten (2006) Creating an Efficient Financial System: Challenges in a Global Economy. World Bank Policy Research Working Paper, No. 3856: pp 1-43

Bell, Clive/ Rosseau, Peter L. (2001) Post-independence India: a case of finance-led industrialization? Journal of Development Economics, 65 (1): pp 153-175

Berglof, E./ Bolton, P. (2002) The Great Divide and Beyond - Financial Architecture in Transition. Journal of Economic Perspectives, 16 (1): pp 77-100

Besley, Timothy (1994) How Do Market Failures Justify Interventions in Rural Credit Markets? The World Bank Research Observer, 9 (1): pp 27-47

Bhalla, A.S. (1998) Sino-Indian Liberalization. The Role of Trade and Foreign Investment. Economics of Planning, 31 (2-3): pp 151-173

Bhattacharya, Prabir C./ Sivasubramanian, M.N. (2003) Financial Development and Economic Growth in India: 1970-1971 to 1998-1999. Applied Financial Economics, 13 (12): pp 925-929

Bhattacharya, Saugata / Patel, Urjit R. (2004) Reform strategies in the Indian Financial Sector. Working Paper Stanford University, No. 208: pp 1-44

Bhaumik, Sumon K./ Dimova, Ralitza (2004) How important is ownership in a market with level playing field? The Indian banking sector revisited. Journal of Comparative Economics, 32 (1): pp 165-180

Bhide, M. G. et al. (2001) Emerging Challenges in Indian Banking. Working Paper Stanford University, No. 103: pp 1-61

Blanchard, Olivier/ Kremer, Michael (1997) Disorganization. Quarterly Journal of Economics: pp 1091-1126

Blejer, Mario (1999) The Financial Sector in Transition. In: Blejer, Mario/ Skreb, Marko (ed): Financial Sector Transformation: Lessons from Economies in Transition. Cambridge (UK), pp 383-392

Boehmer, Ekkehart et al. (2005) Bank privatization in developing and developed countries: Cross-sectional evidence on the impact of economic and political factors. Journal of Banking & Finance, 29 (8-9): pp 1981-2013

Bonaccorsi di Patti, Emilia/ Hardy, Daniel C. (2005) Financial sector liberalization, bank privatization, and efficiency: Evidence from Pakistan. Journal of Banking & Finance, 29 (8-9): pp 2381-2406

Bonin, John P. et al. (2005) Privatization matters: Bank efficiency in transition countries. Journal of Banking & Finance, 29 (8-9): pp 2155-2178

Bonin, John P./ Wachtel, Paul (1999) Toward Market-Oriented Banking in the Economies in Transition. In: Blejer, Mario/ Skreb, Marko (ed): Financial Sector Transformation: Lessons from Economies in Transition. Cambridge (UK), pp 19-92

Bossone, Biagio (2000) What Makes Banks Special? A study on banking, finance, and economic development. Working Paper World Bank: pp 1-60

Boubakri, Narjess et al. (2005) Privatization and bank performance in developing countries. Journal of Banking & Finance, 29 (8-9): pp 2015-2041

Bowers, Tab et al. (2003) Banking in Asia - Acquiring a Profit Mindset. Singapore

Boyreau-Debray, Genevieve (2003) Financial Intermediation and Growth: Chinese Style. World Bank Policy Research Working Paper, No. 3027: pp 1-60

Brandt, Loren / Li, Hongbin (2003) Bank discrimination in transition economies: ideology, information, or incentives. Journal of Comparative Economics, 31 (3): pp 387-413

Bremner, Brian (2005) Betting on China's Banks. Business Week, October 31, 2005: pp 18-26

Bremner, Brian (2006) A Golden Age for China's Banks. Business Week Online Edition, May 31, 2006:

Broadman, Harry G. (2001) The Business(es) of the Chinese State. Working Paper World Bank: pp 1-23

Brownbridge, Martin/ Kirkpatrick, Colin (2000) Financial Regulation in Developing Countries. Journal of Development Studies, 37 (1): pp 1-24

Browning, Martin/ Lusardi, Anna Maria (1996) Household Saving: Micro Theories and Micro Facts. Journal of Economic Literature, 34 (4): pp 1797-1855

Budhwar, Pawan (2001) Doing Business in... India. Thunderbird International Business Review, 43 (4): pp 549-560

Buiter, Willem H. et al. (1999) Financing Transition: Investing in Enterprises during Macroeconomic Transition. In: Blejer, Mario/ Skreb, Marko (ed): Financial Sector Transformation: Lessons from Economies in Transition. Cambridge (UK), pp 150-192

Business Week (2005) China & India. Business Week, August 22-29 2005: pp 29-104

Calderón, César/ Liu, Lin (2003) The direction of causality between financial development and economic growth. Journal of Development Economics, 72 (1): pp 321-334

Cao, Yuanzheng et al. (1999) From federalism, Chinese style to privatization, Chinese style. Economics of Transition, 7 (1): pp 103-131

Caprio, Gerard Jr. et al. (1993) Financial Reform Lessons and Strategies. World Bank Policy Research Working Paper, No. 1107: pp 1-45

Caprio, Gerard Jr. et al. (1994) Policy issues in reforming finance: Lessons and strategies. In: Caprio, Gerard Jr./ Atiyas, Izak/ Hanson, James A. (ed): Financial reform - theory and experience. Cambridge, pp 413-440

Caprio, Gerard Jr. et al. (2001) Introduction and Overview: The Case for Liberalization and Some Drawbacks. In: Caprio, Gerard Jr./ Honohan, Patrick/ Stiglitz, Joseph E. (ed): Financial Liberalization: How Far, How Fast? Cambridge (UK), pp 3-30

Caprio, Gerard Jr./ Klingebiel, Daniela (1997) Banking insolvency: Bad luck, bad policy, or bad banking? , Proceedings of the World Bank Annual Conference on Development Economics 1996, pp 1-29

Carlin, Wendy/ Landesmann, Michael (1997) From Theory into Practice? Restructuring and Dynamism in Transition Economies. Oxford Review of Economic Policy, 13 (2): pp 77-105

Center for the Advanced Study of India (2004) Doing Business in India - Ideology, Politics and Economic Reforms: The National Democratic Alliance 1999-2004

Chan, Vei-Lin/ Hu, Sheng-Cheng (2000) Financial Liberalization in Taiwan. Review of Pacific Basin Financial Markets and Policies, 3 (3): pp 429-449

Chang, Tsangyao (2002) Financial development and economic growth in mainland China: a note on testing demand-following or supply-leading hypothesis. Applied Economics Letters, 9 (13): pp 869-873

Chen, Ji/ Thomas, Stephen C. (1999) Banking on China. The China Business Review, Nov/Dec 1999: pp 16-22

Chipalkatti, Niranjan/ Rishi, Meenakshi (2003) Indian Banking Sector Reform and Liberalization: Pain or Panacea? Working Paper: pp 1-28

Choi, Christina/ Kan, Carmen (2004) Giving a Boost to Foreign Equity Participations in Domestic Financial Institutions. China Law & Practice, March 2004: pp 11-15

Chow, Gregory C. (1997) Challenges of China's Economic System for Economic Theory. The American Economic Review, 87 (2): pp 321-327
Chow, Gregory C. (2004) Economic Reform and Growth in China. Annals of Economics and Finance, 5: pp 127-152
Claessens, Stijn (1996) Banking Reform in Transition Countries. World Bank Policy Research Working Paper, No. 1642: pp 1-28
Clarke, George R.G. et al. (2005) Bank privatization in developing countries: A summary of lessons and findings. Journal of Banking & Finance, 29 (8-9): pp 1905-1930
Coco, Guiseppe (2000) On the use of collateral. Journal of Economic Surveys, 14 (2): pp 191-214
Commander, Simon et al. (1999) Restructuring in Transition Economies: Ownership, Competition, and Regulation. In: Pleskovic, Boris/ Stiglitz, Joseph E. (ed.), Paper prepared for the Annual World Bank Conference on Development Economics 1999, pp 345-373
Cornia, Giovanni Andrea/ Popov, Vladimir (2001) Structural and Institutional Factors in the Transition to the Market Economy: An Overview. In: Cornia, Giovanni Andrea/ Popov, Vladimir (ed): Transition and Institutions - The Experience of Gradual and Late Reformers. New York, pp 3-26
Csaba, Laszlo (1993) On the Normative Theory of Transformation. In: Wagener, Hans-Jürgen (ed): The Political Economy of Transformation. Heidelberg, pp 97-112
Csaba, Laszlo (1997) Economic Transformation: State of Art and some Theoretical reflections. Frankfurt Institute of Transformation Studies Discussion Paper, No. 7/97: pp 1-22
Cygnus Economic & Business Research (2004) Indian Banking. Hyderabad
Das, Dilip K. (2003) Financial liberalisation in the emerging market economies. Journal of Asset Management, 3 (4): pp 345-359
Datta-Chaudhuri, Mrinal (1990) Market Failure and Government Failure. Journal of Economic Perspectives, 4 (3): pp 25-39
de Gregorio, Jose/ Guidotti, P. (1995) Financial development and economic growth. World Development, 23 (3): pp 433-448
de Melo, Martha et al. (1997) Circumstance and Choice: The Role of Initial Conditions and Policies in Transition Economies. Working Paper: pp 1-84
Deckert, Martin (1996) Liberalisierung von Finanzsystemen unter besonderer Berücksichtigung des Faktors Glaubwürdigkeit. Diss., Wiesbaden
DeLong, J. Bradford (2003) India Since Independence: An Analytic Growth Narrative. In: Rodrik, Dani (ed): In Search of Prosperity: Analytical Narratives on Economic Growth. Princeton, N.J., pp 184-204
Demetriades, P.O./ Hussein, Khaled A. (1996) Does Financial Development Cause Economic Growth? Time-series Evidence from 16 Countries. Journal of Development Economics, 51 (2): pp 387-411
Demetriades, Panicos O./ Luintel, Kul B. (1996a) Banking Sector Policies And Financial Development in Nepal. Oxford Bulletin of Economics and Statistics, 58 (2): pp 355-372

Demetriades, Panicos O./ Luintel, Kul B. (1996b) Financial Development, Economic Growth and Banking Sector Controls: Evidence from India. Economic Journal, 106 (435): pp 359-374

Demetriades, Panicos O./ Luintel, Kul B. (1997) The Direct Costs of Financial Repression: Evidence from India. The Review of Economics and Statistics: pp 311-320

Demetriades, Panicos O./ Luintel, Kul B. (2001) Financial Restraints in the South Korean Miracle. Journal of Development Economics, 64 (2): pp 459-479

Demirgüc-Kunt, Asli (2006) Finance and Economic Development: Policy Choices for Developing Countries. Working Paper World Bank: pp 1-55

Demirgüc-Kunt, Asli/ Detragiache, Enrica (1998) Financial Liberalization and Financial Fragility. IMF Working Paper: pp 1-53

Demirgüc-Kunt, Asli/ Sobaci, Tolga (2000) Deposit Insurance Around the World: A Data Base. Working Paper World Bank: pp 1-43

Denizer, Cevdet et al. (1998) The Political Economy of Financial Repression in Transition Economies. Working Paper World Bank: pp 1-32

Deolalkar, G.H. (1999) The Indian Banking Sector: On the Road to Progress. In: Asian Development Bank (ed): Rising to the Challenge in Asia: A Study of Financial Markets - India. Manila, pp 59-109

DeRosa, David F. (2005) China's Defense of the Peg Perpetuates Central Planning. Cato Journal, 25 (1): pp 49-54

Desai, Ashok V. (1999) The Economics and Politics of Transition to an Open Market Economy: India. OECD Technical Paper, No. 155: pp 1-73

Desai, Meghnad (2003) India and China: An Essay in Comparative Political Economy. Paper prepared for the IMF and NACAER Conference "A Tale of Two Giants: India's and China's Experience with Reform and Growth", New Delhi, pp 1-21

DeSombre, Michael G./ Chen, Weiheng (2004) New Capital Rules Bring China's Banking Regulation up to Global Standards. China Law & Practice, April 2004: pp 12-16

Detragiache, Enrica et al. (2006) Foreign Banks in Poor Countries: Theory and Evidence. IMF Working Paper, No. 06/18: pp 1-48

Deutsche Bank Research (2004) China's financial sector: Institutional framework and main challenges. Frankfurt am Main

Deutsche Bank Research (2005) China & India: A visual essay. Frankfurt am Main

Deutsche Bank Research (2006) India's public finances: Do they matter? Frankfurt am Main

Dhanji, Farid (1991) Transformation Programs: Content and Sequencing. The American Economic Review, 81 (2): pp 323-328

Diamond, Douglas W./ Dybvig, Philip H. (1983) Bank runs, deposit insurance and liquidity. Journal of Political Economy, 91 (3): pp 401-419

Diaz-Alejandro, Carlo (1985) Good-bye financial repression, hello financial crash. Journal of Development Economics, 19 (1 2): pp 1-23

Dorn, James A. (2006) Ending Financial Repression in China. Cato Institute Economic Development Bulletin, No. 5: pp 1-4

Echeverri-Gent, John (2001) Political Economy of India's Fiscal and Financial Reforms. Working Paper Stanford University, No. 105: pp 1-26
Economist Intelligence Unit (2005) Country Commerce India. New York
Economist Intelligence Unit (2006) Country Commerce China. New York
Eichengreen, Barry/ Arteta, Carlos (2002) Banking Crises in Emerging Markets: Presumptions and Evidence. In: Blejer, Mario/ Skreb, Marko (ed): Financial Policies in Emerging Markets. Cambridge (Mass.)/London, pp 47-94
Ellman, Michael (1997) The Political Economy of Transformation. Oxford Review of Economic Policy, 13 (2): pp 23-32
Engerer, Hella/ Schrooten, Mechthild (2001) Institutionen, Finanzsysteme und Transformation. Discussion Paper Deutsches Institut für Wirtschaftsforschung, No. 264: pp 1-35
European Bank for Reconstruction and Development (1999) Transition Report - Ten years of transition. London
Fan, Gang (2002) Institutional Reforms in a Developing Country: Transition in China. TIGER Working Paper Series, No. 29: pp 1-23
Fees, Eberhard (1997) Mikroökonomie - eine spieltheoretische und anwendungsorientierte Einführung. Marburg
Feld, Lars P./ Kirchgässner, Gebhard (2003) Die Rolle des Staates in privaten Governance Strukturen. Schweizerische Zeitschrift für Volkswirtschaft und Statistik, 139 (3): pp 253-285
Fernandez, Raquel/ Rodrik, Dani (1992) Resistance to Reform: Status Quo Bias in the Presence of Individual-Specific Uncertainty. The American Economic Review, 81 (5): pp 1146-1155
Ferris, Kenneth R. et al. (2000) Fundamentals of Accounting for Decision Making. New York et al.
Fischer, Stanley/ Gelb, Alan (1991) The Process of Socialist Economic Transformation. Journal of Economic Perspectives, 5 (4): pp 91-105
Fitch Ratings (2003) The Indian Banking System. New York
Fitch Ratings (2005) Chinese Banks: 2004 Review and 2005 Outlook. New York
Forbes, Naushad (2001) Doing Business in India: what has liberalization changed? Working Paper Stanford University, No. 93: pp 1-47
Freebairn, John (1998) Where and Why Government Should Be Involved - A Perspective from Economics. Australian Journal of Public Administration, 57 (4): pp 66-74
Freixas, Xavier/ Rochet, Jean-Charles (1998) Microeconomics of Banking. Cambridge (Mass.)/London
Fry, Maxwell E. (1989) Financial Development: Theories and Recent Experience. Oxford Review of Economic Policy, 5 (4): pp 13-28
Fry, Maxwell E. (1995) Money, Interest and Banking in Economic Development. Baltimore, MD
Fry, Maxwell E. (1997) In Favour of Financial Liberalisation. The Economic Journal, 107: pp 754-770
Frydman, Roman et al. (1999) When Does Privatization Work? The Impact of Private Ownership on Corporate Performance in the Transition Economies. Quarterly Journal of Economics, 114 (4): pp 1153-1191

Funke, Norbert (1993) Timing and Sequencing of Reforms: Competing Views and the Role of Credibility. Kyklos, 46 (3): pp 337-362

Galindo, Arturo et al. (2002) Financial Liberalization and Growth: Empirical Evidence. Paper prepared for the World Bank Conference on Financial Globalization, Washington D.C., pp 1-35

Galindo, Arturo et al. (2003) Does Financial Liberalization Improve the Allocation of Investment? Micro Evidence from Developing Countries. Working Paper: pp 1-42

Ganesan, P. (2001) Determinants of Profits and Profitability of Public Sector Banks in India: A Profit Function Approach. Journal of Financial Management and Analysis, 14 (1): pp 27-37

Ganesan, P. (2003) Impact of Priority Sector Advances on Profitability of Public Sector Banks in India. Journal of Financial Management and Analysis, 16 (2): pp 14-27

Gang, Fan et al. (1999) People's Republic of China: Economic Performance and Prospects. Asian Development Review, 15 (2): pp 43-85

Garcia-Herrero, Alicia et al. (2005) China's Banking Reform: An Assessment of its Evolution and Possible Impact. Documentos Ocasionales Banco de Espana, No. 0502: pp 1-54

Garcia-Herrero, Alicia/ Santabarbara, Daniel (2004) Where is the Chinese Banking System Going with the Ongoing Reform? Documentos Ocasionales Banco de Espana, No. 0406: pp 1-44

Gemech, Firdu/ Struthers, John (2003) The McKinnon-Shaw Hypothesis: Thirty Years on: A Review of Recent Developments in Financial Liberalization Theory. Paper prepared for the Development Studies Association Annual Conference on "Globalisation and Development", Glasgow, pp 1-24

Gerschenkron, Alexander (1962) Economic Backwardness in Historical Perspective. Cambridge (MA)

Ghose, Udoy Michael (2000) Die Transformation der Indischen Union - Eine empirische und theoretische Analyse der Wirtschaftsreformen 1991-96 und ihrer Implikationen für die "Mainstream"-Transformationstheorie. Diss., Frankfurt am Main

Gibson, H./ Tsakalotos, E. (1994) The Scope and Limits of Financial Liberalization in Developing Countries. Journal of Development Studies, 30 (3): pp 578-628

Gilley, Bruce (2005) Two Passages to Modernity. In: Friedman, Edward/ Gilley, Bruce (ed): Asia's Giants: Comparing China and India. New York, pp 19-52

Giovanni, Alberto/ de Melo, Martha (1993) Government Revenue from Financial Repression. The American Economic Review, 83 (4): pp 953-963

Girardin, Eric (1997) Banking Sector Reform and Credit Control in China. Paris

Goldstein, Morris (2006) Renminbi Controversies. Cato Journal, 26 (2): pp 251-266

Gopinath, Shyamala (2006) Approach to Basel II. RBI Bulletin, June 2006: pp 1-10

Gormley, Todd A. (2006) Banking Competition in Developing Countries: Does Foreign Bank Entry Improve Credit Access? Working Paper: pp 1-51

Government of India (1991) Report of The Committee on the Financial System. New Delhi

Government of India (1998) Report of The Committee on Banking Sector Reforms. New Delhi

Government of India (2006) Economic Survey 2005-2006. <www.indiabudget.nic.in/es2005-06/public.htm>, Accessed: August 2006

Greenwood, Jeremy/ Jovanovic, Boyan (1990) Financial Development, Growth, and the Distribution of Income. Journal of Political Economy, 98 (5): pp 1076-1107

Guha-Khasnobis, Basudeb/ Bhaduri, Saumitra N. (2000) A hallmark of India's new economic policy: deregulation and liberalization of the financial sector. Journal of Asian Economics, 11: pp 333-346

Guo, Kai/ Yao, Yang (2004) Causes of Privatization in China: Testing Several Hypotheses. Working Paper China Center for Economic Research, No. E2004004: pp 1-34

Gupta, Ashish/ Jayakar, Roshni (2005) Reddy, Steady, Hold. Business Today, 14 (7): pp 58-62

Gupta, Rajat K. (2005) India's economic agenda: An interview with Manmohan Singh. The McKinsey Quarterly, 2005 special edition: Fulfilling India's promise: pp 115-124

Guriev, Sergei/ Megginson, William L. (2006) Privatization: What Have We Learned. Paper prepared for the Annual World Bank Conference on Development Economics 2006, St. Petersburg, pp 1-45

Halbach, Axel J./ Helmschrott, Helmut (1994) Wirtschaftspolitische Reformen in Indien: Analyse - Kritik - Erfahrungen. München/Köln/London

Hanson, James A. (2001a) Indian Banking: Market Liberalization and the Pressures for Institutional and Market Framework Reform. Working Paper Stanford University, No. 104: pp 1-37

Hanson, James A. (2001b) Indonesia and India: Contrasting Approaches to Repression and Liberalization. In: Caprio, Gerard Jr./ Honohan, Patrick/ Stiglitz, Joseph E. (ed): Financial Liberalization: How Far, How Fast? Cambridge (UK), pp 233-264

Hauner, David (2006) Fiscal Policy and Financial Development. IMF Working Paper, No. 06/26: pp 1-24

Hawkins, J./ Mihaljek, D. (2001) The banking industry in the emerging market economies: competition, consolidation and systemic stability. Overview Paper BIS, No. 4:

Hayami, Yujiro (2004) From the Washington Consensus to the Post-Washington Consensus: Retrospect and Prospect. Asian Development Review, 20 (2): pp 40-65

Haynes, Michael/ Husan, Rumy (2002) Market Failure, State Failure, Institutions, and Historical Constraints in the East European Transition. Journal of European Area Studies, 10 (1): pp 105-129

Heberer, Thomas/ Schubert, Gunter (2006) Political Reform and Regime Legitimacy in Contemporary China. Asien, No. 99: pp 9-28

Henley, John S. (2004) Chasing the Dragon: Accounting for the Under-Performance of India by Comparison with China in Attracting Foreign Direct Investment. Journal of International Development, 16 (7): pp 1039-1052

Hermann-Pillath, Carsten (1993) China's Transition to the Market: A Paradox of Transformation and its Institutionalist Solution. In: Wagener, Hans-Jürgen (ed): The Political Economy of Transformation. Heidelberg, pp 209-241

Hermann-Pillath, Carsten (1999) Was ist und wie betreibt man wirtschaftskulturelle Transformationsforschung? Diskussionspapier der Fakultät für Wirtschaftswissenschaften an der Universität Witten/Herdecke, No. 40

Hermes, Niels/ Lensink, Robert (2000) Financial System Development in Transition Economies. Journal of Banking & Finance, 24 (4): pp 507-524

Holland, Tom/ Lague, David (2004) Wasteful Transfusion. Far Eastern Economic Review, 167 (3): pp 26-29

Holz, Carsten A. (2000) The Changing Role of Money in China and Its Implications. Comparative Economic Studies, 42 (3): pp 77-100

Honohan, Patrick (1997) Banking system failures in developing and transition countries: diagnosis and prediction. BIS Working Paper, No. 39: pp 1-45

Honohan, Patrick/ Stiglitz, Joseph E. (2001) Robust Financial Restraint. In: Caprio, Gerard Jr./ Honohan, Patrick/ Stiglitz, Joseph E. (ed): Financial Liberalization: How Far, How Fast? Cambridge (UK), pp 31-59

Hope, Nicholas/ Hu, Fred (2006) Reforming China's Banking System: How Much Can Foreign Strategic Investment Help? Working Paper Stanford University, No. 276: pp 1-52

Hu, Chia-Hsin (2002) The Direct Effect of Banking System Reforms in Taiwan. Working Paper George Washington University: pp 1-30

Huang, Yasheng (2006) Do Financing Biases Matter for the Chinese Economy? Cato Journal, 26 (2): pp 287-306

Huang, Yasheng/ Khanna, Tarun (2003) Can India overtake China? Foreign Policy, No. 137: pp 74-81

Huang, Yasheng/ Khanna, Tarun (2005) Indigenous versus Foreign Business Models. In: Friedman, Edward/ Gilley, Bruce (ed): Asia's Giants: Comparing China and India. New York, pp 161-179

Hughes, Neil C. (1998) Smashing the Iron Rice Bowl. Foreign Affairs, 77 (4): pp 67-77

Humphrey, David B./ Pulley, Lawrence B. (1997) Banks' Responses to Deregulation: Profits, Technology, and Efficiency. Journal of Money, Credit, and Banking, 29 (1): pp 73-93

ICRA (2004) The Indian Banking Industry. New Delhi

Indian Banks' Association (2003) Banking Industry Vision 2010. Mumbai

International Monetary Fund (2000a) Macroprudential Indicators of Financial System Soundness. IMF Occasional Paper, No. 192: pp 1-49

International Monetary Fund (2000b) World Economic Outlook - Focus on Transition Economies. Washington D.C.

International Monetary Fund (2002) India: Selected Issues and Statistical Appendix. Washington D.C.

International Monetary Fund (2005) Global Financial Stability Report - Market Developments and Issues. Washington, D.C.

International Monetary Fund (2006a) Global Financial Stability Report - Market Developments and Issues. Washington, D.C.

International Monetary Fund (2006b) International Financial Statistics (electronic version)

Jaffe, Dwight/ Levonian, Mark (2001) The Structure of Banking Systems in Developed and Transition Economies. European Financial Management, 7 (2): pp 161-181

Jalan, Bimal (2005) The Future of India - Politics, Economics and Governance. New Delhi

Jayaratna, Jith/ Strahan, Philip .E. (1996) The Finance-Growth Nexus: Evidence from Bank Branch Deregulation. Quarterly Journal of Economics, 111 (3): pp 639-670

Johnston, R. Barry/ Sundararajan, V. (1999) Sequencing Financial Sector Reforms: Country Experiences and Issues. Washington

Joshi, Vijay/ Little, I.M.D (1997) India's Economic Reforms 1991-2001. Delhi et al.

Joshi, Vijay/ Little, I.M.D (1999) India - Reform on Hold. Asian Development Review, 15 (2): pp 1-42

Kamesam, Vepa (2002) Indian Economy - Financial Sector Reforms and Role of RBI. RBI Bulletin, May: pp 375-391

Kaminsky, Graciela/ Reinhart, Carmen (1999) The Twin Crises: The Causes of Banking and Balance-of-Payments Problems. The American Economic Review, 89 (3): pp 473-500

Kaminsky, Graciela/ Schmukler, Sergio L. (2002) Short-Run Pain, Long-Run Gain: The Effects of Financial Liberalization. Working Paper World Bank: pp 1-33

Kapur, Devesh/ Ramamurti, Ravi (2002) Privatization in India: The Imperatives and Consequences of Gradualism. Working Paper Stanford University, No. 142: pp 1-40

Kennedy, Peter (2003) A Guide to Econometrics (5th ed.). Cambridge (MA)

Kim, Byung-Yeon/ Pirttilä, Jukka (2003) The political economy of reforms: Empirical evidence from post-communist transition in the 1990s. BOFIT Discussion Papers, No. 4: pp 1-27

King, Robert G./ Levine, Ross (1993) Finance and Growth: Schumpeter might be right. Quarterly Journal of Economics, 108 (3): pp 717-737

Kirkpatrick, Colin (2005) Finance and Development: Overview and Introduction. Journal of Development Studies, 41 (4): pp 631-635

Kloten, Norbert (1991) Die Transformation von Wirtschaftsordnungen: theoretische, phänotypische und politische Aspekte. Tübingen

Koch, Elmar B. (1998) Banking Sector Reform in the Transition Economies - A Central Banking Perspective. Economic Survey of Europe, No. 2: pp 67-86

Kochhar, Kalpana et al. (2006) India's Pattern of Development: What Happened, What Follows? IMF Working Paper, No. 06/22: pp 1-70

Kohli, Atul (2006a) Politics of Economic Growth in India, 1980-2005 - Part I: The 1980s. Economic & Political Weekly, 1 April 2006: pp 1251-1259

Kohli, Atul (2006b) Politics of Economic Growth in India, 1980-2005 - Part II: The 1990s and Beyond. Economic & Political Weekly, 8 April 2006: pp 1361-1370

Kohli, Renu (2001) Capital Flows and Their Macroeconomic Effects in India. IMF Working Paper, No. 01/192: pp 1-35

Kolodko, Grzegorz W. (1999) Ten Years of Postsocialist Transition. Lessons for Policy Reforms. The World Bank Policy Research Working Paper, No. 2095: pp 1-32

Kolodko, Grzegorz W. (2004a) Institutions, Policies and Growth. TIGER Working Paper Series, No. 56: pp 1-24

Kolodko, Grzegorz W. (2004b) Transition to a Market System: Gradualism versus Radicalism. TIGER Working Paper Series, No. 60: pp 1-11

Kormendi, Roger C./ Snyder, Edward A. (1996) Bank Privatizations in Transitional Economies. William Davidson Institute Working Paper, No. 1: pp 1-23

Kornai, Janos (2000) What the Change of System From Socialism to Capitalism Does and Does Not Mean. Journal of Economic Perspectives, 14 (1): pp 27-42

Krahnen, Jan Pieter/ Schmidt, Reinhard H. (1994) Development Finance as Institution Building - A New Approach to Poverty-Oriented Banking. Boulder, San Francisco, Oxford

Kumbhakar, Subal C./ Sarkar, Subrata (2003) Deregulation, Ownership, and Productivity Growth in the Banking Industry: Evidence from India. Journal of Money, Banking, and Credit, 35 (3): pp 403-424

Kusic, Sinisa et al. (2003) Banking System Reforms in China. Discussion Paper University of Frankfurt: pp 1-13

Küster, Georg H. (1996) Zur Transformation von Wirtschaftsordnungen - Ergebnisse einer zweifachen deutschen Erfahrung. In: European Business School (ed): Erfahrung - Bewegung - Strategie, ebs-Forschung, Vol. 3. Wiesbaden, pp 59-84

Kynge, James (2003) China gives foreign banks wider access to its market. Financial Times, 2 December 2003, pp 15

La Porta, Rafael et al. (2002) Government Ownership of Banks. The Journal of Finance, 57 (1): pp 265-301

Laeven, Luc (2003) Does Financial Liberalization Reduce Financing Constraints? Financial Management, 32: pp 5-34

Lago, Ricardo (2002) The Financial Sector in Transition Economics Ten Years After: The Issues, the Record, and the Challenges. TIGER Working Paper Series, No. 23: pp 1-13

Lal, Deepak (2006) A Proposal to Privatize Chinese Enterprises and End Financial Repression. Cato Journal, 26 (2): pp 275-286

Lane, Timothy D. (1994) Reforming the Financial System. In: Schipke, A./ Taylor, A.M. (ed): The Economics of Transformation - Theory and Practice in the New Market Economies. Heidelberg, pp 233-252

Lardy, Nicholas R. (1998) China's Unfinished Economic Revolution. Washington D.C.

Lardy, Nicholas R. (2000) When Will China's Financial System Meet China's Needs? Working Paper Stanford University, No. 54: pp 1-48

Lardy, Nicholas R. (2005) Exchange Rate and Monetary Policy in China. Cato Journal, 25 (1): pp 41-47

Lau, Lawrence J. (1999) The macroeconomy and reform of the banking sector in China. In: Bank for International Settlements (ed): Strengthening the Banking System in China: Issues and Experiences (BIS Policy Papers No. 7). Basel, pp 59-89

Lau, Lawrence J. et al. (2000) Reform Without Losers: An Interpretation of China's Dual-Track Approach to Reforms. Journal of Political Economy, 108 (1): pp 120-143

Leeladhar, V. (2006) Taking Banking Services to the Common Man - Financial Inclusion. RBI Bulletin, January 2006: pp 73-77

Leung, M.K. et al. (2003) Entry of foreign banks in the People's Republic of China: a survival analysis. Applied Economics, 35: pp 21-31

Levine, Ross (1997) Financial Development and Economic Growth: Views and Agenda. Journal of Economic Literature, 35 (2): pp 688-726

Levine, Ross/ Renelt, David (1992) A Sensitivity Analysis of Cross-Country Growth Regressions. The American Economic Review, 82 (4): pp 942-963

Li, David D. (2001) Beating the Trap of Financial Repression in China. Cato Journal, 21 (1): pp 77-90

Lindner, Christian/ Bösswetter, Urs (1998) Pfadabhängigkeiten im institutionellen Wandel: Eine kritische Würdigung der evolutionstheoretischen Ansätze für die Transformationspolitik. In: Oberender, Peter (ed): Theorie und Praxis der Transformation von Wirtschaftssystemen. Bayreuth, pp 33-47

Llewellyn, David T. (2002) An analysis of the causes of recent banking crises. The European Journal of Finance, 8 (2): pp 152-175

Lo, Wai Chung (2001) A Retrospect on China's Banking Reform. The Chinese Economy, 34 (1): pp 15-28

Loayza, Norman/ Ranciere, Romain (2006) Financial Development, Financial Fragility and Growth. Journal of Money, Credit, and Banking, 38 (4): pp 1051-1076

Lohmann, Gerhard (1997) Wirtschaftliche Transformation als Ordnungsproblem. Diss., Baden-Baden

Long, Simon (2005) The tiger in front. The Economist, 374 (8416): pp 3-4

Lowinski, Felix/ Terberger, Eva (2001) Transformation im chinesischen Finanzsektor: Die Reform der staatlichen Banken zwischen Anspruch und Wirklichkeit. Wittener Diskussionspapiere, No. 86: pp 1-35

Lynch, David (1996) Measuring Financial Sector Development: A Study of Selected Asia-Pacific Countries. The Developing Economies, 34 (1): pp 3-33

Madgavkar, Anu et al. (2001) Revitalizing India's banks. The McKinsey Quarterly, No. 4: pp 113-116

Majudmar, Sumit K. (1998) The Hidden Hand and the License Raj: An Evaluation of the Relationship between Age and the Growth of Firms in India. Working Paper Stanford University: pp 1-33

Makhija, Anil K. (2006) Privatisation in India. Economic & Political Weekly, 20 May 2006: pp 1947-1951

Makin, John H. (2006) Does China Save and Invest too Much? Cato Journal, 26 (2): pp 307-315

Mankiw, N. Gregory (1995) The Growth of Nations. Brooking Papers on Economic Activity, No. 1: pp 275-326

Manor, James (2005) India's Reform Strength. In: Friedman, Edward/ Gilley, Bruce (ed): Asia's Giants: Comparing China and India. New York, pp 97-119

Manove, Michael et al. (2001) Collateral versus project screening: a model of lazy banks. RAND Journal of Economics, 32 (4): pp 726-744

Mavrotas, George/ Kelly, Roger (1999) Financial Sector Development and Savings Mobilisation: An Assessment. Working Paper Finance and Development Research Programme University of Manchester, No. 10: pp 1-37

McKinnon, Ronald (1973) Money and Capital in Economic Development. Washington D.C.

McKinnon, Ronald (1991) The Order of Economic Liberalization - Financial Control in the Transition to a Market Economy. Baltimore/London

McKinnon, Ronald/ Pill, Huw (1997) Credible Economic Liberalizations and Overborrowing. The American Economic Review, 87 (2): pp 189-193

McKinsey Global Institute (2001) India: The Growth Imperative. San Francisco

McKinsey Global Institute (2006a) Accelerating India's Growth through Financial System Reform. San Francisco

McKinsey Global Institute (2006b) Putting China's Capital to Work: The Value of Financial System Reform. San Francisco

Megginson, William L. (2005) The economics of bank privatization. Journal of Banking & Finance, 29 (8-9): pp 1931-1980

Megginson, William L./ Netter, Jeffrey M. (2001) From State to Market: A Survey of Empirical Studies on Privatization. Journal of Economic Literature, 39 (2): pp 321-389

Mehran, Hassanali/ Laurens, Bernard (1997) Interest Rates: An Approach to Liberalization. Finance & Development, June 1997: pp 33-35

Mehrez, Gil/ Kaufmann, Daniel (2000) Transparency, Liberalization and Banking Crises. World Bank Policy Research Working Paper, No. 2286: pp 1-33

Micco, Alejandro et al. (2004) Bank Ownership and Performance. Working Paper Inter-American Development Bank, No. 518: pp 1-48

Minsky, Hyman P. (1991) The Transition to a Market Economy: Financial Options. Working Paper, No. 66: pp 1-23

Mishkin, Frederic S. (1996) Understanding Financial Crises: A Developing Country Perspective. In: Bruno, Michael/ Pleskovic, Boris (ed.), Paper prepared for the Annual World Bank Conference on Development Economics 1996, Washington D.C., pp 29-62

Misra, Biswa Swarup (2003) Allocative Efficiency of the Indian Banking System in the Post-Reform Period: A State Level Analysis. RBI Occasional Papers, 24 (3): pp 161-186

Mitchell, Janet (2000) Theories of soft budget constraints and the analysis of banking crises. Economics of Transition, 8 (1): pp 59-100

Mo, YK (1999) A review of recent banking reforms in China. In: Bank for International Settlements (ed): Strengthening the Banking System in China: Issues and Experiences (BIS Policy Papers No. 7). Basel, pp 90-115

Modigliani, Franco/ Cao, Shi Larry (2004) The Chinese Saving Puzzle and the Life-Cycle Hypothesis. Journal of Economic Literature, 42 (1): pp 145-170

Mohan, Rakesh (2004) Financial Sector Reforms in India: Policies and Performance Analysis. RBI Bulletin, October 2004: pp 851-877

Mohan, Rakesh (2006a) Financial Sector Reforms and Monetary Policy: The Indian Experience. RBI Bulletin, July 2006: pp 1-24

Mohan, Rakesh (2006b) Monetary Policy and Exchange Rate Frameworks: The Indian Experience. RBI Bulletin, June 2006: pp 1-16

Morduch, Jonathan (2000) The Microfinance Schism. World Development, 28 (4): pp 617-629

Morgan Stanley (2004) India and China: A Special Economic Analysis. New York et al.

Mukherji, Joydeep (2002) India's Long March to Capitalism. India Review, 1 (2): pp 29-60

Mukherji, Joydeep (2005) The Causes of Differential Development: Beyond Regime Dichotomies. In: Friedman, Edward/ Gilley, Bruce (ed): Asia's Giants: Comparing China and India. New York, pp 55-75

Mukherji, Joydeep (2006) Economic Growth and India's Future. Occasional Paper Center for the Advanced Study of India, University of Pennsylvania, No. 26: pp 1-23

Muniappan, Shri G.P. (2002) The NPA Overhang - Magnitude, Solutions, Legal Reforms. Paper prepared for the CII Banking Summit 2002, Mumbai, pp 1-11

Murrell, Peter (1995) The Transition According to Cambridge, Mass. Journal of Economic Literature, 33 (1): pp 164-178

Naastepad, C.W.M. (2001) The Macro-Economic Effects of Directed Credit Policies: A Real-Financial CGE Evaluation for India. Development & Change, 32 (3): pp 477-506

Nair, Lekshmi R. (2005) Financial Sector Liberalization and Household Savings in India. In: Sethu, G. (ed.), Paper prepared for the Ninth Capital Markets Conference, Navi Mumbai, pp 1-27

Nanto, Dick K./ Sinha, Radha (2002) China's Banking Reform. Post-Communist Economies, 14 (4): pp 469-493

National Bureau of Statistics of China (2006) Announcement on Revised Result about Historical Data of China's Gross Domestic Products. <www.stats.gov.cn/english/newsandcomingevents/t20060110_402300302.htm>, Accessed: 18 April 2006

North, Douglass C. (1991) Institutions. Journal of Economic Perspectives, 5 (1): pp 97-112

Nsouli, Saleh M. et al. (2002) The speed of adjustment and the sequencing of economic reforms: Issues and guidelines for policymakers. IMF Working Paper, No. 02/132: pp 1-28

Oberender, Peter et al. (2003) Gradualismus vs. Schocktherapie oder lokale vs. globale Optimierung als relevante Alternativen der Transformationspolitik?

Eine theoretische Analyse! Diskussionspapier Universität Bayreuth, No. 15-03: pp 1-46
Olson, Mancur (1965) The Logic of Collective Action - Public Goods and the Theory of Groups. Cambridge (Mass.)
Olson, Mancur (1996) Big Bills Left on the Sidewalk: Why Some Nations Are Rich and Others Poor. Journal of Economic Perspectives, 10 (2): pp 3-24
Opper, Sonja (2004) The Political Economy of Privatization: Empirical Evidence from Transition Economies. Kyklos, 57 (4): pp 559-586
Organization for Economic Cooperation and Development (2003) Developments in Growth Literature and their Relevance for Simulation Models. OECD Papers, 3 (12): pp 1-64
Organization for Economic Cooperation and Development (2005) Economic Survey of China. OECD Policy Brief, September 2005: pp 1-8
Oschinski, Matthias (2003) Economic Liberalization and Globalization vs. India's Poor. TIGER Working Paper Series, No. 36: pp 1-17
Otchere, Isaac (2005) Do privatized banks in middle- and low-income countries perform better than rival banks? An intra-industry analysis of bank privatization. Journal of Banking & Finance, 29 (8-9): pp 2067-2093
Oxford Advanced Learner's Dictionary (1989) 4th edition. Oxford et al.
Panagariya, Arvind (2004) India in the 1980s and 1990s: A Triumph of Reforms. IMF Working Paper, No. 04/43: pp 1-38
Pandit, Ranjit V. (2005) Why believe in India. The McKinsey Quarterly 2005 special edition: Fulfilling India's promise: pp 133-139
Park, Jennifer (2004) New Comparative Advantages. Harvard International Review, 26 (3): pp 34-37
Parker, David/ Kirkpatrick, Colin (2005) Privatisation in Developing Countries: A Review of the Evidence and the Policy Lessons. Journal of Development Studies, 41 (4): pp 513-541
Pei, Guifen/ Shirai, Sayuri (2004) The Main Problems of China's Financial Industry and Asset Management Companies. Working Paper: pp 1-16
Pei, Minxin (2002) China's Governance Crisis. Foreign Affairs, 81 (5): pp 96-109
Pei, Minxin (2006) The Dark Side of China's Rise. Foreign Policy, March/April 2006: pp 32-40
Perotti, Enrico C. (1995) Credible Privatization. The American Economic Review, 85 (4): pp 847-859
Pham-Phuong, Dong (2003a) Konzeptionen der Transformationsökonomie (Teil 1): Transformationstheoretische Ansätze aus Sicht der Neuen Institutionenökonomik. Discussion Paper Research Association for International Agrarian & Economic Development, No. 73: pp 1-44
Pham-Phuong, Dong (2003b) Konzeptionen der Transformationsökonomie (Teil 2): Institutioneller Strukturwandel, Transformation monetärer Ordnung und Rolle der Bankenreform im Transformationsprozess. Discussion Paper Research Association for International Agrarian & Economic Development, No. 74: pp 1-28
Pickel, Andreas (2002) Transformation theory: scientific or political? Communist and Post-Communist Studies, 35: pp 105-114

Platek, Mariusz (2002) Financial Sector Development and Economic Growth in Transition Countries. Diss., Bamberg

Prahalad, C.K. (2005) The Fortune at the Bottom of the Pyramid. Upper Saddle River/NJ.

Prasad, Eswar S./ Rajan, Raghuram G. (2006) Modernizing China's Growth Paradigm. IMF Policy Discussion Paper, No. 06/03: pp 1-16

Pryor, Frederic L. (1985) A Guidebook to the Comparative Study of Economic Systems. Englewood Cliffs

Przeworski, Adam/ Limongi, Fernando (1993) Political Regimes and Economic Growth. Journal of Economic Perspectives, 7 (3): pp 51-69

Qian, Yingyi (1999a) The Institutional Foundations of China's Market Transition. In: Pleskovic, Boris/ Stiglitz, Joseph E. (ed.), Paper prepared for the World Bank's Annual Conference on Development Economics 1999, Washington, pp 377-398

Qian, Yingyi (1999b) The Process of China's Market Transition (1978-98): The Evolutionary, Historical, and Comparative Perspectives. Paper prepared for the Journal of Institutional and Theoretical Economics symposium, Wallerfangen/Saar (Germany), pp 1-35

Qian, Yingyi (2003) How Reform Worked in China. In: Rodrik, Dani (ed): In Search of Prosperity: Analytical Narratives on Economic Growth. Princeton, N.J., pp 297-333

Qian, Yingyi/ Weingast, Barry R. (1996) China's Transition to Markets: Market-Preserving Federalism, Chinese Style. Journal of Policy Reform, 1: pp 149-185

Quah, Danny (1993) Empirical Cross-Section Dynamics in Economic Growth. London School of Economics Working Paper: pp 1-19

Quantitative Micro Software (2004) EViews 4.1 Student Version User's Guide. Irvine (CA)

Quispe-Agnoli, Myriam/ McQuerry, Elizabeth (2001) Measuring Financial Liberalization in Latin America: An Index of Banking Activity. In: Kay, Stephen/ McQuerry, Elizabeth (ed.), Paper prepared for the Domestic Finance and Global Capital in Latin America Conference, pp 1-39

Raiser, Martin (2001) Informal Institutions, Social Capital, and Economic Transition: Reflections on a Neglected Dimension. In: Cornia, Giovanni Andrea/ Popov, Vladimir (ed): Transition and Institutions - The Experience of Gradual and Late Reformers. New York, pp 218-239

Rajan, Raghuram G. (2006) Global Imbalances and Financial Reform with Examples from China. Cato Journal, 26 (2): pp 267-273

Rajan, Raghuram G./ Zingales, Luigi (1998) Financial dependence and growth. The American Economic Review, 88 (3): pp 559-586

Rajan, Raghuram G./ Zingales, Luigi (2003a) The Great Reversals: The Politics of Financial Development in the 20th Century. Journal of Financial Economics, 69 (1): pp 5-50

Rajan, Raghuram G./ Zingales, Luigi (2003b) Saving Capitalism from the Capitalists: Unleashing the Power of Financial Markets to Create Wealth and Spread Opportunity. New York

Raje, Pradeep (2000) Where did India miss a turn in banking reform? Is there a comeback? Working Paper Center for the Advanced Study of India, University of Pennsylvania: pp 1-63

Ram Mohan, T.T. (2004) Privatisation in China: Softly, Softly Does It. Economic & Political Weekly, 6 November 2004: pp 1-14

Ram, Rati (1999) Financial Development and Economic Growth: Additional Evidence. Journal of Development Studies, 35 (4): pp 164-174

Rao, M. Govinda (2002) Dynamics of Indian Federalism. Working Paper Stanford University, No. 140: pp 1-30

Ray, Alok (2002) The Chinese Economic Miracle: Lessons to be Learnt. Economic & Political Weekly, 14 September 2002: pp 1-29

Reddy, Y.V. (2002a) Monetary and Financial Sector Reforms in India: A Practitioner's Perspective. RBI Bulletin, May: pp 357-374

Reddy, Y.V. (2002b) Public Sector Banks and the Governance Challenge: Indian Experience. RBI Bulletin, May: pp 337-356

Reserve Bank of India (1999) Report of the Working Group on Restructuring Weak Public Sector Banks

Reserve Bank of India (2000) Report on Trend and Progress of Banking in India 1999-2000

Reserve Bank of India (2001a) Report of The Advisory Group on Bankruptcy Laws

Reserve Bank of India (2001b) Report on Trend and Progress of Banking in India 2000-01

Reserve Bank of India (2003) Report on Trend and Progress of Banking in India 2002-03

Reserve Bank of India (2004a) Basic Statistical Returns of Scheduled Commercial Banks in India (Volume 33). Mumbai

Reserve Bank of India (2004b) Report on Trend and Progress of Banking in India 2003-04

Reserve Bank of India (2004c) Statistics Relating to Scheduled Commercial Banks at a Glance

Reserve Bank of India (2005a) Database on Indian Economy. <https://reservebank.org.in/cdbmsi/servlet/login>, Accessed: October 2005

Reserve Bank of India (2005b) RBI Unveils Roadmap for Presence of Foreign Banks in India and Guidelines on Ownership and Governance in Private Banks. Press Release, February 28th 2005, pp 1-3

Reserve Bank of India (2005c) Report on Trend and Progress of Banking in India 2004-05

Rodrik, Dani (1995) Getting Interventions Right: How South Korea and Taiwan Grew Rich. Economic Policy, 10 (1): pp 55-107

Rodrik, Dani (1999) Institutions for High-Quality Growth: What They Are and How to Acquire Them. Paper prepared for the IMF Conference on Second-Generation Reform, Washington D.C., pp 1-26

Rodrik, Dani (2000) Development Strategies for the 21st Century. In: Pleskovic, Boris/ Stern, Nicholas (ed.), Paper prepared for the Annual World Bank Conference on Development Economics 2000, Washington D.C., pp 85-108

Rodrik, Dani (2004) Growth Strategies. Working Paper Harvard University: pp 1-57

Rodrik, Dani/ Subramanian, Arvind (2004) From "Hindu Growth" to Productivity Surge: The Mystery of the Indian Growth Transition. IMF Working Paper, No. 04/77: pp 1-43

Rojas-Suarez, Liliana (2001) Can International Capital Standards Strengthen Banks in Emerging Markets? Working Paper: pp 1-42

Roland, Gérard (1994) The role of political constraints in transition strategies. Economics of Transition, 2 (1): pp 27-41

Roland, Gérard (2000) Corporate Governance and Restructuring: Lessons from Transition Economies. In: Pleskovic, Boris/ Stern, Nicholas (ed.), Paper prepared for the Annual World Bank Conference on Development Economics 2000, Washington D.C., pp 331-352

Roland, Gérard (2001) Ten Years After ... Transition and Economics. IMF Staff Papers, No. 48 (Special Issue): pp 29-52

Roland, Gérard (2002) The Political Economy of Transition. Journal of Economic Perspectives, 16 (1): pp 29-50

Romer, Paul M. (1986) Increasing Returns and Long-Run Growth. Journal of Political Economy, 94 (5): pp 1002-1037

Romer, Paul M. (1994) The Origins of Endogenous Growth. Journal of Economic Perspectives, 8 (1): pp 3-22

Roubini, Nouriel/ Sala-i-Martin, Xavier (1992) Financial repression and economic growth. Journal of Development Economics, 39 (1): pp 5-30

Roy, Tirthankar (2002) Economic History and Modern India: Redefining the Link. Journal of Economic Perspectives, 16 (3): pp 109-130

Rybczinski, Tad M. (1991) The Sequencing of Reform: Microeconomics of Transition in Eastern Europe. Oxford Review of Economic Policy, 7 (4): pp 26-34

Sachs, Jeffrey/ Woo, Wing Thye (1994) Structural Factors in the Economic Reforms of China, Eastern Europe, and the Former Soviet Union. Economic Policy, 9 (1): pp 102-145

Saez, Lawrence (2001) Banking Reform in India and China. International Journal of Finance and Economics, 6 (3): pp 235-244

Saez, Lawrence/ Yang, Joy (2001) The Deregulation of State-Owned Enterprises in India and China. Comparative Economic Studies, 43 (3): pp 69-97

Santos, Joao A. C. (2000) Bank Capital Regulation in Contemporary Banking Theory: A Review of the Literature. BIS Working Paper, No. 90: pp 1-32

Schipke, Alfred (1994) The Political Economy of Privatization. In: Schipke, A./ Taylor, A.M. (ed): The Economics of Transformation - Theory and Practice in the New Market Economies. Heidelberg, pp 171-189

Schmidt, Ingo (1999) Wettbewerbspolitik und Kartellrecht, 6., neu bearb. und erw. Aufl. Stuttgart

Schmidt-Hebbel, Klaus/ Serven, Luis (1997) Saving across the World - Puzzles and Policies. World Bank Discussion Paper, No. 354: pp 1-159

Schmidt-Hebbel, Klaus/ Serven, Luis (2002) Financial Liberalization, Saving, and Growth. Working Paper: pp 1-30

Schrettl, Wolfram (1993) On Some Barriers to Transition. In: Wagener, Hans-Jürgen (ed): On the Theory and Policy of Systemic Change. Heidelberg, pp 207-217

Schulders, Guy (1998) Die Besonderheiten der asiatischen Transformationsprozesse. Frankfurt Institute of Transformation Studies Discussion Paper, No. 14/98: pp 1-71

Seitz, Konrad (2000) China - Eine Weltmacht kehrt zurück. Berlin

Seliger, Bernhard (2002) Toward a More General Theory of Transformation. Eastern European Economics, 40 (1): pp 36-62

Sen, Kunal/ Vaidya, Rajendra R. (1997) The Process of Financial Liberalization in India. Delhi et al.

Setser, Brad (2006) The Chinese Conundrum: External financial strength, Domestic financial weakness. Paper prepared for the CESifo Conference "Understanding the Chinese Economy", pp 1-29

Shan, Jordan/ Morris, Alan (2002) Does Financial Development 'Lead' Economic Growth. International Review of Applied Economics, 16 (2): pp 153-168

Shaw, Edward S. (1973) Financial Deepening in Economic Development. New York

Sheng, Andrew (1996) Bank Restructuring Techniques. In: Sheng, Andrew (ed): Bank Restructuring: Lesson from the 1980s. Washington D.C., pp 25-48

Sheshinski, Eytan/ López-Calva, Luis Felipe (1999) Privatization and its Benefits: Theory and Evidence. HIID Discussion Paper, Harvard University, No. 698:

Shirai, Sayuri (2002a) Banking sector reforms in India and China: Does India's experience offer lessons for China's future reform agenda? Asia-Pacific Development Journal, 9 (2): pp 51-82

Shirai, Sayuri (2002b) Banking Sector Reforms in India and China: Does India's Experience Offer Lessons for China's Future Reform Agenda? JBICI Discussion Paper, No. 2: pp 1-94

Shirai, Sayuri (2002c) Road from State to Market - Assessing the Gradual Approach to Banking Sector Reforms in India. Asian Development Bank Insti tute Research Paper, No. 32: pp 1-73

Shleifer, Andrei (1994) Establishing Property Rights. In: Bruno, Michael/ Pleskovic, Boris (ed.), Paper prepared for the Annual World Bank Conference on Development Economics 1994, Washington D.C., pp 93-117

Shleifer, Andrei (1998) State versus Private Ownership. Journal of Economic Perspectives, 12 (4): pp 133-150

Singh, Charan (2005) Financial Sector Reforms in India. Working Paper Stanford University, No. 241: pp 1-63

Singh, N.K. (2003) India's Economy: the Next Five Years. Working Paper Stanford University, No. 186: pp 1-14

Solarz, Jan Krysztof (1998) Transformation of the Banking System in Poland in Comparative Perspective. In: Drobnig, Ulrich et al (ed): Systemtransformation in Mittel- und Osteuropa und ihre Folgen für Banken, Börsen und Kreditsicherheiten. Tübingen, pp 147-152

Solow, Robert M. (1956) A contribution to the theory of economic growth. Quarterly Journal of Economics, 70 (1): pp 65-94

Srivastava, Pradeep/ Basu, Priya (2004) Scaling-up Access to Finance for India's Rural Poor. Working Paper World Bank: pp 1-36

Staude, Leonie (2002) Transformation und Perspektiven des chinesischen Bankensystems. Diploma thesis European Business School (unpublished): pp 1-99

Stiglitz, Joseph E. (1989a) Financial Markets and Development. Oxford Review of Economic Policy, 5 (4): pp 55-68

Stiglitz, Joseph E. (1989b) Markets, Market Failures, and Development. The American Economic Review, 79 (2): pp 197-203

Stiglitz, Joseph E. (1994) The Role of the State in Financial Markets. In: Bruno, Michael/ Pleskovic, Boris (ed.), Paper prepared for the Annual World Bank Conference on Development Economics, Washington, pp 19-52

Stiglitz, Joseph E. (1996) The Role of Government in Economic Development. In: Bruno, Michael/ Pleskovic, Boris (ed.), Paper prepared for the Annual World Bank Conference on Development Economics 1996, Washington D.C., pp 11-23

Stiglitz, Joseph E. (1999) Whither Reform? Ten Years of the Transition. In: Pleskovic, Boris/ Stiglitz, Joseph E. (ed.), Paper prepared for the Annual World Bank Conference on Development Economics, Washington D.C., pp 27-56

Stiglitz, Joseph E. (2004) Information and the Change in the Paradigm in Economics Part 2. The American Economist, 48 (1): pp 17-49

Stiglitz, Joseph E./ Bhattacharya, Amar (1999) The Underpinnings of a Stable and Equitable Global Financial System: From Old Debates to a New Paradigm. In: Pleskovic, Boris/ Stiglitz, Joseph E. (ed.), Paper prepared for the Annual World Bank Conference on Development Economics 1999, Washington D.C., pp 91-130

Stiglitz, Joseph E./ Weiss, Andrew (1981) Credit Rationing in Markets with Imperfect Information. The American Economic Review, 71 (3): pp 393-410

Sulc, Zdislav (1994) Some theoretical issues on transformation. Eastern European Economics, 32 (2): pp 23-38

Sunder Ram, K. (2001) Indian Financial System: Changing Paradigms. NMIMS Journal, July-December 2001: pp 54-62

Svejnar, Jan (2002) Transition Economies: Performance and Challenges. Journal of Economic Perspectives, 16 (1): pp 3-28

Swain, Ranjula Bali (2002) Credit Rationing in Rural India. Journal of Economic Development, 27 (2): pp 1-20

Swamy, Subramanian (2005a) Chasing China: Can India Bridge the Gap? In: Friedman, Edward/ Gilley, Bruce (ed): Asia's Giants: Comparing China and India. New York, pp 77-95

Swamy, Subramanian (2005b) Political Structure and Economic Reforms: A Comparative Appraisal of India and China. Economic & Political Weekly, 40 (10): pp 934-940

Sy, Amadou (2005) Managing the Interest Rate Risk of Indian Banks' Government Securities Holdings. IMF Working Paper, No. 05/78: pp 1-17

Sylla, Richard (2000) Financial Systems and Economic Modernization: A New Historical Perspective. Paper prepared for the World Bank Summer Workshop: pp 1-10

Temple, Jonathan (1999) The New Growth Evidence. Journal of Economic Literature, 37 (1): pp 112-156

The Economist (2004) Non-performing. The Economist, 370 (8367): pp 18-19

The Economist (2005a) A survey of India and China: Two concepts of liberty? The Economist, 374 (8416): pp 11-14

The Economist (2005b) The tiger in front - A survey of India and China. The Economist, 374 (8416): pp 1-16

Tsai, Kellee S. (2005) The Persistence of Informal Finance. In: Friedman, Edward/ Gilley, Bruce (ed): Asia's Giants: Comparing China and India. New York, pp 123-140

United Progressive Alliance (2004) Common Minimum Programme. New Delhi

van Wijnbergen, Sweder (1998) Bank restructuring and enterprise reform. EBRD Working Paper, No. 29: pp 1-19

Varma, Jayanth R. (2002) Indian Financial Sector After a Decade of Reforms. Centre for Civil Society Discussion Paper: pp 1-41

Vittas, Dimitri (1991) The Impact of Regulation on Financial Intermediation. World Bank Working Paper, No. 746: pp 1-25

Wachtel, Paul (2001) Growth and Finance: What do we know and how do we know it? International Finance, 4 (3): pp 335-362

Wachtel, Paul (2003) How Much Do We Really Know about Growth and Finance? Federal Reserve Bank of Atlanta Economic Review, First Quarter 2003: pp 33-47

Wagener, Hans-Jürgen (1993) Transformation as a Political-Economic Process. In: Wagener, Hans-Jürgen (ed): The Political Economy of Transformation. Heidelberg, pp 3-22

Wagener, Hans-Jürgen (1996) Transformation als historisches Phänomen. Frankfurt Institute of Transformation Studies Discussion Paper, No. 7/96: pp 1-19

Wagener, Hans-Jürgen (1997) Privateigentum und Unternehmenskontrolle in Transformationswirtschaften. In: Cassel, Dieter (ed): Institutionelle Probleme der Systemtransformation - Schriften des Vereins für Socialpolitik, Band 254. Berlin, pp 165-188

Wagener, Hans-Jürgen (2000) On the Relationship Between State and Economy in Transformation. Frankfurt Institute of Transformation Studies Discussion Paper, No. 14/00: pp 1-22

Wagner, Christian (1997) Politischer Wandel und wirtschaftliche Reformen in Indien. Rostocker Informationen zu Politik und Verwaltung, No. 7: pp 1-44

Werner, Richard A. (1999) Indian Macroeconomic Management: At the Crossroads Between Government and Markets. In: (ed): Rising to the Challenge in Asia: A Study of Financial Markets - India. Manila, pp 1-56

Williams, Jonathan/ Nguyen, Nghia (2005) Financial liberalisation, crisis, and restructuring: A comparative study of bank performance and bank governance in South East Asia. Journal of Banking & Finance, 29 (8-9): pp 2119-2154

Williamson, John (1994) In Search of a Manual for Technopols. In: Williamson, John (ed): The Political Economy of Policy Reform. Washington, pp 11-28
Williamson, John (2004) A Short History of the Washington Consenus. From the Washington Consensus towards a new Global Governance, Barcelona, pp 1-14
Williamson, John (2005) The strange history of the Washington consensus. Journal of Post Keynesian Economics, 27 (2): pp 195-206
Williamson, John/ Haggard, Stephan (1994) The Political Conditions for Economic Reform. In: Williamson, John (ed): The Political Economy of Policy Reform. Washington, pp 527-596
Williamson, John/ Mahar, Molly (1998) A Survey of Financial Liberalisation. Princeton
Williamson, John/ Zagha, Roberto (2002) From the Hindu Rate of Growth to the Hindu Rate of Reform. Working Paper Stanford University, No. 144: pp 1-44
Woetzel, Jonathan R. (2003) Capitalist China. Singapore
Woetzel, Jonathan R. (2006) Checking China's vital signs: The social challenge. The McKinsey Quarterly, 2006 special edition: Serving the new Chinese consumer: pp 16-23
Wolken, Lawrence C. (1990) The Restructuring of China's Banking System under the Economic Reforms 1979-1989. Columbia Journal of World Business: pp 53-62
Wong, Y.C. Richard/ Wong, M.L. Sonia (2001) Competition in China's Domestic Banking Industry. Cato Journal, 21 (1): pp 19-41
World Bank (1989) Financial Systems and Development. Washington, D.C.
World Bank (1995) Bureaucrats in Business - The Economics and Politics of Government Ownership. Washington, D.C.
World Bank (1996a) The Chinese Economy: Fighting Inflation, Deepening Reform. Washington, D.C.
World Bank (1996b) From Plan to Market. Washington, D.C.
World Bank (1997a) China 2020. Washington, D.C.
World Bank (1997b) The State in a Changing World. Oxford et al.
World Bank (2001) Finance for Growth - Policy Choices in a Volatile World. Oxford et al.
World Bank (2002) Building Institutions for Markets. Washington D.C.
World Bank (2005) Equity and Development. New York
Wu, Friedrich (2003) Chinese Economic Statistics - Caveat Emptor! Post-Communist Economies, 15 (1): pp 127-145
Wu, Jinglian (2006) The road ahead for capitalism in China. The McKinsey Quarterly, 2006 special edition: Serving the new Chinese consumer: pp 116-120
Wyplosz, Charles (1999) Macroeconomic Lessons from Ten Years of Transition. In: Pleskovic, Boris/ Stiglitz, Joseph E. (ed.), Paper prepared for the Annual World Bank Conference on Development Economics 1999, Washington D.C., pp 317-343
Wyplosz, Charles (2001) How risky is financial liberalization in the developing countries. Paper prepared for the 7th Dubrovnik Economic Conference, June 2001, Dubrovnik, pp 1-25

Yang, Ya-Hwei (2004) Development and Problems in China's Financial System. Working Paper: pp 1-24

Yeyati, Eduardo Levy et al. (2004) Should the Government Be in the Banking Business? The Role of State-Owned and Development Banks. Working Paper Inter-American Development Bank, No. 517: pp 1-47

Yusuf, Shahid (1994) China's Macroeconomic Performance and Management During Transition. Journal of Economic Perspectives, 8 (2): pp 71-92

Zhang, Xiaoke (2003) Political Structures and Financial Liberalization in Pre-Crisis East Asia. Studies in Comparative International Development, 38 (1): pp 64-92

Zou, Keyuan (2006) Revamping Laws for the Market Economy in the Post-WTO China. Asien, No. 100: pp 88-93

Lightning Source UK Ltd.
Milton Keynes UK
UKHW020714181219
355581UK00006B/38/P

9 783790 819816